Karl Polanyi and the Paradoxes of the Double Movement

This book offers a critical reconstruction of the double movement, the central thesis of Karl Polanyi's *The Great Transformation*, one of the most influential books of the 20th century. The double movement is the establishment of a free market economy and the subsequent effort by society to ameliorate the destructive effects of the market.

In Polanyi's bold vision, the double movement constituted the hidden gear of social change and historical transformation within capitalism. The book is a forensic examination and critique of Polanyi's argument. It develops an interpretive framework of the double movement as four interrelated social processes: the establishment of the self-regulating market, the rise of a market society that deepens and extends market imperatives, a social protection phase that constrains the market and safeguards society, and the contradictions and crises that result from this clash of social principles.

The book will be an indispensable guide for students and scholars across the social sciences which illuminates the relevance of Polanyi's insights to a critical understanding of the contemporary era –the scourge of insecurity and inequality, the multiple crises of neoliberalism, the rise of right wing populism- as well as those interested in egalitarian and emancipatory alternatives to capitalism.

John Vail is currently a Visiting Professor in the School of Geography, Politics and Sociology at Newcastle University where he was previously a Senior Lecturer of Sociology until his retirement. His research interests are in egalitarian political economy. He has edited volumes on insecurity and alternative approaches to full employment and has written several articles on decommodification and egalitarian political economy. With Professor Robert Hollands, he has written a series of papers on the transformative cultural activism of the Newcastle based film and photography collective, Amber Films.

Routledge Studies in Social and Political Thought

167 Outlines of a Theory of Plural Habitus
Bourdieu Revisited
Miklós Hadas

168 Marcel Gauchet and the Crisis of Democratic Politics
Edited by Natalie J. Doyle & Sean McMorrowl

169 Anatomies of Modern Discontent
Visions from the Human Sciences
Thomas S. Henricks

170 Critical Theory of Coloniality
Paulo Henrique Martins

171 Karl Polanyi and the Paradoxes of the Double Movement
John Vail

172 Nationalism and Hegemony
The Consolidation of the Nation in Social and Political Life
Michaelangelo Anastasiou

173 Lockean Property Ethics and Restitution
David Jarrett

174 Making Citizenship Work
Culture and Community
Edited by Rodolfo Rosales

For a full list of titles in this series, please visit www.routledge.com/series/RSSPT

Karl Polanyi and the Paradoxes of the Double Movement

John Vail

Routledge
Taylor & Francis Group
LONDON AND NEW YORK

First published 2022
by Routledge
4 Park Square, Milton Park, Abingdon, Oxon OX14 4RN

and by Routledge
605 Third Avenue, New York, NY 10158

Routledge is an imprint of the Taylor & Francis Group, an informa business

British Library Cataloguing-in-Publication Data
A catalogue record for this book is available from the British Library

Library of Congress Cataloging-in-Publication Data
A catalog record has been requested for this book

ISBN: 978-0-415-39079-8 (hbk)
ISBN: 978-1-032-24868-4 (pbk)
ISBN: 978-1-003-13318-6 (ebk)

DOI: 10.4324/9781003133186

Typeset in Times New Roman
by Taylor & Francis Books

Contents

Chapter 1

Introduction

The Paradoxes of Karl Polanyi

Introduction: The Crash of 2008

The "seven days that shook the world" in the fall of 2008 began with the ominous announcement on the morning of September 15 that the New York investment firm, Lehman Brothers, was filing for bankruptcy protection with over $600 billion in debts on their books.[1] Coming on the heels of the collapse of another Wall Street firm, Bear Sterns, whose sale to JP Morgan six months earlier had been underwritten by guarantees from the Federal Reserve Bank, the announcement of Lehman's travails and the refusal of the US government to agree to another bailout sent shudders throughout the entire financial system. Serious questions were raised about the viability of other financial institutions and given the interlocking links between financial actors around the world, there was a understandable fear that the distress of a single firm might trigger an unstoppable domino effect that would plunge the entire world financial system into chaos.

Within days, American government officials were forced to broker the sale of another ailing firm, Merrill Lynch, to the Bank of America and negotiated the largest bailout in history, taking close to an 80% equity share in the world's largest insurer, American International Group (AIG) (which had guaranteed over $500 billion in risky insurance portfolios), in return for an infusion of $85 billion to prevent it from going under and sparking a calamitous global banking collapse. Even these steps failed to stem the panic spreading like wildfire: the precarious circumstances of these large financial institutions precipitated a further seizing up of the nation's credit markets with additional bank failures and reorganizations; global stock market capitalization fell to its lowest point since 1929; and the Dow Jones industrial average registered the largest drop in its 120-year history. A financial collapse threatened to plunge the global economy into another Great Depression, which was averted only by the decisive action of political leaders of the advanced nations. By any calculation of the historical imagination, the 2008 crash was the most significant event of the 21st century – the first in a series of worldwide crises, such as the 2020 global pandemic and climate change, that utterly remade the world.

DOI: 10.4324/9781003133186-1

The proximate triggers for the crisis could be located in a series of events stretching back over decades. The first of these was the ever-deepening penetration of financial relations into the fabric of American society as exemplified by several trends: the gradual spread of credit card debt to growing numbers of consumers; the extension of home ownership (via so-called "sub-prime" mortgages and cheap credit) to sectors of the population with modest incomes and little history of debt; an increase in borrowing to pay for the precipitous rise in college fees; and individualized pension arrangements (Krippner, 2011). On the one hand, this new regime of accumulation, which Colin Crouch felicitously termed "privatized Keynesianism" (Crouch, 2009), enabled millions of Americans with stagnating salaries and little job security to maintain their living standards and personal consumption via increased credit and equity borrowing from rising house prices. On the other hand, it left them increasingly vulnerable to the volatility and discipline of the market thereby tying them ever more closely to the vicissitudes of the interdependent global economy.[2] This new system of financialization depended upon an unholy combination of financial wizardry in the creation of new commodities as well as ideological machination. A new technology of "securitization" was designed to transform any debt into a new security that could be bought and sold by investors and institutions: "collaterized debt obligations" (mortgage-based securities packaged into highly complex bundles of standardized financial assets) and credit default swaps (insurance against corporate default) were among the most prominent innovations that constituted an important new revenue stream for banks, investment firms and hedge funds (Tett, 2009). The entire system was predicated on an almost religious fervor that proclaimed markets were inherently self-regulating and self-correcting. Its proponents insisted these new forms of financial commodities distributed risk far more effectively than ever before and that, as a consequence, government regulation of the financial sector should be kept to a bare minimum.

Unfortunately, the idea of self-regulation turned out to be a dangerous illusion. These new instruments underpinning the shadow financial sector proved to be so complex and complicated that even their own creators did not fully understand them and more importantly, could not accurately estimate how much risk was being placed into the system so the potential for self-destructive behavior and crisis grew exponentially (Tett, 2009). Once the housing bubble collapsed in 2006, the entire house of cards collapsed. A precipitous decline in house prices meant that many new homeowners could no longer afford to make their debt payments, thereby precipitating a record number of foreclosures and defaults, which in turn led to a collapse in the price of assets that were tied to underwater mortgage payments resulting in a sharp decline in household spending once house prices collapsed. This saddled financial institutions with a growing mountain of bad investments and debt that they could only offload at reduced prices which only worsened their position. AIG, which had insured many of these mortgage-backed securities, was faced with the calamitous prospect of an unprecedented number of payout claims but were unable to borrow sufficient capital to cover its potential losses because of a downgrade of its credit rating. Similarly, because of their precarious position, banks refused to lend, thereby paralyzing business investment throughout the economy and in effect leaving the entire market economy teetering on a precipice.

In the aftermath of the wreckage, four paradoxes regarding the crisis seemed particularly perplexing to policy makers and commentators alike: the issue of predictive failure, the legacy of self-regulation, the symbiotic relationship of states and markets, and the deeper foundations of the crisis. The first of these concerned the fundamental question of how policy makers and economists failed so grievously to foresee the looming crisis. Even though Warren Buffett (and a handful of contrarians) had presciently warned as early as 2003 about the perils of what he sarcastically called "financial weapons of mass destruction", warning signs were ignored, the very possibility of a catastrophic failure was presumed to have been eradicated from the market economy, and the magnitude of systemic risk was grossly underestimated (Eichengreen, 2015). As one commentator astutely noted: "The true nature of the international system…was not realized until it failed…The awful suddenness of the transformation thus took the world completely by surprise". What explains such a pervasive social amnesia? Ideological blinders certainly played a role: the blind faith in the liberal creed, which exaggerated the self-healing resilience of the market, meant the dangers of a financial tsunami could be blithely overlooked. Nor should sheer greed be underestimated as profit margins and individual bonuses at firms were directly tied to this toxic alchemy, giving all actors a reckless incentive to knowingly maintain a deliberate "social silence" about potential catastrophic risks (Tett, 2009).

But what also seemed inescapable was the role of willful complacency in overlooking the potential for crisis within the new global architecture, a psychological inability to properly appreciate the significance of the periodic crises that had plagued the global economy for well over a decade (stretching from the Asian debt crisis of 1997 to the dot com bubble in 1999–2000, the Enron scandal of 2001 and the Argentine crisis of 2002) and the willingness to discount any countervailing evidence or voices calling for a more prudent course. To other observers, these vertiginous swings demonstrated that crisis was an essential feature of capitalism and that all eras of political and economic stability are plagued by contradictions that carry the seeds of their own downfall (Piketty, 2014).

A related paradox of the 2008 crisis was that, despite the useful fiction of self-regulation espoused by neoliberal acolytes, the entire edifice of the financial system proved to be utterly dependent on the guarantee of *political* protection. "The ferocity of the financial crisis in 2008 was met with a mobilization of state action without precedent in the history of capitalism", argues Adam Tooze. "Never before outside wartime had states intervened on such a scale and with such speed" (Tooze, 2018, 166). The United States government's actions were instructive in this regard. Faced with the very real possibility of a meltdown of the entire banking and financial system and a subsequent world-wide depression comparable to the 1930s, the federal government (spanning both the Bush and Obama administrations) acted swiftly to avert disaster and prevent the crisis from diffusing across the global economy: it committed $700 billion to the Troubled Asset Relief Program to ease credit and money markets; it passed a Recovery Act that committed nearly $800 billion in stimulus spending (a combination of tax cuts, aid to states and infrastructure projects); it pledged billions to the rescue of individual firms (such as Bear Sterns, AIG and Washington Mutual) and private housing financiers (Fannie Mae and Freddie Mac) whose implosion threatened to spread the crisis; it networked with finance ministers and treasury officials around the globe to orchestrate a coordinated response to the crisis (Drezner, 2014).

But, the state was equally implicated in the origins of the crisis as well. The *laissez-faire* model of limited oversight encouraged the perilous overleveraging of financial institutions, the incentives market actors had to engage in risky behavior and the pathways that they took to alleviate their predicament (Krippner, 2011). As one commentator bluntly stated, "The road to the free market was opened and kept open by an enormous increase in continuous, centrally organized and controlled intervention". Even the most ardent of free market ideologues now seemed to accept the valuable lesson, all too easily forgotten in the heady days of market triumphalism, that capitalism is not self-sustaining or self-regulating but rather requires a panoply of political and social institutions to keep it from self-destructing (Block, 2003). As Dani Rodrik insisted: "[M]arkets do not create, regulate, stabilize or sustain themselves. The history of capitalism has been a process of learning and relearning this lesson" (Rodrik, 2011, 237). "No market economy separated from the political sphere is possible" is how a commentator summarized this new conventional wisdom.

However, in reality, the knowledge that governments would rescue market actors, no matter how egregious the risk taking, in effect meant that the people most responsible for the crisis in the first place were bailed out by the public purse. In what Mark Blyth called the "greatest bait and switch in human history", banks were able to privatize their gains to shareholders and executives while socializing their losses back to struggling taxpayers as public debt. This raised a fundamental question of fairness as many reasonably inquired how it was that the very people who created the mess in the first place were rewarded while the vast majority suffered from greater insecurity and austerity (Blyth, 2013). In the new liberal world, individuals were forced to hold multiple jobs, their incomes have stagnated or been subject to increasing volatility, with insecurity inscribed into the everyday practices of a new flexible capitalism (Sennett, 1998). One writer lambasted economic elites for their "mystical readiness to accept the social consequences of economic improvement, whatever they may be". Not surprisingly, the crisis brought questions of rising inequality and the fairness of the economic system back into public discourse (Piketty, 2014) and various social movements – from the Occupy movement in the United States to the *Indignados* in Spain – called for a fundamental restructuring of social and economic priorities. The crisis confirmed yet again that one of the enduring controversies in modern life is adjudicating the proper relationship and boundary between economy and society and the implicit recognition that social needs and stability might not be well served by the narrow bottom lines of market actors.

In the aftermath of the cataclysm, many assumed that the events of 2008 would naturally precipitate a reconsideration of the mystical shibboleths of market self-regulation that dominated political and economic discourse over the past several decades. Early on, both sides of the political spectrum appeared convinced the crisis had once and for all demonstrated that the model of free market capitalism was inherently fragile and unsustainable and that neoliberal hegemony had suffered a fatal blow. On the right, the presiding French President Nicolas Sarkozy pronounced the demise of *laissez-faire*: "A certain idea of globalization is drawing to a close with the end of a financial capitalism that imposed its logic on the whole economy. The idea that the markets are always right was a crazy idea". On the left, Gordon Brown, Labour Party Prime Minister of the UK at the time, signaled a similar paradigm shift:

> "Today we are seeing not just the collapse of failed institutions but the collapse of a failed *laissez faire* dogma. In this first financial crisis of the global age the old free market fundamentalism, no matter how it is dressed up, has been found wanting...[T]he events of the past months bear witness, more than anything in my lifetime, to one simple truth: markets need morals"
>
> (Brown, 2009)[3]

Even the house organs of financial capitalism were guilty of a nervous wobble, with *The Economist* blaring a headline in October 2008 proclaiming – "Capitalism-was it a good idea?" – and the *Financial Times* publishing a series the following year dedicated to the theme of "the future of capitalism". Indeed, many appeared convinced that the crisis might spur a new debate about restructuring capitalism – of creating a new social contract between market institutions and society predicated on fairness, equality and responsibility – that could even revive more radical alternatives representing a systemic alternative to global capitalism (Wright, 2010).

But perhaps the most puzzling outcome of the crisis is that despite the manifest failures of the self-regulating market to ensure prosperity and growth, neoliberalism's demise has been greatly exaggerated. Colin Crouch, in fact, argued that *laissez-faire* is "emerging from the financial collapse more politically powerful than ever" (Crouch, 2011, viiii). In the United States, the most protracted popular mobilization was directed at the Obama

Administration's efforts to ameliorate the effects of unconstrained markets such as the Affordable Care Act and Dodd-Frank legislation. In Europe, the dominant political conversation and policy agenda has emphasized deficit reduction, sound budgets and the inevitability of austerity rather than the construction of feasible alternatives to neoliberal hegemony. Mired in depression-like conditions of slow growth, staggeringly high levels of unemployment, savage cuts to social safety nets and disintegrating living standards as a result of austerity mania, a growing sense of despair and hopelessness pervades the continent, striking many with uncomfortable resonances to the cataclysmic interregnum of the 1930s. As in that era, political paralysis and declining political legitimacy precipitated an inchoate anger and radical disillusionment, leading to the rising popularity of anti-establishment parties of both the left and right, with the election of Donald Trump in 2016 as American president, the defining moment of this development. One commentator articulated the grave danger inherent in this stark historical parallel: "Eventually, the moment would come when both the economic and political systems were threatened by complete paralysis. Fear would grip the people and leadership would be thrust upon those who offered an easy way out at whatever ultimate price".

There is a final puzzle to ponder concerning the origins of the crisis. While most commentators focused on the proximate triggers that sparked the crisis –an unsustainable housing bubble that led to the mortgage meltdown, opaque financial instruments that greatly increased excessive risk taking, sheer blindness to the latent risk of crisis in the system – others contemplated the longer term foundations of the crisis. One commentator recognized the key paradox: "Not even when the cataclysm was already upon them did the leaders see that behind the collapse of the international system there stood a long development within the most advanced countries which made that system anachronistic". In the aftermath, scholars have begun to explore why some historical periods appear more prone to episodes of crisis than others; or how the foundations of the current crisis arose from the unintended consequences of efforts to resolve the earlier crisis of the 1970s, which led to the inauguration of the current round of neoliberalism and commodification (Krippner, 2011; Streeck, 2011); or suggested that excessive risk taking was tolerated because the entire system of financialization underpinned the global expansion of goods production and exchange of services (Panitch and Gindin, 2010); or took a longer-term historical vantage point that revealed recurrent episodes of speculative excess culminating in huge financial crashes have been ever-present in capitalist history (Reinhart and Rogoff, 2009). Beyond the material foundations of the crisis, other scholars have highlighted the pervasive social, cultural and political devastation – social insecurity, environmental degradation, political stalemate, which market fundamentalism has left in its wake (Hall and Lamont, 2013; Somers, 2008).

Twelve years later, in 2020, the worldwide Covid-19 pandemic exposed many of these same dysfunctions and crisis tendencies. Governments struggled to address the dual challenge of halting the spread of the disease (and at the same time preventing the collapse of their health systems) while at the same time averting a complete meltdown of their domestic economies. Businesses shuttered to ride out the storm and economies shutdown around the globe, simultaneously plunging the entire world into a deep recession. With millions furloughed or out of work, people struggled to make rent and pay for basic household expenses including food and heating. Of course, there were millions of people who still needed to go out to work or whose jobs were unsuitable to be done remotely, an important reminder that a great deal of the essential labor in our economies is often performed by workers such as supermarket clerks, carers of the elderly, nurses, waste removal workers and food deliverers, whose contributions are only rarely acknowledged. Drawing on lessons from the 2008 crisis, governments implemented massive fiscal and monetary expansions that even dwarfed the size of the earlier bailouts. Globally over $18 trillion was committed to subsidize business payrolls, assist struggling small businesses, provide direct cash payments for families with children, and increase unemployment benefits and other supports to help to rebuild a frayed social safety net. The miraculous development of effective vaccines, spurred by the timely and efficacious assistance of public seed money, saved countless lives and allowed nations to reopen their economies and return to some semblance of normal life.

Nonetheless, the staggering loss of human lives, with excess deaths as a result of Covid-19 estimated at over 10 million worldwide, was an unfathomable human tragedy, which triggered considerable critical reflection. Some emphasized how the crisis offered a stark lesson about the increasing vulnerability of an interconnected global economy that could be paralyzed at the hands of a single plague. Others highlighted the failure to develop a global vaccination program – not simply an unethical act but also an inexplicable one, given that it was in the self-interest of advanced nations to reduce global infections and thereby minimize the risk of new variants emerging that might endanger their own populations – as further proof of the intractable problem of global inequality. While some wondered whether the decisive political rescue of the global economy represented the long anticipated death of neoliberal orthodoxy, others saw it as convincing evidence that the system did in fact work. For Pope Francis, in his 2020 papal encyclical, *Fratelli Tutti* ("Brothers and Sisters All"), the pandemic offered confirmation that contemporary political and economic systems had to be comprehensively reformed: "Anyone who thinks that the only lesson to be learned was the need to improve what we were already doing, or to refine existing systems and regulations, is denying reality".

Martin Wolf, an influential columnist for *The Financial Times*, surveying the wreckage at the height of the pandemic in July 2020, took a broader view: "We are living in an age of multiple crises: Covid-19; a crisis of economic disappointment; a crisis of democratic legitimacy; a crisis of the global commons; a crisis of international relations; and a crisis of global governance. We do not know how to deal with all of these...because politics cannot deliver the necessary changes". What was urgently required, he insisted, was a historically grounded, analytical perspective that could link together all these overlapping crises into a single explanatory framework that could make sense of our tumultuous times. His nomination for this task: a book, *The Great Transformation*, written over 70 years ago in 1944 by a little known European émigré by the name of Karl Polanyi.

Polanyi Redux

Indeed, the work of Polanyi offers exactly this perspicacious intellectual account. It will come as little surprise that the insights about the 2008 crisis registered in the unattributed commentary above were actually drawn from *The Great Transformation* (1944 [1957]; henceforth GT: see, 206, 140, 196, 33, 143, 20), which went on to become one of the most influential works of the 20th century. What makes this astonishing prescience so remarkable is that he was actually drawing these inferences from an earlier crisis of market liberalism yet his analysis of that epoch is eerily reminiscent of present developments. The core thesis of *The Great Transformation* concerns the evolution of the "double movement", which he believed constituted the primary dynamic of the 19th and 20th centuries (GT, 76, 130). A critical reconstruction of this double movement schema is the primary objective of this book.

The opening phase of the double movement began with the ascendancy in England during the early 1830s of the "self-regulating market", which Polanyi uses to describe the complete commodification of labor, land and money and the universal assertion of market imperatives throughout society, a development which he believed represented a qualitative break in human history. Unlike the neoclassical parables that envisaged the market as a natural evolution, he argued the establishment of the market economy was the product of intentional design, ideological fervor and political determination. "The emergence of national markets was in no way the result of the gradual and spontaneous emancipation of the economic sphere from governmental control", wrote Polanyi. "On the contrary, the market has been the outcome of a conscious and often violent intervention on the part of the government which imposed the market organization on society for non-economic ends" (GT, 250). Once established, this disembedded market contains a totalizing logic that subjects all of society to the values, goals and imperatives of market calculation.

But the creation of such a "market society" proved unsustainable because "such an institution could not exist for any length of time without annihilating the human and natural substance of society; it would have physically destroyed man and transformed his surroundings into a wilderness" (GT, 3). In the face of this existential peril, society spontaneously mobilized a counter-movement for social protection that pressured governments to moderate the destructive workings of the market and safeguard the continued reproduction of society. Factory legislation, pensions, unemployment insurance, and health care were all the logical outgrowth of this protective instinct. For over 100 years, institutional change was largely the outcome of this contestation between two competing principles of social organization: "economic liberalism, aiming at the establishment of a self-regulating market" and "the principle of social protection aiming at the conservation of man and nature as well as productive organization" (GT, 132). It is this schism, Polanyi claims, which sparked a headlong spiral of contradictions culminating in the cataclysm of the First World War and Fascism.

The Great Transformation unquestionably has been one of the most influential, widely cited books in the social sciences of the 20th century. "No work of economic history," argues Santhi Hejeebu and Deidre McCloskey, "except *Capital* and *The Protestant Ethic*...has had more influence" (Hejeebu and McCloskey, 1999, 286). It has inspired important contributions across a wide range of academic disciplines, including anthropology, sociology, economic history and comparative political economy. Polanyi is considered one of the founders of the important sub-field of economic sociology (Smelser and Swedberg, 1994; Krippner and Alvarez, 2007) where he was believed to have pioneered a non-Marxist analysis that envisaged markets as social and political projects that required a range of non-market institutions to flourish. "Few economic sociologists would disagree with the statement 'We are all Polanyians now'", claims Jens Beckert (Beckert, 2009, 40). He was a significant inspiration for work in economic anthropology (Dalton, 1968) as well as in comparative political economy in its concern for the historical/institutional variation of capitalist economies (Hollingsworth and Boyer, 1997, for instance, dedicated their edited collection to "Karl Polanyi, for teaching us about the dynamics of capitalism"). Claus Offe explicitly acknowledged Polanyi's influence on his work on the welfare state (Offe, 1984, 262) as did Gosta Esping Andersen in his paradigmatic writings on decommodification (Esping Andersen, 1990, 36). The most widely cited article in international political economy, John Ruggie's paper on "embedded liberalism" (Ruggie, 1982), drew its starting point from Polanyi as did James O'Connor's seminal contribution to green theory which openly admits his debt (O'Connor, 1988, 12-13). The important ideational turn in political economy that underlines the importance of ideas, beliefs and ideology in the social and cultural construction of markets has been greatly influenced by Polanyi's work (Blyth, 2002; Callon, 1998; Krippner, 2007; Somers and Block, 2005). His argument about "fictitious commodities", which implied the abiding importance of the non-market realm to the social reproduction of labor, inspired a generation of feminist economists in their work on caring and household relations (Folbre, 2001; Fraser, 2016). These examples could be added to with ease – indeed, it would take an entire chapter in itself to do justice to the amazing breadth of his intellectual influence, so it is not entirely surprising that *The Great Transformation* is routinely cited as one of the most influential books of the 20th century.[4]

Scholars have returned to Polanyi because of the profound resonance which the grand narrative of the double movement has for the contemporary era (as discussed more extensively in Chapter 6). Recent critiques of the second coming of *laissez-faire* and the utopian idea that economic activity (nationally and globally) should be organized through self-regulating markets have received ample support from his writings (Lacher, 1999; Randles, 2007). His central emphasis on the extraordinary scope and intensity of market imperatives as a cornerstone of capitalist development rings true for many observers who similarly note the contours of an era of market fundamentalism where everything is for sale and anything can be commodified (Kuttner, 1997; Sandel, 2012; Satz, 2010). The cognate belief that there is a finite limit to the amount of uncertainty and upheaval that human beings can adapt to (which receives strong support in Polanyi's withering admonition against market corrosion that is discussed in considerable detail in Chapter 3) has been the cornerstone of critiques against the new insecurity that has profoundly damaged social resiliency in this era (Bourdieu, 1998; Somers, 2008). The diverse forms of resistance arrayed against the forces of commodification and neoliberalism – from struggles against the privatization of core services such as water and electricity in Brazil and South Africa to workers' protests in the developing world – are said to demonstrate the potential for a newly emergent Polanyian countermovement (Arrighi and Silver, 2003; Burawoy, 2010; Webster et al., 2008).

There have been calls for a renewed attention to the double movement as a means of better understanding the rise of right wing populism in the aftermath of the 2008 financial crisis (Berman, 2021; Gidron and Hall, 2020; Hopkin, 2020; Yarrow, 2017). Such are the destructive levels of insecurity and disruption of everyday lives by the *force majeure* of the free market that the countervailing powers of governments and civil society are seemingly compelled to impose greater regulatory constraints and to search for more efficacious forms of social protection rooted in well-being and solidarity (Hacker, 2006; Hall and Lamont, 2013). Indeed, this search to bridge the innovative energy of markets with social stability – what Peter Evans calls the "Polanyi problem" (Evans, 2008, 238) – extends to the very capitalist system itself as many scholars have insisted that there is a formidable challenge in ensuring that globalization and international economic integration do not jeopardize domestic social and political stability or undermine the very prospects for economic prosperity and growth (Rodrik, 2011). A new generation of public intellectuals/activists have used Polanyi as an inspiration for the renewal of the social democratic project (Konzcal, 2020; Kuttner, 2018) while others have seen him as a prophet of a radical, anti-capitalist politics that would transform the entire capitalist social order (Fraser, 2018, 2021; Lacher, 2019).

Nearly two decades ago, Ira Katznelson lamented that one of the key paradoxes of the reception to Polanyi's masterpiece was that *The Great Transformation* had failed to be "considered and evaluated primarily as analytical and historical social science. [It has] been understood and appreciated, only partially, even by admirers, usually consigned…to boxes of political economy…too small to contain [it]" (Katznelson, 2003, 59). Indeed, with notable exceptions (Block and Somers, 1984, 2003; Block, 2003; Burawoy, 2003; McRobbie, 2006; Munck, 2002), the double movement framework had not been subject early on to the kind of close, forensic textual readings that other notable works in the social sciences typically received. But this omission has been partially rectified in the last decade. Based on extensive archival research and consultation of previously unpublished papers, Gareth Dale has exhaustively detailed the arguments in the book via two incisive chapters (2010, chapter 2; 2016, chapter 5) and numerous articles (2010, 2011, 2012, 2017) alongside the first major biography of Polanyi (2016). Fred Block and Margaret Somers published a major recapitulation of their decades long ground-breaking scholarship on Polanyi (Block and Somers, 2014). There has been a tremendous outpouring of new Polanyian scholarship that has sparked multiple reinterpretations of his work and its contemporary significance (Brie and Thomasberger, 2018; Hann and Hart, 2009; Harvey et al., 2007; Polanyi Levitt, 2013).

At the same time, other scholars have begun to use Polanyi as a springboard for their own intellectual projects. This has included major restatements of the key events of the era: the origins of capitalism in Europe (Lacher, 2006); the evolution of 19th century political economy culminating in the cataclysm of World War I (Halperin, 2004); the political trajectories of fascism and social democracy in the interwar years (Berman, 2006). Other scholars, meanwhile, have explicitly used the double movement as a framework to engage with developments in the contemporary period such as the trajectory of 20th-century labor movements (Silver, 2003), the resurgence of anti-globalization movements (Webster et al., 2008), the contradictions of the global political economy (Birchfield, 1999), the ideological foundations of institutional change (Blyth, 2002), privatization of citizenship rights (Somers, 2008), transformations in the American political economy (Block, 2007) and alternatives to neoliberal globalization (Evans, 2008). Wolfgang Streeck, who has used Polanyi as inspiration for the micro-foundations of a new capitalist history (Streeck, 2009, 2011, 2016), argues that the double movement offers a superior interpretation of institutional change within contemporary capitalism:

> "The reason why the notion of capitalist development as a 'double movement' appears so fruitful today as we try to understand institutional change in an era of liberalism is not only that it specifies, in a historically concrete way, the forces that drive it… It also conceives of these same forces as being in systematic conflict with one another, allowing for

> theory to be dialectical, and for change to result from contradiction and to be accounted for as the uncertain event of an ongoing contest between mutually incompatible tendencies, or social needs."
>
> (Streeck, 2009, 250)

Despite these valuable efforts at reconstruction and revision, Polanyi's own argument of the double movement can still seem under-developed as the all-too-familiar formula of the double movement – the onset of *laissez-faire* followed seamlessly in turn by a protectionist countermovement – is ritualistically cited as a helpful heuristic without any attempt to unpack the specific arguments he made about each of these processes (Dale, 2010). As I discuss more fully in the following section, a comprehensive examination of his argument about the double movement requires us to envision it as the ensemble of *four* interrelated processes: the establishment of the self-regulating market; the subsequent rise of a market society that deepens and extends market imperatives; the development of social protection to safeguard society and constrain the market; and the contradictions and crises that occur from the clash of opposing social principles within the double movement.[5] This expanded framework offers an opportunity to deepen our understanding of his work; to suggest avenues for how the double movement framework could be revised so as to underpin future comparative-historical research; and how it might illuminate the contours of our contemporary era. I want to stress that my objective herein is to mount a critical reconstruction not to defend a reverential orthodoxy. As Block and Somers have admirably pursued in their invaluable Polanyian scholarship (Block and Somers, 2014, 2021), the first task in a properly critical evaluation of his towering accomplishment is to view his work without what E. P. Thompson called "the enormous condescension of posterity" (Thompson, 1966, 12). This would be a fitting testament for a work whose bold queries, the scope and passion of its intellectual engagements, and the acuity of its intellectual judgments put to shame most modern writing in the social sciences.

My goal is therefore to offer an extensive reconstruction and critique of *The Great Transformation*: although I will have occasion to refer to some of his other writings, the focus is almost exclusively on this book alone. By subjecting the conceptual and historical foundations of the double movement to a forensic examination, I believe we are better equipped to situate Polanyi's formidable intellectual achievement. At the same time, it is only when we delineate the strengths and weaknesses of his analysis that a more coherent, plausible and politically nuanced explication of the relevance of the double movement to our present circumstances can be accomplished. I need to register a preliminary caution that my goal herein is to offer an interpretive framework and analytical reconstruction of Polanyi's argument about the double movement; it is not conceived as a work in historical sociology itself and therefore does not attempt to offer a systematic historical or analytical account of any of the core phases of the double movement (even if there is ample reflection about what such an account might entail). Similarly, I willingly accept that no amount of textual critique (of this major work or his other writings) can ever produce a definitive interpretation given that Polanyi's open ended intellectual program lends itself to multiple readings (Block and Somers, 2014; Dale, 2010; Peck, 2013).

As with any critique, there is always the danger that the value of what is being scrutinized might get lost in the morass of counterargument. My critical judgments are by no means intended to slight his work; indeed, for the truth of the matter is that I am indebted to Polanyi for stimulating me to draw out these arguments more carefully. I have consciously attempted to be appreciative, balanced and accurate in my critique especially when I disagree with him and to engage with the spirit of the book rather than impose my own critical agenda on it.

In the next section of the Introduction, I analyze the centrality of the double movement within his work. I argue for an extensive reconstruction of the double movement and discuss the rationale for such an interpretive project; I then explore the specific historical methodologies employed by Polanyi in his depiction of the double movement; and finally, I examine the relationship of the double movement to historical change. The final section explores his intellectual world, with particular emphasis on his contested relationship with Marxism and then offers an overview of the remaining chapters of the book.

The Double Movement and Historical Change

The animating spirit of *The Great Transformation* is Polanyi's desire to comprehend what he called in his subtitle the "political and economic origins of our times". In actual fact, there are several social transformations that hold center stage in his treatise that relate directly to the evolution and dynamic of the double movement (Blyth, 2004; Katznelson, 2003). "Yet, it is perhaps the openness of Polanyi's analytic", suggests Blyth, "that allows scholars to differ over exactly what the great transformation actually was, which is no small consideration" (Blyth, 2004, 120). Hannes Lacher sees it as the establishment of modern capitalist social relations in Europe in the 19th century (Lacher, 2006); for Sandra Halperin, it refers to the collapse of the 19th-century international order that precipitates World War I (Halperin, 2004); for John Ruggie, it is the post war re-embedding of markets, the creation of a system of 'embedded liberalism' that constitutes Polanyi's legacy (Ruggie, 1992). Michael Burawoy (2010) points to three successive transformations: from the establishment of the self-regulating market in 1830s; to the period from late 1930s-1970s when the market was in effect embedded; to the last three decades that has witnessed the resurgence of market fundamentalism. In Blyth's own judgment, which I share, there are multiple transformations predicated on cycles of disembedding and embedding that occur over time. However, in his book, it took Polanyi's prodigious leap of imagination to perceive the hidden connections between the central "great transformations" of his book –the historically unprecedented establishment of a self-regulating market economy in England and the triumph of Fascism in the 1930s. "In order to comprehend German Fascism", he claimed, "we must revert to Ricardian England" (GT, 30). The double movement, the driving force of change in the 19th and 20th centuries, remains the central concern of *The Great Transformation*.

In order to challenge the familiar assumptions and misleading understandings of the double movement that have become inscribed as conventional wisdom, I argue that we need to both deepen and expand our analysis of the double movement. The contours of the double movement that are most ritualistically cited in the scholarly literature – the establishment of a system of free market capitalism and the subsequent rise of social protection to re-embed the market – actually contain quite sophisticated explanatory frameworks regarding the origins of both the self-regulating market and social protection (Dale, 2010). These require ample explication to do proper justice to his argument as well as to evaluate the efficacy of this framework in accounting for future episodes of the double movement that arise within capitalism.

At the same time, I maintain that these familiar understandings of the double movement obscure what is the most critical aspect of the concept: that it is actually an intricate ensemble of not *two* but rather *four* interrelated processes. For Polanyi, social protection becomes an urgent demand only once the scope and intensity of market imperatives become so utterly devastating that a societal campaign for "protective covering" is provoked but this presupposes the specific social arrangements and processes of a *market society* to generate and transmit these pressures. However, these cannot be automatically inferred from and indeed have a distinct causal relation to the initial establishment of a *self-regulating system*. Likewise, once a regime of social protection is inaugurated to constrain the free market, it is incumbent to discuss how these competing social principles coexist in a single social formation. Because market actors regularly seek to weaken or escape from the confines of political and social embedding, discovering effective means of binding them to social obligations and ensuring both the material resources and political capacity for social protection is a perpetual dilemma that can always be undermined and overturned. Hence, instability and crisis are enshrined within the heart of the double movement and the fundamental opposition between social reproduction/social rights and the dynamics of the free market is enshrined within capitalist democracy itself. The final phase therefore is constituted by the contradictions, social upheaval and political stalemate that lead inexorably to crisis and cataclysm. Therefore, I argue the framework of the double movement should be expanded to a constellation of *four* phases: (1) the establishment of the self-regulating market; (2) the processes of a market society that deepen and extend market imperatives; (3) the promulgation of social protection; and (4) the ensuing clash between these mutually contradictory social principles of the market and social protection.

This perspective might appear to be a counterintuitive one: *four* component stages of a *double* movement seems at the very least a clear sign of an imprecise logic and thus requires some justification on my part. I hope to demonstrate that this framework reflects arguments that lie within the complex architecture of *The Great Transformation*; indeed, I believe that it is the very taken–for-granted nature of the book that has mandated a certain degree of critical reconstruction in order to more consistently present the core dynamics of the double movement, which are often obscured by the dramatic shape of Polanyi's narrative. For readers with more than a passing acquaintance with the book, there are bound to be some uneasy juxtapositions, yet I hope that my unconventional approach will not just stimulate novel insights and understandings but highlight areas where his formidable contributions have not been properly acknowledged.

In my first four chapters, I illuminate the hidden threads of this approach. In Chapter 2, I delineate Polanyi's multi-causal explanatory framework (employing analytical factors such as technology, social power, the state, ideology and the contradictions of the old regime) regarding the origins of the self-regulating market. In Chapter 3, I explore the interactive dynamic between embedding and disembedding in the double movement and specify three key social processes of disembedding (*market imperialism, market corrosion, market insulation*) that extend and deepen market relations and constitute the foundation of a market society. In Chapter 4, I uncover an immanent argument regarding the political foundations of social protection that challenges the functionalist reasoning of the "spontaneity" account that is also prominent in his framework. Finally, in Chapter 5, I explore the internationalization of the double movement and investigate the contradictions of the double movement that lie at the heart of his account of long term historical change and crisis. But the core dynamic of the double movement – the contested relationship and recurrent oscillation in national politics and the international market system between the oppositional forces of disembedding and embedding – is played out in every one of these chapters.

Reconstructing the double movement

Admittedly, the writings of all important social theorists contain ambiguities, inconsistencies and contradictions and thus are always open to multiple interpretations and readings. Polanyi is no different and it is a hallmark of the contemporary resurgence of interest in his work that these differences are being more clearly articulated and debated (Block and Somers, 2014, 2021; Dale, 2010; Lacher, 2019). The reconstruction that I am proposing is not intended to offer a definitive account of the double movement but rather constitutes an interpretive enquiry that can hopefully generate useful insights as opposed to entrenching a specific Polanyian orthodoxy.

I argue that this expanded framework of the double movement offers a number of distinct advantages. *First*, a reconstruction of the double movement allows us to do proper justice to the brilliant, albeit flawed, framework of the double movement in the first place and enables us to appreciate his formidable insights, which can be somewhat obscured in academic commentaries. As I trace in Chapter 2, Polanyi was among the first scholars to explicitly advocate that capitalism represents an unprecedented qualitative break in human history and he offers a multi-factor account of the origins of the self-regulating market. The critical processes of disembedding outlined in Chapter 3 presciently anticipated many significant developments in the social sciences. As an example, in documenting the cultural devastation of the free market and insisting that a rise in material standards could obscure a cultural cataclysm, he prefigured work in the moral economy tradition of E. P. Thompson (1966) as well as contemporary political economists who call for a new paradigm of development that prioritizes the social dimensions of economic growth (access to public goods, citizenship rights, community integration, well-being, environmental sustainability and the like) as opposed to the prevailing fixation on GDP (Fitoussi et al., 2010; Hall and Lamont, 2013). As I discuss in Chapter 4, his emphasis on how countermovements for social protection are mobilized from all segments of society on the basis of the deleterious consequences of commodification represents a challenge to Marxist explanations stressing exploitation and social class; these "Polanyi movements" have received renewed attention in recent decades against the backdrop of the continual expansion of market fundamentalism (Burawoy, 2009; Silver, 2003; Webster et al., 2008). His argument about the central role of contradictions and crisis within capitalist democracies, the unstable equilibrium between market and society, as traced in Chapter 5, has been the inspiration for numerous works in political economy (Fraser, 2013, 2014; Offe, 1984; Streeck, 2009, 2011, 2014).

Equally, an expanded perspective enables us to better identify the enduring weaknesses of the book. As highlighted in forthcoming chapters, Polanyi's general framework can be faulted on any number of grounds, which might also have been levelled at European scholars of his intellectual generation (Dale, 2010): it sometimes fails to properly elaborate causal arguments in a clear and systematic manner but instead relies on dramatic rhetorical assertions to support his conclusions; it occasionally relies on either-or reasoning that privileges false binaries at the expense of explanatory complexity; it can be internally contradictory and prone to functionalist argument that minimizes the scope of human agency and political strategy; it does not always employ historical-comparative analysis in a rigorous manner but instead falls back on a structural perspective that has difficulty in adjudicating diverse pathways. As discussed in further detail in later chapters, his specific treatment of the dynamics of the double movement also suffers from a number of flaws. On the disembedding side, for example, his depiction of a market society downplays the process whereby the corrosive effects of commodification might be mitigated by wider social and cultural contexts or the ways in which marketization might actually generate beneficial outcomes; on the embedding side, he is plagued by an overly optimistic belief in the inevitability of social protection and he does not always acknowledge that the broad coalition behind the countermovement might well obscure forms of social protection that reinforce social oppression and domination (Fraser, 2013). The unresolved tensions between these opposing social principles, as we shall see in Chapter 5, often has a greater descriptive rather than explanatory power to depict the formidable social change of the epoch. But the wider reconstruction that I am proposing herein allows us to properly identify these inconsistencies, correct mistaken impressions of his argument, as well as to reveal areas where he actually offers competing accounts to familiar scholarly claims.

Second, an expanded portrait of the double movement reveals what a formidable challenge – epistemological, analytical and normative – Polanyi's work represented to conventional approaches in the social sciences (Block and Somers, 2014; Somers, 2008). "Nothing obscures our social vision as effectively as the economistic prejudice" insisted Polanyi (GT, 159). What he called the "economistic fallacy" is founded on the belief that market values, incentives and structures are an ever-present feature of human history; that "economic" mechanisms are the central organizing principles of all societies; and that human nature can essentially be comprehended by rational self-interest, material concerns and productive activity. In the classical economist's worldview, the market is seen as an elemental, inexorable force of nature yet, all the while, "society as a whole remained invisible" (GT, 258). As discussed in Chapter 3, Polanyi had nothing but scathing contempt for free market ideologues whose "icy silence" (GT, 98) and "perversion of cruelty" (GT, 224) callously disregarded the suffering and hidden injuries engendered by a rapacious market and who proved all too willing to countenance any amount of social and material insecurity in the name of economic "improvement". Against their indifference, he insisted there was a moral imperative to improve our capacity for social learning:

> "We find ourselves stultified by the legacy of a market economy which bequeathed us oversimplified views of the function and role of the economic system in society. If the crisis is to be overcome, we must recapture a more realistic vision of the human world and shape our common purpose in light of that recognition."
>
> (Polanyi, 1947, 17)

Indeed, one of Polanyi's enduring strengths is the way that intellectual and moral questions are seamlessly intertwined in his work (Block and Somers, 1984, 2014; Dale, 2010; Katznelson, 2003). As discussed more fully in Chapter 3, his indictment of capitalism is premised on a series of normative propositions: that the market system represents a tragic waste of human potential; that the relentless objectification and subordination of human beings by the scythe of commodification is morally wrong and socially unsustainable; that the discovery of paths to human liberation and autonomy, which should constitute the fit aim of every society, is cruelly thwarted by the market. In the Polanyian world view, complex freedom and security is predicated on shared fate and social reciprocity and a belief that individual freedom could only be achieved via social cooperation and mutual obligations. Because of this fierce emancipatory stance, he was insistent that adjudicating the proper scope of the market and the spheres of social life open to commodification is an urgent political, social and moral question for all societies (explored more fully in Chapter 7) (Sandel, 2012). Chapters 4 and 5 discuss the crucial role of states in setting collective constraints on the market yet given the very unpredictability of market relations, these will always be contingent and dynamic and therefore political life in the Polanyian universe requires a permanent capacity for innovation and reinvention.

Third, given my aim to reinstate the double movement as the primary hallmark of Polanyi's theoretical enterprise, I argue that extending and deepening our understanding of the double movement is necessary to advance the efficacy of a Polanyian approach (both as an explanatory and interpretive framework) to the study of social change within capitalist societies (Fraser, 2013; Streeck, 2016). At its heart, the double movement postulates an endemic tension between capitalist markets and democratic politics; between capitalist development and social reproduction and the natural order; between contrasting principles of social organization, one based on profit maximization, accumulation and the self-regulating virtues of market forces and another predicated on social needs and equality. The expanded account I offer moves beyond the conventional emphasis on the establishment of the self-regulating market to properly delineate the continual widening and deepening of market relations that lie at the heart of every market society (Somers, 2008). A hallmark of our current era of market fundamentalism is the relentless transformation of social spheres into "fictitious commodities" – the new forms of financialization (derivatives, securitization of loans, credit swaps) and the gradual spread of market relations into everyday lives that were the proximate cause of the 2008 crash are a telling illustration of this trend, but this development is coeval with the increased commodification of labor around the globe (alongside an unwanted decommodification as many are driven out of the work force altogether) and the deepening commodification of land, water, and natural resources that have left in their wake a rising tide of insecurity and inequality across the globe. A diverse amalgam of social and cultural forces, marshalling distinct social and political motivations, struggle to design appropriate measures to counter market expansion and disintegration. But a regime of social protection must be continually adaptive, innovative and encompassing in order to match the innate dynamism of the market and to shelter society from the destabilizing and destructive consequences of the deepening and intensification of market relations (Block and Somers, 2014; Evans, 2008; Streeck, 2011, 2016).

The double movement perspective therefore stresses the perpetual volatility, if not fundamental incompatibility, of coexistence within the same social formation of two competing social principles (Fraser, 2013). Offe perfectly captures the instability inscribed into the very nature of the double movement: "Certain indispensable elements of a social structure cannot be integrated because they are at odds with each other; i.e., the social structure paralyzes itself because the elements necessary for its survival at the same time render it impossible" (Offe, 1984, 262). A vital problematic for all democratic capitalist societies is how to integrate a ruthlessly expansive and disembedded market with the primary needs of social reproduction and an egalitarian society. Each era might arrive at distinct means of reconciling these tensions through particular forms of cultural, political and social embedding.

Nevertheless, as delineated more fully in Chapter 5, Polanyi seemingly implies that all institutional solutions within the double movement to this "Polanyi problem" are ultimately self-defeating and thus a systemic imperative for crisis and disequilibrium lies at the heart of a system that incorporates two competing principles of social organization within the same social formation (Streeck, 2016). In Chapter 7, we explore whether the double movement system can be transcended by an alternate political economy of decommodification and if the inherent undermining and destabilizing tendencies can be constrained or arrested. But it is the wider lesson I want to underscore here: in the double movement world, moments of economic prosperity, social harmony and international peace might actually prove to be much more short-lived than anticipated, which means a vital political and moral task of every era is to continually rediscover new ways of creating and sustaining these periods. In the Polanyian world view, the possibilities of hope are always tempered by a historically grounded realism, a perspective that feels increasingly resonant in our crisis plagued era.

Historical methodology and the double movement

In the scholarly literature, Polanyi has been claimed on behalf of partisans in economic anthropology, economic history, economic sociology and political economy but, given his overriding emphasis that the dynamics of the double movement (if not capitalism more broadly) impart a specific direction and rhythm to modernity, I primarily situate his work within the grand narratives of historical sociology (Block and Somers, 1984, 2014; Dale, 2010; Katznelson, 2003). His subject – the transformation of capitalism into a social, institutional and historical order – was, alongside the formation of nation states, the key historical development of the 19th and early 20th centuries (Tilly, 1984, 14–15). It is incumbent therefore to highlight the conceptual and methodological foundations of Polanyi's analysis of the double movement that will be discussed in much greater detail in each of the opening chapters.

Charles Tilly's influential typology of historical explanation is a helpful guide to analyze the strengths and weaknesses of Polanyi's explanatory perspective (Tilly, 1984). In terms of Tilly's classification schema, Polanyi seems at first glance to fit the profile of two approaches, those of *universalizing comparisons* and *encompassing comparisons.* If we focus on the first of these, *universalizing comparisons* are employed in situations where multiple cases exhibit sufficient similarity for them to be treated as a common pattern; the intent of the scholar is to demonstrate that the same set of processes and institutions recur across widely disparate settings. In this framework, the researcher typically begins with a critical juncture that initiated the historical dynamic in question; this is then broken down into a set of discrete events or stages; and then the process is extended to other cases that can be shown to exhibit the same common properties of the initial circumstances. The universalizing comparison method, suggests Tilly, has an important advantage in that it obviates the requirement for a separate explanatory framework for each setting yet at the same time it heightens awareness of the similarities and differences across distinct historical and comparative contexts (1984, 145).

The double movement argument bears all the hallmarks of this approach. A paradigmatic statement of the universalizing approach comes in the opening pages of his book:

> "Nothing could seem more inept than the attempt to reduce a civilization, its substance and ethos, to a hard and fast number of institutions; to select one of them as fundamental and proceed to argue the inevitable self-destruction of civilization on account of some technical quality of its economic organization. Civilizations, like life itself, spring from the interaction of a great number of independent factors which are not, as a rule, reducible to circumscribed institutions. To trace the institutional mechanism of the downfall of a civilization may well appear as a hopeless endeavor. Yet it is this we are undertaking. In doing so we are consciously adjusting our aim to the extreme singularity of the subject matter. For the civilization of the nineteenth century was unique precisely in that it centered on a definite institutional mechanism."
>
> (GT, 4)

Polanyi claimed that the entire world civilization of the 19th and 20th centuries was locked into the institutional order of the double movement, which acted as the hidden "gear of social change" (GT, 237) subjecting all nations, no matter their distinct societies and polities, to its imperatives. "From such uniformity of underlying institutional arrangements derived the intriguing similarity in the pattern of events which in the half-century 1879–1929 was spread out over an enormous expanse", he wrote. "An endless variety of personalities and backgrounds, mentalities and historical antecedents gave local color and topical emphasis to the vicissitudes of many countries, and yet, over the greater part of the world civilization was of the same fabric" (GT, 209; see also 162, 218, 244).[6]

Critical junctures certainly play a major role in Polanyi's work (Block, 2003). The onset of the self-regulating market in 1834, the transition from free trade to protectionism and inter-imperialist rivalry after the Great Depression of 1873, the return to *laissez-faire* in the 1920s that precipitated the descent into barbarism: all are watershed moments that trigger profound historical transformations. In the opening pages, he highlights his determination to focus on these key turning points:

> "Ours is not a historical work; what we are searching for is not a convincing sequence of outstanding events but an explanation of their trend in terms of human institutions. We shall feel free to dwell on scenes of the past with the sole object of throwing light on matters of the present; we shall make detailed analyses of critical periods and almost totally disregard the connecting stretches of time..."
>
> (GT, 4)

He believed these critical junctures were moments when the ability of policymakers and the populace to perceive the outlines of change became particularly opaque; when the role of political and social agency took on heightened significance; and when opportunities for radical institutional upheaval were considerably enhanced. In this regard, Polanyi anticipated the important work of David Collier and Ruth Berins Collier on critical junctures (Collier and Collier, 1991): they also stress how these periods produce polarizing reactions among various social agents which act as a tipping point sparking political processes and social developments that exercise a strong legacy on future events. Ira Kaztnelson helpfully clarifies the analytical stakes involved in this approach:

> "The issues bundled in the word 'origins' include matters of *descriptive* inference –identifying objects of analysis and providing a scheme of periodization – and of *causal* inference, entailing simplified but powerful analytical models of history and its sequencing. In identifying a particular moment as the time of origins, two sets of causal problems are raised: the *sources* of this constituting moment and the *mechanisms* governing its subsequent effects."
>
> (Katznelson, 2003, 51, fn 13, my emphasis)

My expanded framework follows on from this insight, with Chapter 2 investigating Polanyi's brief for 1834 as the Year Zero of the free market and the following chapters detailing the processes diffusing from this original tipping point that constitute the double movement dynamic including the development of a market society, inauguration of social protection and internationalization of the double movement system.

But, as Tilly cautioned, the universalizing approach also entails significant drawbacks. One particular concern is that systematic differences between cases are often used to illustrate the general principle at stake rather than to explore variations in depth (Tilly, 1984). In a sense, this seems to contradict the familiar perspective of Polanyi that situates him as one of the forefathers of comparative political economy that stresses the enduring differences between nations (Hollingsworth and Boyer, 1997; Block and Somers, 1984). Certainly, there are ample moments in the book where his focus is on comparison and variation. To take but a single example, I explore in Chapter 4 how he employs a historical-comparative framework to explain the origins of social protection, yet his overriding emphasis is to validate the significance of the double movement as a universal system. As we shall see, Polanyi only sporadically investigates whether variation in the underlying conditions of the double movement – not just the presence or absence of factors, but qualitative differences in the character and intensity of particular sequences of commodification, the corrosiveness of the market or distinct forms of counter-movements or policies of social protection – might generate systematic differences in outcomes.

A related critical lacuna arises from this universalizing perspective. As I highlight across several chapters, a persistent problem in his analysis of the double movement is the difficulty Polanyi encounters in "specifying the phenomena" (Merton, 1987; Tilly, 1984). As discussed in Chapter 2, his definition of the self-regulating market sometimes suffers from being insufficiently differentiated from that of capitalism more generally or industrialization; in Chapter 5, the internationalization of the double movement (in other words, the contention that all nations participated in the international market system and adopted social protection and that therefore the same cause and effects of the double movement system occurred across disparate settings) is not rigorously established in his account. These omissions have real consequences for his framework because it is much harder to argue for the universalizing impact of the double movement if its constituent elements are not adequately established.

At the same time, Polanyi's argument about the double movement features a related methodological approach. "*Encompassing comparisons*", suggests Tilly, "place different instances at various locations within the same system, explaining their characteristics as a function of their varying relationships to the system as a whole" (Tilly, 1984, 115). Within large-scale processes, such as the development of capitalism or industrialization, the similarities and differences of particular cases might reflect more their systematic interconnection to an overall system rather than to intrinsic characteristics of the cases themselves. Because all units and events are conceived as part of a larger social entity, the character and agency of each aspect is determined and constrained by their relationship to the wider social process itself. And by delineating the interconnections between ostensibly disparate events, this method gives scholars an incentive to ground their analyses in the specific historical contexts they are researching (1984, 147).[7]

Again, there is no question that Polanyi utilizes this approach throughout the book.[8] "The utopian springs of the dogma of *laissez-faire*", he wrote, "are but incompletely understood as long as they are viewed separately. The three tenets – competitive labor market, automatic gold standard, and international free trade – formed one whole. The sacrifices involved in achieving any one of them was useless, if not worse unless the other two were equally secured. It was everything or nothing" (GT, 138). The double movement constitutes a holistic system with interlocking components that structure social action and circumscribe the feasible set of policy options. As noted earlier, he insisted that the origins of 20th-century fascism were to be found in the establishment of the free market in 19th-century England. In his analysis of the contradictions that emerge from the dialectical tension between market and social protection, he suggests that domestic outcomes (class tensions, political instability, economic depression) can be traced to the particular insertion of each nation within the global double movement system rather than to purely national developments. "It will be easy to see", he wrote, "in what manner Germany and Russia, Great Britain and the United States, as power units, were helped or hampered by their relation to the underlying social process" (GT, 29).

However, as Tilly suggests, there are particular hazards to this approach as well. Encompassing comparisons are vulnerable to problems of functionalism in that the units of analysis are often assumed to act in a certain way because of the consequences of its behavior for the system as a whole. Polanyi certainly falls prey to this inclination at various moments in the book (Burowoy, 2003; Dale, 2010; Hechter, 1981; Katznelson, 2003). "And yet by functional determination", he wrote, "it fell to haute finance to avert general wars" (GT, 13). As I discuss in Chapter 4, this is one of the main drawbacks of his analysis of the origins of social protection, which relies in part on functionalist reasoning; it emphasizes the inevitability of social protection once such an urgent social need was demonstrated, even though the mere presence of an urgent necessity by no means ensures that such a solution will be identified, forthcoming or efficacious. However, an immanent critique, discussed more fully in Chapter 4, offers a competing framework for social protection that more closely establishes an explanatory link between structural need and collective action.

There is also the concomitant dilemma of specifying how the fate of social and political actors owes more to their particular insertion into the double movement system rather than to the peculiar development of idiosyncratic national contexts (Halperin, 2004). As an example, Polanyi argued that the rise of fascism could be traced to the structural imperative of the double movement and insisted that the political trajectory of nations depended on their particular insertion into the double movement system, which led to multiple pathways and solutions. He stressed the pernicious dilemmas and unsolvable paradoxes faced by all reform governments in the 1920s: in order to solve their desperate economic crisis, they could either cut wages and social services, which was politically unpalatable, or abandon the gold standard and embark on more expansive monetary policies, which was equally sacrilegious (GT, 228, 233). All potential options were sharply conditioned by the institutional and intellectual legacies inherited from the dynamics of the double movement in the 1920s, even if the precise political pathways chosen to avoid crisis owed as much to long term historical and political legacies (Berman, 2006), a debate we address more fully in Chapter 5.

The double movement and historical change

Unquestionably, one of Polanyi's primary aims in writing *The Great Transformation* was to examine the underlying patterns and regularities of history in order to make sense of the chaos unfolding before his eyes. "Yet in spite of all its wealth and variety", he insisted:

> "the flow of history has its recurrent situations and alternatives which account for the broad similarity in the texture of events of an age. We need not trouble about the fringe of unpredictable eddies, if we can account to some degree for the regularities which governed currents and countercurrents under typical conditions."
>
> (GT, 218)

The rebirth of the self-regulating market in the 1920s, which took center stage in the last section of his book, might have led him to emphasize the cyclical nature of the double movement yet he was convinced that society had learned the harsh lessons of the past and henceforth the utopian experiment of the free market would be forever banished from history. "In retrospect, our age will be credited", wrote Polanyi, "with having seen the end of the self-regulating market...The restoration of the past is as impossible as the transferring of our troubles to another planet" (GT, 142, 250–1).

Of course, his confidence in the vanishing act of market society has been belied by the present day apparition of neoliberalism as we highlight in Chapter 6. But we might reasonably attribute his oversight to an understandable bout of wishful thinking amidst the horrors of World War II rather than as a logical outcome of his own model of the double movement. "After all, if disembedding the market led to a double movement where labor demanded protection through an institutional re-embedding, then was it not reasonable to expect, in turn, another reaction against those embedding institutions by those most affected, namely capitalists?", writes Blyth. "In fact, the political struggle between disembedding and embedding the market continues today, even though its contours have shifted" (Blyth, 2002, 4). Beyond the "Great Transformation" of Polanyi's remit, the entire 20th-century (and the first decades of the 21st) could be viewed as a "pendulum-like motion" of successive great transformations and iterations of the double movement (Silver, 2003, 17): from the golden age of "embedded liberalism" (Ruggie, 1982; Marglin and Schor, 1990) stretching from the 1940s until the late 1970s followed by the counter-reaction of *laissez-faire* that has dominated economic policy and social life in the last five decades (Blyth, 2002; Burawoy, 2010) (see the discussion in Chapter 6). Certainly, this is the tack recommended by Streeck whose account of institutional change under capitalism is explicitly modeled on the double movement:

> "I propose that institutional development and institutional change under capitalism are the outcome of a struggle between processes for an expansion of markets and increasing commodification of social relations on the one hand, with the uncertainty and instability these entail, and with social demands for political stabilization of relative prices and extant social structures on the other."
>
> (Streeck, 2009, 5)[9]

The trajectory of change and the balance of power *within* the double movement system, which remains one of the least theorized aspects of the double movement, is also critical to the relationship between the double movement and historical change (Arrighi and Silver 2003; Block 2003, 2007; Blyth, 2002; Lacher, 2019). In Chapter 5, I use the Gramscian term "unstable equilibrium" to describe the balance of forces within the double movement (Gramsci, 1971, 182) and throughout the opening chapters, I detail the areas in which the reconstructed framework can flush out the contours of this combustible oscillation. This requires specifying and delineating any number of social processes – the origins of *laissez-faire*, the scope of market imperatives, the destructiveness of market relations, the extent and efficacy of the market's adaptive capacity, the range of political and social interests mobilized on behalf of embedding the market, the innovative design of social protection, the forms and duration of state failures, the ideological machinations of supporters of both embedding and disembedding, to analyze the timing and direction of change within the cycle (Hirschman, 1982). But we also need to clearly specify the contours of this mutual interdependence, the ways in which these durable interactions might become self-reinforcing or undermining, and the points at which the institutional order comes under challenge and contestation. Equally, it is incumbent to explore the ways in which these opposing principles mutually contaminate each other's respective spheres, infusing political authority with market calculations and market relations with political dictates (Offe, 1984; Cohen and Rogers, 1983).

As Fred Block emphasizes, the outcomes of the dynamic between these contrasting poles can never be predicted in advance and can produce divergent political and historical outcomes:

> "The relative strength of the two sides of the double movement at any particular time can produce a range of different outcomes. These include…periods of political stalemate in which neither side is able to

> exert enough power to make institutions work effectively, and periods of relatively benign balancing where the victories of countermovements help create the conditions for sustained economic growth. In a word, there is no automatic mechanism that pushes societies to the proper balance between these contending forces."
>
> (Block, 2007, 7)

Nor, given the dynamic interactions of embedding and disembedding in every cycle, is it so straightforward to adjudicate which is in the ascendancy or on the wane and scholars might well draw distinct lessons about these matters (Block and Somers, 2021; Lacher, 2019). As discussed in Chapter 6, the post war "golden age" of social protection might have installed an unprecedented period of security and equality but it also led to a massive widening and deepening of market relations and commodification; while the neoliberal era represents the triumph of market ideology and policy making, it has also fostered ground breaking initiatives of social protection that have reduced poverty and inequality.

Polanyi envisages change within the double movement system as the product of persistent, systemic, and dialectical change: a long term, endogenous transformation of a slowly disintegrating institutional system alongside radical, discontinuous breaks where tumultuous tipping points can precipitate a systemic collapse (Block and Somers, 2014; Streeck, 2009).[10] In the Polanyian world view, historical change has no teleological endpoint, no fixed outcomes; the balance of power with the double movement and transitions between cycles remain unpredictable and politically contingent.

Nevertheless, the assertion of a common pattern across such disparate time periods raises complex methodological issues that require careful attention. "A cycle is presumably defined", suggested Albert Hirschman, "as a process in whose course identical forces are responsible over and over again for moving economy or society from one point to the next" (Hirschman, 1982, 15). In the case of the double movement, we would need to delineate the common process underpinning each repeat occurrence and "to be persuasive, such a theory must be endogenous, that is, one phase must be shown to arise necessarily out of the preceding one" (1982, 4). The validity of the periodization also needs to be properly established: it has to be shown not only that these eras can be properly bounded historically, but that a similar set of problems and processes that are identified in the earlier period are still of consequence in the present. Even if similarities are not based on false analogies or superficial affinities that obscure deeper differences, we cannot assume that present day events will be explained by the same causal relationships, or that the findings of the earlier period will automatically substantiate the causal claims of the current period, or that these processes will necessarily take the same form in both times or generate the same effects (Tilly, 1984).

Given these complexities, this contention of a recurrent cycle in capitalism begs an even more fundamental set of paradoxes. If the double movement is indeed a structural regularity within capitalism's history, then how do we account for this development and how do we explain transitions within the double movement itself?[11] William Sewell succinctly poses the essential quandary:

> "In spite of the eventful, even hyper-eventful, character of the capitalist economy, there appears to be a recurrent logic at the centre of the flux that generates a continuous, monotonous repetitive pattern. This recurrent logic must, in some sense, be extremely abstract, since the concrete institutions and materials through which the repetitive pattern manifests itself change radically over time."
>
> (Sewell, 2008, 521)

In order for the double movement to constitute such a cyclical logic, it would need to demonstrate several processes: that the relentless forces of market expansion and market corrosion are ubiquitous throughout capitalist history (although the precise forms that they assume and the kinds of social and cultural disruption they engender can vary considerably); that economic and political actors (with distinct ideologies, institutional practices and capacities) repeatedly view economic liberalism as a feasible and favored solution to crisis across various historical periods; and that there are compelling reasons why feasible alternatives are not selected by political and economic elites. At the same time, the social and political forces inscribed in democratic societies must continually search for a *rapprochement* that ensures social reproduction and stability without jeopardizing economic prosperity or dynamism even if this too will require an efficacious combination of political coalitions, social resistance and institutional innovation whose outcome can neither be guaranteed or predicted in advance. The reconstructed framework of the double movement proposed herein, with its primary emphasis on the ways in which the underlying dialectic of disembedding and embedding play out across every one of the four phases, is an attempt to partially address this problematic. In this expanded framework, the double movement operates as both a *structural* regularity within capitalism and as a *contingent* political project.

The stipulation of the double movement as a critical recurrence within capitalist history reveals a final paradox. *The Great Transformation* is honeycombed with salutary examples of how 19th- and 20th-century actors were not only unable to comprehend the wave of change that enveloped them, they also failed abysmally to learn the lessons of the past. Although social agents are instrumental in driving historical change forward, they are also partially blinded by the very complexities and operations of the double movement which obscures their ability to perceive the contours of change: "on the eve of the greatest industrial revolution in history, no signs and portents were forthcoming. Capitalism arrived unannounced" (GT, 89). "Nowhere has liberal philosophy failed so conspicuously", he wrote, "as in its understanding of the problem of change" (GT, 33). As we shall see in Chapter 5, political leaders under the spell of liberal dogma in the 1920s remained singularly blind to the dangers of a return to *laissez-faire*: in this period, people "continued to exist in an almost indescribable state of confusion" and "awareness of the essential nature of the problems of politics sank to an unprecedented low point" (GT, 21, 189). "Not even when the cataclysm was already upon them", wrote Polanyi, "did their leaders see that behind the collapse of the international system there stood a development within the most advanced countries which made that system anachronistic; in other words, the failure of market economy itself still escaped them" (GT, 20).

Polanyi's faith in the ability of historical analysis to illuminate the hidden trajectory of social change was not merely a conceptual claim but represented a core philosophical and political stance within his work. He believed that the perverse logic of capitalism was objectionable, not merely because of its innate destructiveness, but because it impaired our societal capacity for learning. *Laissez-faire*, he remarked, "is paralyzing our social imagination by more or less fostering the prejudice of economic determinism" (GT, 73). The hegemony of market life, he implied, cast a long shadow over the future: setting constraints (material, institutional, spiritual) on the very possibility of change and exercising a tyranny over our perception of the efficacy and feasibility of alternatives. The underlying message of his work is that human societies need to find new ways of improving the ability to interpret the past and present, of discovering again and again a rejuvenated capacity for problem solving, innovation and social learning that can properly tame the market. The historical imagination, in this sense, is inextricably aligned with hope: an abiding conviction that societies will continue to demonstrate an amazing resiliency and spark of invention and the promise that a fairer, more egalitarian, and peaceful form of social cooperation lies within our reach, a question we revisit in the final chapter.

Polanyi's Intellectual World

Like many great social thinkers, Polanyi was, in Hirschman's elegant phrase, a "trespasser of boundaries": a writer equally comfortable in discussing the economic livelihood of the Kula community, the intricacies of the gold standard and the international monetary system in the 19th century, or the origins of Fascism.[12] *The Great Transformation* is a veritable primer in interdisciplinary scholarship, encompassing anthropology, historical sociology, economic history, and political economy. Its historical reach is audacious, traversing the enclosure movement of the late 16th century to the 100 years peace of the 19th century to the onset of fascist movements in the 20th. It cuts against the grain of the dominant paradigm of disciplinary specialization and the contemporary enshrinement of the short term that has made genuinely interdisciplinary work and scholarship of historical and disciplinary reach along the lines of Polanyi an anathema. Its passionate commitment to historical critique and moral engagement is deeply unfashionable at a time when the influential post-modern paradigm denies the very existence of orderly processes in the social world or the possibility of achieving cumulative and reliable social knowledge.

Polanyi in many ways bears a close kinship with the classic European founders of sociological thought – there are echoes of many of the great social theorists (Marx, Durkheim, Weber) in *The Great Transformation*, even if his eclectic intellectual sensibilities are such that his argument is never predicated on any single one of these influences (Dale, 2010). As an example, the opening chapters demonstrate a distinctive resonance with Durkheim: his emphasis on the importance of non-market relations of trust, reciprocity and cooperation as key elements in the sustenance of a market economy; his claim that the cultural devastation of a market society leads to anomie, insecurity and the collapse of traditional values; his assertion that collective action against the market emerges "spontaneously" in response to the "disruptive strains" of social distress. Likewise, there are numerous examples within his work of an affinity with Weber: his insistence on the centrality of the state in the development of the market and regulation of economic activity, his recognition that capitalism represented a qualitative break from the past, and the denial of human subjectivity and social relations via commodification.

But, unquestionably, it is Marxism that exerted the most sustained influence on his theoretical agenda, historical methodology and moral sensibilities (Block and Somers, 1984; Block, 2003; Burawoy, 2003; Dale, 2010, 2016; Lacher, 2019).[13] Polanyi believed he was articulating a distinct alternative to Marx, one that equally recognized and opposed the inequality and irrationality of capitalism yet managed to avoid the dangers of economism and determinism which he thought plagued the Marxist approach. For instance, he debunked the idea that class was the primary basis of group solidarity or the key agent of social and political change; he believed classes were cultural rather than purely economic institutions and reflected broader social interests based on their wider social function and organization. He insisted that both Marxists and classical political economists fell prey to the economic determinism of the "economistic fallacy" and emphasized instead the enduring importance of broader social institutions and relationships in the formation and development of market activity. And, despite his argument about the centrality of the double movement to historical change, he denied that there was any substance to Marxist theories of history predicated on the law-like dynamics of modes of production.

This contrarianism is somewhat forced in several respects. First, it tends to blur the extent to which Polanyi could be chastised for many of these same flaws: one of the paradoxes of his work is that some of the things he dislikes most about opposing theoretical positions – the "spontaneity" argument of liberals, the economic determinism of Marxism, the reification of the economy by classical economists – are unconsciously emulated in his own analysis from time to time. Second, it detracts attention from the areas in which he was offering a genuine alternative to the Marxist tradition. For instance, Polanyi highlighted (as discussed in Chapter 3) the role of international finance in securing pacific relations which countered Lenin's belief that it had led to imperialism and war. One might cite as well his argument (detailed in Chapter 4) that the inspiration for the protectionist counter-movement arose as a societal response to the perils of commodification that threatened all of society as opposed to the class-based emphasis on exploitation that characterized the Marxist approach to collective action and struggle (Burawoy, 2009; Webster et al., 2008). Or for that matter his insistence on the centrality of the double movement as the motor of historical change rather than the Marxist emphasis on transformations in class structure and class conflict.

Perhaps, most importantly, this gambit obscures the real legacy of the Marxist tradition on Polanyi. As I highlight throughout the book, the writings of Marx and other leading Marxists, notwithstanding his repeated protestations to the contrary, offer numerous affinities to his work. His emphasis on the perils of commodification, the view of capitalism as a historical break in modernity, the corrosive power of capitalism that collapses everything in its wake, the unparalleled ability of the market system to insinuate its values and imperatives into the entire society, the contradictory, destabilizing nature of capitalism as a social order: all can be traced directly to Marx's own problematic. In his emphasis on discontinuity and upheaval, in his desire to perceive the hidden motor of change in the critical moments of transition of each age, Polanyi certainly can be identified with the other leading Marxists of the early 20th century, such as Bloch, Gramsci and Lukacs, all of whom shared similar preoccupations (Birchfield, 1999; Burawoy, 2003; Dale, 2010; ; Mendell and Salee, 1991).

One vital trait that he also shared with the Marxist tradition was his abiding appreciation of the role of paradoxes in social life (Block and Somers, 1984; Dale, 2010).[14] There are innumerable examples throughout the book that evidence his inordinate fondness for these kind of intellectual and historical puzzles. Sometimes it might be a historical oddity that needs to be explained: how was it that the Speenhamland system of poor relief persisted long after it had been demonstrably proven to be a calamity; how did the pursuit of self-interest lead to the unprecedented hundred years' peace of the 19th century; how could the establishment of the free market produce both higher living standards and a cultural catastrophe? At other times it might be the wrong-headed interpretations attributed to events by social commentators: in the dominant explanation of the onset of *laissez-faire,* he insisted that "the logic of the case is, indeed, almost the opposite of that underlying the classical doctrine" (GT, 58) and he lambasted 19th-century liberals "whose minds habitually missed the characteristics of the world they were living in" (GT, 202). On other occasions, it might be the puzzling behavior of individuals, social groups or even nations that requires clarification, as when he attempts to explain the "seeming paradox of imperialism – the economically inexplicable and therefore allegedly irrational refusal of countries to trade together indiscriminately, and their aiming instead at the acquisition of overseas and exotic markets" (GT, 214). Polanyi had an abiding appreciation of the "cunning of history", the ways in which social action can systematically produce unintentional consequences that undermine institutional orders and unlock social change. "Much genuine idealism sprang from the sphere of barter and trade", he wrote, "by a supreme paradox, man's selfish wants were validating his most generous impulses" (GT, 198). He appears to positively revel in demonstrating how all of social life seems to be saturated by the incongruous and the absurd. This ubiquitous feature is consciously echoed in his prose style, as dialectical pairs square off in elegant clauses and the stark absurdity of these historical conundrums is driven home by brute repetition. "*Laissez faire* was planned, planning was not" (GT, 141), he wrote. "Instead of economy being embedded in social relations, social relations are embedded in the economic system" (GT, 57).

If Polanyi was both an amazingly provocative and synthetic thinker, he could be an untidy one as well. He typically dispenses with classical narrative form in *The Great Transformation*. The opening themes are developed in the first few chapters, and then unceremoniously dropped, only to resurface in the last section of the book with little fanfare. With rare exceptions, which demand particular scrutiny because they are often so revealing of his intentions, his arguments are not marshaled in classic social science style (first…, second…, third, etc.) nor is there any systematic exposition of the causal arguments, which has necessitated a certain amount of reconstruction in my own analysis. Polanyi's conceptual intentions are often foreshadowed by the rhetorical device of repetition: in order to drive home the significance of a particular idea (the spontaneity of social protection, the leading role of haute finance in the 100 years' peace, the lacerating effects of the Speenhamland system), he typically makes the same argument over and over again in slightly different formulations over the course of a handful of pages. In all these respects, he is in the great tradition of European thought – these same charges could be leveled at Marx or Weber – yet it makes him harder to appreciate in the context of modern social science discourse in which historical evidence and causal claims are no longer used in such a wide-ranging fashion. This is no way diminishes the literary accomplishments of the book: it is immensely quotable, full of pithy epigrams, memorable metaphors and stirring phrases, a biting irony and wit, and polemical force (McRobbie, 2000). Even the disjointed structure enhances its attraction, transforming academic puzzle into nail biting cliffhanger, and as his narrative breathlessly evokes the historical drama, so too are the analytical elements fused with a moral jeremiad.

What Lies Ahead

The Great Transformation is a magisterial work that deserves, if not demands, a forensic examination of its formidable strengths and weaknesses, which is the task I have set myself in this monograph. The book is structured along the lines of the four phases of the "double movement". The first is the establishment of the free market economy, what Polanyi refers to as the "self-regulating market". Chapter 2 ("The Origins of the Self-Regulating Market") examines his conceptualization of the self-regulating market, his account of its origins, and a general overview of his historical method. I begin with his insight that capitalism, as a system of economic activity and a nexus of social relations and institutions, represented a qualitative break in human history. This has long been a matter of intense historiographical debate and I discuss his original contribution to the transition question. I explore the three factors that Polanyi identified as the distinctive elements of capitalism – the commodification of the critical aspects of social life (land, labor and money), competition, and the universalizing aspects of the market – and explore his account of the critical juncture of 1834, which witnessed the birth of the self-regulating market. In the middle section of the chapter, I offer an extensive scrutiny of the explanatory framework that he used to explain the rise of the self-regulating market: featuring technology, social power, the state/political power, contradictions of the preceding regime of political economy, and ideology as key factors. Finally, I undertake a broader overview of the conceptual and methodological implications of his framework.

The second phase of the double movement is the creation of a market society: the set of social arrangements that facilitate the subordination of all of society to the dictates of the market. Although closely associated with Polanyi, the concept of the "market society" is considerably underdeveloped in his work and the contours (both conceptually and empirically) of this entity are not elaborated in any consistent or rigorous fashion. In Chapter 3 ("The Dynamics of Market Society"), I begin by exploring the dichotomy of embedding and disembedding within his argument and suggest ways in which these concepts can be usefully united within a single framework. I then present a critical reconstruction of diverse threads within the book to argue for three core processes of a market society. The *imperialism of the market* investigates the way in which market imperatives are progressively extended and deepened into more and more spheres of social and cultural life. The *corrosion of the market* investigates the way in which the market erodes non-market domains, practices and norms. The *insulation of the market* examines how market actors and institutions are protected from social obligations and political oversight and the process whereby market power is translated into political power. In these sections, I offer a critical reading of some of Polanyi's most celebrated insights about 19th-century society: the social and cultural calamity of industrial capitalism, market driven famines in India, and the evolution of the contradictory system of capitalist democracy. I then conclude with a critique of his unique account of the "hundred years' peace", a period of pacific international relations from 1814 until 1914, which he argued was the result of the crucial influence of the double movement system.

The third phase of the double movement is the growth of social protection to ameliorate the wreckage of the market. Chapter 4 ("The Politics of Social Protection") begins by investigating the contours of social protection: identifying the specific initiatives that constitute social protection, the varied agencies that deliver this protection, and the way in which the very need for social protection is ideologically and politically constructed. The discussion then proceeds to an extensive critique of Polanyi's conceptual and empirical argument about social protection: namely, that the establishment of social protection resulted from the spontaneous act of all sectors of society to protect itself against the depredations of the market, a claim that was substantiated, he argued, by the historical evidence that all European governments, regardless of political ideology and state structures, implemented similar protection policies during the 19th and early 20th centuries. I maintain this argument is flawed because of its functionalist inclinations but at the same time, insist that the book actually offers an immanent perspective that is sensitive to institutional variation and historical discontinuity. This framework explores the extent to which the distinct nature of marketization and disembedding shape the nature of the countermovement and design of social protection. Finally, I consider the structural and historical limits to the design of social protection.

The fourth phase of the double movement concerns the contradictions that arise from the clash of competing social principles exemplified by the market and social protection. Chapter 5 ("Contradictions and Crisis within the Double Movement") explores Polanyi's account of how an international market system was established, his conceptual argument about the centrality of contradictions to social change, and the way in which these systemic tensions eventually culminate in the cataclysm of World War I and European fascism. In the first section, I explore the internationalization of the double movement, with special attention paid to the creation of the new social relations of the international system and his account of the relationship between the double movement and imperialism. I then examine the centrality of contradictions to his discussion of the double movement, explore how these impaired the international economy and chart how they precipitated a widespread social and political crisis. In the final section, I offer a forensic examination of his empirical arguments regarding the causal link between the breakdown of the double movement and the massive historical transformations of World War I and the rise of fascism.

Chapter 6 ("The Double Movement in the Contemporary Era") explores the contemporary relevance of the double movement. It begins with an exploration of whether the post war and neoliberal interregnums constituted a new double movement cycle. In the second section, I explore the efficacy of a Polanyian framework to two key concerns of the present era: the scourge of insecurity and inequality as viewed through the works of Polanyi and Thomas Piketty; and the rise of right wing populism. In a final section, I explore whether the double movement is likely to emerge as the "gear of social change" in the contemporary crisis and if, and when, a successor to neoliberalism is at all imminent.

Finally, the concluding Chapter 7 ("Transcending the Double Movement") offers a speculative discussion of what a feasible institutional design for transcending the double movement in the 21st century might entail. I believe that *decommodification*, which once animated social policy in the 1970s, will need to be rediscovered and reconceptualized as the critical principle for a new social protection. Inspired by Polanyi's concept of "complex freedom" and his speculations about a post-market future, I trace five institutional principles of a reconstructed framework for decommodification – boundary protection, enhanced public good provision, decommodified economic circuits, new forms of social protection and market transparency – and investigate the extent to which it represents a Polanyian agenda for egalitarianism and emancipation.

Notes

1 I am paraphrasing the title of John Reed's famous account of the Russian Revolution. For excellent accounts of how the crisis unfolded, consult Cassidy, 2009; Tett 2009.

2 A wider point to be highlighted is that the entire process greatly increased the centrality of the financial sector within the structure of the American economy; at the height of the crisis, the total value of global financial assets far outstripped (by over a four to one ratio) the total worth of global GDP (Panitch and Konigs, 2009).

3 One could cite any number of scholars, public intellectuals and journalists putting forth essentially the same claim. The Nobel prize-winning economist, Joseph Stiglitz, to take a single example, insisted in an article in *The Guardian* (September 20, 2008): "The fall of Wall Street is for market fundamentalism what the fall of the Berlin Wall was for communism."

4 In a survey by the International Sociology Association of the top 100 books of the 20th century, *The Great Transformation* came in at 26 just behind Antonio Gramsci, Jurgen Habermas and Barrington Moore.

5 Gareth Dale (2010) has also argued for a four stage process, albeit with significant differences, which includes marketization, countermovement, disruptive strains and socialist/fascist resolution.

6 There is a rhetorical corollary in his penchant, almost a guilty pleasure it seems given its repeated use, for depicting circumstances where the structural force of the double movement produces a uniformity in outlook among diverse actors despite very different political ideologies. As an example, in describing the return to the gold standard in the 1920s, he states: "Bismarck and Lasalle, John Stuart Mill and Henry George, Phillip Snowden and Calvin Coolidge, Mises and Trotsky equally accepted the faith…It would be hard to find any divergence between the utterances of Hoover and Lenin, Churchill and Mussolini, on this point" (GT, 25). As we shall see, he similarly employs this "strange bedfellows" rhetorical gambit to describe the overlap in anti-imperialist positions, the endorsement of social protection and the misperception of pauperism.

7 Peter Gourevich's influential article "The Second Image Reversed" attempts to delineate precisely this kind of interrelationship between international relations and domestic politics arguing that "they should be analyzed simultaneously as wholes" (Gourevich, 1978, 911).

8 Block and Somers underscore this point: "Polanyi seeks to demonstrate the structural relationship among all parts of the social whole, while rejecting the genetic determinacy of any one aspect" (Block and Somers, 1984, 62–3).

9 For a critique of this argument regarding the pendular motion of the double movement, see Dale 2012 and Lacher, 2019.

10 Mark Blyth has argued in a different vein that Polanyi's vision of the double movement lacks a clear understanding of institutional change: "The double movement, in common with other interest-based explanations of institutional change, sees change as a problem of comparative statics. That is, in order to explain institutional change, the elements of a present set of institutions are juxtaposed to those of a previous set, and then a (usually exogenous) variable is imputed that 'explains' why the latter emerged out of the former" (Blyth, 2002, 7). Although I offer a different interpretation, there is no question that this problem does surface in the text, most notably in his discussion of the 1920/1930s conjuncture that I trace in Chapter 5.

11 The problematic of recurrent cycles within capitalist history has long been a subject of scholarly investigation, with proponents postulating various factors (business cycles, financial accumulation, change in institutional regimes) as the engine behind this development. Particularly prominent is the work of Joseph Schumpeter on business cycles (Schumpeter, 1943), Giovanni Arrighi on long term cycles of financial accumulation (Arrighi, 1994) and the French regulation school (Boyer, 2008).

12 Both Fred Block and Gareth Dale rightly call attention to the fact that Polanyi's biography also represented a trespassing of geographical boundaries – from Hungary to Austria to England, the United States and Canada – and this peripatetic life as a displaced global citizen significantly impacted on the conceptual formulations in the book (Block, 2003, 4; Dale, 2010, 2016).

13 Critical judgments about Polanyi often hinge on what a scholar considers to be his relationship with Marx. Sandra Halperin essentially faults him for being insufficiently Marxist in terms of ignoring transformations in class structure, class conflict and a class-based view of the state when considering the evolution of the long 19th century (Halperin, 2004); Fred Block and Margaret Somers, for their part, emphasize Polanyi's overly close attachment to Marxism that led him to the intellectual cul de sac of embedding/disembedding discussed in Chapter 3 (Block, 2003) but generally regard the book as a distinctive break with Marxism (Block and Somers, 2014).

14 Marshall Berman argues just this point in case of Marx: "the basic fact of modern life, as Marx experiences it, is that this life is radically contradictory at its base… Our nineteenth century theorists were simultaneously enthusiasts and enemies of modern life, wrestling inexhaustibly with its ambiguities and contradictions; their self-ironies and inner tensions were a primary source of their creative power. Their 20th-century successors have lurched far more toward rigid polarities and flat totalizations" (Berman, 1982, 19, 24). This to my mind is a perfect description of Polanyi's quintessential 19th-century mentality.

Acknowledgments

This book has had far too long a gestation period but there are a number of people along the way who helped bring it to realization. I owe a special debt of thanks to Fred Block whom I approached out of the blue with a cheeky inquiry if he might be willing to read various chapters in progress. In an incredible act of generosity and graciousness, Fred agreed and proceeded to send me a series of incisive and helpful critiques of the chapters that greatly aided my thinking. I am proud to be another in a long line of scholars who have been the beneficiary of Fred's exemplary kindness and erudition. Stephen Eric Bronner of Rutgers University performed a similar feat of generosity and his thoughtful critiques challenged me to write a much better book than I would have contemplated. At Newcastle University, Jane Wheelock, is owed a special gratitude for encouraging me to read Polanyi in the first place and she, along with my colleagues Dariusz Gafijczuk, Peter Philimore and William Outhwaite, gave me the benefit of careful readings of the manuscript. For their irreplaceable intellectual camaraderie and friendship through the years, I also owe thanks to Seraphim Alvanides, Nick Arnold, Meg Aubrey, Jackie Bernard, Chris Brown, Isa Buchstaller, Toby Cann, Colin Clark, Isabel Clough, Kate Degnen, Naomi Diamond, Roberto Fernandez, Alan Gordon, Claire Gordon, Zak Gordon, Chris Gomez, Richard Greeman, Robert Hollands, Micheline Ishay, Michael Karluk, Carlangelo Liverani, David Ost, Simon Philpott, Gary Pritchard, Bruce Rafeek, Tom Reagan, Monica Santoro, Jackie Leach Scully, Peter Smith, Elaine Snaith, Paul Summers, Ash Summers, Jen Tarr, Suzanne Thompson, Michael Underhill, John Veit-Wilson, Simon Veit-Wilson, Chris Wilkins. I'd like to thank audiences at various conferences and departmental seminars for their helpful comments, including the American Political Science Association, British Sociology Association, Society for the Association of Socio-Economics, the Karl Polanyi International Conference, Lancaster University and Newcastle University. For their emotional support and countless acts of kindness, I dedicate this book to the entire Vail clan: Bridget Sheridan Vail, John Vail, Peggy Sheridan, Cathi Vail, Bernadette Vail, Michael Vail, Luke Burns, Martin Burns, Will Burns, Hannah Vail, Emma Vail, Matthew Vail, Dawn Vail and Marina Tempelsman.

Chapter 2

The Origins of the Self-Regulating Market

Our journey begins with a reconstruction of the first strand of the double movement, namely the establishment of the "self-regulating market" in England. Polanyi argued that this represented "an entirely new institutional mechanism" (GT, 40), a unique "institutional principle" (GT, 37) of social life. It was initiated only when the following conditions were met: economic activity was controlled, regulated, and directed by markets alone; all aspects of production (such as land, labor, money) were commodified, in other words, were for sale on the market and all incomes primarily derived from such sales; all economic actors were compelled to maximize their self-interest; and there was no political interference in the formation of markets or setting of prices (GT, 43, 68–9, 72–3).[1] Polanyi dates the inception of the self-regulating market to 1834, when the newly enacted New Poor Law overturned the Speenhamland system of poor relief and thereby guaranteed the complete commodification of labor and a fully competitive labor market in England.

The 1834 conjuncture occupies a crucial organizing principle in the book, especially as regards his approach to historical change. Polanyi believed the establishment of the self-regulating market represented a crucial watershed in history: for the first time, the material life of a society was dictated by the imperatives of a market economy and an entirely new set of values and practices became inscribed within society. "Nineteenth century civilization… chose to base itself on a motive only rarely acknowledged as valid in the history of human societies", he wrote, "and certainly never before raised to the level of a justification of action and behavior in everyday life, namely gain" (GT, 30). The evolution of the double movement is utterly dependent on this radical break as well: the contours of a market society are shaped by the establishment of the self-regulating market and the succeeding phase of social protection is precipitated by the calamity these events leave in their wake. It thus represented the first step in what he called the "social history of the nineteenth century": from this moment onward, the full dynamic of the double movement was unleashed across the globe, culminating in the horrific cataclysm of World War I.

DOI: 10.4324/9781003133186-2

In this chapter, I begin by examining Polanyi's argument about how the self-regulating market constituted a qualitative break in human history. I explore the three factors he identified as the distinctive elements of capitalism – the commodification of the critical aspects of social life (labor, land and money), capitalist competition and the totalizing aspects of the market – and then discuss the historical and conceptual implications of his emphasis on the paramount importance of the critical juncture of 1834. In a lengthy middle section, I offer a forensic scrutiny of his causal explanation of the rise of the self-regulating market – featuring the interplay of five distinct factors: technology, social power, the state, ideology and the contradictions of political economy – that challenges the view that his framework is devoid of such a perspective.[2] Finally, I present a wider overview of the conceptual implications of Polanyi's framework of historical change.

But before we begin, a brief caveat regarding terminology is worth highlighting. In addition to the term "self-regulating market", Polanyi also employs a number of other formulations that have typically been used to describe the general system of capitalism itself: "market economy", "market system", "competitive system", "capitalist economy" and "industrial capitalism". The confusion, as we shall demonstrate, arises because he persists in using the specific and the general terms interchangeably even when he is clearly referring to developments that he says are unique to the specific case of the self-regulating market. While he acknowledges the long evolutionary process whereby capitalism established its pre-eminence, Polanyi is specifically concerned with the installation of the self-regulating market, which he views as a qualitatively distinct social formation within capitalist history (which others, as we shall see, have suggested only refers to capitalism itself).

This definitional impreciseness is hardly a trivial matter. The nature, form and timing of the "Great Transformation" to capitalism has long been a matter of scholarly debate and controversy, with each century mustering its own partisans (R. H. Tawney and Robert Brenner for the 16th, Christopher Hill and Joyce Appleby for the 17th, Polanyi for the 19th) and indeed the bulk of the first third of *The Great Transformation* is dedicated to these debates. As I argue below, these terminological evasions reflect critical tensions in Polanyi's conceptual framework and therefore warrant careful consideration. It is important therefore to be clear that when I use the terms "market economy" or "marketization", I am referring to the general evolution of capitalism as an economic and social system which includes the process of commodification, extension of competition, and the like. I use the term "self-regulating market" to refer specifically to the 1834 epoch (also known as *laissez-faire*); and I use the term "market society" to characterize the wider transformations in social, cultural and political life that occur after this period.

Conceptualizing the Self-Regulating Market

The origin of the self-regulating market is inextricably entwined with the historical debate about the origins of capitalism itself. Two broad schools of thought dominate this discussion (Wood, 1999). The first argues that the transition to capitalism was a gradual development: the expansion of inter-state trading, the rise of urban commercial centers, a widening division of labor, alongside the increased commercialization of economic life, all slowly undermined the foundations of feudalism and created the conditions for the supremacy of the capitalist mode of production. This stance can incorporate a variety of bedfellows: economists (such as Adam Smith) who maintain that the pursuit of self-interest and the inclination to "truck and barter" were timeless characteristics of human nature; historians (such as Ferdinand Braudel), sociologists (such as Immanuel Wallerstein) and economists (such as Sanjay Hejeebu and Deidre McCloskey) who point to the evidence of commercial exchange, price differentials, profits and wages in previous historical epochs as proof that markets predated the modern era; and even Marxists (such as Paul Sweezy or Maurice Dobb) who argue that capitalist elements were buried deep within the interstices of feudal society and the transition to capitalism simply a matter of overcoming the obstacles that prevented this economic system from emerging. What links each of these perspectives is that they all describe capitalism as a more or less natural, continuous outcome that does not require a specific transition from one historically specific social formation to another.

The second perspective envisages capitalism as a historically and structurally specific institution, what Ellen Meiksins Wood depicts as "a complete transformation in the most basic human relations and practices, a rupture in age-old patterns of human interaction with nature" (Wood, 1999, 69). As she astutely notes, Polanyi is an outright proponent of this view, consciously drawing a sharp discontinuity between the character of "market society" and the non-market societies that preceded it: "the change from regulated to self-regulated markets at the end of the 18th century represented a complete transformation in the structure of society" (GT, 71).[3] In earlier societies, economic activity was enmeshed in a nexus of non-market relationships such as communal ties, kinship relations, and religious commitments, and was oriented towards goals and incentives other than profit or material gain; what he called "habitation" rather than "improvement" (GT, 33–42, 46). As Polanyi details in Chapter 4 of *The Great Transformation*, economic activity was organized around different core principles (reciprocity, redistribution and household) than market exchange and the securing of livelihoods was so penetrated by non-market institutions and practices that it was impossible to speak of the economy as a separate sphere. Although commercial activity certainly existed in some form in pre-capitalist societies, markets did not exercise a directive role in the economic life of these societies and "were merely an accessory feature of an instituted setting controlled and regulated more than ever by social authority" (GT, 67). "No society could, naturally, live for any length of time unless it possessed an economy of some sort", he insisted, "but previously to our time no economy has ever existed that, even in principle, was controlled by markets" (GT, 43). Time after time, he repeats the same thesis: the development of the market economy in the 19th century represented a critical watershed in world history (GT, 30, 40–41, 43–4, 49, 56, 68, 71, 84). Even so, the thrust of this discussion largely concerns the long transition to capitalism where the actual establishment of the self-regulating market was deemed a momentous period within this capitalist history.

Polanyi argued that those who proclaimed that market values, incentives or practices were an ever-present feature of human history suffered from what he called the "economistic prejudice" (GT, 159) or alternatively the "economistic fallacy" (Polanyi, 1947). The assumptions of economic rationality, scarcity-driven optimizing choices, and individual self-interest are historically and culturally bounded; they prevail only when market processes and social relations are dominant; and they cannot be generalized to periods in which these imperatives do not apply. "In spite of the chorus of academic incantations so persistent in the nineteenth century", he maintained, "gain and profit made on exchange never before played an important part in human economy…the alleged propensity of men to barter, truck and exchange is almost entirely apocryphal" (GT, 43–44). While the pursuit of wealth certainly existed throughout history, only under capitalism did gain become largely equated with market transactions and practices. The ascendancy of capitalism should not be seen as the culmination of some benign evolution but rather was the outcome of a brutal imposition on society at the behest of the state and social actors (GT, 250).

The singularity of capitalism

The supposition that capitalism represents a qualitative break in history must of course be underpinned by a conceptual and historical argument about what precisely it is about capitalism – as a structure of activity and social relations, system of power, institutional rules and incentives – that makes it so singular in history (GT, 68–9) (Sewell, 2008). Polanyi's framework, which followed quite closely the general contours of arguments first raised within the Marxist tradition, stressed three features: commodification, competition and the totalizing aspect of the market economy.

If we take these in order, the commodification of the key elements of social life (the process of "fictitious commodities" will be discussed more fully in Chapter 3) – whereby labor, land and money are "produced for sale in the market" – represented the "vital organizing principle" of a market economy (GT, 72, 73). The one indispensable condition for generalizing market relations is the commodification of labor power: "no market economy was conceivable that did not include a market for labor" (GT, 77).[4] The transformation of human beings into commodities engendered a new form of social dependency whereby life chances and basic needs became utterly dependent upon market imperatives (Wood, 1999). Polanyi challenged the liberal view of the market as a realm of freedom and insisted it was a historically new form of coercion and social discipline capable of subjecting all human actors and relationships to its requirements. Workers are certainly free to choose an employer in the formal sense (and this did represent a true measure of liberty from slavery, serfdom and bounded labor) but they were equally compelled to enter the labor market on pain of suffering all the attendant ills of being unemployed, what Polanyi called the application of "nature's penalty" (hunger and the threat of starvation) (GT, 165, 224).

The commercialization of land (via property rights and property transfer) was also essential. In England, direct producers had become fully market dependent by the late 16th century, producing for exchange rather than for their own use, and once subject to competition, they depended on the systematic improvement of productivity to increase their wealth (Brenner, 1986). Many direct producers, dispossessed of their means of subsistence in the land (through enclosure of common lands and other forms of coercion), were compelled to hire out as agricultural laborers or work in cottage industry in order to survive. Private property rights granted individual landowners the ability to control or disperse their property as they saw fit regardless of the wider social relationships that historically embedded land within communal responsibility. Indeed, Polanyi viewed the commodification of land in its widest possible connotations:

> "the economic function is but one of many vital functions of land. It invests man's life with stability; it is the site of his habitation; it is a condition of his physical safety; it is the landscape and the seasons. We might as well imagine his being born without hands and feet as carrying on his life without land."
>
> (GT, 178)

Commercialization irrevocably damaged the historic link that people had established with the land. It destroyed the sustainable strategies that communities had adopted over the years to deal with resource scarcity; it abolished patterns of land tenure that had constituted security for generations of peasants; and it subordinated the land to the needs of the urban population.

Finally, the commodification of money became an essential component in the development of a market economy. Price making and profit making in the market are utterly dependent on the monetary arrangements that make market exchange possible. Until money becomes the embodiment and measure of all values, where all forms of commodities can be compared in price independently of place or time, a system of competitive exchange cannot emerge. “All transactions are turned into money transactions”, Polanyi wrote, “and these in turn require that a medium of exchange be introduced into every articulation of industrial life” (GT, 41). The gold standard, which he denoted as “international commodity money” (GT, 193), similarly underpinned the expansion of competitive trade and capitalist social relations around the globe.

As regards the second unique feature of the capitalist social formation, the nature of competition under capitalism was a qualitatively different phenomenon from previous epochs. Pre-capitalist commercial exchange traditionally involved a transfer of goods from one area where they were available to another where they were not; in other words, trade remained a question of *complementary* exchange – a matter of wine for wool or cotton for spices – and typically was restricted to the exchange of luxury goods (GT, 60). Specialization might have occurred, and there might even have been goods on offer from various producers at different prices (and hence a limited form of profit making) yet this did not constitute competition in the capitalist sense. There was no in-built, structural incentive for producers to innovate, to produce at lower costs, or to improve productivity; profits were achieved by striking better terms of exchange or locating cheaper sources of materials rather than from differentials in labor productivity or capital intensity (and these were in turn guaranteed by non-economic methods such as government sponsored monopoly privileges and military strength) (Wood, 1999).

A market economy however entailed the presence of *competitive* exchange: “similar goods from different sources are offered in competition with one another” (GT, 60). Henceforth, trade became organized according to competitive pressures, with all economic agents compelled to produce efficiently, innovate continuously, and maximize productivity in order to stay afloat on the market. The development of a national market was the vital stage in this process, integrating economically more specialized regions into a coherent whole and permitting the exchange of goods for mass consumption. Once a fully commodified, competitive market is established, the supply and demand of goods and services is determined by the operation of price-making mechanisms that bring markets into balance.[5]

In a competitive market, not only were all factors of production bought and sold, but the supply and demand for these items was also subject to what Polanyi called “compensating effects”. What this implied was that obstacles and problems generated by action in the market economy were redressed by the mutual adjustment of other market forces. The enclosure of common lands typified this process. While it might have temporarily increased the number of landless peasants, it also laid the basis for new opportunities for sheep production; this in turn sparked a cottage industry that provided new employment opportunities for these displaced workers and thereby created a new incentive for labor mobility. The wider point Polanyi stressed was that “only in a market economy can such compensating effects be taken for granted” (GT, 34); only in a self-regulating market can this equilibrating mechanism be ensured. The idea of compensating effects also plays an important ideological and political role as well. The presumption of a frictionless, automatic adjustment of factors of production obscured not only the indispensable role of the state in assisting private adjustments but also the devastation that such adjustments unthinkingly imposed on the rest of society. If the market's automatic mechanism is impaired in any way by political intervention, then the beneficial nature of these compensating effects can no longer be taken for granted and the result will be a series of destabilizing contradictions (an argument I trace at greater length in Chapter 5).

Finally, Polanyi emphasizes the dramatic totalizing aspect of a market system. Capitalism represented a complex social order and coordination of material life. It featured a powerful expansionary logic quite unlike any other social system in history (Sewell, 2008). It continually imposes its dictates on new lands and new spheres of social life: the market "developed in leaps and bounds, it engulfed space and time, and by creating bank money, it produced a dynamic hitherto unknown" (GT, 130). As we shall discuss more fully in the following chapter, it has an unparalleled ability to subject all social actors to its prerequisites and to infect all of human existence with its demands. "A new way of life spread over the planet", Polanyi wrote, "with a claim to universality unparalleled since the age when Christianity started out on its career, only this time the movement was on a purely material level" (GT, 130).

The critical juncture of 1834

It is equally incumbent on proponents of the qualitative break hypothesis to detail the timing and sequencing of this radical break. This should not rely on an arbitrary periodization but rather needs to be premised directly on the conceptual argument regarding what constitutes a qualitative break in the first place. If the market economy represents a unique turning point in history, then it is necessary to determine when this system came into existence. The sticky dilemma in this regard is that these momentous social transformations rarely occur overnight or can be dated with pinpoint precision. Indeed, the consensus among British social historians is that the transition occurred in the early modern period (16th–18th centuries), which "witnessed the fuller emergence and increasing dominance of the structures and culture characteristic of a 'market society'" (Wrightson, 2002, 22), and just as importantly, it occurred in overlapping stages when market and non-market relations co-existed rather than a single either-or transformative moment. There is no question that Polanyi acknowledged the gradual transition to capitalism that took centuries to unfold and he offers numerous examples of this process in the text. However, he also makes a very strong case that the transformative moment was most readily identified as the early decades of the 19th century with the Year One of the self-regulating market arising in 1834 with the passage of the New Poor Law. "Chronologically, Speenhamland antedated market economy", he wrote:

> "the decade of the Poor Law Reform Act was a transition to that economy...Not until 1834 was a competitive labor market established in England; hence industrial capitalism as a social system cannot be said to have existed before that date."
>
> (GT, 82, 82–83)

Polanyi's insistence on the critical juncture of the self-regulating market is intended to support three broad claims. *First*, it is only with the establishment of the self-regulating market that market imperatives become truly ubiquitous. *Second*, it is only after 1834 that all aspects of social life, especially labor power, are completely commodified and placed in a competitive market. *Third*, it is only after the self-regulating market is established that the innate destructiveness of the market becomes truly evident and the double movement cycle is initiated. Each of these questions involves not just the thorny issue of how to adjudicate the timing of the radical transformation but also returns us to the contested debate about what constitutes a capitalist system in the first place, a discussion that continues to have great political significance in the contemporary era.[6]

If we begin with the *first* claim, that market forces only become operative after the self-regulating market is instituted, Polanyi states this point quite bluntly in several passages:

> "In no case can we assume the functioning of market laws unless a self-regulating market is shown to exist...Market economy implies a self-regulating system of markets; in slightly more technical terms, it is an economy directed by market prices and nothing but market prices. Such a system capable of organizing the whole of economic life without outside help or interference would certainly deserve to be called self-regulating."
>
> (GT 38, 43)

> "A market economy is an economic system controlled, regulated and directed by markets alone; order in the production and distribution of goods is entrusted to this self-regulating mechanism. An economy of this kind derives from the expectation that human beings behave in such a way as to achieve maximum money gains...Every element of industry is regarded as having been produced for sale; as then and then only, will it be subject to the supply-and-demand mechanism interacting with price."
>
> (GT, 68, 72)

As we explore more fully below, he claims the embedded social and economic institutions of the old regime (Speenhamland laws, parish relief) made commodity production and capitalist markets impossible. Only with the inception of the "One Big Market" (GT, 72, 178), when all factors of production were fully commodified, could a self-regulating system be said to truly exist.

It is important to state at the outset what a striking contention this actually is. On the one hand, he insists that the imperatives of a market economy only operate when a self-regulating mechanism prevails; furthermore, a market economy is not feasible unless economic activity is completely directed by market criteria. The tendency herein is to equate the market economy, what other historians have termed "capitalism", with the self-regulating market. This argument, reiterated in numerous places in the text, is so smoothly executed that its inherent assumptions might not be immediately evident. Either an economy is totally dominated by market prices (or market "laws" more generally, which are curiously left undefined) or it is by definition excluded as a market economy, even if this weakens the case for a framework that envisages the self-regulating market as a particular moment within capitalism.

What are we to make of this contention? I believe that Polanyi's framework can be challenged on both historical and conceptual grounds. In the first place, if we take "market laws" to refer to processes such as market dependence, specialization, profit maximization, expansionary tendencies and the like, Robert Brenner convincingly argues that many market imperatives were already well in force considerably before the 19th century. English farmers in the 16th century, faced with economic leases and rents subject to market criteria, were forced to specialize for the market and produce competitively in order to guarantee access to the means of subsistence. Over time, this process in turn created the systematic imperative for accumulation and innovation that underpinned future agrarian and industrial transformations (Brenner, 1986, 1977).

Indeed, the causal relationship that Polanyi posits – market dictates become manifest only after the system becomes self-regulating – might actually be the inverse of what occurred. Brenner maintains that it was market dependence which underpinned the development of commodification and unleashed the peculiar imperatives of a capitalist system. Once direct producers were dependent upon the market for their economic inputs, their very survival therefore required them to sell successfully in a competitive market (Brenner, 1997). This transformation in property relations laid the basis for the unprecedented levels of investment, innovation and productivity gains that were achieved in agriculture (which dramatically reduced the percentage of the population working in this sector by half at a time when the population increased nearly threefold). As Wood argues, the complete dispossession of the direct producers that created a mass proletariat was the *result* not the *cause* of this new market dynamic (Wood, 1999) (Dale, 2010). Polanyi clearly appreciates this logic – his discussion of the devastating consequences of agricultural rationalization specifically highlighted the disappearance of non-market income (GT, 92) – yet it is overshadowed by his rather dogmatic stance on the pre-eminence of self-regulation.

What is clear is that his perspective implies a peculiar mode of transition to capitalism. "[T]here was the startling abruptness of the change", he wrote. "Predominance of markets emerged not as a matter of degree, but of kind"

(GT, 67). This is perhaps best viewed as a historical corollary to the big bang hypothesis of cosmology: the dating of the universe of the market economy can be firmly traced back to the explosive impact of 1834 rather than to the gradual build-up of a critical mass that occurred over centuries. His argument begs the immediate question of why an economy that was say 50%, or 75% or even 99% "controlled" by markets (not that it is so straightforward to make such estimates) should be disqualified as "capitalist"; or why only the slightest "contamination" of the market by non-market factors necessarily invalidates its powers of compulsion or makes its imperatives any less determining. It should be noted that Polanyi is very careful not to make the same argument in respect to pre-capitalist social formations. In these periods, various modes of economic integration might "occur in a society without being prevalent in it" (GT, 56) and he insists that the "market pattern was found to be compatible with it [pre-capitalist society]" (GT, 68).[7]

Indeed, market imperatives might be invidious even when markets are not self-regulating. Governmental regulation of the price at which labor power is bought or sold (minimum wage statutes) or the form of contract workers might enter into with their employers (unfair dismissal protection) does not in any way mitigate the need for a worker to enter the labor market in the first place. If there is no doubt that 1834 represented a key moment in political economy that intensified market dependency and enhanced market autonomy, at the same time these market forces had been grievously affecting workers and their livelihoods well before this period. Of course, the converse should not be overlooked either. Even if markets became increasingly disembedded after 1834, this did not necessarily mean that all economic activity was uniquely controlled by market forces. Many allocative decisions after 1834 did not occur in price making markets and the state's role in many markets was still paramount (North, 1977). We will return to this tension between embedding and disembedding at greater length in the following chapter.

This leads us directly to Polanyi's *second* claim that labor commodification did not fully exist until after 1834 (GT, 77, 81, 86, 129). Prior to this juncture, labor was enmeshed in legal and social constraints that restricted full mobility, limited the proper functioning of a national labor market, and "making the very concept of an independent working class an incongruity" (GT, 224; 77).[8] To get at this question requires us to first ask what labor commodification (proletarianization) requires. Charles Tilly defines proletarianization as a two stage process involving two key components: the dispossession of workers from control of the means of production (expropriation) and the dependence of workers on the sale of their labor power for their livelihoods (wage work) (Tilly, 1979).[9] This is essentially the approach Polanyi takes as well and it appears as if he too envisages both of these processes being considerably advanced by the late 18th century. "The English countryside in Adam Smith's time", he wrote:

> "had become part and parcel of a commercial society; the rent due to the landlords as well as the wages of the agricultural laborer showed a marked dependence on prices; only exceptionally were wages or prices fixed by the authorities."
>
> (GT, 115)

He stresses how the parliamentary enclosures intensified wage dependency by eliminating the last vestiges of the remaining open field systems and common lands that served as an alternative source of income (GT, 92).[10] In this, he is merely confirming the scholarly consensus that the majority of English workers were proletarianized long before the 19th century (Pollard, 1978; Thompson, 1993; Tilly, 1997; Wrightson, 2002).

However, despite the fact that both expropriation and wage dependency was nearly universal for the vast majority of the English population, Polanyi nevertheless insisted that the commodification of labor was incomplete because of his claim that no national labor market existed until 1834. His rationale is that Speenhamland in effect prevented the creation of such a market by limiting the mobility of labor and by augmenting their livelihoods (GT, 77, 82). However, as discussed more fully below, recent scholarship has questioned the conclusions he drew regarding the pernicious effects of the relief system: only a small percentage (less than 10%) of the rural population actually collected relief; in the decades preceding Speenhamland, rural out-migration rates were quite high; and the "most mobile group of rural labourers was the group least affected by poor relief" (Boyer, 1990, 182) (Somers and Block, 2005; Block and Somers, 2014). If a labor market can be said to exist when the majority of workers are compelled to sell their labor power in order to obtain their means of subsistence, when the supply and demand of labor is coordinated primarily by market forces, and when the price of employment is largely set by the market, then there seems to be little question that a national labor market existed in England well before 1834 (Pollard, 1978).

This is not to say that mobility was entirely free; or that unemployment was not a constant presence; or that some workers in some industrial districts managed to combine their paid work with possession of a small holding or access to common lands that enabled self-provisioning (Wrightson, 2002). But the imperfect operation of a labor market does not invalidate the fact that individuals are dependent on the market for their livelihoods, or that they are being exploited, or that their autonomy over life choices and life chances is severely circumscribed by their commodified status. Certainly the specter of an all-or-nothing argument is at work here as well: a factor can only be commodified if it is *fully* commodified, which Polanyi argues can only occur if the market in question is self-regulating. However, the weight of the historical evidence would seem to seriously weaken this contention – markets can function according to market laws (in this case, expropriation, exploitation, market dependency) even if they are not self-regulating in the sense that Polanyi means – and thereby weakens his own argument that the 1834 conjuncture constituted a significant moment in capitalist history.

The *third* proposition regarding the primacy of the self-regulating market is that the full destructive effects of marketization on English society were felt only after 1834. The difficulty in this instance is that Polanyi is not merely content with identifying the self-regulating market with capitalism generally; now it is conflated with the industrial revolution as well. The two are linked chronologically – the high point of the industrial revolution, he argues, occurs in 1795–1835, the same period as the transition to the self-regulating market – and via their consequences. The "middle passage" of suffering, which he argues is a consequence of the self-regulating market, is in actual fact linked very closely in his analysis to the specific features of the industrial revolution. "[L]aboring people had been crowded together in new places of desolation, the so-called industrial towns of England", he wrote:

> "the country folk had been dehumanized into slum dwellers; the family was on the road to perdition; and large parts of the country were rapidly disappearing under the slag and scrap heaps vomited forth from the satanic mills…a veritable abyss of human degradation."
>
> (GT, 39)

He goes on to emphasize: "cataclysmic events like the Industrial Revolution – an economic earthquake which transformed within less than half a century vast masses of inhabitants of the English countryside from settled folk into shiftless migrants" (GT, 157).

His repeated use of the terms "industrial civilization", "industrial capitalism" and the like tends to blur the important historical and analytical distinction between the establishment of the capitalist system (or even the more limited phenomena of the self-regulating market) and the subsequent development of industrial capitalism; in other words, his model obscures the fact that there were two different qualitative breaks in capitalist history.[11] Polanyi's own definition of the self-regulating market cannot possibly be expanded to explain the extraordinary transformations –the colossal leap in the scale and scope of production, the dramatic changes in production relations, the widespread introduction of revolutionary new technology, the massive upheaval in rural and urban livelihoods that occurred as a result of the industrial revolution. Nor is there such a straightforward causal relationship between these two events. Societies can be capitalist without being industrial (Netherlands in the 18th century is the operative case) or industrial without being capitalist (the Stalinist road to industrialization being a case in point). And even if these two processes followed a longer temporal trajectory in the English case than in the rest of Europe, one could still argue that Britain had a predominantly capitalist economy long before the industrial revolution.

A more conclusive judgment is now required. I would argue that his analysis of the self-regulating market is seriously flawed because it offers a selective definitional schema that has the effect of predetermining the analytical result. This would appear to give some credence to the caustic remark of Braudel who maintained that Polanyi possessed "an almost theological taste for definition" (Braudel, 1982, 227). It should also alert us to the possibility that the defects of this perspective might well plague additional aspects of his explanatory framework of the double movement.

Origins of the Self-Regulating Market

I now turn to the question of Polanyi's explanation of the origins of the self-regulating market. I believe Polanyi offers a complex argument for the rise of the self-regulating market deploying *five* distinct but interrelated factors: the role of technology as the prime mover; the importance of social power; the critical impact of the state; an emphasis on the influence of ideology; and finally, the contradictions of the preceding political economy system.[12] One reason why this causal framework has attracted less attention is rooted in the character of his narrative. Given his penchant for elliptical discussion, none of these factors (with the exception of the chapters on Speenhamland) are presented in any straightforward exposition; nor for that matter are they treated with equal attention in terms of either pages or analytical focus. Furthermore, it is not immediately apparent that they are actually being offered as causal explanations; or whether he envisions these accounts as competing explanations rooted in distinct theoretical premises; or even if he has chosen this particular constellation of factors on the basis of any overarching conceptual framework (Block and Somers, 2014). Nevertheless, I believe that an examination of each of these factors provides a unique insight into the first phase of the double movement and equally importantly, offers an explanatory framework for understanding the conditions under which subsequent iterations of the double movement might be forthcoming.

Technology and marketization

"We do not intend to assert that the machine caused that which happened", wrote Polanyi, "but we insist that once elaborate machines and plant were used for production in a commercial society, the idea of a self-regulating market was bound to take shape" (GT, 40). Notwithstanding that his discussion of the role of technology is limited to a handful of pages (and the occasional aside), he certainly emphasizes this factor in his account of marketization. In fact, in Chapter 6 when the argument about the self-regulating market is first presented, it is technology that takes center stage (GT, 74–5).

In the early period of capitalist development, the machinery used in production was relatively simple and inexpensive, individual merchants dominated their own supply and demand chains, and production existed as a profitable hobby of commercial interests. It is the development of complex, "elaborate" machinery – "an almost miraculous improvement in tools of production" (GT, 33) – that irrevocably altered these dynamics, ushering in the factory system and creating an inevitable momentum for the self-regulating market. Because purchasing these machines meant incurring substantial financial risks, owners would only undertake such ventures under very limited conditions. They needed to be able to ensure the continuous use of these tools, which required a stable and predictable supply of raw materials, labour and credit; and they needed to guarantee the production of large amounts of goods which in turn presupposed the presence of competitive exchange to sell these goods. In other words, profits could only be safeguarded if all the factors involved in production were supplied through competitive markets and transformed into commodities. "Machine production in a commercial society", he argued, "involves, in effect, no less a transformation than that of the natural and human substance of society into commodities" (GT, 42). "The extension of the market mechanism", he concluded, "to the elements of industry – labor, land and money – was the inevitable consequence of the introduction of the factory system into a commercial society" (GT, 75).[13]

His emphasis on the driving force of technology places him squarely within a hotly contested historiographical debate about the origins and nature of the Industrial Revolution and the link between technical change and social change (Hudson, 1992; Mokyr, 1994). On the one hand, historical evidence casts doubt on the causal link he posits. E. P. Thompson, in a brilliant discussion of the fate of the weavers in his classic text *The Making of the English Working Class,* describes how these workers were subjected to an intense process of commodification in the early part of the 19th century (Thompson, 1966). The weavers faced longer hours, loss of control over their own labor, continual wage reductions, and greater insecurity but the actual villain was cutthroat competition and capitalist exploitation rather than technology. Manufacturers outsourced work to the weavers who were desperate to find labor at any price; oversupply and falling prices were the logical consequence, forcing the weavers to work even longer hours in order to make less, yet by working longer, each worker increased the likelihood of a fellow weaver becoming unemployed. "It is an over-simplification to ascribe the cause of the debasement of the weaver's conditions to the power loom", wrote Thompson. "The status of the weavers had been shattered...at a time...when the competition of power with hand was largely psychological" (Thompson, 1966, 279).

By the 1820s only about a tenth of employees in the manufacturing sector worked in large-scale establishments, but labor commodification, as I highlighted earlier, was fully advanced in nearly every sector of the economy.[14] It is Polanyi's eclectic periodization of capitalism that once again leads to difficulty in specifying the proper causal chain. Although he admits that industrial production had expanded across Britain, he insisted that until the end of the 18th century industry was "a mere accessory to commerce" so of course commodification could not exist fully (GT, 74). Wood argues this analysis is flawed because:

> "what fails to emerge from all this is an appreciation of the ways in which a radical transformation of social relations *preceded* industrialization. The revolutionizing of productive forces *presupposed* a transformation of property relations and a change in the form of exploitation that created a historically unique need to improve the productivity of labor...His order of causation suggests a failure to treat the capitalist market itself as a specific social form."
>
> (Wood, 1999, 24–5)

Stephen Marglin in a similar vein suggested that the purpose of the factory system was not to employ complex technology but rather to transform social relations by destroying the worker's control over their product and eliminating their control over the labor process. Heightened discipline and supervision of the labor force, not increased productivity gains via technology, was the modus operandi here (Marglin, 1974). In his view, the factory system was the *result* of commodification and the transformation of social relations not its *cause*. Maxine Berg contended that "what was striking in nineteenth century Britain was not the power of machines in displacing labour but the dependence of most work processes on more and more labour" (Berg, 1994, 185). Even where new machinery was introduced and a new workplace instituted, the intensification of labor still remained the key to raising surplus value.

Finally, one would want to probe the relevance of this factor to his overall framework of the origins of the self-regulating market. The technological argument is largely limited to the specific example of labor commodification, but Polanyi makes no attempt to extend this account to the other elements of commodification. A closer look at the commercialization of land however would raise doubts about the validity of this argument. The leap forward in agrarian capitalism was not accomplished because of any technological revolution analogous to the transition to the factory system. Before 1840 there was little mechanization in British agriculture (with the exception of the introduction of threshing machines at the turn of the century) and virtually no application of steam power. Greater productivity in the land occurred from creating new land for cultivation (via the seizure of commons lands through the enclosures); by consolidation into larger holdings that permitted new techniques; and by obtaining the maximum rents from tenant leases (Hobsbawm and Rude, 1968). I am inclined to agree with Michael Hechter's critique that the role of technology is not properly grounded in Polanyi's own theoretical premises but rather constitutes an *ad hoc* explanation (Hechter, 1981).

Social power and marketization

"Sectional interests", maintained Polanyi, "are…the natural vehicle of social and political change" (GT, 152) and indeed the contribution of social interests and resources to the onset of a market economy is highlighted in several places in his text. As regards the long term commercialization of English agriculture, he argues the enclosure movements, which triggered the commodification of land, could be seen as "a revolution of the rich against the poor" and follows the lead of Marx and Tawney in depicting them as legalized robbery (GT, 35). The Speenhamland system of outdoor poor relief, which supposedly prevented the full onset of labor commodification, is described in similar class terms as a "device contrived by the squirearchy" to reinforce the paternalistic system of social control and dependency that had dominated the British countryside for centuries (GT, 89, 94). He makes transparent the intra-class considerations which informed these policies: "politically, the squire's pull with the village poor was strengthened by Speenhamland while that of the rural middle class was weakened" (GT, 96). Because workers were tied to the parish, labor-hiring farmers enjoyed a reliable supply of cheap labor during seasonal downturns and at the same time, could keep wages as low as possible because the cost of maintaining the poor was foisted on all ratepayers in the parish. This in effect subsidized the politically dominant labor-hiring farmers at the expense of non-labor hiring rate payers (GT, 97, 122, 298; see also Boyer, 1990). But over time, as the system of poor relief devastated the countryside (see below), all sections of rural life supported the imposition of the New Poor law.

Polanyi noted a similar transition within the manufacturing classes. Manufacturing capital initially found the Speenhamland system to their liking as a means of sustaining an adequate supply of labor: workers not needed during periodic downturns were laid off or put on short term work and then provided outdoor relief, a large proportion of which was paid for by non-labor hiring tax payers. "The Old Poor Law…was a help to manufacturers", he wrote:

> "It …permitted them to divest themselves of responsibility towards their dismissed employees, thus throwing much of the burden of unemployment on public funds…The evidence points to an urban policy more or less consciously directed towards the building up of an industrial reserve army in the towns, mainly in order to cope with the sharp fluctuations of economic activity…Just as village authorities preferred high rates to high wages, the urban authorities also were loath to remove the non-resident pauper to his place of settlement."
>
> (GT, 136, 302)

Of course, while employers were keen to see poor relief maintained in the cities, they supported its eradication in the agricultural regions where it was believed to hinder the migration of surplus labor to the urban labor market and led to large rural-urban wage gaps (GT, 301). Indeed, he attributed the promulgation of the New Poor Law in 1834 to the "work of a new class entering the historical scene, the middle classes of England. Squirearchy could not do the job these classes were destined to perform: the transformation of society into a market economy" (GT, 101).

There are some noticeable omissions in Polanyi's "social" account. Although he does highlight the wider social *consequences* of the enclosures, his "social" explanation of the *cause* of this development is essentially a class explanation, which despite his desire to surmount Marxist economistic formulations of class in favor of a perspective that stresses the "social substances" of classes, makes little systematic effort to incorporate wider social or political forces or interests into an account of why "the easy prevailing of private interest" occurred (GT, 36).[15] As an example, while he briefly mentions the importance of merchant capitalists to the growth of industrial production, he does not explore the qualitatively distinct social organizations and relations (merchant competition, open markets, entrepreneurial middlemen) that played a key role in advancing commodity exchange via a process that represented "commercialization from below" (Lie, 1991). Nor does he discuss how changes in the wider social structure might have stimulated the development of a market economy. Harold Perkin emphasized the greater fluidity of the British social structure (a larger and more prosperous middle ranks than on the Continent) and the diffusion of the capitalist spirit so beloved of Weber and Tawney; both factors contributed to the gradual diffusion of wealth that gave independent, skilled craftsmen the opportunity to accumulate a modest outlay of capital which they used to become the leading entrepreneurs of many of the new industries. It also underpinned an emerging alliance in the 18th century between landed interests and the emerging bourgeoisie, cemented around such common interests as the national debt, mercantile enterprise and the corrupt political system, which inculcated a shared momentum for marketization.

Polanyi also paid scant regard to the critical role played by protests from below in realigning elite interests in favor of self-regulation. Many scholars have described the promulgation of the New Poor Law as the direct consequence of a deep crisis of social control and class relations (Hobsbawm and Rude, 1968; Mandler, 1987; McNally, 1993). In 1830 the so-called Captain Swing revolts erupted across southern England (particularly in those counties that faced the highest poor relief expenditures), unleashing an orgy of machine breaking, sabotage, arson, extortion and violence against landlords and enveloping rural elites in a climate of fear. Indeed, at the initial meetings of the Royal Commission on the Poor Law that were held in this period, many landlords openly testified to their change of heart about retaining the system of subsistence payments, which they regarded as a rioter's charter. Government leaders feared that rural unrest might combine with labor agitation into a widespread movement for reform, leading directly to renewed calls for drastic reform of the relief system .

On a more general note, it is incumbent upon a social explanation to detail the specific mechanisms whereby social power (be it class power or other forms of social advantage) is translated into political change (via lobbying influence, links to political elites, indirect structural power and the like). The reciprocal relationship is equally critical to detail: political institutions are instrumental in shaping the resources, interests and strategies of all social groups and play a vital role in configuring the terrain of workplace social control and the employment relationship as specifically pursued by employers through the courts and the legal system (Somers, 1993). Despite his affinity for this sort of dialectical approach – the double movement is indebted to this kind of explanatory framework – the interrelationship of social and political power, as it concerns both the long transformation to capitalism and the specific conjuncture of 1834, is not articulated in any rigorous fashion.

The state and marketization

"The road to the free market", said Polanyi, "was opened and kept open by an enormous increase in continuous, centrally organized and controlled interventionism" (GT, 140). He sought to disprove the assertion of liberal ideologues that competitive markets emerged spontaneously as a natural outcome of individual market actor's pursuit of their self-interest. "The nineteenth century…naively imagined that such a development was the natural outcome of the spreading of markets", he wrote:

> "It was not realized that the gearing of markets into a self-regulating system of tremendous power was not the result of any inherent tendency of markets towards excrescence but rather the effect of highly artificial stimulants administered to the body social…[T]he market has been the outcome of a conscious and often violent intervention on the part of government which imposed the market on society for non-economic ends."
>
> (GT, 57, 250)

Indeed, it was a crescendo of legislation – the New Poor Law of 1834, Peel's Bank Act of 1844, the Anti-Corn Law Bill of 1846 – that proved decisive in institutionalizing the core tenets of *laissez-faire*: a competitive labor market, the gold standard and international free trade. Mark Blyth summarized this Polanyian conventional wisdom: "None of this happened by accident. It was politics all the way through" (Blyth, 2004, 119).

Polanyi begins by highlighting the mercantile state's role in the creation of a national market in England via: developing an efficient transport infrastructure of roads, canals and ports; creating an effective credit and taxation system; establishing a national legal system and set of effective property rights; and eliminating particularistic barriers to trade erected by municipalities. By the late 18th century, economic and political elites were in broad agreement that the proper remit of the state should include the regulation of the economy for the public good through the development of favorable bases of trade, promotion of exports, support for industries that enhanced England's military might, and the maintenance of social order (Brewer, 1989).

Political action, whether by legislation, administrative fiat, or war, was critically implicated in the commodification process as well. Commercialization of the land in England began with changes in the legal order during the 16th and 17th centuries that gradually eroded customary rights. "More often than not", he wrote, "common law insisted on the owner's right to improve his land profitably even if this involved grave dislocation in habitations and employment" (GT, 181). The Parliamentary enclosures of the 18th century likewise eliminated all customary rights that interfered with the process of capitalist accumulation. This granted landlords the right to assert private ownership of common lands, which eliminated the rights of peasants to hunt, fish, and gather wood or graze their animals on the commons. It was precisely these customary rights that acted as a safety net for rural communities and made all the difference between a life of subsistence and one of abject poverty. Their decimation, he argued, led inexorably to the creation of a landless class of wage laborers that incipient industrialists were anxious to benefit from.

Labor commodification began in very similar ways with changes in the legal sphere that expunged the non-contractual rights workers had enjoyed for centuries; as Polanyi wittily noted, "the commodity theory of labor was first stated emphatically not by economists but by lawyers" (GT, 181). The rights of apprenticeship, which gave workers significant control over the terms and conditions of their labor, were severely weakened in favor of employer control of the labor process. The law criminalized as theft and embezzlement the long standing practice which allowed workers to take the by-products of production and at the same time guaranteed the right of the employer to the full ownership of all the products of the labor process, a move that virtually assured workers became wholly dependent on their money wages for their livelihood (Thompson, 1993). The Master and Servant Act of 1823 enabled coercive labor contracts that more tightly bound workers to employers, intensified labor discipline, and outlawed workplace resistance (Steinberg, 2016).[16] Worker's rights of free association were whittled away by various legislative acts (conspiracy laws, combination acts) and the final road to total labor mobility and proletarianization was enacted by the legislative fiat of the New Poor Law that abolished Speenhamland subsidies and imposed harsh new standards of workhouse assistance.

A final plank in his argument was to deride the hypocrisy of the liberals who lamented any interference with the market as a recipe for disaster yet proved all too eager to countenance state interference that "would destroy non-contractual relations between individuals and prevent their spontaneous re-formation" (GT, 163). As he documented in ample detail, "economic liberals must and will unhesitatingly call for the intervention of the state" (GT, 149). While marketization supposedly demanded the "expulsion of politics" from the economic realm, it was actually accompanied by a simultaneous expansion of the state's powers in the regulatory and administrative arenas (Block and Somers, 2014). "The introduction of free markets", Polanyi concluded, "far from doing away with the need for control, regulation and intervention, enormously increased their range" (GT, 140). The New Poor Law, as an example, abandoned local relief subsidies but at the same time expanded punitive standards that forced workers to choose between factory discipline or the dreaded workhouse. It also inaugurated many of the administrative devices which proved the hallmark of the British state over the next century: central control by a Board of Commissioners, centralized inspection and finance, and the development of a professional service bureaucracy (GT, 139).

Despite the considerable attention he devotes to the state – indeed, this tends to be the explanation for the origin of the self-regulating market most often attributed to Polanyi in the literature – the disparity in his work between epigrammatic ambition and conceptual rigor is perhaps most pronounced in this discussion of political power. There is no question that he is convincing in his demolition of the liberal's spontaneity thesis (although as I describe in Chapter 4, he embraces a different sort of "spontaneity" argument to explain the origins of social protection). Nor do I have any quibble with his insight that political institutions are essential to the development and maintenance of a market economy. However, as was the case in previous sections, his analysis is scattered throughout the book and the consistent absence of a coherent analytical focus is telling. What is lacking is an analytical framework of the range of state actions that might be instrumental in creating the self-regulating market or the extent to which these might generate cross-cutting or reinforcing interests.

Polanyi recognizes that the state both actively abets the process of disembedding and acts to slow it down; as we will see in later chapters, the state is simultaneously rolled back from the economy yet rolled forward to protect society from the market (Dale, 2010). There are numerous examples of this dialectic in the text. In the case of enclosures, the Tudor state harnessed the power of the Crown to slow down the economic improvement of land: "employing the power of central government to relieve the victims of the transformation, and attempting to canalize the process of change so as to make its course less devastating" (GT, 38). The role of the common law shifted from encouraging marketization in the 16th and 17th centuries to acting "as a conserver of the past in the face of modernizing legislation" in the 18th century, only to give way to the freedom of contract in the *laissez-faire* period of the 19th (GT, 182). The speedy transformation from the protectionist period of Speenhamland to the rapacious disembedding of the New Poor laws is further evidence of the process.

Although I will return to the contradictory role of the state in future chapters, the immediate point to stress is that Polanyi has very little to say about what might account for this differential role. The question of how these diametrically opposed (yet complementary) tasks could be promoted without creating an unsustainable incoherence inside the state itself was a prevalent feature of the debates on the state in the 1980s (Offe,1984). As many highlighted at the time, such an explanation needed to unlock many challenging puzzles: to specify the agencies within the state that had responsibility for accomplishing these divergent goals; to detail how political elites generated the appropriate knowledge to adjudicate these dilemmas; or the criteria they utilized to decide these complex trade-offs. Polanyi's work served as an inspiration to this literature because he stipulated precisely this difficulty and implied that considerable institutional variation within capitalist economies could be traced to the distinct choices different state elites made in this regard. Yet at the same time, he himself offers little in the way of a conceptual framework to evaluate these decision making conundrums.

One could, as an example, postulate a number of explanations rooted in class coalitions and the state to explain this process. Some social elites might enjoy enhanced influence with state actors or a group might ally with state elites to further their rivalry against other social groups; or state actors might seek to advance their own interests against those of dominant social groups. None of these are systematically discussed in the book. The "state capture" approach is enlisted to explain the case of the Tudor state, whose "commitment was to the commonalty", gave way to "government by a class – the class which led in industrial and commercial progress" (GT, 38). He similarly insists one of the preconditions of the 1832 Reform Bill was that "the middle class had forced its way to power, partly in order to remove this obstacle to the new capitalistic economy" (GT, 78; see 287) and attributes the passage of the New Poor Law to the "political victory of the middle class in 1832" (GT, 137). However, in neither case is this class victory within the state detailed in any convincing fashion. There is also a passage endorsing the "state-class rivalry" perspective: he argues that the anti-enclosure policy had to be viewed in the context of a fight for political control between the monarchy and the gentry (GT, 35). Yet this explanation would still need to describe the reason why class strategies had shifted or why the state had the capacity to represent the wider interest against entrenched social power and Polanyi does not discuss either possibility.

Nor is it apparent why political elites within the state come to see marketization in a more favorable light. Is it because formerly antagonistic elites are now joined in an alliance with the state or because these social groups enjoy greater access to decision making inside the government; or because protectionist policies lose their effectiveness; or because the state faces external pressures (for example, the need to raise increased revenues to wage war) which give it greater incentive to search for new growth strategies; or because political leaders are won over to the allure of the new ideology of political economy? Each of these would be a plausible account but none are explored systematically by Polanyi. The state's dual role is undoubtedly related to the nature of the state itself – the fact that over different time periods, the locus of political power or state capacity might shift considerably – but again these possibilities are not addressed even though they relate directly to a more comprehensive account of the onset of the double movement.

Similarly, Polanyi does not comprehensively link state action back to the question of social power. The New Poor Law freed up elites to impose even greater restrictions on the freedom of action of those most affected by marketization in order to minimize disruptions (Block, 2003). Indeed, although this receives only perfunctory attention in his work, the onset of the market economy went hand in hand with substantial changes to the repressive capacity of the English state between 1750 and 1840 (Tilly, 1995). Levels of direct coercion (disruption of political meetings, surveillance of activists, bans on marches, meetings and demonstrations) increased dramatically, exile and incarceration were employed to a much greater extent, and the formation of a unified London police force ushered in new forms of control over public space.

Lastly, any emphasis on the primacy of the state is predicated on an essential precondition: that it has the capacity to fulfill this historic role. Some of the conceptual oversights in this regard have previously been alluded to but Polanyi offers no comparable historical focus either. Although he makes a passing remark about the Tudor state's innovative and efficient administration (GT, 38–9), he does not seem to truly appreciate the exceptional strength of the English state in this period. It enjoyed a unified central state, with a national parliament and single legal system, centuries before many of its rivals on the Continent. It enjoyed a substantial comparative advantage over its European rivals in terms of its unparalleled ability to extract fiscal resources from society (which underpinned its ability to wage war and promote economic growth) (Brewer, 1989; Mann, 1986). Way before its European competitors, it was able to dismantle pernicious feudal restrictions and monopolies that hindered the growth of a national market (Appleby, 2010). It possessed a virtual monopoly of coercive force over society because, unlike other European countries where aristocracies fought a bitter war of attrition against the absolutist state to preserve their independent capacity for violence, the English landed classes had relied on central state power to sustain their property rights (Wood, 1999). Far more than any other state in Europe, sociopolitical might and economic prowess was inextricably linked in the English polity which immeasurably assisted the transition to a market economy.

Ideology and marketization

"The discovery of economics was an astounding revelation", proclaimed Polanyi, "which hastened greatly the transformation of society and the establishment of a market system…" (GT, 119). This bold claim that ideas and consciousness play a critical role in social transformation would seem at first glance to run against the grain of his materialist/structural stance. But, a number of commentators have stressed the abiding importance of ideology in his framework (Blyth, 2002, 2004; Somers and Block 2005, 2014). Blyth argued in this vein: "Polanyi's singular methodological contribution to economic history was the insight that thinking and action are not separable, even analytically speaking, without inserting the very categories one seeks to explain back into the history one seeks to understand" (Blyth, 2004, 130; see also Blyth, 2002). Michel Callon similarly stressed his unique perspective:

> "But it is also, and above all, one of the rare attempts to link up economics and economy, with a convincing analysis of the role of economic theories, such as that of Ricardo, in the establishment of a labor market."
> (Callon, 1998, 2)

Block and Somers use the term "ideational embeddedness" to stress the centrality of ideas, ideologies, and narratives to the establishment of the market system (Block and Somers, 2014, Chapter 6).

Indeed, he devotes considerable attention to this factor and I believe he envisages ideology as a key causal factor in the establishment of the self-regulating system. Social change requires not just significant transformations in the material world, but in the realm of consciousness as well. In this case, the particular ideology is that of "political economy": generally speaking, this is the ideology of the self-regulating market, *laissez-faire*, individualism and free trade. I have taken the liberty of organizing Polanyi's loosely developed themes in terms of various ideological mechanisms (recurrent patterns whereby an ideology is expressed and disseminated) that contributed to the transition to the self-regulating market (Eagleton, 1991).

The first of these envisions ideology as an *interpretive* and *ordering* mechanism. In transitional periods, when a new socio-economic system is emerging but the old regime still holds sway, comprehending the contours of social change can be a profound challenge. "But the contemporaries did not comprehend", he wrote, "the order for which they were preparing the way… The complicated economies of Speenhamland transcended the comprehension of even the most expert observers of the time…The pitfalls of the market system were not readily apparent" (GT, 81–2). Ideology plays several important functions in these critical junctures. The first is to impose a semblance of order onto the melee of paradoxical tendencies. To accomplish this, an ideology needs to be *imperialistic in scope* – in other words it can be flexibly applied to explain a great many different occurrences – and *simplifying in practice* – in other words, it offers a parsimonious portrait that accounts for nearly all instances. In Polanyi's view, economic liberalism purported to be just this sort of "organizing principle" (GT, 135).

In the midst of such paralyzing uncertainty, ideology operates as a *therapeutic device*, a means of providing psychic security. "Out of the horrors of Speenhamland", Polanyi said, "men rushed blindly for the shelter of a utopian economy" (GT, 102). This is not to suggest that this new interpretation in any way constituted a valid explanation for these events. Polanyi almost gleefully notes that this new body of theory proved a "rich source of misunderstandings" and unabashedly suggests that "neither Ricardo nor Malthus understood the working of the capitalist system" (GT, 123–4). Indeed, he insisted the specific nature of the transition, which contained contradictory principles of social organization, precluded such an understanding:

> "no unitary system could have explained the facts, as they did not form part of any one system, but were actually the result of the simultaneous action on the body social of two mutually exclusive systems, namely a nascent market economy and a paternalistic regulationism in the sphere of the most important factor of production, labor."
>
> (GT, 125)

Ideology is also an *action-oriented* mechanism whereby elites develop rationales for their prescriptions and political imperatives. "As Albert Hirschman points out", wrote Blyth, "capitalism did not simply evolve, it was argued for" (Blyth, 2004, 125). Polanyi focused specifically on the way *laissez-faire* advocates premised their ideology on a modernizing ethic, a key tenet of which was the belief that change was imperative no matter the consequences. Several related passages take up this theme:

> "Fired by an emotional faith in spontaneity, the common sense attitude toward change was discarded in favor of a mystical readiness to accept the social consequences of economic improvement, whatever they might be" (GT, 33); "A blind faith in spontaneous progress had taken hold of people's minds, and with the fanaticism of sectarians, the most enlightened pressed forward for boundless and unregulated change" (76); "Hope-the vision of perfectibility…was embodied in a concept of progress so inspiring that it appeared to justify the vast and powerful dislocations to come."
>
> (GT, 84)

The ideologues of political economy insisted that not only should change be embraced as a positive accomplishment in itself but the primary threat society faced during this momentous interregnum came from those who sought to prevent this change from taking place at all. "[T]hat not the competitive system and the self-regulating market", he wrote, "but interference with that system and interventions with that market are responsible for our ills" (GT, 143). Heretical deviations from liberal orthodoxy were condemned with religious zeal by the "enlightened" and opponents denounced for postponing the one true heaven. As Somers and Block note, *laissez-faire* in this way became immune to the very countervailing evidence that under normal conditions would have undermined it (Somers and Block, 2005).

The chiliastic ardor of the market missionaries is perfectly captured in several passages that characterize liberalism/political economy/laissez-faire in quasi-religious terms as: "a blind faith" (GT, 76), an "evangelical fervor" (135), "militant creed" (137), "emotional faith" (33), "secular religion" (102), and a "crusading passion" (137) (Blyth, 2002). Ideology represented an intentional device by social and political elites to justify the profound changes that were contemplated in the name of progress. The more devastating and damaging the undertaking for society, the greater the need for a convincing ideological cover for such precipitate action. "*Laissez faire* waxed into a fervently held creed", he wrote, "when the uselessness of any other but extreme solutions became apparent" (GT, 137). On three separate occasions, Polanyi links the "vast scope of the interlocking changes involved in the establishment of the new order" to the "magnitude of the sufferings" that result from the transformation (GT, 135–38). Only an ideology that brooks no hesitation, which refuses to accept anything "less than complete acceptance", would have been successful in this epoch.

It is equally true that those who direct such perilous experiments can be persuaded of the justness of their cause only if they can convince themselves that they are enthralled in a sacred mission, which, at the same time, constitutes a willful disregard of the horrors that this transition will unleash. Polanyi acknowledges in this regard elites' "mystical readiness to accept the social consequences of economic improvement, whatever they might be" (GT, 33). Ideologies that conduct moral crusades bind proponents to policies from which they might instinctively recoil, demonstrating that market discipline operates not just as a *material compulsion* but as an *emotional imperative* as well. There is a hint of this insight in the following passage: "The creation of a labor market was an act of vivisection performed on the body of society by such as were *steeled* to their task by an assurance which only science can provide" (GT, 127, my emphasis).[17]

A related ideological mechanism is *legitimation.* One of the primary aims of any ideology is to construct a plausible justification for social behavior that otherwise might encounter severe criticism and opposition.[18] It is often engaged by dominant classes anxious to promote the indefensible and thereby vouchsafe their power in the cloak of rationality. Polanyi highlights the dramatic transformation of everyday common sense: the way in which the ideas of the moral economy, especially the notion of a basic right to security and subsistence that was deeply rooted in common beliefs, customary practices and institutional practices, became hideously perverted by the new ideology in order to de-legitimate these popular ideas of fairness and social justice. Security no longer was identified with a guaranteed right to subsistence but rather became a way of ensuring an employer's right to a steady supply of workers and the free hand to exploit them. Instead of being seen as a menace to social order, poverty became "the price to be paid for the highest stage of prosperity" (GT, 118). Whereas traditional societies organized their economies to safeguard against outbreaks of famine, the threat of starvation was now harnessed as a whip to heel the masses to the discipline of the labor market.

A lengthy quote from Townsend's *Dissertation on the Poor Laws* regarding the positive virtues of hunger (a sentiment that reappeared in the works of Malthus, Bentham and other leading lights of political economy) is given prominence in the text:

> "Hunger will tame the fiercest animals, it will teach decency, civility, obedience and subjection to the most perverse. In general it is only hunger which can spur and goad them [the poor] onto labor; yet our laws have said they shall never hunger. The laws, it must be confessed, have likewise said, they shall be compelled to work. But then legal constraint is attended with much trouble, violence and noise; creates ill will, and never can be productive of good and acceptable service: whereas hunger is not only peaceable, silent, unremitting pressure, but, as the most natural motive to industry and labor, it calls forth the most powerful exertions; and when satisfied by the free bounty of another, lays lasting and sure foundations for good will and gratitude."
>
> (quoted in GT, 113)[19]

Polanyi used Townsend and others to demonstrate a further corollary to the legitimation mechanism, namely that all ideologies attempt to render their beliefs as *natural laws.*[20] There is ample evidence that he saw this as a ubiquitous leitmotif of political economy:

> "The laws governing a market economy…were put under the authority of nature herself…economic society was founded on the grim realities of Nature; if man disobeyed the laws which ruled that society, the fell executioner would strangle the offspring of the improvident."
>
> (GT, 125)

"[T]he drive for a competitive market acquired the irresistible impetus of a process of Nature. For the self-regulating market was now believed to follow from the inexorable laws of nature, and the unshackling of the market to be an ineluctable necessity."

(GT, 126–7)

> "scholars proclaimed in unison that a science had been discovered which put the laws governing man's world beyond any doubt. It was at the behest of these laws that compassion was removed from the hearts, and a

> stoic determination to renounce human solidarity in the name of the greatest happiness of the greatest number gained the dignity of secular religion."
>
> (GT, 102)

This naturalizing rhetoric accomplished three critical tasks. *First,* it represented a sleight-of-hand, a "Potemkin imaginary" that obscured the brutal political engineering that created the market system in the first place, what Margaret Somers calls an "alchemy of misrecognition" (Somers, 2018, 92). *Second*, naturalism was designed specifically to justify the extraordinary trauma wrought by marketization; indeed, so long as the laws governing the market were envisioned as natural and spontaneous, any attempt to regulate the market in order to reduce social suffering was deemed an arbitrary and coercive interference that prevented the unfolding of these natural laws (GT, 115). The emerging market system appeared immune to change and overturning it seemed as futile as trying to change the laws of gravity. *Third,* the aura of inevitability of these natural laws also acted as an important unifying device, wielding opposing partisan outlooks into a cohesive identity. "What made economic liberalism an irresistible force", he insisted, "was this congruence of opinion between diametrically opposed outlooks" (GT, 127) (here referring to the conservative Burke, the reformer Bentham and the liberals Malthus and Ricardo). All agreed that aiding the poor violated these natural laws and called for the restoration of the only valid "natural" right, namely the right of property.[21]

Lastly, a *universalizing* mechanism is an enduring feature of all ideologies. The dominant values of a historical epoch are projected as the ideals and interests of all humanity (if not throughout all history). This too became an enduring feature of political economy (and of economics as a discipline) and was a hallmark of the "economistic fallacy". "Economic liberalism labored under the delusion that its practices and methods were the natural outgrowth of a general law of progress", Polanyi wrote. "To make them fit the pattern, the principles underlying a self-regulating market were projected backward into the whole history of human civilization" (GT, 274). He ridiculed the ideologues of political economy for insisting that the Smithian "propensity to barter, truck and exchange one thing for another" was a timeless virtue of human society; that markets were an ever-present feature of history; or that the intrinsic dynamics of capitalist behavior (optimizing, scarcity, rationality) were essentially present in all societies. As highlighted earlier, he devoted an entire chapter to a comprehensive debunking of this proposition, aptly illustrating its historical inaccuracy and analytical flaws. But historical errors aside, the ideological force of this universalist fallacy is quite potent because it provides illusory comfort and reinforcement of market constrained choices.

A related component of the universalizing dictum is the projection of the interests of a single group as the common interests of all; the more accomplished an agent/group/class is in universalizing its aims, the less likely it will be perceived as a sectional interest engaged in selfish pursuits. Polanyi wryly lampoons the rhetoric of liberal leaders who denounced "the blindness of the working people to the ultimate beneficence of unrestricted economic freedom to all human interests, including their own" (GT, 144). Lastly, a universalizing ideology must engender a sense of unity – a conviction that individuals are all striving for the same goals, even if the fundamental nature of social life is rooted in conflict. He saw this as a key proposition of the political economists as well:

> "Harmony was inherent in economy, it was said, the interests of the individual and the community being ultimately identical – but such harmonious self-regulation required that the individual respect economic law even if it happened to destroy him. Conflict, also seemed inherent in economy, whether as competition of individuals or as struggle of classes –but such conflict, again, might turn out to be only the vehicle of a deeper harmony immanent in present, or perhaps, future society."
>
> (GT, 85)

While I greatly admire his discussion of the formative contribution of ideology to the establishment of the self-regulating market – indeed, the passages in this regard are among my favorite parts of the book for their coruscating wit and memorable phrasemaking – there are a number of issues that warrant further consideration. The first is to ask under what conditions the triumph of a new ideology can be consolidated. Polanyi implies that the articulation and resonance of an ideology will vary depending upon the precise historical juncture. As an example, he posits a qualitative break in the development of the ideology of political economy, as exemplified by the yawning divide he identifies between the stances of Adam Smith and Joseph Townsend (GT, 92, 111–13). Smith, he maintains, still viewed the "wealth of nations" in terms of the social, political and moral bases of the community:

> "there is no intimation in his work that the economic interests of the capitalists laid down the law to society; no intimation that they were the secular spokesman of the divine providence which governed the economic world as a separate entity. The economic sphere, with him, is not yet subject to the laws of its own that provide us with a standard of good and evil...A broad optimism pervades Smith's thinking since the laws governing the economic part of the universe are consonant with man's destiny as are those that govern the rest. No hidden hand tries to impose upon us the rites of cannibalism in the name of self-interest."
>
> (GT, 111–12)

Just ten years later, amid growing pauperism, unemployment and the disruptive effects of external trade, Townsend and the other members of the political economy school propagated the belief of the economy as an independent sector and completely abandoned Smith's "humantistic foundations" (GT, 115). Classical political economy properly begins he insisted, with Malthus and his followers in 1798 (GT, 121).

Like Weber in his discussion of the "elective affinity" between capitalism and Protestantism, which suggested religious ideals were adopted by certain social groups because these ideas conformed to their own lived experience, Polanyi implies that the popular reception of political economy (as well as the rich vein of misunderstandings that so characterized it) owed directly to its tight fit with the character of the transition to a market economy. "The new foundations", he wrote, "closely fit the society that was emerging" (GT, 115). Liberal ideology undermined the moral claims of the old moral economy; it offered an ideological justification for the suffering that resulted; it gave a reasonably persuasive account of the critical factors involved in the transition; and it helped create a coalition for change among very divergent perspectives.

While I heartily endorse the valuable proposition that the social/political context exerts immense influence on the propagation of an ideology, there is considerable ambiguity in Polanyi's account. In the first place, the alleged discrepancy between Smith and the emerging political economy school exemplified by Townsend seems considerably overstated. Smith's "Digression Concerning the Corn Trade" (Book 4, Chapter 5 of *The Wealth of Nations*) is particularly revealing of the *laissez-faire* foundations that Polanyi is a bit too hasty to discount.[22] Smith confidently asserted that in times of food shortage there was an overwhelming requirement for "the unlimited, unrestrained freedom of the corn trade, as it is the only effectual preventative of the miseries of a famine so it is the best palliative of the inconveniences of a dearth" (Smith, 1937 [1776], 493). He specifically cautioned against government action (such as emergency food relief, bans on food exports, and the like) that interfered with the workings of the free market to alleviate food shortages, maintaining that this would only make the situation worse: "a famine has never arisen from any other cause but the violence of government attempting, by improper means, to remedy the inconveniences of a dearth" (Smith, op. cit., 492–3). Smith's position, E. P. Thompson remarked, acquired "oracular authority" among the indoctrinated British colonial authorities and:

> "were among the most influential writings in history, with a global influence which was sometimes baneful. Their arguments discredited and disallowed traditional protective interventions in time of dearth, could be used to justify profiteering and hoarding, and could serve as apologetics to soothe the troubled consciences of the authorities by commending inactivity as correct political economy."
>
> (Thompson, 1993, 279, 282)

It might well be the case, as Polanyi maintains, that Smith's normative concerns could be distinguished from Malthus or Ricardo yet his tenets of liberalism and its concrete policy orientations in these pages was virtually identical to any political economist.

One might claim that Polanyi was simply unaware of this section of Smith's book yet since his incisive discussion of the *laissez-faire* underpinnings of famine policy in India (discussed at length in Chapter 3) supports nearly all the charges leveled by Thompson, I doubt that this position can be sustained. Indeed, if one returns to his comment about Smith quoted earlier – "no hidden hand tries to impose upon us the rites of cannibalism in the name of self-interest" – an unseemly assertion in light of the appalling carnage incurred by the Indian and Irish populations as a result of these liberal policies, it is almost as if the passage actually represents an unconscious acknowledgment of this very work. And surely, as keen as he was to dissect the obfuscations and double-speak of political economy, one has to ask how Polanyi could possibly have avoided lambasting such a ghastly non-sequiter as the "*inconveniences of a dearth*". I am inclined to view this "oversight" as the product of his dogmatic insistence that the real transition to the market economy began only after 1795. Given that he seeks to link the emergence of liberal ideology to the onset of the self-regulating market, Polanyi has no choice but to posit the distinctiveness of Smith's work vis-à-vis the political economy school even if it results in such transparent problems of interpretation.

There are additional problems with the "context" argument that relate directly to the qualitative break question. If we take the historical grounding of ideology seriously, then there is no question that an ideological justification for the market economy generally, and the commodification process specifically, predated Smith by at least a century and that these were articulated in terms highly reminiscent of political economy. The erosion of common property rights in the land and the state's committed support from the late 17th century onwards for the relentless process of enclosures was paved by an ideological metamorphosis in beliefs about the proper role of land and nature. John Locke is a pivotal figure in this regard: he offered invaluable support for the appropriation of land and labor power as an inalienable right which presupposed an awareness of a commercial economy in which both factors were already in the process of being commodified (Macpherson, 1962, 211–220; McNally, 1993). In his *Second Treatise on Government*, Locke specifically links the development of property rights in the land to the question of "improvement". Any person who is able to take "unimproved" land (such as the commons) and make it productive and profitable for any use has added to the nation's wealth and therefore should be supported by the full weight of the law. The cult of improvement acted as a justification for landed interests to engage in the brutalizing enclosures with clean hands and at the same time was employed as a new modernizing ethos (and basis of political opposition) against landed rivals who had no abiding interest in productivity-enhancing activities.

Joyce Appleby similarly documents how 17th-century pamphleteers in favor of the market were forced to confront the deeply entrenched cultural beliefs of the moral economy which represented a serious impediment to commodification: the dangers of usury for the commodification of money; the intrinsic value of the commons and a regulated grain trade for the commodification of land; the customs and norms of fair work and wages for the commodification of labor. She argues it was the specific historical context of the transition to capitalism that explains *why* particular ideological mechanisms were commonplace. The legitimacy of capitalism as a "natural" progression had everything to do with the fact that the transition took place over centuries in England:

> "This dimension of time powerfully affected the perception of the change. For those on the continent, industrialization was a radical force that required explanation; for the English, the final stages of advanced capitalism appeared as the end product of what seemed a predictable and wholly natural progression…"
>
> (Appleby, 1978, 9)

Regrettably, Polanyi does not address this historical evolution of liberal ideology in any sustained manner, a consequence of his dogmatic embrace of the big bang of the self-regulating market. Liberalism, he insists, remained "a spasmodic tendency" only until a "fully deployed market economy" was in place (GT, 135).

Finally, it must also be argued that stipulating the various social mechanisms of an ideology does not automatically constitute an explanation of why a specific ideology is able to become the dominant ideological regime. "Only some ideas", argue Block and Somers, "can exercise the causal power to undermine, dislodge and replace a previously dominant ideational regime" (Block and Somers, 2014, 156). A more rigorous account of the triumph of political economy would have to posit a series of direct processes (in the cultural, social and political realms) that create a set of favorable conditions for its propagation. For instance, it would be necessary to explain the way in which the new ideology sunk its roots in the wider population. There is quite a substantial puzzle to overcome in this regard. In early capitalist societies, where the literacy of the population was low and the information industries (mass media, education) highly underdeveloped and unsophisticated, the capability to transmit dominant ideologies was considerably circumscribed (Abercrombie et al., 1980). Polanyi does not elaborate how the ideology of political economy became the new common sense or the way in which the broad popular attachment to moral economy was in fact weakened and challenged.

Now, one might offer a tentative hypothesis that the symbiosis of the market economy and the liberal state, and in particular the way in which the gradual extension of suffrage was coeval with the development of individual economic opportunities, bound people to the market. It might be possible as well to stipulate a series of cultural mechanisms that had this effect. E. P. Thompson, as an example, cited Weber to the effect that "even piece rates and other incentives lose effectiveness at a certain point if there is no *inner compulsion*...the laborer must be turned into 'its own slave driver'" (Thompson, 1966, 357). In industrializing England, it was the powerful compulsion of Methodism that played this unexpected role. Although it might have seemed paradoxical that a religion which stressed the virtues of discipline, order, and self-reliance would have such wide appeal in a time of exceptional hardship, Methodism, as Thompson so eloquently describes, proved a powerful force of indoctrination in the workplace, community, leisure and Sunday schools. A further explanation might stress the enduring *political* weakness of the ideological system that political economy succeeded. Thomas Paine's stirring defense of the moral economy, *The Rights of Man*, rather than Malthus's *Treatise on Population*, was the runaway best seller of the day and demonstrated the formidable hold which the ideas of the moral economy exerted over poor people's lives. But as an organized political and economic force, moral economy did not possess an effective "counter-hegemonic" strategy. In other words, it did not possess a compelling alternative political economy (a viable system of production, exchange and trade that could ensure economic prosperity and social justice) and thus it is not entirely surprising that it succumbed to liberalism. I am not suggesting that any or all of these constitute sufficient explanations but rather to highlight the fact that Polanyi does not explore the conditions for ideological success in any sustained way, which weakens the overall efficacy of an ideological explanation for the onset of the market economy.

The contradictions of political economy

"No wonder that the contemporaries were appalled at the seeming contradiction", wrote Polanyi, "of an almost miraculous increase in production accompanied by a near starvation of the masses. By 1834 there was a general conviction – with many thinking people a passionately held conviction – that anything was preferable to the continuance of Speenhamland" (GT, 80–1). The centerpiece of his argument regarding the provenance of the self-regulating market is certainly his extended treatment over two chapters of the Speenhamland system.[23] In 1795 the British government repealed the Act of Settlement that required workers to find employment in their home parish; by restoring the mobility of labor, this promised to be the first step in the creation of a national labor market. At the same time, in response to the demands of rural elites, a system of relief allowances tied to the price of bread, which became known as the Speenhamland system, was implemented to prevent pauperism in the countryside and ensure an adequate supply of labor for farmers during seasonal fluctuations (GT, 89). However, by shielding the rural population from the full force of the market, Polanyi argued

Speenhamland forestalled the creation of a labor market and set in motion a catastrophic spiral of social dislocation, economic devastation and cultural depredation. "Speenhamland precipitated a social catastrophe", he wrote. "By the time of its repeal huge masses of the laboring population resembled more the specters that might haunt a nightmare than human beings" (GT, 98, 105). As the contradictions of the old system festered, the impetus for a radical shift to the self-regulating market took on an unstoppable momentum.

Polanyi actually highlights three different sorts of contradictions (self-undermining/destabilizing tendencies) of the Speenhamland political economy (not all of which have the same causal relation to the origin of the market economy). In the *first* instance, there are the contradictions that occur as the direct result of the faulty institutional design of the traditional social protection regime. *Second*, there is the mutual incompatibility of competing principles of social organization – in this case, the emerging market economy and traditional social protection – where the protection of labor clashed with a system that treated it as a commodity. *Third*, there are the contradictions that are precipitated by the broader transformations in the domestic and global economy.

If we begin with the *first* set of contradictions, Polanyi, in detail that mirrors any classic policy implementation study, describes the multitude of weaknesses that plagued the administration of poor relief under Speenhamland (Block and Somers, 2003; Somers and Block, 2005). The jurisdictional scale of the programs proved hopelessly inadequate to the task: because relief was administered at the parish level, variability in local coverage heightened the risk of purposive mobility on the part of the poor. "The greater the variety of local provisions for the poor", he wrote, "the greater the danger to the well-kept parish that it would be swamped by the professional pauper" (GT, 88). Eligibility rules were applied indiscriminately and failed to distinguish between different components of the impoverished. "The various categories of paupers and able bodied employed", he said, "now tended to fuse into one indiscriminate mass of dependent poverty" (GT, 95–6). He draws the appropriate conclusion about the scope of coverage: "Accordingly, only in those short periods, when the administration of the Poor Law was both *national* and *differentiated* could it be more or less satisfactory" (GT, 95).

The financing of the allowance system was similarly plagued with grievous faults. "The craziest aspect of the system", he wrote, "was its economics proper" (GT, 96). In actual fact, the burden of paying for poor relief fell on all ratepayers indiscriminately without regard to their ability to pay. Many rate payers were poor tenant farmers, just one bad harvest from being "on the rates" themselves; wealthier landlords, on the other hand, were able to deduct part of their rates and derived the extra advantage (highlighted above) of using relief as an indirect subsidy which allowed them to keep their wage bills to a minimum. "On the whole, the relationship of the ratepayer and the pauper", Polanyi interestingly notes, "was somewhat similar to that of the employed and unemployed of our times under various schemas of insurance which make the employed bear the burden of keeping the temporary unemployed" (GT, 96).

The construction of the program also created a series of perverse incentives for both employers and workers alike. Farmers refused to hire agricultural laborers with small plots who were ineligible for relief with the consequence that "those who tried to keep off the rates and earn a living by their own exertions were hardly able to secure a job" (GT, 97). Given that parish relief supposedly guaranteed a livable income, landlords had every incentive to keep their wages as low as possible and to keep them below that of their fellow farmers because this meant that others subsidized their wage bill (GT, 122). This precipitated a vicious cycle of wage cutting that depressed wages well below the subsistence level. Polanyi was distinctly aware of this distorted logic which "should have stopped wage labor altogether. Standard wages should have gradually dropped to zero, thus putting the actual wage bill wholly on the parish" (GT, 81). Employers hired as few workers as possible, and for the briefest periods, and relied on the parish to care for the indigent but doing so increased the level of rates so rate payers cut down on their labor requirements even further thereby exacerbating the original dilemma.

Speenhamland also destroyed labor productivity and created a premium for shirking in the workplace. Workers had no incentive to work in unsatisfactory jobs, so long as relief was available to support their income, and because productivity was so low, employers had no reason to raise wages (even if they had been so inclined). Parishes put the unemployed to work in tawdry makeshift schemes that were degrading and demeaning: moving stones from one side of the road to the other was a familiar boondoggle. Speenhamland fatally damaged worker's personal autonomy and self-respect and helped cultivate habits of dependency. "Little by little, the people of the countryside were pauperized", he wrote, "the adage 'once on the rates, always on the rates' was a true saying" (GT, 80). It proved fatal for economic growth given that only the most ambitious and skilled workers had the wherewithal to migrate to the higher paying jobs in the urban manufacturing centers. It also occupied a profound legacy in the historical memory of the British working class: "The hatred of public relief, the distrust of state action, the insistence on respectability and self-reliance, remained for generations characteristic of the British worker" (GT, 101).

Beyond this specific critique of Speenhamland's failings, Polanyi is asserting a broader claim about the nature of social change: that before any new social system can be established and legitimated, the old one must first be systematically undermined (Lukacs, 1971). In this case, the moral economy system, which permeated political institutions, economic life and culture, and had sunk deep roots in the population, had to be discredited before a new one could possibly function. While this delegitimation process certainly functioned at the level of ideology, he also implies that it must also imbue everyday life as well. The desolation of Speenhamland was so disastrous and demoralizing that people were ready to contemplate any alternative, even the radical shock of liberalism. As if to prove the validity of the claim by sheer repetition, Polanyi presses this point in related formulations throughout the text:

> "This final step was taken only when market economy was set to start, and when the absence of a labor market was proving a greater evil to the common people themselves than the calamities that were to accompany its introduction."
>
> (77)

> "Only when a grave deterioration of the productive capacity of the masses resulted – a veritable national calamity which was obstructing the progress of machine civilization – did the necessity of abolishing the unconditional right of the poor to relief impose itself upon the consciousness of the country."
>
> (81–2)

> "And yet the success of this lacerating operation [marketization] was due to the deep seated convictions of the broad strata of the population, including the laborers themselves, that the system to which all appearances supported them was in truth despoiling them, and that the 'right to live' was the sickness unto death"
>
> (101)

The *second* contradiction was the clash between two mutually exclusive organizing principles of society (GT, 130). While the destructive dialectic between the market economy and social protection, the twin poles of the double movement, becomes the central plank of Polanyi's explanation of the great transformations of the 19th and 20th centuries, he utilizes a similar argument in the case of Speenhamland. 1795, in his conception, was still an "essentially pre-capitalist age" and he contrasts the paternalistic instincts of Speenhamland to the emerging market economy. "Under Speenhamland, society was rent by two opposing influences", he maintained:

> "the one emanating from paternalism and protecting labor from the dangers of the market system; the other organizing the elements of production including land, under a market system, and thus devastating the common people of their former status, compelling them to gain a living by offering their labor for sale, while at the same time, depriving their labor of its market value."
>
> (GT, 80)

On several occasions, Polanyi cites the paradox, which so confused contemporary observers of the period, whereby a simultaneous rise in both pauperism and wages occurred, a feature he claimed was symptomatic of a transitional period where elements of a capitalist economy existed but a fully competitive labor market had not yet been achieved (GT, 94). The contradictions at this stage were not as severe as those which will spark the apocalyptic spiral of the 19th century – because the double movement had not yet been fully internationalized, tensions did not bleed into the international arena quite so easily – but they nevertheless provoked an economic crisis, a deepening of social conflict and a collapse of political legitimacy. "There was a stark contradiction between the two industrial policies", he wrote, "what else but a social enormity could have been expected from their simultaneous continued application" (GT, 89).

Finally, Polanyi hints at a very different kind of argument – admittedly one that does not attain the same prominence in his narrative as these other factors – that posited Speenhamland was not just a *cause* of severe contradictions but was itself a *product* of the contradictions generated by the transformations in the wider political economy. In the first instance, he stressed the destabilizing effects of the transition to an urban-based manufacturing economy. This precipitated the demise of the rural putting-out industries, which hastened higher levels of rural unemployment and drained the countryside of its labor reserve as workers were drawn to the cities by the promise of employment and higher wages (GT, 287). Transformations in agricultural production were also instrumental, featuring new rounds of enclosures that extinguished commons rights, advances in farming methods and techniques, and new forms of specialization. These changes led to a higher concentration of landholding, reduced agrarian employment and created new patterns of seasonal unemployment, increased the wage dependency and poverty of laborers, and made all rural actors more vulnerable to volatility in the price of food and agricultural commodities (GT, 92). Polanyi stressed that these tensions of the domestic economy could be further traced to the instability of the global economy: "much of the social damage done to England's countryside sprang at first from the dislocating effects of trade directly upon the countryside itself" (GT, 92).[24] It was against this backdrop of social instability that Speenhamland was contemplated. "A dam had to be erected to protect the village from the flood of rising wages", he argued.

> "Methods had to be found which would protect the rural setting against social dislocation, reinforce traditional authority, prevent the draining off of rural labor, and raise agricultural wages without overburdening the farmer…its social implications met squarely the situation as judged by the ruling village interest – the squires."
>
> (GT, 94)

There is no question that Polanyi's argument here is the most substantial of any of the factors stipulated, not merely as a consequence of the space allocated to the presentation, but because the question of contradictions is so obviously central to his entire inquiry and method. I will be devoting ample discussion to this question in Chapter 5, so my critique here is limited to the specific contribution of Speenhamland to the rise of the self-regulating market. There are a number of historical and conceptual objections that could be leveled against his emphasis on Speenhamland. In the past four decades, there has been a burgeoning literature on the Poor laws that has essentially undermined his fundamental contention that poor relief precipitated a cultural, economic and social calamity (Blaug, 1963; Block and Somers, 2003; Boyer, 1990; Somers and Block, 2005).[25] Many of his claims, which had underpinned the deliberations of the Poor Law Commission as well, can no longer be sustained: the labor disincentive effects of the allowance system were minimal and rural employers were quick to deny assistance to anyone suspected of work shirking; productivity did not decline as a result of the old poor law; relief did not constitute a meaningful alternative to employment (indeed, as noted earlier, only a small percentage of the population was ever on relief) nor did it hinder labor mobility as much as he maintained; the specific system of bread allowances was never as widespread as he believed; and cut-throat wage cutting did not occur to the extent that he claimed. Speenhamland was only a single policy in a broad array of relief measures (seasonal unemployment insurance, employer subsidies, workfare), none of which had the same detrimental consequences he stipulated (Block and Somers, 2014, 127). Nor was the old system of relief ever as de-legitimated as he assumed: worker agitation (both urban and rural) against the New Poor Law was a persistent feature of the decades after 1834, and indeed these protests fed into the Chartist movement that emerged in the 1840s .

A further historical objection could be raised as well. Once we look beyond the big bang version of marketization, it would seem logical to assume that there might well have been earlier conjunctures where contradictions arising from either previous regressive programs of social protection or wider crises in the political economy would have similarly spurred the further expansion of commodification and the growth of the market. While Polanyi neglects to take such a path, Douglas North and Barry Weingast offer just this perspective for the key period of the Glorious Revolution in the mid-17th century (North and Weingast, 1989). The Stuart monarchy, which could no longer sell off crown lands to compensate for revenue shortfalls, was faced with a massive financial crisis that forced them to enact a series of hasty policies: forcible loans, seizure of properties, sale of monopolies, expansion of the peerage and sale of hereditary peerages (which merely decreased the value of both, stimulating even further cut rate initiatives). Each of these was viewed by the aristocracy and Parliament as an attempt by the crown to forcibly expropriate private wealth and subsequent political upheavals could be traced to these injudicious policies. The aftermath of the 1688 settlement witnessed a veritable institutional revolution within the state: Parliament gained the exclusive right to raise new taxes and to scrutinize the crown's finances; an independent judiciary was established to limit the royal prerogative; and a system of political liberties safeguarded. These had profound consequences for the development of the market economy: with private property rights now in effect sacrosanct, capital accumulation and the growth of financial markets took a giant leap forward in the ensuing decades.

An important analytical question is how to explain the presence of competing social principles and their harmonization into a new regime. How, in other words, does crisis lead to reform? Polanyi implies this process was essentially a tug of war between opposing social interests, each pulling in their own direction for distinct policies (agrarian elites for social stability, urban manufacturing interests for a mobile work force) with the end result a stalemated system that had partial advantages for each group yet produced overall chaos that ultimately benefited no one. Hobsbawm and Rude, in their classic work *Captain Swing*, posit just this kind of social paralysis:

> "A fundamental contradiction lay at the heart of English agrarian society in the period of the Industrial Revolution. Its rulers wanted it to be both capitalist and stable, traditionalist and hierarchical. In other words, they wanted it to be governed by the universal free market of the liberal economist....but only to the extent that suited nobles, squires and farmers; they advocated an economy which implied mutually antagonistic classes, but did not want it to disrupt a society of ordered ranks."
>
> (Hobsbawm and Rude, 1968, 47)

However, one of the abiding weaknesses of Polanyi's explanation of the 1834 conjuncture is that these conflicting interests of the dominant classes are never comprehensively detailed. His prevailing assumption appears to be that as the cultural, economic and social harm of poor relief intensified, political and manufacturing interests became alert to the need for radical change. But he seems to imply that this was not the case for rural elites: "by 1833, the farming community was solidly in favor of retaining Speenhamland", despite the rise in rural unrest and the paralyzing effects of the system (GT, 298–9). Of course, this leaves us with a curious puzzle: why would a Parliament, which was dominated by these very agrarian elites, nonetheless countenance such a radical overhaul of a program that they believed was still representing their interests (Boyer, 1990)?

The answer lies in the mutual relationship between ideological, political, and social power in the decades leading up to the critical rupture of 1834. Peter Mandler has described how the landed gentry, formerly passionate adherents of paternalism, surrendered to the allure of the Malthusian ethos as early as 1815. Many forward looking members of their class had already begun experimenting with innovative forms of poor relief premised on these ideals. "Landlords...found many of their traditional norms to be crippling encumbrances", Mandler argued.

> "In the drive to enclose common lands, to introduce technological innovations and to cope with the cheapening of grain in a freer market, they could no longer afford their muddled, half-Lockean, half-paternalist view of a labourer's right to land, a job, a fair wage."
>
> (Mandler, 1987, 137)

Yet despite the compelling economic and political incentives that the gentry had to embrace a complete reform of poor relief, no reform was forthcoming until several decades later.

The resolution of this paradox can be traced to the *political* calculations of this social group:

> "institutional change was bound to lag behind ideological change, especially in times of political instability, for if landlords had much to fear for the long term economic effects of poor law rights, they had more to fear from the short term political effects of seeking to abrogate them."
>
> (Mandler, 1987, 139)

As noted earlier, the gentry feared any significant change was bound to be political dynamite, precipitating massive unrest and jeopardizing their political authority in the countryside. Inter-class considerations were also paramount: reform minded agrarian elites were unable to achieve meaningful change so long as the administration of relief was controlled by a local magistracy dominated by paternalist interests and while a stalemate existed within the Parliament regarding the proper course of action. Institutional obstacles were equally important: modernizing farmers could not rely on the central government for assistance given that this scale of action was historically unprecedented and presupposed too great a leap of faith in the capacity of the central state. What was required for reform was not only a new understanding in relations between state and society but also the specific catalyst of the Swing unrest that threatened the social fabric of the countryside, a political crisis that ushered in a new reform minded government, and the proselytizing mission of the Royal Commission that cemented the new consensus for radical change.

A related solution to the "agency" issue would be to argue that the contradictions, even if not as uniformly detrimental as Polanyi supposed, nevertheless constituted such a serious obstacle for policy makers that they were compelled to engage in an accelerated strategy of social learning. This is reminiscent of Albert Hirschman's notion of "blocked development", whereby policy makers achieve greater innovation when forced to confront seemingly insurmountable challenges (Hirschman, 1979). There is a glimmer of this in his analysis in terms of the way social classes shift their attitudes toward marketization in response to the challenges thrown up by Speenhamland, although this transformation in political elites is left largely unspoken. In fact, as Somers and Block detail, parishes did experiment with a variety of different ways of distributing relief (a minimum guaranteed income such as Speenhamland, seasonal unemployment insurance, public works subsidies) and these incremental steps produced a strong momentum for reform (Somers and Block, 2005).

However, this perspective is predicated on an implicit assumption, namely that a turn to the free market is chosen precisely because this new institutional framework is able to resolve these formidable contradictions. Certainly, Polanyi believes this to be the case. "In the end, the free labor market", he wrote, "in spite of the inhuman methods employed in creating it, proved financially beneficial to all concerned" (GT, 78). The sustained cut in relief expenditures in the transition to the workhouse under the New Poor Law improved the financial status of agrarian elites. The brutality of the workhouse enhanced the appeal of migration from rural areas and millions of rural workers (particularly the young and skilled) moved to urban areas between 1831 and 1851 and thereby increased their standard of living (Boyer, 1990, 209–210). Greater labor mobility released the pressures of unemployment in the countryside and also led to a reduction of wages in urban manufacturing that generated higher profits for employers. Industrial workers faced much higher levels of insecurity, working much longer hours for less money and with less control over their labor (Thompson, 1966). However, there is a further paradox at the heart of this contention. No matter the gains engendered by the promulgation of the free market, it can never be guaranteed that all contradictions are automatically reconciled in the following era or that the force of these anachronistic problems might not exert a persistent influence for decades to come (Bloch, 1970). If this is indeed the case, then many of the tensions and problems that Polanyi associated with the *laissez-faire* regime (see the following chapters) might actually have been the residue of this previous epoch's unresolved contradictions.

Conclusion

I want to conclude this chapter by exploring some general methodological and conceptual implications suggested by the foregoing discussion. In the analysis of large-scale events, one can quite unproblematically enumerate the range of factors that might be relevant to the transformation but this is only a starting point for developing an adequate explanation. Even if no one variable can be said to be primary, we still need to ask whether *all* of the factors are necessary in order to bring about the outcome under investigation. Albert Hirschman referred to such moments of *contingent causation* where a series of factors are seemingly involved in an explanation: "Any substantial change in course requires an exceptional convergence of numerous favorable conditions such that looking backward, change looks overdetermined when in actual fact, every one of those conditions was indispensable for it to occur" (Hirschman, 1982, 72). One of the limits of Polanyi's account is that he gives no indication of whether the origins of *laissez-faire* are best understood as an example of this sort of contingent causality or whether any of the five factors are more central than others (Lacher, 2006).

As an example, although the commodification of land, labor and money are all critical to his account of the great transformation, it is only in the case of labor commodification that all five causal variables (technology, social power, the state, contradictions and ideology) are implicated. The role of the state and social power are mentioned with respect to land and there is an oft-handed remark about the importance of technology when the case is made for the extension of land commodification to the international sphere. But the commodification of money receives virtually no discussion in terms of these causal variables even though financial commodification was immeasurably aided by the growing sophistication of communications and transport technologies in the 16th and 17th centuries. The state played a paramount role as well: an open door immigration policy during the Elizabethan period enabled the emigration of European refugees who had originated the social networks that created a transnational capital market and certainly the Bank of England played a determinative role in the development of English finance (a feature he returns to in his discussion of the gold standard).

Similarly, any account of social change should delineate how the causal variables differ in type and significance. The explanatory scope of each variable might vary considerably – for instance, one factor might have little relevance to the onset of labor commodification but have everything to do with the commodification of money, so a preliminary investigation is required to sketch out these connections, which if done properly, would complement the contingent approach suggested above. Furthermore, outcomes might be differentially affected by the causal variables in different ways at different stages in the commodification process, a feature that Polanyi highlights but never develops in any systematic manner. In other words, one would want to utilize this causal analysis as a means of generating a set of hypotheses that might suggest the conditions under which a transition to a self-regulating period within capitalism in the future is more likely to occur, a critical necessity for any theory of the double movement itself. As I suggested in the Introduction, it is the absence of such analytical ambitions that partly explains why his model of the double movement has not often served as the foundation for comparative-historical sociological studies.

Finally, Lawrence Stone argued there was an additional requirement to ensure the validity of multiple causation. "They [multiple explanations] are convincing", he insisted, "provided that they form a set of elective affinities, held together not by mere random chance but by a system of logical integration that points them all in the same direction and makes them mutually reinforcing" (Stone, 1989, 592). Polanyi comes closest to this in his argument about Speenhamland, which clearly integrates many of these factors as noted earlier. As an example, he noted the close relationship between ideology and the contradictions of the Speenhamland era, insisting that the "foundations of economic theory were laid down during the Speenhamland period", a development which "had the most far-reaching consequences for the understanding of the nature of economic society" (GT, 124, 125). The liberal assertion of the "iron law of wages", the assumption that the bare subsistence level of laborer's livelihood was the consequence of a "law" that kept wages so low, might have been utterly misleading yet the recourse to naturalism could be directly attributed to the widespread confusion that marked the era. "The naturalistic element in the foundations of orthodox economics", he maintained, "was the outcome of the conditions primarily created by Speenhamland" (GT, 123). But this interactive model is by no means applied to all the factors impacting on commodification, a serious omission at the heart of his analysis.

If we move beyond the immediate account of the origins of the self-regulating market to consider his broader historical sociological approach, Polanyi's conceptual framework embodies two distinct explanatory stances. On the one hand, he clearly emphasizes the importance of intentional action in the marketization process. "Only when one can point to the group or groups that effected a change", he wrote, "is it explained *how* that change has taken place" (GT, 152). However, as this chapter has already noted, one of the persistent weaknesses of his exposition is the difficulty he sometimes has in detailing the precise rationale for group actions. Polanyi makes it quite clear that social preferences for marketization change over time but he does not fully explicate the way in which these are "structured" by the changing dynamic of the expanding market or by transformations in political, social and cultural relations. An explanation in this regard would need to explain the precise ways in which individual (or group) interests and ideas are shaped by structural positions and how preferences are continuously evaluated and prioritized, not simply as a result of these structural positions but by a *strategic* evaluation of the likelihood of success and failure in the immediate circumstances (which is culturally and historically conditioned).

At the same time, Polanyi maintains that the origins of *laissez-faire* can also be traced to long-term historical trends that acted as deep structural imperatives for change. In his discussion of the 16th century enclosures, he differentiates between the "*rate of change*" and the "*direction of change*":

> "The rate of change is often of no less importance than the direction of change itself; but while the latter does not depend on our own volition, it is the rate at which we allow change to take place which may well depend upon us."
>
> (GT, 36–37)

At the same time, he insisted that the direction of change in Western societies was clearly foreshadowed: "In retrospect nothing could be clearer than the Western European trend of economic progress which aimed at eliminating an artificially maintained uniformity of agricultural technique, intermixed strips, and the primitive institution of the common" (GT, 37). In other words, even at the time of the enclosures, he seems to imply that there was a structural advantage that capitalist economic relations already enjoyed which subsequently influenced the strategies and interests of all agrarian actors. Capitalist social relations were the intentional product of human agency yet, at the same time, the ascendancy of capitalism generated a structural imperative that was not reliant on human agency.

In a related manner, the Speenhamland conjuncture is presented as a case where the momentum of history set in motion inevitable processes of social change (discussed more fully in the conclusion to Chapter 4). The attempt to forestall the onset of the market economy was ultimately doomed to fail because it contradicted the general trajectory of history. "The attempt to create a capitalistic order without a labor market had failed disastrously", he commented.

> "The laws governing such an order had asserted themselves, and manifested their radical antagonism to the principle of paternalism. The rigor of these laws had become apparent and their violation had been cruelly visited upon those who had disobeyed them."
>
> (GT, 80)

There are other places in which the transition to the self-regulating market is depicted in similarly deterministic language: "in 1834, industrial capitalism was ready to be started, and Poor law reform was ushered in...the mechanism of the market was asserting itself and clamoring for its completion; human labor had to be made a commodity" (GT, 102).

These passages bear all the flaws of naturalistic arguments employed by liberal ideologues in favor of the free market: the assertion of the blind operation of historical laws outside of human intervention and the futility of human agency against the inviolability of such laws. The difficulty in sustaining such a precarious balancing act – of employing a species of naturalism on behalf of a long term explanation of the dynamics of capitalism yet condemning its use by the architects of this very process – should be apparent. But more critically, Polanyi never specified any particular structural imperatives underpinning historical change that might link such temporally distinct events as the enclosures and Speenhamland: as an example, an assumption about the technological superiority of capitalist social relations and an innate tendency to replicate those relations over time (Cohen, 1978). Nor did he detail with sufficient precision or generality the "laws governing a capitalist order" or explain the ways in which these trends might have acted to circumscribe political action and strategy (I am not suggesting that the search for such laws would have been at all fruitful, merely that it was not a feature of his own argument). The single moment where the "direction of change" appears to be vulnerable to transformation is when an existing system has seemingly exhausted its potential and its demise is imminent; but this is simply tantamount to defining what a transitional period constitutes rather than explaining the reproduction and deterioration of the system. There is no *a priori* reason why the direction of any historical process, even the evolution of capitalism, cannot be altered in substantial ways.[26] "Capitalism is a contingent – and also a temporary product of history", argues William Sewell. "Its emergence as a system was the product of a far from necessary conjunction of developments in agriculture, commerce, industry, politics and culture over the course of the sixteenth, seventeenth and eighteenth centuries" (Sewell, 2014, 2).

By framing the issue in terms of the indomitable unfolding of a historical law, Polanyi weakens his overall argument: it undermines his own emphasis on the singularity of the critical juncture of 1834; it undercuts the historical methodology of the double movement which stresses the fundamental discontinuity of social change; and it violates his self-stated purpose of historical investigation which was to "reintegrate society into the human world" (GT, 126).

Notes

1 There is an additional complication to note. Polanyi maintained the self-regulating market had three features: a competitive labor market, automatic gold standard and free trade (GT, 139). In essence, the latter two components represent the means by which the commodification process is extended outwards by the spread of the market mechanism in the 19th century and therefore should not be considered within the general definition itself. This is discussed in Chapter 5.

2 Sandra Halperin, for example, writes: "Absent in Polanyi's analysis is a detailed explanation of the 'first transformation' that, at the end of the 18th century, brought about the rise of an unregulated market system" (Halperin, 2004, xvi). For an exception to this, see Dale, 2010.

3 Wood comments: "The fact remains that *The Great Transformation* is a significant departure from conventional historiography on the 'transition" (Wood, 1999, 25). But this is not to say that Polanyi is completely immune to the tug of the opposing tradition (Dale, 2010). In accounting for the commercialization of agriculture, he emphasizes the formative role of urban centers as opposed to shifting class relations: "corn markets up to the fifteenth century had a strictly local organization. But the growth of towns induced landlords to produce primarily for sale on the market…" (GT, 181). There is also a distinct Wallerstein-like flavor to the following quote: "The Commercial revolution, so closely connected with the rise of capitalism, became the vehicle to power for Portugal, Spain, Holland, France, England and the United States, each of them benefiting from the chances offered by that broad and deep seated movement, while on the other hand, capitalism itself was spreading over the planet through the instrumentality of these rising Powers" (GT, 28).

4 Marx made precisely the same argument: commodity production "becomes inevitable from the moment there is a free sale, by the worker himself, of labour power as a commodity…Only where wage labour is its basis does commodity production impose itself upon society as a whole" (Marx, 1973, 733).

5 Polanyi's argument is limited in two key respects. He attributes the evolution of the internal market to mercantilist policies but ignores the ground breaking role of merchant entrepreneurs in diffusing commodity relations and extending the scope of market activities (Lie, 1991). The relationship of the internal and external

markets is largely unexplored as well. Polanyi suggests that external markets were "unrelated to the internal organization of the economy", a claim that has been challenged by recent scholarship that highlights the importance of the slave trade and trade with the colonies America and India) to the overall economic development of English capitalism (Pomerantz, 2000).

6 These debates have considerable relevance for contemporary political life and are not merely the province of "transition" anoraks. Certainly, the question of whether China has crossed the threshold into a capitalist economy is a matter of vital social and political concern. To adjudicate this claim, one would have to carefully trace the way in which social and political life there is being shaped and constituted by markets. Likewise, the important debate in developing societies about the extensiveness of bonded labor or the penetration of commercial practices into agricultural relations, is essentially a critical judgment about the extent to which commodification exerts a formidable influence on these societies.

7 Polanyi's conceptualization of pre-market societies is curiously incomplete, especially in light of how many scholars have utilized his tripartite framework wherein economic activity could be organized according to the principles of reciprocity, redistribution or by markets. While most of the transition debate postulated a shift from feudalism (which he argues was dominated by either reciprocity or redistribution [GT, 55]) to capitalism, it is not entirely clear what type of society or mode of economic activity is implicated in his analysis of the period directly before 1834. He speaks of "pre-capitalist" or "semi-commercial" period (GT, 81, 104), yet this essentially defines the period purely by reference to what is to come rather than by the intrinsic dynamics of the era. Polanyi tends to utilize the term "mercantilism" to describe this period yet he never actually details which of his three modes of economic activity best characterizes this kind of regime (see GT, 54–5, 62–70, 73–4).

8 Polanyi is not alone in making this argument. William Reddy, in a fascinating critique of E. P. Thompson's famous discussion about the fate of the English weavers, argued that despite a precipitate fall in their wages and the opportunity of alternative employment elsewhere, the weavers were not induced to employ their labor power elsewhere but instead chose to die of near starvation and exposure. He maintains that this demonstrates that "the handloom weavers were not disposing of their labor in a market" (Reddy, 1987, 5).

9 Although expropriation and wage work have strong historical connections, Tilly argues that these processes occurred in distinct historical sequences and represented different outcomes of strategic behavior by social actors (Tilly, 1979).

10 Recent scholarship has questioned the extent to which the common lands were available to laborers on the eve of the parliamentary enclosures. Leigh Shaw-Taylor has argued that even before 1700 "over 80% of labouring households in these villages neither owned nor rented common rights. Thus the great bulk of labouring households was overwhelmingly dependent on wage labour" (Shaw-Taylor, 2001, 98). The enclosure movement certainly immiserated agricultural workers but it did not proletarianize them since their dependence on wage work was nearly complete by the turn of the 18th century.

11 Historians of the industrial revolution have their own transition debate, featuring the same heated arguments about the nature of the transition (gradualists squaring off against adherents of radical discontinuity) and what the core dynamic of the transition might be (technological determinists versus institutionalists) (Hudson, 1992). Polanyi was clearly aware of these terms of debate: "The very term 'Industrial revolution' was now framed upon as conveying an exaggerated idea of what was essentially a slow process of change. No more had happened, these scholars suggested, then that a gradual unfolding of the forces of technological progress

transformed the living of the people" (GT, 161). What is actually remarkable is how little these two transition debates actually reference each other, an intriguing oversight given their parallel concerns. Historians of the industrial revolution insist that this was the real transformation that mattered – "The changes that occurred in Britain between 1760–1830 dwarfed in virtually every respect the change that had occurred in the previous seventy years" (Mokyr, 1994, 3) – and as such give little attention to the remarkable changes in lifestyles, life chances and life experiences which the onset of a market economy created. For their part, the capitalist transition historians have not convincingly demonstrated the way in which their qualitative break underpinned the later transformation to an industrial economy.

12 Gareth Dale (2010) discusses four key factors (technology, elite opinion, role of political elites and problems of the protective regime) that overlap considerably with my own account even if our emphases and discussion of Polanyi's framework lead in distinct directions.

13 Of course, Polanyi is not the only social theorist to be attracted to such an account. Marx's writings betray the same kind of technological determinism as this famous quote from the *Poverty of Philosophy* demonstrates: "Social relations are closely bound up with productive forces. In acquiring new productive forces men change their mode of production; and in changing their mode of production, in changing their way of earning a living, they change all their social relations. The hand mill gives you society with the feudal lord; the steam mill society with the industrialist capitalist" (Marx, in Tucker, 1972, 236).

14 Many historians have noted the surprising resilience of the domestic system and outwork that persisted well into the mid-19th century. In sectors where these forms dominated, productivity gains were achieved through intensification of the labor process not by technological improvements and the real driving force of workplace reorganization and commodification was the competitive dynamic of the market. Indeed, Patrick Joyce argues the advance of capitalist relations of production occurred less through the impact of large manufacturers and factory mechanization than by the capitalist middlemen who dominated the outwork trades: "Capitalism in the nineteenth century made headway as much if not more by the tightening hold of the middlemen rather than the large manufacturer. In the trades and in outwork, the worker often confronted not the capitalist employer but the much more immediate figures of the merchant, the putter-out, the clerk, inspector and agent. These were the bearers of unfettered competition and degraded status" (Joyce, 1991, 165).

15 E. P. Thompson's account of the parliamentary enclosures extends the "social" explanation by highlighting factors such as the changing social attitudes among the aristocracy, higher social pretensions aligned with ostentatious consumption which created an urgent need for greater rental income, as well as the general counter-revolutionary tone of the entire political period ("reflexes of panic and class antagonism") (Thompson, 1993, 218).

16 However, Mark Steinberg draws the opposite conclusion from Polanyi. "Contrary to Polanyi's story of the double movement {the inevitable rise of social protection}", he wrote, "unions largely sought refuge from rather than in state institutions, opting for what became known as 'collective laissez faire'" (Steinberg, 2016, 142).

17 Albert Hirschman makes a similar observation: "the idea that the public happiness is best served by everyone pursuing private gains may have served not so much as a glorifying function for the new class of capitalists; it also fulfilled the more pressing need to relieve acute guilt feelings experienced by many a so-called 'conquering bourgeois' who actually had long been exposed to a non-bourgeois moral code" (Hirschman, 1982, 128–29).

18 Eagleton makes the important distinction between ideologies, which serve, and those, which *legitimate* social interests (Eagleton, 1991, 55). An ideology that purports a belief in the beneficial role of hunger in society might serve dominant interests without necessarily legitimating them in the minds of its subjects.

19 I cannot resist offering the following riposte written by another Englishman at roughly the same time period, but drawing very different lessons about the educational merits of hunger: "Poverty, in defence of principle, begets a degree of meanness that will stoop to almost anything. A one hundred refinements of argument may be brought to prove that the practice of honesty will be still the same, in the most trying and necessitous of circumstances. He who was never hungry may argue finely on the subjection of the appetite: and he who was never distressed may harangue as beautifully on the power of principle. But poverty, like grief, has an incurable deafness. The oration loses all its edge; and 'to be or not to be' becomes the only question". This was written by Thomas Paine in his first published work in a pamphlet entitled *The Case of the Officers of Excise.*

20 Eagleton makes an incisive point about the wider implications of the naturalizing rhetoric. He writes: "it is interesting, incidentally, that the concept of naturalization itself rests upon a particular ideology of nature, which tells it in the manner of William Wordsworth to be massively immutable and enduring; and it is ironic that this view of Nature should prevail in an historical epoch where the stuff is continually being transformed" (Eagleton, 1991: 59). Polanyi is not at all predisposed to this kind of sentimentality and indeed sees nature as inseparable from human's lived experiences: "Natural is that which is in accordance with the principles embodied in the mind of man; and the natural order is that which is in accordance with those principles...Political economy should be a human science; it should deal with that which was natural to man, not to Nature" (GT, 112).

21 The assertion of natural laws was hardly the sole province of liberal ideologues. French revolutionaries invoked the natural rights of equality, liberty and fraternity against custom and privilege and this species of naturalism became a powerful ally of progressive change. See Micheline Ishay's *Internationalism and Its Betrayal* (Minnesota, 1995) for an illuminating discussion.

22 E. P. Thompson called this writing of Smith "the most lucid expression in English of the standpoint of the new political economy" (Thompson, 1993, 282).

23 In a series of thorough, richly detailed articles, Block and Somers present the centrality of the Speenhamland case within his work and offer an exhaustive review of the empirical and causal gaps within Polanyi's argument (Block and Somers, 2003, 2014; Somers and Block, 2005).

24 Another contributing factor would have been the destabilizing effects of the demobilization of hundreds of thousands of soldiers at the end of the Napoleonic wars that increased competition for jobs in already impoverished rural areas.

25 Dale (2010) and Rogan (2017) detail how Polanyi's original draft of the book was strongly criticized by G. D. H. Cole and Richard Tawney who both believed he had over exaggerated the impact of Speenhamland.

26 Some historians, as an example, have claimed the open field system, which was eliminated by the enclosures ostensibly because of the latter's inherent productive superiority, actually generated yields that were as efficient as their proto-capitalist counterparts and could possibly have constituted an alternative pathway to agrarian capitalism (Allen, 1992). Similarly, Charles Sabel and Jonathan Zeitlin argued that the growth of the factory system was not an inevitable or irreversible development and that a system of "flexible production", rooted in a small scale

artisanal economy, might very well have provided similar increases in goods and resources yet with less rapid centralization and smaller increases in the standard of living (but with far less onerous cultural effects) (Sabel and Zeitlin, 1985). Of course, there are compelling reasons, rooted in the specific social, political and technological circumstances of English history, why neither of these alternative roads were chosen.

Chapter 3

The Dynamics of a Market Society

Once the self-regulating market had been constituted, the development of a "market society" represented the next critical step in the evolution of the double movement. Polanyi offers a characteristically trenchant epigram of this process:

> "Ultimately, that is why the control of the economic system by the market is of overwhelming consequence to the whole organization of society; it means no less than the *running of society as an adjunct of the market*. Instead of economy being embedded in social relations, *social relations are embedded in the economic system*...For once the economic system is organized in separate institutions, based on specific motives and conferring a special status, *society must be shaped in such a manner as to allow that system to function according to its own laws.* This is the meaning of the familiar assertion that a market economy can function only in a *market society.*"
>
> (GT, 57, my emphasis)

A market society, whereby all of social life is subordinated to the dictates of the market (via commodification, accumulation, competition, profitmaking), represented a radical departure in human history. "Nineteenth century society, in which economic activity was isolated and imputed to a distinctive economic motive", he wrote, "was, indeed, a singular departure" (GT, 71). It was only when the consequences of this new social formation became so destructive that an urgent need for social protection was thereby triggered.

While numerous scholars have identified "disembedding" as a core theme within Polanyi's work (Barber, 1995; Block, 2001, 2003; Block and Somers, 1984, 2014, 2021; Dale, 2010; Deutschmann, 2019; Krippner, 2001; Krippner and Alvarez, 2007; Lacher, 1999, 2019), the question of whether a market society represents a unique institutional setting and tendency within capitalist history, as well as a core component of the double movement, is still very much a debated question. The concept of a market society (and its corollary, disembedding) has been conflated with the inauguration of the self-regulating

DOI: 10.4324/9781003133186-3

market, or seen as an ideal type (Dale, 2010; Hann and Hart, 2009), or belief system, or viewed as a rhetorical device or myth (Holmes, 2012), or regarded as a utopian project and a logical impossibility given that all markets are embedded and an untrammelled market would devastate society (Block and Somers, 2003, 2014). Others locate his framework within a "hostile worlds" view that depicts market society as an antagonistic realm whose relentless imperatives of commodification and market discipline are innately destructive of other social and cultural domains (Fourcade and Healy, 2007; Zelizer, 2005). It is clear that scholarly views of Polanyi will vary considerably depending on how we adjudicate the question of the market society's significance to the double movement.

I envision market society as a unique analytical and historical entity, with a set of core dynamics and social processes, which needs to be understood as analytically and historically separate from the establishment of the self-regulating market as a key moment within capitalist history. To properly comprehend the nature of disembedding as a social process in its own right (and the double movement as a structural regularity within capitalist history), it is necessary to first delineate the specific processes and dynamics wherein market supremacy is enshrined within a market society. My starting point therefore is to organize Polanyi's tentative ideas into a more cohesive discussion and to suggest what an appropriate analytical framework might be to explore this phenomenon. I begin with a general discussion of the centrality of market society within his work, focusing on the tensions and contradictions of embedding and disembedding in his approach and maintain that disembedding should be understood as a distinct social process within the double movement. I then argue that Polanyi's elaboration of a market society is best understood in terms of three interrelated social processes (Tilly, 2008). *Market imperialism* concerns the expansionary logic whereby more and more spheres of social, political and cultural life are brought within the market orbit. *Market corrosion* explores the way in which the market is utterly destructive of social life and corrosive of non-market domains, norms and practices. *Market insulation* examines how the market becomes protected against the reciprocal influence of society and particularly how the "separation of the economic and political" generates profound consequences for political life and culture. While it is true that Polanyi did not himself use this specific terminology to describe these processes, I have utilized them as helpful means of organizing what is often a diffuse and vague conceptual apparatus into a more coherent framework although I would caution that my presentation is not intended to be a full explication of any of these processes. Nonetheless, this conceptual framework is elaborated, based on a careful reading of the text that I believe is respectful of the overall tenor of his argument.

There are several rationales for including such a detailed examination of market society within an expanded framework of the double movement. *First*, a market society is a specific institutional configuration within capitalist history, wherein the scope and intensity of market imperatives can vary considerably across different historical eras. *Second,* only by unpacking the dynamics of disembedding into discrete social processes can we truly understand the sequence of events leading to the inception of social protection and at the same time the dialectic of instability and crisis inscribed into the heart of the double movement that dominates Polanyi's account of the long 19th century. In each of these processes, we explore the contradictory interplay of disembedding and embedding that is central to the double movement. *Third,* because commodification lies at the heart of Polanyi's account of the double movement (if not of modernity itself), exploring the specific social mechanisms whereby the elemental force of the market extends its imperatives, visits its destructive consequences and separates itself from social obligations is vital to a more nuanced understanding of the double movement as a form of institutional change. *Fourth,* by exploring the social processes that constitute a market society, it is possible to highlight aspects of his argument that are often overlooked, underappreciated or even misinterpreted and to recognize the analytical, epistemological and normative challenge that his work represented to conventional social science approaches. Indeed, some of Polanyi's most celebrated insights –his portrait of the cultural devastation of marketization, the *laissez-faire* foundations of the cataclysmic famines in 19th-century India, the emergence of a hundred years peace in Europe – are best appreciated within the context of a broader discussion of market society. Finally, the entire political and moral thrust of the double movement framework – that society cannot be left to the mercy of market imperatives; that social and political institutions must be continually designed to safeguard society; that true freedom and autonomy demands a transcendence of the market – can be more readily observed via an elaboration of the dynamics of a market society.

I recognize that this emphasis on disembedding and the centrality of a market society perspective puts me at odds with some influential Polanyian scholarship (Block and Somers, 2014). On the face of it, this is not necessarily problematic; as a general rule, distinct, if not contradictory, readings of a scholar are not automatically a sign of intellectual confusion (on the part of either the author or their critic) but rather a hallmark of the richness and engaging quality of a work that naturally throws up distinct interpretations and analytical pathways. As I stressed in the Introduction, this tendency has been the hallmark of the secondary literature of other well-known social scientists, who have elicited competing intellectual tendencies and passions, and it is a sign of the revival of interest in Polanyi's work that these divergent approaches are now being more clearly debated. And I want to caution that my own perspective on market society as articulated in this chapter is by no means a brief for a definitive interpretation of his work, which thereby castigates opposing scholarly positions as the work of dangerous heretics, but I do believe it can offer us new insights into the dynamics of the double movement.

In the first section, I explore the tensions and contradictions inherent in his discussion of the processes of disembedding and embedding. Over the following three sections, I trace the core processes of a market society and finally, in the last section, I discuss his argument about the "hundred year's peace", which is the single most prominent example in the text where he discusses a beneficial outcome of a market society.

Constituting a Market Society

Any discussion of the centrality of market society within Polanyi's framework leads us directly to one of the key ambiguities in his work: namely the tension between *disembedding* (the dynamics that construct the market as an autonomous realm in society) and *embedding* (the nexus of social, cultural and political arrangements that shape and constrain market actions). This disembedding/embedding dichotomy has been prominently identified by many scholars as a key strand in his work; as Greta Krippner and Anthony Alvarez note: "Polanyi's views, regarding the conditions under which economies might be said to be disembedded- and what substantively is implied by such a statement- remain controversial issues" (Krippner and Alvarez, 2007, 221; see also Block and Somers, 2014, 2021; Gemici, 2008; Krippner, 2001; Lacher, 2019).[1]

While the received wisdom tends to emphasize him as the inspiration for the concept of embeddedness, this chapter emphasizes the centrality of *disembedding* within his framework.[2] My starting point, given this book's central focus on the dynamics of the double movement, is to explore how these debates about market society illuminate the complex terrain of the double movement. Disagreements between the embedding/disembedding positions, in large part, represent contested debates about the nature of the double movement itself and the ambiguities that are inherent in Polanyi's own attempt to depict it as a holistic system. But if a "disembedding" perspective is to have any purchase, it must suggest how this approach can be unpacked into discrete social processes that underpin the foundation of a market society; these social processes must detail the relational dynamic between disembedding and embedding that occurs in each; and trace how the specific historical evolution of a market society impacts on the core dynamics of the double movement itself. In this section, I begin first with an overview of the embedded position, then present a rationale for the salience of disembedding, and conclude with some provisional thoughts about how a holistic approach to the double movement might bridge both perspectives.

Polanyi's concept of "fictitious commodities", which Block and Somers among others have argued is the central premise of his work, is the appropriate place to begin this discussion (Block and Somers, 2014; Dale, 2010). He summarized his perspective in this famous passage:

> "But labor, land and money are obviously *not* commodities; the postulate that anything that is bought and sold must have been produced for sale is emphatically untrue in regard to them. In other words, according to the

> empirical definition of a commodity, they are not commodities. Labor is only another name for a human activity which goes with life itself, which in turn is not produced for sale but for entirely different reasons, nor can that activity be detached from the rest of life, be stored or mobilized; land is only another name for nature, which is not produced by man; actual money, finally, is merely a token of purchasing power which, as a rule, is not produced at all, but comes into being through the mechanism of banking or state finance...The commodity description of labor, land and money is entirely fictitious."
>
> (GT, 72)

Of course, Polanyi acknowledged that, in reality, labor, land and money were being continually converted into commodities (with the intentional hand of the state) and bought and sold on a market: "It is with the help of this fiction that the actual markets for labor, land and money are organized" (GT, 72). However, he ascribed to these core social entities (nature, human creativity, tokens of exchange) a "fictional" status because he insisted that they possessed a prior social existence whose character is fatally compromised when allocated an exchange value on a market (GT, 73).[3]

To take labor commodification as a representative case, treating individuals as if they were commodities ignores the full range of resources, interests and capabilities that people possess and, as such, represents a diminished portrait of human flourishing. This fiction obscures the extent to which waged work is dependent upon the realm of social reproduction. "Wage labor could not exist", argues Nancy Fraser, "in the absence of housework, child rearing, schooling, affective care and a host of other activities which help to produce new generations of workers and replenish existing ones... Social reproduction is an indispensable background condition for the possibility of capitalist production" (Fraser, 2016, 61). Once labor is regarded as a commodity like any other with a market price that rises and falls, owing to supply and demand, all the heightened uncertainties that result from market fluctuations – stagnating wages, unemployment, job restructuring, workplace injuries, relocation – threaten the very substance of individuals and their communities. But, at the same time, labor is unique among commodities in that it is capable of safeguarding itself against these vertiginous forces via collective organization, social struggle and protective social legislation.

It is these wider connotations of social life that are irrevocably decimated by the onset of a market society. "To allow the market mechanism to be the sole director of the fate of human beings and their natural environment", wrote Polanyi, "indeed, even of the amount and use of purchasing power, would result in the demolition of society" (GT, 73). He is not only signposting here the next stage of the double movement – the broad countermovement for social protection, which is generated by the grievances and hardships imposed by commodification – but he is also stipulating the more fundamental postulate that a market system cannot be sustained unless these social elements are safeguarded. *No aspect of commodification can be undertaken or sustained without the vital resources of the non-commodified world* (Block, 2003; Block and Somers, 2014; Fraser, 2013).[4]

As such, many scholars have seen within these passages the kernel of a broader contention about the embedded nature of a market economy, namely, that all market exchanges and relations are saturated with cultural, social and political relations. Markets require social structures to operate; the transformation of key social domains into commodities requires the instrumental action of the state and crucial forms of cultural work; and market activity is itself embedded within legal, political and social relations that are vital to its very activity. Polanyi makes this argument in many places in the book (even if the actual term "embedded", as others have noted, is used only sparingly) (Barber, 1995; Krippner, 2001). He argues that "the economic system is, in effect, a mere function of social organization" (GT, 49) and "No market economy separated from the political sphere is possible" (GT, 196). In a later work, he reiterated this insight: "the inclusion of the non-economic is vital. For religion or government might be as important for the structure and functioning of the economy as monetary institutions or the availability of tools and machines themselves that lighten the toil of labor" (Polanyi, 1957, 250).

This Polanyian insight has become a fundamental staple of economic sociology, where markets are said to be routinely entangled with and constrained by social norms, institutional rules and political regulations. States are critical to markets in terms of facilitating cooperation among market actors, establishing property rights, maintaining a monetary and credit system, providing a proper infrastructure for trade and exchange, and enacting rules and legal codes that guide market behavior. In the business world, transnational firms coordinate their far flung inter-firm interests according to hierarchical rules and criteria; exchange networks and supplier chains depend crucially on relations premised on reciprocity and trust; and small businesses organize entrepreneurial networks on the basis of ethnic and kinship ties. Shop floor relations are permeated by notions of morality and fairness while everyday consumption is saturated with non-material meanings (social conformity, autonomy, individuality, ethical stances) that people attach to commodities. Even in the most market-like of economic processes, such as the financial market, scholars have demonstrated that this sector is imbued with social relations, power dynamics, cultural rules and symbolic activities (Ho, 2009; Mackenzie, 2006). Markets, in other words, are best viewed as *social* structures in their own right, with Douglas North drawing the appropriate historical lesson for the case at hand: "Price-making markets have never completely dominated economic decision making through history, including the nineteenth century. We do not observe resources being allocated by market prices inside households, voluntary organizations and governments through history" (North, 1977, 709).

Fred Block and Margaret Somers argue that the term "always embedded economy" is the most effective way of capturing this dynamic within Polanyi's own work and "provides the most powerful and enduring way to make sense of Polanyi's core arguments in *The Great Transformation*" (Block, 2003, 276; Block and Somers, 2014; see also Barber, 1995; Somers 2008). Their strong version of the embedded thesis maintains the very claim of disembedding is not logically feasible within Polanyi's framework: "This formulation rejects conceptualization of the economy as an analytically autonomous-or even potentially autonomous realm…The project of disembedding was an impossibility; it would ultimately destroy both human beings and their natural environment" (Block, 2003, 5).[5] In this view, market society is envisioned as a convenient fiction, an ideological cover used by liberals to cordon off the market from outside interference. However, because of the existential threat of the "demolition of society", the establishment of such a market society could only be short lived; a system of social protection would be instantaneously forthcoming to protect society against the ravages of the market and indeed, no market society could exist for long without these non-market institutional bulwarks.

Of course, any assertion of the centrality of embeddedness within his conceptual framework has to square this account with the numerous claims for an autonomous economic realm and disembedding social processes that are so prominently made by Polanyi throughout *The Great Transformation.* Even if one was inclined to dismiss the bold assertion of the quote with which I began this chapter as a characteristic rhetorical flourish, there are countless passages where the clear emphasis is placed on the process of disembedding. As I detail more fully throughout this chapter, there are multiple instances within the text where he identifies the separation of the economic sphere as a distinct feature of a market society; where the acute social distress and cultural devastation of the market is amply highlighted or the rampant diffusion of market relations and values is taken for granted.

Indeed, what is puzzling and frustrating in equal measure is that Polanyi often presents contradictory embedding/disembedding accounts in close proximity of each other in the text (Dale, 2010). To offer a single example, although he first declares that the "separation of the political and the economic" is "the outstanding characteristic of market society" (GT, 195), this is followed just a page later by his claim that "the institutional separation of the political and economic spheres had never been complete, and it was precisely in the matter of the currency that it was necessarily incomplete" (GT, 196). Krippner and Alvarez astutely note that Polanyi was well aware that his argument about disembedding was likely to be misinterpreted. They quote from a revealing passage from a later work that attempts to guard against such inconsistency: "On the face of it, such a proposition must appear almost self-contradictory. It may seem to imply that very overestimation of the importance of the economy against which it ostensibly wishes to forewarn. However, this is by no means the case" (Polanyi, 1977, xlvi; Krippner and

Alvarez, 2007, 228). But, even this caution betrays the same exact tendency because a few pages later, Polanyi goes on to claim: "For all practical purposes, the economy *did* now consist of markets and the market *did* envelop society " (Polanyi, 1977, 9).

How are we to account for these considerable ambiguities and is there a satisfactory solution to this conundrum? Block accepts that the text is internally contradictory but suggests that it is symptomatic of an "epistemological break" within Polanyi's intellectual evolution, that he had not yet broken free from the shackles of conceptual frameworks inherited from the Marxist tradition that were antithetical to his own evolving theoretical approach. "Polanyi glimpsed the idea of the always embedded market economy", claims Block, "but he was not able to give that idea a name or develop it theoretically because it represented too great a divergence from his initial theoretical starting point" (Block, 2003, 276). Richard Swedberg and Mark Granovetter, for their part, claim that the confusion represents a more fundamental incoherence at the heart of his work: "Although in many places, he argued that the 19th century ushered in an utterly new type of society, dominated by the 'self-regulating market', he also made the incompatible argument that such a situation was never really possible except as an ideological construct or rhetorical device because society had to immediately intervene to prevent such an awful outcome" (Granovetter and Swedberg 1992, 22).

In fact, both positions actually point to a similar conclusion. Either a market society is a logical impossibility and a short-lived phenomenon, given the instantaneousness of social protection; or it is merely a misplaced rhetorical flourish – a synonym for any society that embraces the market system, i.e., a capitalist society, which cannot survive without a panoply of social and cultural institutions. In neither case, is there any special urgency therefore to survey the contours of this specific social entity with the consequence that the unique *force majeure* of commodification – its universal scope, its ferocious pace of change, its destructive onslaught- is curiously obscured and the acute *political* challenge that is actually required to re-embed the market is considerably downplayed (Deutschmann, 2019; Streeck, 2011). Krippner argues that there is "a certain tendency in economic sociology to give analytical priority to the social institutions – social norms, network ties, forms of state regulation – that provide a foundation for market transactions, while under-attending to the market that is disarticulated from said institutions at various moments in the historical development of capitalism" (Krippner, 2020, 208).

This categorical standpoint strikes me as deeply unsatisfying. The implication seems to be that if we accept the possibility of disembedding as a discrete social process, we therefore must underestimate the influence of the social sphere and the manner in which markets are socially constituted; or if we favor the always-embedded position, we therefore lose sight of the specific dynamics that constitute commodification and a market society. Yet this occludes what is central to Polanyi's argument about the double movement, namely that the entire system depends on the contested, dialectical tension between the market *and* society. What is inscribed into the very heart of this system is the recognition that there are core dynamics operating in conflicting directions within the double movement. Market actors (who are fundamentally *social* actors) struggle to expand market imperatives and logic into new domains, to subvert political constraints and insulate themselves from social oversight, and to mold social relations in their own image; at the same time, social, cultural and political agents are constantly seeking to design effective means of constraining the market's range of action and influence while attempting to preserve the cohesion of non-market domains (Somers, 2008; Streeck, 2011). This tug-of-war not only creates a perpetual incentive for instability and crisis within the double movement, which we discuss more fully in Chapter 5, it becomes the central dynamic within each of the four phases of the double movement. In this perspective, the narrative inconsistency noted earlier, rather than a fatal sign of intellectual incoherence, is best viewed as a rhetorical equivalent of the contested dialectic inherent in the double movement and, unlike a static either-or position, is eminently suited to capturing Polanyi's abiding interest in the dynamic process of *transformation*.

Even if these oppositional principles and forces are inextricably linked, if not mutually constituted, within the double movement system, it is still incumbent to precisely delineate the key processes involved in disembedding. In the first instance, we must carefully distinguish the concept of a market society from that of the self-regulating market for they are not analytically equivalent (Deutschmann, 2019, 75). In the same way that Chapter 2 argued the self-regulating market was not identical to capitalism itself but rather represented a particular moment within capitalist history, a market society is first and foremost an array of *social* arrangements and institutional practices that "make the market the only organizing power in the economic sphere" (GT, 69), which in practice means "to subordinate the substance of society itself to the laws of the market" (GT, 71). To use a different kind of analogy, the onset of war and the evolution of war cannot be traced to the same set of factors but rather require distinct analytical strategies to carefully unpack the continuities and discontinuities inherent in the course of the conflict. Similarly, the inception of a self-regulating system in 1834 did not on its own determine the scope and depth of market relations throughout society; nor did it guarantee the extent to which the market would begin to influence individual motives and social practices or corrode existing social domains; or the precise ways in which market actors were able to escape from or weaken social and political oversight. To properly understand these dynamics, disembedding has to be understood as both a *social* process with distinct mechanisms that are interactive and interlocking and as a new *political* configuration of power and domination.[6]

Once we embrace this perspective, it follows that we need to take more seriously the implicit injunction embodied in the phrase "society must be *shaped in such a manner* as to allow that system to function according to its own laws" (GT, 57). In a fundamental sense, all capitalist societies are "market societies" given that markets are the dominant means of organizing economic activity and market imperatives (to secure a livelihood through labor market participation, to allocate social resources via decentralized mutual exchange, to privately accumulate capital, to foster competition, and the like) are ubiquitous. But Polanyi seems to be implying something more than this: in some specific historical periods, prevailing social arrangements and institutional orders might enable market actors to extend and deepen commodification as well as to subject social life to even greater doses of market discipline as the processes and institutions of a "market society" remake society in its own image (Block, 1990; Streeck, 2011). Market actors can go to extraordinary lengths to extend the sway of the market to further areas of social life, which means that the price mechanism and market ways of thinking will dominate, market dependency could intensify, and other realms of social life, such as knowledge or nature, might be transformed into fictitious commodities (Burawoy, 2010; Somers, 2008; Streeck, 2016). As market imperatives deepen, this could consequently subvert, weaken and even decimate non-market forms of economic, social and cultural activity and political and social actors intent on defending non-market social traditions might prove incapable of resisting this market juggernaut (Beckert, 2009). "Although it is true, in this version of Polanyi as in any other, that capitalism cannot exist without a non-capitalist 'embedding'", writes Wolfgang Streeck, "it cannot create or preserve it either, and in fact, tends to erode and consume it- which makes capitalism, if unchecked, a self-destructive social formation" (Streeck, 2016, 224).[7]

In short, some capitalist societies might be more market like (more capitalist), more self-destructive, more destabilizing than others (Block, 1990; Dale, 2010; Wright 2010). For Polanyi's claim that the 19th-century market society represented just such a historical conjuncture, North offers his support: "the stubborn fact of the matter is that he was correct in his major contention that the nineteenth century was a unique era in which markets played a more important role than in any other time in history" (North, 1977, 706). A fuller comprehension of these periods and processes cannot be automatically read off the inception of the self-regulating market nor can the outcomes of the perpetual oscillation between embedding and disembedding be predicted *a priori*. Neither does a recognition that markets are permanently instantiated as "social" entities (in fact, require the social in order to exist in the first place) necessarily invalidate the postulate that market societies across historical periods might vary considerably in the scope and intensity of market imperatives.

There will always be significant differences in the extent to which capitalist societies more or less resemble "market societies". The scope of market penetration or the corrosiveness of market relations depends not only on the intentional strategies of market actors to circumvent social obligations but also on the "countervailing forces of civil society" (Somers, 2008) such as: the resiliency and adaptability of social domains to resist market imperatives (Zelizer, 2010); the scope and strength of institutional structures and regulations that condition the autonomy of market action (Streeck, 2009); the vitality of normative principles of equality and the common good that combat market hegemony; and the success of counter-movements to decommodify and protect society from the ravages of the market. Disembedding therefore is context specific and sensitive to local variations and historical agency. An emphasis on disembedding is by no means a brief for the inevitability and supremacy of market rationality but rather a recognition of how contingency and indeterminacy are inscribed into the very nature of the double movement, a theme we return to in Chapter 5. The central point to emphasize is that the core processes of a market society (market imperialism, market corrosion and market insulation) remain fundamentally *social* processes – they are aided and abetted by social and political agents, shaped by the adaptive capacities of social institutions, constructed by prevailing ideologies and cultural meaning, contested by social and political actors – but equally, they are essential components of a *market* dynamic given that they are devoted to extending and deepening market imperatives. They are not merely an elite exercise in ideological obfuscation or a rhetorical strategy but rather an intentional program of deepening market dependency and extending the scope of market power, of making the world in a market image.

At the same time, a more thorough treatment of market society also offers an improved understanding of its opposing tendency within the double movement, namely the drive for social protection. The fact that the market needs to be insulated from societal interference infers that it must be so naturally intrusive and damaging of social life that people will instinctively recoil from it and seek to challenge its supremacy. Without this cultural devastation, there would be no call for a protective response yet again these destructive effects cannot be automatically inferred from the mere existence of the self-regulating market. The scope and depth of this cataclysm, as Polanyi recognized, is shaped by existing institutional arrangements as well as by the nature of marketization itself. However, as discussed more fully in the following chapter, the onset of social protection was anything but instantaneous but rather reflected hard fought political contestation and there might well be periods where social policies designed to alleviate the consequences of disembedding are ineffective or even non-existent given the perpetual scheming of market actors to denude or escape these arrangements. Similarly, without a fuller reckoning of the disembedding and embedding dynamic, it is impossible to appreciate the clash of social principles within the double movement that produces the contradictions that constitute the driving force of 19th-century history.

To be sure, I do not want to overemphasize any of these analytical distinctions. Many of these insights have been embraced, albeit with slightly different emphases, by other scholars, all of whom acknowledge that the real work of exploring this dialectical relationship occurs precisely at the intersection of these opposing principles (Beckert, 2009; Block, 2003; Block and Somers, 2014; Dale, 2010; Fraser, 2013; Somers, 2008). Polanyi might not always strike the proper balance in his analysis – the "hostile worlds" tendency is quite pronounced in places and there are elisions and omissions in his depiction of market society highlighted throughout this chapter – yet his fundamental premise remains a promising pathway forward. The reconstruction proposed herein also has the advantage of enhancing an improved understanding of the political and normative complexity at stake in his argument. Markets could intensify social distress, insecurity and inequality, but equally they might foster autonomy and weaken oppression. In some periods, the precarious balance of forces of disembedding and embedding could be conducive to economic growth and social justice; in others, it could lead to widespread social injury and political turbulence. This does not mean that we lose the critical capacity to challenge market fundamentalism as a political/ideological project or to promote alternatives to its political hegemony but rather it accepts that the emancipatory thrust of the Polanyian approach will be more persuasive when aligned with a more rigorous framework of market society that accurately accounts for this abiding social complexity (Fraser, 2013).

Yet the foregoing discussion suggests an even more fundamental analytical tension within the disembedding/embedding framework that was highlighted in the Introduction. From the advantage of historical hindsight, it appears that capitalism has a structural predilection to expand its imperatives outward no matter the distinct political incentives, motivations of social actors or institutional contexts to promote or resist it (Sewell, 2008; Streeck, 2016). Similarly, there is ample evidence that the corrosive impact of the market has consistently occurred across diverse social realms, across divergent social and cultural contexts, and across distinct historical periods. Given these tendencies, the thorny conceptual dilemma, which this chapter is not intended to resolve, is how one explains these deep, structural regularities. If market systems possess a unique trans-historical logic, how do we avoid falling prey to the same *cul de sac* that Polanyi cautioned about in his withering admonition against the classical economist's proclamation of a natural economic sphere? And how, and under what conditions, do these structural imperatives actually become manifest in concrete social and political formations that privilege one aspect of the double movement rather than the other?

Surely though, the political regulation of markets, normative foundations of consumption, or the adaptive capacity of social arenas in no way precludes the routine functioning of market compulsion: workers are still dependent on the market for their livelihood; firms still depend upon the market for the allocation of their inputs and outputs; enterprises are still subject to competitive pressures to innovate and accumulate in order to prosper. Even in the most institutionally embedded market economy, there remains the presence of what Charles Lindblom calls the vast "market sea" of coordination and direction of economic activity conducted primarily by virtue of the mutual adjustment processes of market actors alone (Lindblom, 2001, 75). Polanyi hints at this form of autonomy in numerous places when he speaks of "processes of economic self-healing" (GT, 207), of "autonomous and automatic mechanisms" (GT, 218) or of the self-correcting aspects of international trade (GT, 201). However, as he also insisted, the dialectic works in the opposite direction as well: even when markets are at their most impersonal, they are still embedded in a larger institutional framework and culture that constrains market action. The formidable challenge is how to acknowledge a structural imperative that underpins the processes of disembedding yet still recognize that markets are themselves socialized, regulated, and constituted as social processes. Even if Polanyi was not entirely successful in resolving this dilemma, his argument offers a useful starting point in thinking through how such solutions could be formulated and it is his analysis of the core processes of market society, to which we now turn.

Market Imperialism

Ever since the establishment of a market economy, it has become a commonplace notion among social scientists that capitalism has an unparalleled ability to insinuate its norms, values and practices into the fabric of everyday life. As Albert Hirschman highlighted, there is a handy supply of metaphors that have been employed by scholars to depict the pervasiveness of capitalism: "contamination", "contagion", "infection", "infiltration", "intrusion", and "imperialism" (Hirschman, 1982). Similar themes resurface in most accounts: capitalism has an expansionary logic, unique in history, which enables it to expand its reach around the globe; to widen and deepen the force of market imperatives and practices into spheres of life where previously it did not exist; and it has an unrivalled capacity to induce individual behavior and beliefs that are consistent with its own needs (Deutschmann, 2019; Sewell, 2008; Streeck, 2011, 2012). This essential feature of capitalism occurs via multiple structural imperatives –innovation, competition, capital accumulation, entrepreneurship – that does not require collective deliberation or cooperation among capitalists but is rather an existential requirement to innovate and expand or else face the ultimate penalty of extinction. It is this process that I am calling *market imperialism* (Waltzer, 1983, 120).

This contention has a long lineage within the social sciences. Marx's famous lines from *The Communist Manifesto* evoke this tendency: "The need for a constantly expanding market for its products chases the bourgeoisie over the surface of the globe. It must nestle everywhere, settle everywhere, establish connections everywhere" (Marx, in Tucker 1972, 338). Max Weber, in his classic *The Protestant Ethic and the Spirit of Capitalism*, emphasized the way a market economy encouraged the development of particular character traits (the instrumental, rational calculating individual) and penalized those which did not fit the operation of capitalism:

> "In order that a manner of life so well adapted to the peculiarities of capitalism could be selected at all, i.e. should come to dominate others, it had to originate somewhere, and not in isolated individuals alone, but as a way of life common to whole groups of men."
>
> (Weber, 1967, 55)

Joseph Schumpeter maintained that "capitalists can never rest; opening new markets, creating new capacities, constant pressure for innovation…incessantly revolutionize the economic structure *from within*, incessantly destroying the old one, incessantly creating a new one" (Schumpeter, 1950 [1943], 83).

In the contemporary era, David Harvey echoes this familiar theme: "precisely because capitalism is expansionary and imperialistic, cultural life in more and more areas gets brought within the grasp of the cash nexus and the logic of capital circulation" (Harvey, 1999, 344). Streeck insists: "[T]he tendency to expand is a fundamental property of capitalism. Any capitalism that is worth its name, or its money, is necessarily on the move and always from within" (Streeck, 2011, 5). William Sewell likewise stresses the same dynamic:

> "Another dimension of capitalist expansion is the continuing extension of its logics to ever-wider aspects of social life…whole areas of life previously governed by institutions other than capitalist markets have been commoditized…In short, there is a clear, secular tendency for capitalist logics to spread over an ever-wider range of activities and to ever-greater psychic depths of social existence. The imagination, the personality, the family, and affective relations are increasingly subjected to capitalist logics."
>
> (Sewell, 2008, 523)

And as Harvey, Streeck and Sewell all emphasize, this "systematic restlessness" also engenders a systematic tendency for disorder, instability and uncertainty, a point we treat at length in the next section and in Chapter 5.

There are numerous instances in *The Great Transformation* where Polanyi identifies market imperialism as a prominent feature of a market society (Dale, 2010; Deutschmann, 2019). As noted earlier, the very act of treating nature or human beings as fictitious commodities that could be produced or exchanged on a market, which was the essence of commodification, greatly extends the reach of the market. Once the core relations of social life – labor, land, money (as a store of value) – could be commodified, the frontier of the market could be extended into other core social domains. Like Marx, Polanyi conceived of this ubiquitous process of commodification in terms of an implacable expansionary dynamic, with the emphasis on the spatial dimensions of this process. He speaks of the "unrelenting pressure to spread the fabric of market economy and market society elsewhere. Consequently, by the end of the 19th century, the peoples of the world were institutionally standardized to a degree unknown before" (GT, 253). "The mechanism which the motive of gain set in motion", wrote Polanyi, "was comparable in effectiveness only to the most violent outburst of religious fervor in history. Within a generation the whole human world was subjected to its undiluted influence" (GT, 30). Indeed, he echoes many of the most extravagant claims made by contemporary globalization theorists in his depiction of 19th-century internationalization:

> "That system [laissez faire] developed in leaps and bounds; it engulfed space and time, and by creating bank money it produced a dynamic hitherto unknown. By the time it reached its maximum extent, around 1914, every part of the globe, all its inhabitants and yet unborn generations, physical persons as well as huge fictitious bodies called corporations, were comprised in it. A new way of life spread over the planet with a claim to universality unparalleled since the age when Christianity started out on its career, only this time the movement was on a purely material level."
>
> (GT, 130)

Although he succinctly posed the problematic of market imperialism as a core disembedding feature of a market society, Polanyi was not especially inclined to explain how commodification colonizes other areas of social life beyond labor, land and money or to speculate under what conditions this process would be more or less encompassing. Nor did he fully investigate the dynamics of this process by either charting the full range of political intervention or cultural work implicated in extending the market's reach or conversely by exploring the ways in which the domain of the market might be limited by pre-existing cultural and social institutions that successfully resist the market onslaught or embed them with social and cultural meanings (Zelizer, 2010). This strikes me as a notable omission that detracts quite a bit from his own ambitions, especially as regards the intrinsic relationship of marketization to the historical cycle of the double movement. Clearly, he recognized that the more the market extends its reach, the greater its destructiveness might be and consequently the more urgent the need for social protection (and the more complex its delivery would entail); and he certainly understood that the internationalization of market relations (discussed more fully in Chapter 5) generated serious contradictions and crises. Nevertheless, there are some intriguing Polanyian insights concerning the process of market imperialism that are worth exploring.[8]

Polanyi maintained the extension of market imperatives could be accomplished through social mechanisms of standardization and reinforcement, involving the use of political prerogatives, institutional configurations and structural power. Once the market becomes entrenched, various locking-in processes limit the range of permissible behavior of market actors and bind all citizens to market practices and standards. This can be achieved in several ways: by limiting the benefits of market activities to only those who participate in market institutions, by imposing penalties on those who choose to remain outside the market's orbit, or by penalizing would-be defectors from the market regime. While such objectives can be achieved by strategic action, the structure of the market itself is also instrumental in furthering this dynamic without the conscious intervention of social actors. In this regard, Polanyi highlighted the coercive impact of the "peaceable, silent, unremitting pressure" of hunger, what he called "nature's penalty", which was automatically imposed on anyone foolhardy enough to remain out of the labor market (GT, 113, 165).

These locking-in mechanisms were instrumental to the spread of the market across many social spheres. As Polanyi highlights in the case of the enclosure movement, one of the critical steps in extending the scope of the market came in the granting of private property rights that delegated to individuals the legal right to fully control and dispose of their assets and more importantly, to convert common lands into private property controlled exclusively by a single landowner (GT, 181). Property rights essentially constitute a means of empowering certain individuals by augmenting their freedom to impose market criteria while concurrently raising the costs to others of resisting the extension of market imperatives. There could be considerable material and power advantages that accrue to social agents who promote the extension of commodification into hitherto protected areas. Landlords might be keen to extend the commercialization of land into previously protected spheres because this augments their ability to generate value from these holdings. New land can be brought under the control of the market through the full range of coercive measures that landed interests (typically in cahoots with political compulsion) have the power to employ: dispossession of small landholders of their own means of production, expropriation of the commons, and intimidation and repression of dissidents (GT, 35). Land can also be commercialized through its transformation into a site of commodity production itself: constructing factories, shopping malls, housing developments and the like.[9]

Polanyi highlights in several places the "rigid determinism" of the self-regulating market, the operation of the "blind act of soulless institutions" that so irrevocably structured social life at home and abroad (GT, 218, 219). One of the critical institutions in this regard was the gold standard – "the supreme vehicle of the expansion of market economy" (GT, 214) – that constituted the international monetary system of the 19th and early 20th centuries. "The organization of world commodity markets, world capital markets, and world currency markets under the aegis of the gold standard", wrote Polanyi, "gave an unparalleled momentum to the mechanism of markets" (GT, 76). The gold standard, which operated according to a uniform system of fixed exchange rates, locked all states into a narrow constellation of market friendly policies. It established the goals of sound currency and low inflation as the epitome of proper economic management and threatened economic ruin to anyone who sought to challenge the gold standards' supremacy. This is not to underestimate the complex coordination problems required to sustain this mechanism or the extent to which its actual practice varied considerably from this idealized depiction (see Chapter 5 for a fuller discussion). But the wider point to reiterate is that when the force of a single material standard can be asserted unilaterally across the entire globe with the complete authority of nearly all states, it significantly circumscribed the capacity of national governments to opt out of this arrangement.

If markets were extended by reinforcement, they also spread by virtue of ideological diffusion through social mechanisms such as emulation and contagion. The interdependence of the market economy, embodied by the roller coaster turbulence of commodity prices and currency exchanges, played a critical role in this regard. When the fate of individuals throughout the globe is determined in large part by the fluctuating fortunes of the market, and when minute price changes can be experienced as monumental upheavals, it is not entirely unexpected that individuals exhibit a keen awareness of the market and that material concerns occupy a prominent place in their world view. Polanyi repeatedly emphasizes the demonstration effect of global integration:

> "By the fourth quarter of the nineteenth century world commodity prices were the central reality in the lives of millions of Continental peasants; the repercussions of the London money market were daily noted by businessmen all over the world; and governments discussed plans for the future in light of the situation on the world capital markets."
>
> (GT, 18)

The lived experience of market society acted as a transmission belt for the propagation of market values as well. Submission to the exigencies of the labor market and the authority relations inside the workplace engendered competitive relations and an unvarnished pursuit of self-interest. Given that the grounds for successful progress, if not survival itself, on a competitive market depend upon relentless innovation, it comes as no surprise that the ideals of entrepreneurship –enterprise, diligence, a willingness to take risks, delayed gratification – became so dominant in the 19th century. Marx similarly argued that capitalism's success owed to its extraordinary capacity to engender new structures of feeling and desires that closely emulated the spirit of the market. "In place of the old wants, satisfied by the products of the country, we find new wants, requiring for their satisfaction the products of distant lands and climes", said Marx. "In place of the old local and national seclusion and self-sufficiency, we have intercourse in every direction, universal inter-dependence of nations…National one-sidedness and narrow mindedness becomes more and more impossible…" (Tucker, 1972, 338–9).[10]

Indeed, one of the principle mechanisms of diffusion is that every market society disseminates values that are commensurate with its own reproduction. "The true criticism of market society", wrote Polanyi, "is not that it was based on economics – in a sense every and any society must be based on it – but that its economy was based on self-interest" (GT, 249). He went on to claim:

> "Nineteenth century civilization alone was economic in a different and distinctive sense, for it chose to base itself on a motive only rarely acknowledged as valid in the history of human societies, and certainly never before raised to the level of a justification of action and behavior in everyday life, namely, gain."
>
> (GT, 30)

Once economic rationality and private gain were enshrined as the quintessential practices of a market society, the market became the objective reality against which all other values and actions should be measured. All the "innumerable forms of public and private life that do not affect profits" are in danger of being crowded out in favor of the market (GT, 133).[11] But as we shall see in the following section, this process also encounters specific limits in that the perpetual upheaval and unpredictability of economic and cultural change in the wake of market encroachment generates unsustainable pressures on even the most flexible of cultural values and social arrangements.

However, it is not merely that the satisfaction of new cultural desires are predicated on extending the scope of the market or that non-market relationships might be more difficult to sustain as societies become more complex and interrelated. It is also that the creation of these new wants and desires could be something that is positively emulated by individuals rather than merely as an act of compulsion. From my reading, it must be stated quite clearly that Polanyi singularly underestimates the extent to which the values of the market exert a gravitational field of attraction. "Economic motives *per se*", he insisted, "are notoriously much less effective with most people than so-called emotional ones" (GT, 219). He downplays the ways in which the tenets of the market (freedom, opportunity, choice, self-enrichment, merit) develop wide cultural, if not affective, appeal and are embraced as a matter of individual authenticity and expression or the extent to which market relations are instrumental in shaping everyday dreams, experiences and imaginations.[12]

Market Corrosion

The claim that the values and practices of the market are fundamentally antagonistic to and corrosive of non-market institutions, the process I am calling *market corrosion*, has a long lineage within the social sciences. Durkheim believed market relations jeopardized collective goods such as trust and cooperation that could not be provided by the system itself. Weber argued that secularism and economic individualism were corrosive of Christianity's hold over European populations. Schumpeter insisted that capitalism undermined the very foundations of its success – "an atmosphere of almost universal hostility to its own social order", primarily because it destroyed the protective institutional framework (of family, small firms, farmers) the market needs to survive and made individual entrepreneurial innovation harder to achieve in huge, bureaucratic corporations (for an overview, see Hirschman, 1982; Fourcade and Healy, 2007).

Polanyi similarly believed that the extension of market relations into additional arenas of social life, would grievously undermine the dominant practices, institutions and values of non-market society (Fraser, 2013; Sandel, 2012; Somers, 2008). "To separate labor from other activities of life", he wrote:

> "and to subject it to the laws of the market was to annihilate all organic forms of existence and to replace them by a different type of organization, an atomistic and individualistic one…In practice this meant that the noncontractual organizations of kinship, neighborhood, profession and creed were to be liquidated since they claimed the allegiance of the individual and thus restrained his freedom."
>
> (GT, 163)

In his view, the market erodes all relationships, such as trust, cooperation, solidarity, altruism, and friendship, which are not predicated on instrumental calculation or self-interest. This process of *market corrosion* not only makes the mutual reciprocity of community life harder to achieve but it has the potential to undermine the very success of the market system itself, which requires the indispensable relationships of trust and reciprocal obligation to enable market relations to function. One cannot underestimate the importance of this process to his double movement framework given that it is responsible for sparking the countermovement for social protection, so a careful delineation of this process of market corrosion is certainly warranted.

Polanyi's primary contention, based largely on the case study of England, is that the inauguration of a market society unleashed a pervasive *cultural* devastation. While acknowledging the substantial economic improvements and rise in living standards that occurred as a result of the transition to industrial capitalism in Britain, Polanyi nevertheless insisted that a true accounting of the effects could not be adjudicated by quantitative data alone, which "obscured deeper social and cultural problems". "[A] social calamity", he wrote, "is primarily a *cultural* not an economic phenomenon that can be measured by income figures or population statistics" (GT, 157, my emphasis).[13] His thesis is worth quoting at length:

> "[W]hat appeared primarily as an economic problem was essentially a social one. In economic terms, the worker was certainly exploited; he did not get in exchange that which was his due. But important though this was, it was far from all. In spite of exploitation, he might have been financially better off than before. But a principle quite unfavorable to

> individual and general happiness was working havoc with his social environment, his neighborhood, his standing in the community, his craft; in a word, with those relationships to nature and man in which his economic existence was formerly embedded… The economic process may, naturally, supply the vehicle of destruction, and almost invariably economic inferiority will make the weaker yield, but the immediate cause of his undoing is not for that reason economic; it lies in the lethal injury to the institutions in which his social existence is embodied."
>
> (GT, 129, 157)

The significance of this cultural nightmare is underscored by the repetition of synonyms for this cultural collapse: "catastrophe" (GT, 4, 33, 35, 39–40, 157), "calamity" (82, 157, 297), and "cataclysm" (4, 157, 303), all of which feature alongside peril, desolation, and havoc. Marketization precipitated the "wholesale destruction of the traditional fabric of society" (GT, 77): uprooted from their familiar environment and disconnected from their traditional means of subsistence, people became atomized, family life collapsed, social safety nets and reciprocal norms disintegrated, and workers lost all semblance of self-respect, becoming "transformed into a nondescript animal of the mire" (GT, 99). This dehumanization too is captured by any number of rhetorical formulations such as "moral debasement", "degradation", "destitution", "inhuman means" and "perdition" and "scourge" (GT, 39, 76–7, 80, 129, 157, 169) (McRobbie, 2000).

To explore Polanyi's argument about this complex process of corrosion, it is essential to disentangle the causal and consequentialist arguments embedded in the text.[14] First, we need to identify the specific processes (economic, political, social) that acted as the "vehicle of destruction" of the cultural and social environment. Second, it is essential to investigate the extent to which the corrosion process was mitigated by pre-existing institutional and social factors. Finally, we need to enumerate the diverse forms of "lethal injury" that accompanied marketization.

If we start with his explanatory argument first, Polanyi suggests the evolution of commodification, with roots stretching back into the 18th century, was directly responsible for this cultural shock wave. The radical transformation of the English labor process was one such factor. The expansion of the division of labor and specialization precipitated widespread deskilling, greatly intensified exploitation and work intensity, and decimated entire trades (Tilly, 1979). This profound transition in work fortunes, and the concomitant "scourge of fluctuating employment", eliminated the limited autonomy and self-reliance that workers enjoyed. They were forced into even greater submissiveness to employer's wishes and their abiding fear of the workhouse induced them to accept employment at whatever wages were on offer. The secular shift in the economy from agriculture to manufacturing (alongside the decline of rural industries) completely uprooted rural life, with continuous out-migration to cities and the rapid growth of unemployment and pauperism in the village.

The intensification of market dependency was another critical process accelerating cultural upheaval. The second wave of enclosures, the so-called parliamentary enclosures that reached their apogee in the years 1760–1815, perfectly illustrates this development.[15] Polanyi argued this process generated a "powerful unsettling effect" on the rural population:

> "as long as domestic industry was supported by the facilities and amenities of a garden plot, a scrap of land, or grazing rights, the dependence of the laborer on money earnings was not absolute...and family earnings acted as a kind of unemployment insurance. The rationalization of agriculture inevitably uprooted the laborer and undermined his social security."
>
> (GT, 92)

He insisted the enclosure movement destroyed the sense of common fate and community that cooperation in the open field system had fostered and widened social differentiation and stratification. Whereas previously there had been little perceptible divide between villagers, after enclosure, the farmers who prospered were elevated in the social hierarchy and a yawning gap emerged between these yeoman and those who had only their labor to exchange (Snell, 1985; Wrightson, 2002).

When considering how the wider institutional context impacted on market corrosion, Polanyi acknowledged there could be considerable variation in a society's vulnerability to this cultural cataclysm. He particularly stressed the way in which marketization occurred in different social and political contexts. "Whether the dislocation was swiftly healed or whether it caused an open would in the body social depended primarily on the measures taken to regulate the process", he wrote. "Powerful factors of change and adjustment were introduced by governments themselves" (GT, 180). National features also played a critical role. On the continent, peasants were not forcibly removed from the land by enclosures but rather chose to migrate to cities because of high wages and the allure of urban life. European workers were able to preserve their solidaristic institutions and thereby cushion the impact of the market and so avoided the moral and cultural catastrophe that devastated English workers (GT, 183). "Far from being debased, he felt elevated by his environment", wrote Polanyi.

> "Doubtless housing conditions were abominable, alcoholism and prostitution were rampant among the lower strata of town laborers as late as the beginning of the twentieth century. Yet there was no comparison between the moral and cultural catastrophe of the English cottager or copyholder of decent ancestry, who found himself hopelessly sinking in the social and physical mire of the slums of some factory neighborhood..."
>
> (GT, 173–4)

Another noticeable difference was that "the continental laborer had not passed through the degrading pauperization of Speenhamland nor was there any parallel in his experience to the scorching fires of the New Poor Law." (GT, 175). Finally, the divergent nature of social stratification and class differentiation played a vital role. In England, Polanyi bemoaned the absence of a mobile middle stratum as existed on the continent: "there was in the new towns no settled urban middle class, no such nucleus of artisans and craftsmen, of respectable petty bourgeois and townspeople as could have served as an assimilating medium for the crude laborer..." (GT, 98).

Beyond these mediating factors, Polanyi's primary interest was to delineate the horrific consequences of this cultural upheaval on English society. He repeatedly emphasized the furious acceleration of uncertainty and insecurity that accompanied marketization. In pre-capitalist economies, economic relationships were enmeshed in a social context where rights and obligations were clearly tied to wider community needs and the ebb and flow of economic activity could be readily comprehended by individuals. This recognition became fatally compromised in a market economy. Once individuals were confronted with the bewildering multiplicity of options and choices engendered by the market, no single individual or group could possibly be expected to possess a deep understanding of the pattern of choices or preferences of an entire society. This was further exacerbated by the disorienting interdependency which marketization brought in its wake. Given a growing number of decisions affecting an individual's fate were now decided outside their immediate orbit, as with the disciplinary force of commodity prices transmitted via global interchanges, insecurity and uncertainty increased exponentially. Economic activity became largely incomprehensible to the average person (Reddy, 1987).

One of the most telling aspects of a market society is the way in which commodification is imposed on a population with exceptional speed and intensity (Glasman, 1996). Polanyi returns again and again in the text to the "inconceivable rapidity of change", the way in which this radical transformation occurred overnight in an "avalanche", "maelstrom", "torrent", and "vortex" of upheaval and dislocation (GT, 40, 82, 158, 178). Industries rise and fall, workers are tossed about on the labor market like tiny boats in a tidal wave, and land that had been enjoyed in common for centuries is appropriated for private use and transformed for other purposes. Specialization and dependency on the market made all participants vulnerable to roller-coaster swings in prices and competitive pressures. Over time, insecurity became enshrined ideologically as a natural, if not preferred, feature of economic life; perpetual change was envisioned as the linchpin of economic prosperity; and wage dependency seen as tantamount to an elevated moral standing.

However, Polanyi insisted that this perpetual insecurity was profoundly debilitating. Individuals were incapable of coping with such impermanence and instability without suffering ill health, stress, anomie and demoralization

(Block, 2003). "Huge masses of the laboring population", he wrote, "resembled more the specters that might haunt a nightmare than human beings" (GT, 102). Indeed, rapid social change not only disrupted the fabric of social life, it damaged the very character of individuals, robbing them of their "physical, psychological and moral entity" (GT, 73) (Case and Deaton, 2020; Sennett, 1998). Polanyi favorably quotes Robert Owen to this effect:

> "the general diffusion of manufacturers through a country generates a new character in its inhabitants; and as this character is formed upon a principle quite unfavorable to individual and general happiness, it will produce the most lamentable and permanent evils."
>
> (GT, 128)

Amid this gale force of insecurity, the dense web of communal, ecological and normative ties became severed and people became increasingly detached from nature and their fellow citizens. Polanyi insisted there are discrete social and cultural limits to the amount of change and insecurity any community, society or polity can endure before their resiliency and efficacy are irrevocably damaged, a process that, as we shall see in Chapter 5, has powerful political ramifications as well.

There is actually a stronger version of the corrosion argument in the text. It is not just that the vertiginous character of the market corrodes all established institutions and social arrangements, or that it perverts individual character; even more importantly, this maelstrom, if left unchecked, has an irresistible momentum that threatens to cannibalize the very foundations of society that the market requires for its own existence (GT, 130) (Block and Somers, 2014; Fraser, 2013). "Such an institution could not exist for any length of time without annihilating the human and natural substance of society", he wrote, "it would have physically destroyed man and transformed his surroundings into a wilderness" (GT, 3). This is particularly acute in the case of the individual worker who is in danger of being worked to the outer limits of their physical strength: "robbed of the protective covering of cultural institutions, human beings would perish from the effects of social exposure" (GT, 73). Each individual capitalist has an interest in extracting the most value from their work force that they possibly can, even if this literally entails working their labor force to the death, but this collectively endangers the very basis of social reproduction itself (GT, 132–33).[16] This was no less true for the land as well: the exploitation and disequilibrium of the natural world, which enclosure and commercialization brought in its wake, destroyed the sense of belonging with nature that had been an integral feature of the moral economy and "made them [the poor] strangers in their own land" (Thompson, 1993, 184). Indeed, it is the economic system itself that faces a dire threat from the unleashing of the market: "Paradoxically enough, not human beings and natural resources only but also the organization of capitalistic production itself had to be sheltered from the devastating effects of a self-regulating market" (GT, 132; see also 192).

Polanyi extended his treatment of the English cataclysm to the case of developing societies. In repeated formulations, he insists there was a direct corollary between the origins of capitalism and the process of colonialism, a link which he claimed had been grievously ignored by many economic historians. "The cultural catastrophe of black society today", he wrote, "is closely analogous to that of a large part of white society in the early days of capitalism" (GT, 159). Once again, the true culprit was cultural in nature:

> "not economic exploitation, as often assumed, but the disintegration of the cultural environment of the victim is the cause of the degradation... Who, for instance, would care to deny that a formerly free people dragged into slavery was exploited, though their standard of life, in some artificial sense, may have been improved in the country to which they were sold as compared to what it was in their native bush."
>
> (GT, 157, 159)

"Indian masses in the second half of the nineteenth century did not die of hunger because they were exploited by Lancashire", reiterated Polanyi, "they perished in large numbers because the Indian village community had been demolished" (GT, 159–60).

The economic inferiority of these nations plays a key role in explaining the severe dislocations created by the market juggernaut. In his discussion of developing societies, Polanyi insisted the market economy enjoyed higher productivity and efficiency, enabling it to offer the same (or even better) products at cheaper prices and with more reliable delivery. It destroyed people's independent livelihood, making them increasingly dependent on the fluctuations of the market (GT, 164). The market generated higher prices for land holdings, thereby making individual strategies of survival more attractive than cooperative ones and fatally weakened the collective solidarity of these societies (GT, 159–60). Brute political power by colonial authorities acting to safeguard the material interests of their own national capital also underpinned economic dependency: "thus the colonists may decide to cut the breadfruit trees down in order to create an artificial food scarcity or may impose a hut tax on the native to force him to barter away his labor" (GT, 164). And surely the vicissitudes of the world economy played an important part, with fluctuating commodity prices acting as a transmission belt for insecurity and uncertainty.

As in England, the sudden incidence of massive change unleashed on these societies was a palpable feature of social life. "The catastrophe of the native community", he wrote:

> "was a direct result of the rapid and violent disruption of the basic institutions of the victim...These institutions are disrupted by the very fact

> that a market economy is foisted upon an entirely differently organized community; labor and land are made into commodities, which, again, is only a short formula for the liquidation of every and any cultural institution in an organic society."
>
> (GT, 159)

Polanyi similarly emphasized the perversion of individual character that occurs as a result of the contamination of the market. The "noble savage" of African tribes was reduced to "a human variety of half-domesticated animal…a nondescript being, without self-respect or standards, veritable human refuse" (GT, 157). The cultural debasement of the "valiant black tribes" was accomplished through the decaying of traditional industries and institutions, and the utter collapse of the social and political foundations of their existence. Despite the problematic "imperial" baggage that his vocabulary seemingly implied, he had nothing but contempt for the familiar colonialist view that the coming of white civilization represented the triumph of development. Nothing could be further from the truth, he argued, for these societies had already discovered a successful way of organizing economic activity albeit one that was predicated on very different institutional principles than the market.

One of Polanyi's most brilliant and original insights came in a brief excursus where he illuminated the catastrophic impact of the market on food security in 19th-century India. In his brilliant book, *Late Victorian Holocausts*, Mike Davis celebrates Polanyi's unique insight: "Yet the only twentieth century economic historian who seems to have clearly understood that the Great Victorian famines (at least in the Indian case) were integral chapters in the history of capitalist modernity was Karl Polanyi" (Davis, 2001, 9). The inception of market relations calamitously weakened the capacity of Indian society to prevent famines. "The three or four large famines that decimated India under British rule since the Rebellion", writes Polanyi:

> "were thus neither a consequence of the elements, nor of exploitation, but simply of the new market organization of labor and land which broke up the old village without actually resolving its problems. While under the regime of feudalism and of the village community, *noblesse oblige*, clan solidarity, and regulation of the corn market checked famines, under the rule of the market the people could not be prevented from starving according to the rules of the game."
>
> (GT, 160)

In subsistence societies, starvation could be averted because traditional systems of household and village grain reserves, organized along complex networks of communal obligation, alleviated food shortages (GT, 163). The Moghul state as well actively intervened to prevent famine: storing grain, regulating food prices, subsidizing relief operations, embargoing grain exports, and forcing merchants to sell their supplies. The cash nexus imposed on India by its British rulers demolished these safeguards; hopelessly enamored of liberal orthodoxy, they refused to countenance any interference with the operation of the market. Grain speculation by merchants was so endemic that the population was unable to buy food at the skyrocketing prices. Food surpluses were exported, where they could fetch a higher price, instead of being transported to domestic areas of dire need. The British government banned private relief donations and what meager relief was offered was made as repugnant and ineffective as possible. In fact, the "Temple rations" (named in honor of the British high commissioner at the time) that were distributed to the population had a lower calorie content than that which was given to inmates at the Buchenwald concentration camp (Davis, 2001).

Polanyi attests to the horrific human cost of such a fateful embrace of liberal dogma. "Under the monopolists the situation had been fairly kept in hand with the help of the archaic organization of the countryside, including free distribution of corn", he wrote, "while under free and equal exchange Indians perished by the millions" (GT, 160). Davis estimates that the Indian death toll from the two cataclysmic famines of the late 19th century (1876–79, 1896–1902) reached between 15–30 million (Davis, 2001, 165). Its social and cultural consequences were no less catastrophic: family breakdown intensified as men abandoned their families in search of gainful employment; social solidarity degenerated into intercaste and class violence as groups waged a primitive struggle for survival. Davis argues the costs of forcibly incorporating Indian peasants into the world economy had even wider consequences: namely, the vast inequality that marked the historical creation of the underdeveloped world could be dated to these dramatic events.

If we extend our focus beyond the specific empirical cases, Polanyi's analysis of market corrosion represents a fundamental challenge (analytical, epistemological and normative) to the conventional social sciences (Somers, 2008). "Nothing obscures our social vision", wrote Polanyi, "as effectively as the economistic prejudice" (GT, 159). It is an enduring hallmark of this economistic fallacy, he insisted, that this cultural catastrophe had been long relegated to a sideshow among economic historians, whose narrow yardstick of changes in productivity growth, GDP, wages and consumption, obscured the "inferno of early capitalism" (GT, 156) and downplayed the "magnitude of suffering" (GT 135) that had taken place. The "pressure of an unfeeling mechanism" (GT, 83) could not be expected to take into account the way in which millions of lives were crushed, the psychological torture and violence they endured, the misery and degradation to which they were subjected. One of Polanyi's critical insights was that historical accuracy and a fuller understanding of this transformation demanded that these *hidden injuries* be illuminated; indeed, only when social scientists committed themselves to the "reintegration of society into the human world" (GT 126) could an accurate account of social change be achieved.

To accomplish this task, an epistemological break with conventional thinking was required. In the classical economist's explanatory schema, "vision was limited to the market" yet "society as a whole remained invisible" (GT, 258). As discussed in the previous chapter, the operation of the market was couched in naturalistic terms by its proponents – "essentially, economic society was founded on the grim realities of nature" (GT, 125); "the self-regulating market was now believed to follow from the inexorable laws of nature" (GT, 127), as a means of enshrining it with a super-human rationality that placed it beyond the understanding of the average person. Polanyi insisted on moving beyond the "inexorable brute laws" of the market (GT 84), the "blind action of *soulless* institutions" (GT, 219, my emphasis), to emphasize the market as a form of human activity, constituted by human action and therefore capable of being regulated, shaped and even overturned by human action.

His plea to overcome the "icy silence" of economists who ignored, if not intentionally obscured, this onslaught (GT, 98) was predicated on a fierce normative commitment and emancipatory stance as well. Polanyi lambasted both economic elites and their academic apologists for their "mystical readiness to accept the social consequences of economic improvement, whatever they might be" (GT, 33) and insisted that this belief in naturalism and rational calculus meant "compassion is removed from hearts" (GT 102). Indeed, the more destructive the transformation, the greater the need for elites to acquire the "blind faith" that served them as both justification and exculpation. While Polanyi's critique of "fictitious commodities" invoked an ethical injunction against commodification, his entire book can be seen as a vehement indictment of the callous disregard of these "hidden injuries" of capitalism. His analysis of the double movement, therefore, is predicated on an emancipatory critique of the ways in which the impersonal juggernaut of the market tramples individual autonomy and social cooperation, a point to which we return in Chapter 7.

Interrogating the corrosion argument

Because of the centrality of the corrosion argument to Polanyi's double movement framework, it is essential to critically reflect on the broader analytical issues raised by his discussion. In the first instance, the persistent question of periodization needs to be raised yet again. Many of the cultural and social consequences that he so abhorred actually predated the 1795–1834 conjuncture and could be traced to the long process of capitalist development rather than the explicit onset of *laissez-faire* (GT, 33–42). In other instances, Polanyi attributes these problems not to the advance of market society or the inception of the New Poor Law but rather to the general ills of industrialization and urbanization. "Laboring people had been crowded together in new places of desolation", he wrote in language barely distinguishable from the narrative of market corrosion:

> "the so-called industrial towns of England; the country folk had been dehumanized into slum dwellers; the family was on the road to perdition; and large parts of the country were disappearing under the slack and scrap heaps vomited forth from the 'satanic mills'...a veritable abyss of human degradation."
>
> (GT, 39)

The cumulative effect of this tendency is to somewhat weaken the direct association between cultural devastation and the process of market corrosion (and implicitly between market corrosion and social protection as well) (GT, 156–7).

It is true that Polanyi explicitly cautioned that the consequences of distinct periods of social transformation had to be carefully differentiated:

> "[W]e must distinguish between the various vicissitudes to which the laboring people were exposed to in England since the coming of the machine: first, those of the Speenhamland period, 1795–1834; second, the hardships caused by the Poor law reform, in the decades following 1834; third, the deleterious effects of a competitive labor market after 1834, until in the 1870s the recognition of the trade unions offered significant protection. Chronologically, Speenhamland antedated market economy; the decade of the Poor Law Reform Act was a transition to that economy. The last period –overlapping the former – was that of market economy proper."
>
> (GT, 82)

Yet his discussion only sporadically adheres to his own admonition, and even then, largely through the terse epigrammatic statements that he often favored. "In short, if Speenhamland meant the rot of immobility", he wrote in this vein, "now the peril was that of death through exposure" (GT, 83). Indeed, a close examination of the text reveals only the slightest of differences in his discussion of these distinct periods: it is not easy to differentiate between the putative ills attributed to the defects of the Speenhamland system of social protection, or the Industrial revolution, or the cultural tsunami that took place after the inception of the market economy. While the distinct culprits are clearly identified, the divergent pathways of corrosion are not carefully specified.

Beyond this omission lies a more general flaw in his approach. Even though this argument about the cultural cataclysm is absolutely central to the double movement framework –without such a catastrophe, the subsequent rise of a countermovement for social protection would never be triggered – Polanyi did not offer a rigorous explanation of how this process actually transpired. Although the very format of the book is predicated on key aspects of commodification, he never explored the question of whether the specific nature or scope of market imperialism was likely to generate more or less distress. As an example, not all forms of agricultural commercialization are alike: some might lead to greater displacement through upheavals in land tenure while others might augment diversification of rural livelihoods that minimize cultural distress. Polanyi did not seem inclined (aside from the broad generalizations highlighted at the beginning of this section) to catalogue the various social mechanisms, such as the distortion of incentives, change in valuation processes or preference formation, crowding-out of non-market alternatives, shifts in strategies of domination, whereby the corrosion of the market actually takes place (Bowles, 2011).

What is curious is that Polanyi offers a precis of just this sort of account in analysing how the dominant mode of economic activity within a pre-capitalist society could be safeguarded against market incursions. In a fascinating passage on the Melanesian political economy, he writes:

> "The individual's economic interest is rarely paramount for the community keeps all its members from starving unless it is itself borne down by catastrophe, in which case interests are again threatened collectively, not individually. The maintenance of social ties, on the other hand, is crucial. First, because by disregarding the accepted code of honor, or generosity, the individual cuts himself off from the community and becomes an outcast; second, because in the long run, all social obligations are reciprocal, and their fulfilment serves also the individual's give-and-take interest best. Such a situation must exert a continuous pressure on the individual to eliminate economic self-interest from his consciousness to the point of making him unable…even to comprehend the implications of his own actions in terms of such interest. This attitude is reinforced by the frequency of communal activities such as the partaking of food from the common catch or sharing in the results of some far-flung tribal expedition. The premium set on generosity is so great when measured in terms of social prestige as to make any other behaviour than that of utter self-forgetfulness simply not pay."
>
> (GT, 46)

In essence, Polanyi is postulating a series of concrete social mechanisms in this passage – reinforcement (through the imposition of penalties), incentive transformation, closure, fusion of individual and collective interests, the diffusion of reciprocity via myriad social and inter-personal networks, crowding out of competing alternatives, preference formation – that limit the spread of the market. However, he offers no comparable framework to explain why the process of corrosion or these sort of adaptive strategies were not efficacious in resisting the onslaught of a market society.

Indeed, although Polanyi offers a few examples of how specific institutional constellations mitigate the effect of this market onslaught, this is not elaborated in any systematic fashion. The conceptual schema of pre-market societies laid out in the book does not differentiate between the various characteristics of these cultures that might make them more or less vulnerable to marketization such as the vitality of existing institutional arrangements, the strategic capability of the state, legitimacy of traditional arrangements among the population, density of social networks, community adaptability and the like (Hall and Lamont, 2013). Polanyi appears to severely underestimate the resiliency of traditional societies. Local cultures are not automatically overwhelmed by markets: they might modify traditional practices or reconfigure social relations in ways that imbue market relations with social content and cultural meanings (Zelizer, 1994). Even in the case of Speenhamland, it is the widespread failure of specific actors to adapt to change (the stubborn adherence of elites to outworn aims, their inability to perceive the crisis, the inept response by politicians and policy makers) that makes adaptability less efficacious. When the specific mechanisms of market corrosion intersect with the institutional nexus of the non-market realm, the outcomes that are generated are likely to be highly contingent and historically bounded in ways that militate against a "hostile worlds" perspective, such as Polanyi's, that stipulates the automatic contamination by all forms of market penetration (Fourcade and Healy, 2007; Williams and Zelizer, 2005).

It is in this sense that Polanyi's insistence on the cultural ills that accompanied the self-regulating market seems slightly overwrought. E. P. Thompson confirmed many of these same vices that marred the English working class in the period of industrialization – "dissipation, thievishness, lack of thrift and providence, slovenliness, low productivity of labor, lack of self-respect and stamina" – yet whereas Polanyi emphasized anomie, social disintegration and culture shock, Thompson also envisaged the makings of solidarity and social cohesion fused by class organization and consciousness that emerged alongside the market economy (Thompson, 1966, 273). Although Polanyi clearly recognized that non-market elements continued to exercise a formidable hold on the working class even after the self-regulating market was instituted (GT, 172), he did not extensively explore how the degrading effects of market society were often mitigated by class solidarity and community (Calhoun, 1982).

In fact, there is a paradox that Polanyi implicitly poses yet does not explicitly address: namely, that if the working populace/community was so thoroughly demoralized and weakened by the ordeal of Speenhamland and the 1834 liberal reforms, how is it that they also found the resilience and collective cohesion to launch a countermovement (Burawoy, 2003)? In this vein, Somers argues that were it not for the continued vitality of community, the cohesiveness of family structures, and the reassertion and ongoing validity of traditional rights and obligations, the social fabric of 19th-century society might very well have collapsed (Somers, 1993; Block and Somers, 2014). As we discuss in Chapter 4, Polanyi is certainly aware of this dynamic – in his discussion of Owenism, he highlights the "intellectual and emotional vigor" of the populace (GT, 169), yet he tends to subsume many of these characteristics into the realm of the countermovement and of social protection more generally and minimizes the way in which they constituted an institutional nexus that directly influenced the contours and evolution of commodification in England even in advance of the articulation of a social protectionist instinct. More generally, Polanyi's depiction of the "society" component of market society is curiously flattened. The durability or vulnerability of communal arrangements, the cohesiveness or dissolution of social stability, the vitality or passivity of social resistance – in short, the very dynamics of how a market society is constituted – is shorn of its complexity (Burawoy, 2003; Fraser, 2013).

At the same time, Polanyi sometimes seems trapped by a romanticized vision of what pre-capitalist societies were really like. Traditional societies were no less insecure or less prone to the vertiginous fluctuations of fortune as under capitalism. The nature of economic activity in these pre-industrial agricultural systems was equally brutal and the pastoral idyll supposedly ripped asunder by market relations masked social relations that could be every bit as exploitative and inegalitarian (Popkin, 1979). In his marvelous study of industrial workers in contemporary India, Jonathan Parry details how traditional agricultural life, which most workers were just a single generation removed from, was disparaged by these workers for "its backwardness, bigotry, illiteracy and lack of 'civilization'" (Parry, 1999, 117). As many of the youngest workers acknowledged, agricultural work was viewed as even less humane and undesirable than the formidable rigors of industrial life and certainly no one exhibited the slightest interest in returning to this world. Compulsion was built into the very fabric of rural life and was even more severe than the discipline of the labor market:

> "when the weather conditions are right, it is *now* that the fields need ploughing or the seed to be sown. But if one's body aches, we may well decide that one's presence on the building site can wait until next week."
>
> (Parry, 1999, 118)

Pierre Bourdieu likewise argues that unlike the overt discipline of the labor market, domination ("symbolic violence") in pre-capitalist societies was disguised under the veil of "enchanted relationships". "Violence is both more present and more hidden", he writes:

> "Because the pre-capitalist economy cannot count on the implacable, hidden violence of objective mechanisms, it resorts simultaneously to forms of domination which strike the observer as more brutal, more primitive, more barbarous, or at the same time, as gentler, more humane, more respectful of persons."
>
> (Bourdieu, 1990, 191)

But this view of non-market life, which is by no means exceptional, does not feature extensively within *The Great Transformation*.

Paradoxically, it is the vitality of traditional cultures that sometimes gets exaggerated in his analysis, with the case of famine in India instructive in this regard. While his remarkable insight about the devastating effects of the free market and the liberal state on food security in India should certainly be applauded, it does not immediately follow that the contrast he drew between market society and non-market society had the same validity. Despite his claims to the contrary, famines were not unknown in pre-colonial India: traditional society did not typically include sufficient economic opportunities for all its citizens nor were its protective arrangements always so robust as to be able to effectively shelter its most vulnerable members from catastrophic food insecurity. Famine relief might have had a long history but its operations were far from systematic or comprehensive and it is certainly an open question whether the Moghul state could have staved off the serious ecological crisis of the late 19th century when nearly half to three quarters of the Indian harvest was wiped out (Davis, 2001).[17]

It is because of the foregoing complexity that one would also want to question the normative implications of his argument as well. Polanyi's view of market corrosion seems to suggest that every non-market encounter with the market juggernaut is bound to end in disaster yet, as we have argued, it is hard to validate such a claim *a priori*. There are instances where economic transactions are not corrosive – where instrumental rationality, calculation and self-interest do not crowd-out, destroy or damage other valued social relations – and, more to the point, valuable social relations might well be constituted and sustained by markets (Zelizer, 2010). For-profit dating services help people fall in love, assigning a market value to caring activities can heighten public appreciation and recognition of this work, creating a market in carbon trading might actually reduce harmful emissions. The precise balance of harm or benefit generated by disembedding might not be fixed in advance and could well depend on a variety of contingent factors: whether capitalist social relations spread as a result of compulsion or choice; the speed at which non-market institutions are dislodged; the extent to which the existing society or social sphere in which market penetration is contemplated is marred by relations of exploitation, authority and dependency (Streeck, 2011). Indeed, the more people embrace the market as a realm of freedom rather than coercion, the more likely that the constraints on market imperialism will be porous and the corrosive effects diffused.

This general critique can be applied to his specific treatment of the English case. Even if we grant his argument that the processes of marketization, industrialization and urbanization proved a force of cultural devastation, there is still a more complex interpretation of this historical case to be registered. Polanyi admits, albeit begrudgingly, that economic improvement might have occurred as a result of a market society, but concomitant improvements in the cultural or social realm are not broached in any comprehensive manner. The commercialization of agriculture and development of industrial enterprises might very well have shattered the traditional community of rural England, but it also eliminated the isolation and seclusion of rural life. Marketization might have heightened insecurity, but it also weakened paternalist ties of dependency and status that distorted social relations. Market society might have increased vulnerability yet, at the same time, it offered new vistas and opportunities for mobility, education and greater cultural awareness (Snell, 1985).

Indeed, the introduction of markets might very well precipitate a collapse of a cultural system but, if in so doing it decimates traditional forms of exploitation, subordination and "coercive harmony", then improved opportunities (especially for women) for autonomy and independence could be one beneficial outcome. Along these lines, Jean Ensminger (1992) details the effects of market encroachment on the Orma tribe in Kenya. In many ways, their traditional culture did disintegrate in the wake of the introduction of market relations: privatization of common lands and services weakened tribal social cohesion; their egalitarian subsistence ethos was damaged as a result of growing income inequality; and the authority of the tribal elders was seriously undermined by the spread of individualism. But at the same time, she details how market relations also created the foundation for improved autonomy and independence, especially for women members of the tribe. Young women were now able to assert their right to choose their own partners and marry for love; or to divorce freely; or to refuse to be betrothed in arranged marriages; or if widowed, to refuse to be inherited by their brothers-in-law. There is no question that the traditional culture, in particular the patriarchical hold of the male elders, had been debased, degraded, and decimated, but just the same, women had been empowered by the extension of market relations.

In short, what we deem to be the appropriate scope of the market must also include a frank evaluation of what the alternative to the market might be and what its broader cultural and social consequences for emancipation and equality might be (Bowles, 2011). Even while I applaud Polanyi's fierce appreciation of the moral deficit that markets might sometimes entail, it is equally fair to say that his inability to develop a more comprehensive account of market corrosion revealed a fundamental weakness in his overall perspective of the double movement.

Market Insulation

In Polanyi's framework, the market has an unparalleled capacity to influence all of society and its destructive aspects are exceptionally pervasive. But the establishment of a market society also rested on the extent to which the market realm could be insulated from the reciprocal influence of the non-market world. "Hence there must not only be markets for all elements of industry, but no measure of policy must be countenanced that would influence the action of these markets", wrote Polanyi. "Neither price, not supply, nor demand must be fixed or regulated; only such policies and measures are in order which help to ensure the self-regulation of the market by creating conditions which make the market *the only organizing power in the economic sphere* (GT, 69, my emphasis). Disembedding the market from the collective constraints (cultural, social, ideological and political) of the non-market realm was an active process of a market society, separate from the establishment of the self-regulating market; and it was subject to intense political and social contestation that ebbed and flowed depending upon the balance of political forces. The following account of what I call *market insulation* investigates the extent to which it is successful in ensuring market prerogatives, deepening market dependency, and structuring the very nature of social and political action.

Polanyi, following the lead of Hobbes, Smith and Marx, emphasized the formal institutional separation between the economic and political realms, which he termed the "outstanding characteristic of market society" (GT, 195).[18] "A self-regulating market", he wrote, "demands nothing less than the institutional separation of society into an economic and political sphere" (GT, 71). One means of achieving this bifurcation was through an ideological maneuver that conceptualized both the economic and political spheres as realms of freedom (Somers, 2008, 2018; Block and Somers, 2014). The market, as intoned regularly by its acolytes, is a sphere of freedom, choice and opportunity, with market forces coercive only in the sense that they compel economic actors to maximize choice and opportunity. Workers can choose the job they want, purchase the products they desire, or become self-employed depending on the availability of their material resources and alternative employment. Polanyi recognized that the liberal state offered valuable protections in the form of civil rights and formal political equality and, indeed, speculated in later writings that this institutional separation made these even more likely to be safeguarded. "As division of sovereignty between pope and emperor", he said, "left medieval princes in a condition of freedom sometimes bordering on anarchy, so division of sovereignty between government and industry in the nineteenth century allowed even the poor man to enjoy freedoms that partly compensated for his wretched status" (Polanyi, 1968, 75).

But he also argued that market notions of free exchange offered a restricted, if not deceptive, notion of what freedom actually entailed. "The institutional separation of politics and economics" he wrote:

> "which proved a deadly danger to the substance of society, almost automatically produced freedom *at the cost of justice and security.*"
>
> (GT, 254–255, my emphasis)

Whereas in the pre-1834 moral economy, the relationship between employers and workers was subject to a host of normative, political and social constraints developed over centuries of contestation, market discipline exerted a formidable constraint on political autonomy in the *laissez faire* era. This institutional separation guaranteed that the prerogatives of market actors would be insulated from popular control; private property would be put under "the highest conceivable *protection*" (GT, 225, my emphasis).

This meant that vast areas of everyday life – where people work, the conditions under which they toil, the wages received in compensation, where investments and firms are located, how productive systems impacted on nature – were *de facto* considered illegitimate matters for political and social oversight (Cohen and Rogers, 1983). "The separation of politics", wrote Polanyi, "was used to separate the people from power over their own economic life" (GT, 225).

Market insulation circumscribed the policies that were available to embed and regulate market actors. "This is ultimately why the reform of capitalist economy by socialist parties is difficult even when they are determined not to interfere with the property system", wrote Polanyi. "For the mere possibility that they might decide to do so undermines that type of confidence which in liberal economy is vital, namely, absolute confidence in the continuity of titles to property" (GT, 234) (Kalecki, 1943). As discussed more fully in Chapter 5, Polanyi offers an insightful portrait of how a combination of ideological fealty and institutional incentives sharply circumscribed the range of available policies for social democratic reformers in the inter-war years. Lindblom, in his wonderful article entitled "The Market as Prison", talks in distinctly Polanyian ways about how this market discipline operates in macro-political terms, exerting a formidable constraint on policy making and punishing non-market alternatives that seek to challenge its directives. In fact, Lindblom specifically cites Polanyi in this article but laments that he did not go far enough in his analysis of market determination: "I am arguing that the crippling of policy making in a market society may be more serious than he [Polanyi] thought" (Lindblom, 1982, 329). "As for the ubiquity of the punishment, its swiftness and severity, there is nothing like it elsewhere in the social system", Lindblom argues. "Nowhere else is there so effective a set of automatic punishments established as a barrier to social change" (326). Governments, which want to impose tighter regulation on environmental pollution, or seek higher corporate taxes, or regulate business competition, could face the unpleasant consequences of capital flight to more accommodating regions, disinvestment and the attendant problems of unemployment and a reduced revenue base.

The rationale for this, as Lindblom argues (echoing Polanyi quite closely as we shall detail in Chapter 5), is quite simple: these restrictions directly impinge on profitability, which cannot be tolerated by market actors, so "punishment" must inevitably follow. The discipline imposed by this market tyranny is automatic; it does not require cooperation among elites, or deliberation about the proper course of action, or even a declared intention to exact such a penalty. "Business people do not have to debate whether or not to impose the penalty", said Lindblom. "They need do no more ...than tend to their businesses, which means that, without thought of effecting punishment on us, they restrict investment and jobs simply in the course of being prudent managers of their enterprises" (ibid, 327). Indeed, this mechanism creates a debilitating anticipatory effect that paralyzes the ability to conceive of alternatives to the market: citizens do not contemplate, never mind explore, alternatives because in their estimate such initiatives have no hope of succeeding against market compulsion (Kalecki, 1943; Konzcal, 2020).

But, more broadly, this process of insulation implies that the political containment of the market is always a precarious, uphill battle (Beckert, 2009; Streeck, 2011). Capitalists wage a perpetual battle to escape from regulation and social obligations. In Streeck's evocative imagery:

> "their true nature must come to the fore again, revealing them to be the live predators that they are, for which politically imposed social obligations are nothing but the bars of a cage bound to become too small for them and for their insatiable desire for the hunt."
>
> (Streeck, 2009, 234–5)

He locates this "true nature" in the relentless pressures of competition at the heart of capitalism that mandate continual expansion, innovation and the search for new profit opportunities. While the market's unique capacity to universalize its precepts and practices is directly related to its liberation from the bounds of political authority, this separation partially accounts for the "corrosive" character of market society highlighted earlier. With the ascendancy of market values, the vitality of non-market institutions and practices (such as the notion of the public good or even the public sphere itself) can be grievously weakened (Sandel, 2012). But Polanyi sought to extend this insight to the whole of society, which as a result of this process of insulation, becomes utterly reliant on the economic realm. "Since no human aggregation can survive without a functioning productive apparatus", he wrote, "its embodiment in a distinct and separate sphere had the effect of making the 'rest' of society dependent on that sphere" (Polanyi, 1968, 63). "This 'structural' separation", writes Ellen Meiksins Wood, "may, indeed, be the most effective defence mechanism available to capital" (Wood, 1995, 20).

In Polanyi's vision, this process of market insulation was evidenced as well in the precarious balance between the institutional forces of democracy and capitalism that foreshadowed the dialectics of the double movement. The growth of a class of independent wage earners and the expansion of middle class entrepreneurship in the 19th century reduced the share of the population living under the direct control of the landed classes and provided a permanent incentive for the extension of democracy across the industrialized nations

(Rueschmeyer et al., 1994). But elites realized that as long as citizenship rights could be harnessed as a weapon of struggle by the working classes to defend their non-market heritage and thwart the spread of the market itself, they had a permanent incentive to limit the extent and efficacy of these political freedoms. Polanyi argues that the denial of political rights to the working class was directly related to the extension of the market realm: "from the point of view of the spreading of the market forms of existence, this might have been justified, since it helped to overcome the obstacles presented by the surviving organic and traditional forms of life among laboring people" (GT, 172). Yet at the same time, capitalism also requires the democratic state to organize consent to its rule and channel economic antagonisms along "harmless" democratic lines; this might be more difficult if ruling interests let their narrow material interests interfere with their wider hegemonic ambitions and therefore impose restrictions on democratic participation which weakens the social fabric of market society. In the 19th century, Polanyi claimed "the ruling classes had committed the error of extending the principle of uncompromising class rule to a type of civilization which demanded the cultural and educational unity of the commonwealth if it should be safe from degenerative influences" (GT, 172). As we shall discuss in greater detail in Chapter 5, this tug of war between universal democratic rights and particularistic economic interest led to the deep social polarization and paralysis of political life in the inter-war years.

Polanyi explicitly acknowledged the importance of this bifurcation to the specific case of British political culture. "The separation of economics and politics ceased to be an academic issue", he wrote, "and became the irrefragable condition of the existing system of society" (GT, 225). Whereas liberal freedoms had previously acted as a bulwark against the unlawful, arbitrary behavior of the state, in the 19th century they were utilized to enforce this institutional separation and to deflect any political action that sought its transcendence. The political reform that negotiated the entry of the middle classes into political life delayed the extension of suffrage rights to the working class for decades: "In England, it became the unwritten law of the constitution that the working class must be denied the vote...there was not a militant liberal who did not express his conviction that popular democracy was a danger to capitalism" (GT, 226). The British state brutally repressed the Chartist movement, which promoted a wider democratization of the state and economy, "in the name of the institution of property on which all civilization rested" (GT, 225). The defeat of the Chartists, the last working class movement in England to fuse political and economic issues in a single campaign, left an indelible mark on the English working class. Henceforth, working class struggles called on the power of the state merely to ensure their ability to act autonomously in the industrial realm. British unions never sought for themselves an institutional political capacity to intervene in wage bargaining affairs, a fatal weakness that went a long way to explaining the militant economism of the British working class in comparative terms.[19] Polanyi well understood this development:

> "While the British workers developed an incomparable experience in the personal and social problems of unionism, including the tactics and strategy of industrial action, and left national politics to their betters, the Central European worker became a political socialist, used to handle problems of political statecraft…"
>
> (GT, 174)

Beyond the specific frame of political culture, Polanyi's analysis of market insulation also offers a fascinating account of the complex dialectic of political authority inscribed within the state itself. In his view, the state is actually implicated in two distinct forms of "protection" involving distinct institutional approaches that correspond to the dialectic between disembedding and embedding (Block, 2003; Dale, 2010). "Market protection", which is essentially the process of market insulation discussed in this section, consists of guaranteeing the autonomy of market actors to dispose and control their private assets as they see fit; to consolidate these rights within an appropriate legal framework that grants them discretion over their material interests; to ensure that other social actors have limited ability to judge or influence this decision making; and to instantiate an institutional framework to make this possible (eg., the administrative apparatus of the New Poor Law, intensified repressive capacity, and the like). At the same time, because of the destructive aspects of market corrosion, the state must offer "social" protection which entails nearly the complete opposite norms and institutional principles (discussed more fully in Chapter 4). In this instance, the state constrains the actions of market actors and sets limits on the pursuit of their self-interest; places boundaries on the scope of market imperatives; alleviates the burdens imposed on society by market failures; and provides the services and goods which markets find it difficult to deliver in sufficient quantity and at an affordable price.

As noted in Chapter 2, Polanyi does not offer any systematic account of the state's differential role, yet there are several features of this dialectical relationship that deserve further comment. This process of market insulation represents a delegation of a particular form of "political" power to economic actors (GT, 133; Wood, 1995). Relations of domination and coercion, previously the exclusive province of the state, are now vested in private actors. As an example, the relations of authority that occur within a business enterprise – the ability to dismiss workers at will, to discipline them for various infractions, to determine the wages and work conditions under which they toil – can essentially be traced back to the property rights adhering to owners (and indirectly to the managers making these decisions) (Anderson, 2017). Market insulation might also mean that the state no longer has at its disposal the full range of powers that can impact on economic activity, which as Claus Offe suggests, "results in an increase in the veto powers and opportunities for obstruction of those individual and collective actors whose cooperation on the one hand is *indispensable*, but on the other hand, *cannot be enforced*" (Offe, 1984, 107).[20] This displacement of political power also requires a key ideological maneuver: like the classical political economists who discovered the 'economy' in the abstract and therefore obscured the social and political content of capitalism, so too does the institutional separation postulate that this exercise of power is not political at all but rather a "natural" prerogative of the business community (Somers, 2008). Indeed, this exercise of power by private actors is never explicitly acknowledged as a form of domination in the first place.

Although as we shall see in Chapter 5, Polanyi places considerable emphasis on the fundamental contradictions between marketization and social protection, his work actually implies that there is a structural contradiction that is logically prior to this dynamic (Dale, 2010). This is the tension that necessarily exists within any social system that seeks to combine both capitalism (private property, commodification, private control of the means of production and investment decisions) and democracy (regular elections, political participation, citizenship rights and civil liberties) . This relationship, variously conceptualized as "capitalist democracy" (Cohen and Rogers, 1983; Przeworski, 1985), "liberal capitalism" (Bowles and Gintis, 1986) and "democratic capitalism" (Streeck, 2009, 2011), was a central focus of academic debate (and certainly illuminated the key political divide as well) within political economy during the 1980s. Once workers enjoy the right to vote, join political parties and form trade unions, they can infringe on the private prerogatives and decisions of capital through their political control of the state. Of course, the institutional separation still exercises a determinative influence on preferences and strategies: workers tend to pursue short term material improvements as their major political goals and democracy is often equated with liberal freedoms (protection of individual rights, civil liberties, limited government) rather than the active exercise of popular control. But these democratic possibilities present formidable problems for capital accumulation, creating a permanent bias to limit them in the name of economic growth and the universal interests of business.

The critical point in the discussion of "capitalist democracy", which Polanyi implicitly foreshadows in his approach to the double movement (Block and Somers, 1984), was the recognition that it constituted a holistic system. Joshua Cohen and Joel Rogers insist:

> "Capitalist democracy is not a system in which a capitalist economy persists alongside a democratic political system, each unaffected by the other. Nor is it a system in which capitalism and democracy are only temporarily joined in an unstable structure of inner antagonism, each striving to forsake the other. Capitalist democracy is not just capitalism, nor just democracy, nor just some combination of the two that does not change its component parts. Indeed, even to think of such separate 'parts' is to miss the vital integrity of the system."
>
> (Cohen and Rogers, 1983, 49)

This hybrid system represented a distinct process of decision-making and of aggregating preferences and a set of principles for how to organize economic activity and political life. The precise manifestation of this combustible mixture can never be predicted in the abstract but rather arises from the complex institutional mediation that guides its operation, which changes over time as a result of transformations in the dynamics of capital accumulation, commodification and state formation (Esping-Andersen, 1990; Streeck, 2011). Each aspect of capitalist democracy was furthermore liable to suffer what Offe called a process of "mutual contamination" whereby political authority became infused with market criteria and competition and market decision making became increasingly hierarchical and rule bound (Offe, 1984). There is a tug of war – between the market and democracy, disembedding and embedding – within every market society that constitutes a perpetual source of instability and conflict. As we shall discuss more fully in the following chapters, the very nature of the double movement itself is predicated on such an eternal cycle.

The Hundred Years' Peace

It should be clear from the foregoing discussion that the normative lessons Polanyi drew from his analysis of market society are nearly always negative; only rarely does he highlight aspects of market society that are conducive to human freedom and autonomy (Dale, 2010; Hann and Hart, 2009). This perspective is somewhat at odds with the work of many historians and social theorists who, even while highlighting the detrimental consequences of capitalism, nevertheless celebrated the market for multiple reasons. Marx envisioned the arrival of market society in terms of both promise and disaster. He accepted that remorseless exploitation went hand in hand with an enhanced potential for subjectivity: although bourgeois society impoverished and destroyed its workers, it spiritually enriched and inspired them as well. Capitalism for Marx, as Frederick Jameson so felicitously suggested, is "at one and the same time the best thing that has ever happened to the human race and the worst" (Jameson, 1984, 86). Sewell, building upon Habermas's influential work, has persuasively argued that commercialization, expanded commodity exchange and abstract market rationality in France in the 18th century underpinned a vibrant civil society and public sphere (coffee houses, fashion, newspapers, promenade) that promoted a widespread civic equality which anticipated the revolutionary events of 1789 (Sewell, 2021).

The 19th century witnessed the enlargement of the scope or personal autonomy and decision making through market activities. Young people enjoyed a greater freedom to form affective relationships that lie outside traditional class and gendered strictures; modern friendships, as Adam Smith insisted, were premised, not on necessity, but rather on equal standing and esteem, a 'natural' sympathy that enriched and deepened moral ties; the cross fertilization of ideas and culture as a result of the new consumerism offered an opportunity for new cultural possibilities and the potential for a felicitous cosmopolitanism; the ability to participate on the labour market was seen as an extension of freedom for many who previously had been forcibly excluded or trapped in the captivity of bound labour; competition could be championed for its role in fostering empathy, strong social ties and inclusive communities (Hirschman, 1982).

It is somewhat surprising, especially given his keen eye for paradoxes, that there are only occasional glimpses of this dialectic in Polanyi's book. He grudgingly accepted that some worker's lives (specifically in the instance of the Continental peasant noted earlier) could be enriched by commodification and likewise acknowledged that civil liberties and democratic freedoms were a fortuitous "by-product of the 19th century economy" (GT, 254). However, these passing comments are not pursued at any great length or with sufficient analytical rigor. Polanyi is not especially keen to document the manifold ways in which a market society corroded durable social and cultural hierarchies; nor is there any sustained effort to conceptualize the conditions under which the positive attributes of the market might be as important to political and social life as the destructive aspects. It would not be an injustice to argue that Polanyi's passionate animosity towards the self-regulating market partially blinded him to the positive aspects of a market society.

The one notable exception to this general rule was the elective affinity that Polanyi posited between marketization and peaceful international relations, which leads off the opening chapter to *The Great Transformation*.[21] In the 19th century, he argued, the European powers enjoyed a "phenomenon unheard of in the annals of Western civilization, namely a hundred years' peace" during 1815–1914 (GT, 5). Although the obstacles to peace were no less pressing than in the past – revolutionary upheavals marked the age, empires were on the brink of dismemberment, new nations were being created out of the maelstrom of nationalist energies– he maintained the wars that occurred in this period were contained within distinct boundaries, time periods and with (in historical terms) minimal bloodshed. This unique turn of events was not the result of a more judicious use of the familiar repertoire of realist stratagems, but rather was rooted in the "emergence of an acute peace interest" (GT, 7), *haute finance*. This new social group constituted a material and social foundation that transformed the balance of power into an instrument of peace not war (GT, 9–11, 15–18). "[M]uch genuine idealism sprang from the sphere of barter and trade", wrote Polanyi, "by a supreme paradox, man's selfish wants were validating his most generous impulses" (GT, 198). The world of international finance became a "permanent agency of peace" for the 40 years leading up to World War I because their material interests, if not the entire edifice of the emerging international economy, would have been jeopardized if a general war broke out between the Great Powers (GT, 10).[22]

Polanyi offers a nuanced account of how this peace mechanism was channeled through the "position, organization and techniques" of *haute finance* itself.[23] In the first place, international finance had an unparalleled ability to bridge the realms of national politics and the global economy. "Independent of single governments, even of the most powerful, it was in touch with all", writes Polanyi, "independent of the central banks, even of the Bank of England, it was closely connected with them" (GT, 10). No other social agent possessed such "amphibious capacity" (GT, 15): this guaranteed not just ease of movement between the interdependent levels of the global political economy but also granted them a structural access to information that could be harnessed to promote cooperation across various domains. Banks and private lenders actively monitored military spending and used it as a sign of a state's credit worthiness. Second, the more national governments relied on international finance for vital investment funds and credit, the more extensive the reach of this peace interest was and the greater its efficacy in extracting a *quid pro quo* of pacific policies in return for its magnanimity (GT, 13, 18). This peaceful intrigue took a more overt form outside the sphere of influence of the West where "business success involved the ruthless use of force against weaker countries, wholesale bribing of backward administrations, and the use of all the underhand means of gaining ends familiar to the colonial and semicolonial jungle" (GT, 13). Because of their de facto control of financial administration and total control over infrastructural investment – an "iron grip of finance on the most prostrate governments of backward regions" (GT, 15) – dollar diplomacy was able to mold imperialist rivalries to their own interest. Finally, *haute finance* was successful in promoting peace because they provided the institutional foundations, the "social organs", to establish, coordinate and maintain peaceful relations between nations.

Nevertheless, as Polanyi bluntly acknowledges, the peculiar form of "peace" achieved was of a very limited sort. *Haute finance's* primary interest was to prevent an outbreak of conflict between the major powers of the West; the potential (real or otherwise) of war in other parts of the globe could be blithely ignored. As Polanyi writes: "The chief danger…was…war – not war between small countries (which could easily be isolated) nor war upon a small country by a Great Power (a frequent and often convenient occurrence) but a general war between the Great Powers themselves" (GT, 14–15). Only this level of warmaking posed a sufficient threat to financial interests: other forms of conflict might actually prove to be profitable avenues of investment. Indeed, Polanyi never insinuates that *haute finance* promoted peace for anything other than purely material reasons. "They were anything but pacifists", he wrote, "they had made their fortunes in the financing of wars; they were impervious to moral consideration; they had no objection to any number of minor, short or localized wars" (GT, 10). Even the wars that did occur proved the general rule. During the Crimean war, as British and French troops fought against Russians, the British government nevertheless gave permission to its Russian counterpart to raise a loan on the London stock market in order to continue its prosecution of the war (GT, 264).[24]

His argument is provocative and fascinating yet there is still work to be done before what is essentially a working hypothesis can be transformed into a proper causal explanation (although it should be clear that I am not offering such an account here, merely stipulating what such an explanation might require). In actual fact, there is quite a broad causal argument being offered by Polanyi, even if it is not developed in any systematic way: despite significant differences among European states in terms of their divergent state structures and political cultures, varying levels of dependency on financial capital (a function of the health of its public finances, economic policy making and war-making ambitions) and positions within the global economy, *haute finance* was nevertheless able to exert its influence over key political actors in exactly the same direction.

To demonstrate such a bold claim, Polanyi would have to first explicate the relative weight of other salient factors aside from finance capital that might have promoted this normative solidarity between governments; these might include the Enlightenment legacy, the development of secularism, the rise of democratic/liberal institutions and values, and the like (Mann, 1993). He would need to investigate the extent to which other social groups (industrial capital, the working class, agricultural interests) were similarly inclined to support pacific international relations and the success or failure of brokering political coalitions across these divergent class lines. Most importantly, he would have to demonstrate the specific measures whereby the pressures of financial capital were translated into actual political decision-making within the appropriate ministries, or to sketch out specific examples where the influence of finance was actively sought and welcomed, or cases in which war was averted by virtue of their propitious intervention. Polanyi certainly recognized this last challenge – "even an organized balance of power system can ensure peace without the permanent threat of war only if it is able to act upon those internal factors directly and prevent imbalance *in statu nascendi*...It is a commonplace that to insure peace one must eliminate the causes of war; but it is not generally realized that to do so the flow of life must be controlled at its source" (GT, 9), even if he did not devote systematic attention to this or any of these other factors.

The collective entity of *haute finance* itself would also need to be more carefully developed than what is sketched in his book. As an example, international finance might have had shared interests in common but such a predisposition does not automatically lead to cooperation or coordinated action. Collective action typically presumes some pre-existing bonds of solidarity that make it easier to minimize free riding and this cannot be automatically read off structural interests. Polanyi, as detailed more fully in Chapter 5, emphasized the decisive role of British hegemony in constructing the elaborate hive of banks and financial intermediaries that underpinned *haute finance* (GT, 252)."Gold standard and constitutionalism were the instruments", he wrote, "which made the voice of London heard in many similar countries which had adopted these symbols of adherence to the new international order. The *Pax Britannica* held its sway sometimes by the ominous poise of heavy ship's cannon, but more frequently it prevailed by the timely pull of a thread in the international monetary network" (GT, 14).

But within the international market system, Polanyi accorded special privilege to the Rothschild banking dynasty whose "metaphysical extraterritoriality" (GT, 10) specifically ensured the success of the peace faction. His insight has been largely confirmed by Niall Ferguson's history of the Rothschild dynasty. During these hundred years, they were far and above the largest bank in the world, with resources that dwarfed all competitors: "the twentieth century has no equivalent: not even the biggest of today's international banking corporations enjoys the relative supremacy enjoyed by the Rothschilds in their heyday" (Ferguson, 1998, 3). The foundation of the Rothschild's colossal fortunes was their creation, and subsequent domination of, the world's first international bond market. All governments of the world were forced to enter this market in order to finance war, bridge budget deficits, construct elaborate infrastructural improvements and the like. The Rothschilds exerted tremendous structural leverage over governments as a result of their pre-eminent status and they used this quite consciously to avert war. Their "amphibious capacity" was equally unprecedented. They assiduously cultivated close relationships with prominent political figures of the day – aided on occasion by the surreptitious disbursement of personal "loans" to these leaders – and met routinely with government officials across Europe to lobby for their interests. They developed a remarkably sophisticated internal information service that gave them up to date news about political and economic affairs. This gave them a distinct advantage over their commercial rivals, allowed them to manipulate and influence the politicians who were equally desperate for such accurate knowledge, and meant they were often asked to serve as diplomatic couriers in the heart of the political establishments of Europe, all of which immeasurably aided their efforts to preserve peace.

And yet, the decisive role of the Rothschilds actually creates a striking paradox. What gave this financial intermediary such unprecedented sway to promote peace was not just their material affiliations but their familial ones. Ferguson delineates the abiding importance of kinship ties in furthering their economic interests: despite the occasional tensions that developed between different nationally-based family partnerships, the far-flung Rothschild empire maintained an impressive cohesiveness and solidarity. In essence, Polanyi's premise about the hundred years' peace relies on the unity and coherence, not of financial capital itself, but of a particularly non-capitalist form, the family, a rather peculiar denouement to say the least but one that perfectly encapsulates the dynamic of disembedding/embedding stressed throughout this chapter.[25]

Notes

1 Indeed, it has been argued that the topic of embeddedness (and implicitly the issue of disembedding as well) constitutes the core intellectual debate within the field of economic sociology that has been shaped so much by Polanyi's work (Krippner, 2001; Krippner and Alvarez, 2007).

2 Greta Krippner astutely noted: "In this regard, it is probably unfortunate that the literature has tended to describe this transformation using the language of 'dis-embeddedness' rather than Polanyi's own preferred terminology of 'institutional separation'. The language of disembeddedness suggests a view of the economy as a free standing mechanisms not an institutional ordering as Polanyi clearly intended" (Krippner, 2020, 249). Nancy Fraser's framework of capitalism as a complex social order with persistent boundary struggles between the market economy and other social spheres is a salutary intervention in this regard (Fraser, 2013).

3 Although Polanyi explicitly took pains to differentiate his argument about "fictitious commodities" from Marx's notion of commodity fetishism (GT,72, FN), there are surely commonalities in his approach. Marx argued that all commodities combine both use values and exchange values, with the use value dimension subjected to a market logic of exchange value in the abstract process of commodification. Once a monetary value can be attached to a thing, it can subsequently be exchanged for (and compared with) anything else with a price. Gareth Dale also traces the formative influence of Tonnies on Polanyi's conception of the fictitious commodities (Dale, 2010).

4 Gosta Esping-Andersen employs this kind of Polanyian language to highlight the essential problematic: "An unfettered labour market may jeopardise societal survival. The pure market is unlikely to 'clear' unless all participants are effectively commodified, meaning that they adjust perfectly to supply and demand. Distortions will emerge if people command alternative sources of welfare such as a guaranteed income. The *contradiction* is that if individuals do not have access to non-market guarantees, their capacity to be free, unconstrained market agents is reduced, even nullified. A first principle in free exchange is that the actor has the possibility of withholding the product until the 'price is right'. However, this is not possible if basic existence is at stake. The labor market can therefore only be a real market when, paradoxically, it has been distorted, reduced and tamed; when participants have access to sources of welfare other than earnings" (Esping-Andersen, 1999, 38).

5 Greta Krippner and Anthony Alvarez maintain that this "always embedded" stance has become paradigmatic among those of a Polanyian persuasion: "For Polanyians, the notion that markets could exist outside of state action is simply inconceivable. This is not a matter of some markets being more or less social than others…nor is it a matter of the state simply setting the context for market transactions. Rather…the state's management of fictitious commodities plants the state inside the market" (Krippner and Alvarez, 2007, 233).

6 Christoph Deutschmann (2019) is one of the few scholars that has emphasized the importance of disembedding within Polanyi's work. But rather than identify discrete social processes of a market society, as I have proposed, he stresses key dimensions of disembedding: territorial, social, material and temporal, the first three of which I consider under the heading of market imperialism.

7 As explored in the following chapters, there are also periods in which the material interests of market actors might be advanced by various forms of *embedding* that enhance their profitability at the expense of their competitors or similarly eras when the balance of political forces (the strength of oppositional forces, the legitimacy of the state and the like) might entice intra-class calculations towards forms of compromise which they might otherwise oppose (Przeworski, 1986).

8 There are any number of additional social mechanisms that could be implicated in the general process of market imperialism, many of which are now the subject of sociological investigation: commensuration (Espeland and Stevens, 1998); justification (Boltanski and Thevenot, 2006); (Krippner, 2011); and valuation (Lamont, 2012).

9 Of course, sheer economic power is often not enough to successfully establish a commodification regime. In a wonderful story utterly redolent of contemporary bio-piracy of third world bio-diversity, English settlers in New Zealand planned to expropriate the indigenous knowledge of the Maori for flax production which they hoped to market widely. Accordingly, settlers kidnapped two Maori tribesmen to force them to reveal their secrets only to discover that they had mistakenly stolen the wrong members of the tribe because this knowledge was the exclusive province of the Maori women! (Brewer, 1989).

10 Sidney Mintz offers a marvelous portrayal of this process in his book *Sweetness and Power* (Mintz, 1985), which details the way in which sugar became entrenched as an indispensable commodity in all Western societies. From 1650 onwards, sugar became an important linchpin for England's ruling strata: they mobilized political and economic support for the colonization of lands where sugar was plentiful; they mounted furious resistance against demands for the abolition of slavery on which the sugar trade (if not the wider development of the English miracle) was predicated; and they conspicuously eliminated duties and lowered tariffs to widen opportunities for commerce and profit-making. The end result of these political shenanigans was a rapid increase in the supply of the commodity and a gradual lowering of prices that enabled sugar to become part of the everyday lives of the English masses, first as a supplement to tea consumption and later as a vital component in more and more foodstuffs. Once employers realized that sugar had a notable effect on worker's energy and productivity, its centrality in working class diets became even more pronounced and other substitutes were crowded out.

11 The ubiquity of market values is wonderfully exemplified by the way even language itself becomes imbued with capitalist meaning. In the case of the word 'interest', Raymond Williams found it indicative that "our most general words for attraction or involvement should have developed from a formal objective term in property and finance…this now central word for attention, attraction, and concern is saturated with the experience of a society based on money relationships" (Williams, 1983, 173). Ellen Wood similarly noted the cultural implications for a society where the word for "making better" (i.e. improve) was first used to denote monetary gains and profit (Wood, 1999, 80). Joan Thirsk highlighted the use of the word "project", which became coeval with "a practical scheme for exploiting material things; it was capable of being realized through mastery and ingenuity" (Thirsk, 1978, 1). Thomas Richards emphasizes that in the new world of commodity culture of the 19th century, a whole new class of words originated in order to explain this emerging process of objectification and "things" in general: gadget, dingus, thingamajig, and the like (Richards, 1991).

12 Polanyi did not address in any meaningful way how political authorities, economic elites and cultural entrepreneurs intentionally disseminated market values and in so doing created a new commodity culture, a new psychology of consumption and an ideology of consumerism in 19th century Britain. Thomas Richards, as an example, discusses the formidable role played by the Great Exhibition of 1851 in this process. A cross between a modern day department store and shopping mall, the Great Exhibition was housed in the magnificent Crystal Palace and featured over 100,000 separate commodities drawn from England and from nations around the world. Although none of the items were for sale, and nothing as crass as a price tag was allowed to mar the spectacle, visitors were encouraged to roam the

miles of exhibits in a haze of fantasy consumption. Richards wittily links being set loose in the Palace as the Victorian equivalent of "channel surfing" and argues that the exhibition ensured that the coveting and purchasing of commodities became an enduring feature of everyday life.

13 The originality of Polanyi's argument should be acknowledged (Burawoy, 2003; Dale, 2010). Twenty years later, his contention was replicated as the central, and most controversial, thesis of E. P. Thompson's *The Making of the English Working Class.* Echoing Polanyi's exact sentiments, Thompson insisted: "Over the period 1790–1840, there was a slight improvement in average material standards. Over the same time period, there was intensified exploitation, greater insecurity, and increasing human misery. By 1840, most people were 'better off' than their forerunners had been fifty years before, but they had suffered and continued to suffer this slight improvement as a catastrophic experience" (Thompson, 1966, 212). This "standard of living" debate, whose partisans still mount incendiary battles in the pages of academic journals, became essentially a judgment about the nature of the free market economy, where Polanyi's unequivocal condemnation of this process stood in stark contrast to the "optimistic" contingent, led by his neoliberal rival Hayek, who saw the transition to industrialism as a universally benevolent development (Taylor, 1975).

14 Michael Sandel maintains that corrosion arguments usually proceed from two distinct standpoints: an argument from *coercion*, which emphasizes the problems that arise when exchanges are impacted by power and unequal resources; and an argument from *corruption*, which insists that exchanges degrade and denigrate that which is being exchanged (Sandel, 2012). Polanyi employs both kinds of arguments as we shall see in this section.

15 Polanyi also highlighted the cultural devastation that resulted from the 16th-century enclosures: "the fabric of society was being disrupted. Desolate villages and the ruins of human dwellings testified to the fierceness with which the revolution raged, endangering the defenses of the country, wasting its towns, decimating its population, turning its over-burdened soil into dust, harassing its people and turning them from decent husbandmen into a mob of beggars and thieves. Though this happened only in patches, the black spots threatened to melt into a uniform catastrophe" (GT, 35). The conversion of small holders and crofters into seasonal wage laborers uprooted a way of life that had endured for centuries.

16 Polanyi's debt to Marx, whose edifice of political economy was predicated on a similar "gravedigger" thesis, is quite obvious in these passages. As Marx himself wrote: "Capital cares nothing for the length and life of labour power. All that concerns it is simply and solely the maximum of labour power that can be rendered fluent in the working day. It attains this end by shortening the extent of the labourer's life as a greedy farmer snatches increased produce from the soil by robbing it of its fertility…capital that has such good reasons for denying the sufferings of the legions of workers that surround it, is in practice moved as much and as little by the sight of the coming degradation and final depopulation of the human race, as by the probable fall of the earth into the sun" (Marx, 1977, 265, 269).

17 It is also worth noting that, despite the thorough going commercialization of Indian agriculture at present, there has not been a major famine in India since after independence in 1948, a fact which Amartya Sen attributes to the influence of robust democratic institutions in the country (Sen, 2001).

18 In a series of brilliant articles, Nancy Fraser postulates that there are a series of multiple separations within the capitalist social order between market production and social reproduction, human society and non-human nature (Fraser, 2013,

2014, 2015, 2018). In each of these, the contested relationships between the spheres creates destabilizing tendencies that undermine the functioning of the spheres, a point we return to in Chapter 5.

19 Ellen Meiksins Wood argues that working class economism should be seen as a structural feature of this separation: class conflict at the point of production tends to be local and particularistic because militancy and political consciousness are separated and political issues of domination and exploitation are transformed into purely economic concerns. Of course, there might be institutional structures that counteract these tendencies but she insists the expulsion of political struggles from the economic arena is a permanent feature of capitalism (Wood, 1995).

20 Of course, this delegation of power requires political orchestration and might very well represent a calculated effort by political elites to avoid having to make politically unpalatable decisions regarding resource allocation and distribution (Krippner, 2011; Streeck, 2009, 2011).

21 It has often struck readers of *The Great Transformation* as a curiosity that Polanyi should begin his book, a treatise about the horrors of market society, with such a lengthy first chapter affirming the positive contribution that marketization made to peace. To my mind, it recalls the rhetorical device that Marx employs at the beginning of *The Communist Manifesto*: the breathless exposition of the wondrous accomplishments of the bourgeoisie there serves only to heighten the effect of the 'middle passage' of proletarianization. Similarly, Polanyi is keen to stress the paradox whereby the "breakdown of civilization" that occurs as a result of the barbarous conflagrations of World War I originates with the extension of the market mechanism in the 19th century.

22 This elective affinity between the market and peace has a long intellectual history as well. Montesquieu first proposed that commerce was a moralizing agent and that civilized behavior was both a precondition for and the result of free trade. Kant, in *Perpetual Peace*, argued that the "commercial spirit", along with republican constitutions and the spread of international law, would produce peaceful harmony.

23 The tension in his work between functional explanation and historical comparative accounts is evident in this discussion as well. Even though his account of the hundred years' peace is grounded in concrete mechanisms, he falls prey to the functionalist habit on occasion. By way of illustration, see the following passages: "and yet by functional determination, it fell to haute finance to avert general wars" (GT, 13); "because this system needed peace in order to function, the balance of power was made to serve it" (GT, 18); "the success of the Concert of Europe sprang from the needs of the new international organization of the economy, and would inevitably end with its dissolution" (ibid).

24 While she is one of the rare scholars to appreciate the significance of the hundred years' peace to his overall perspective on the 19th century, Sandra Halperin goes beyond a critique of his causal framework to challenge Polanyi's entire argument about this period (Halperin, 2004). She maintains that he grievously underestimates the number of wars that took place between European states (both inside the continent and outside it) and completely overlooks the high levels of domestic conflict (strikes, coups, violent demonstrations) that were commonplace in this epoch. Nevertheless, she implicitly accepts the validity of his core argument – that in this period, military conflict between the major powers was minimal, of a limited duration and with little loss of life in comparison to the devastating wars in previous periods – and does not fully account for these seemingly anomalous circumstances. For a viewpoint that is more sympathetic to

Polanyi, see Michael Mann's argument in the second volume of *The Sources of Social Power* (1993) about the roots of World War I, which follows Polanyi very closely in his emphasis on the hegemonic role of the British empire and the actions of transnational capital in preserving the long peace.

25 But a related paradox, which goes unspoken, is that familial connections exerted a gravitational tug in the opposite direction as well. Europe's monarchs who ultimately decided for war were linked by overlapping kinship relations that exacerbated conflict and precipitated the rush to war.

Chapter 4

The Politics of Social Protection

In Polanyi's vision of the double movement, the triumph of the self-regulating market and the consolidation of a market society triggered a fateful spiral. Once entrenched, the devastating effects of a market society imperiled all of society. "To allow the market mechanism to be the sole director of the fate of human beings and their natural environment", he wrote:

> "indeed, even of the amount and use of purchasing power, would result in the demolition of society...no society could stand the effects of such a system of crude fictions even for the shortest stretch of time unless its human and natural substance as well as its business organization was protected against the ravages of this satanic mill."
>
> (GT, 73)

To safeguard itself against the cannibalistic instincts of the unbridled market, society was compelled to avert a total social meltdown. Polanyi spoke of a "countermovement", composed of all segments of society, which spontaneously "calls upon" the state to initiate policies of "social protection" to regulate the destructive vagaries of commodification. He insisted this protective response was a universal development irrespective of political ideologies, partisan governments or political cultures (GT, 150) and represented a distinct "organizing principle in society", with "specific institutional aims...the support of definite social forces and...its own distinctive methods" (GT, 132).

The origins and dynamics of social protection underpinned Polanyi's theoretical framework of the double movement and of social transformation in general. "It is agreed that the liberal movement, intent on the spreading of the market system", he wrote, "was met by a protective counter-movement tending toward its restriction; such an assumption, indeed, underlies our own thesis of the double movement" (GT, 144). The rise of the free market presupposed, indeed, could not have proceeded without an account of the rise of social protection. The universalization of social protection was also a bedrock of Polanyi's political and moral engagement. In direct contradiction of liberal mythology, he insisted that only an activist state could counter the debilitating effects and

DOI: 10.4324/9781003133186-4

dynamics of a capitalist economy, and that in the absence of this intervention, all of society risked obliteration in the wake of the market onslaught.

Despite its importance to his work and life, there has not been as much sustained discussion of his analysis of social protection as other aspects of the book.[1] Many scholars who use the double movement formula simply repeat the mantra of the social protection phase of the double movement as if his main claim – in *every* case in which a free market economy has been established, a protective countermovement has been forthcoming as well – is either self-evident, and therefore above criticism, or sufficiently established by Polanyi's theoretical and empirical arguments. I hope to demonstrate that substantial questions can be raised about the dominant explanatory framework he utilized to account for this outcome. Indeed, the difficulties he experienced in developing a proper conceptual account of the nature and origins of social protection challenge not only his own theoretical assumptions about the double movement but also the possibilities for political engagement with *laissez-faire*.

Indeed, Polanyi's discussion of the "social protection" phase of the double movement is one of the most revealing sections of *The Great Transformation*. There are actually two contrasting analytical frameworks to account for the origins of social protection. The first, which is often given central focus in the text (if not in most academic accounts), insists that social protection emerged spontaneously out of the perils of the market society and is heavily reliant on a flawed functionalist reasoning (Burawoy, 2003; Dale, 2010). But, as I argue in this chapter, there is also an alternative Polanyian perspective on social protection, an immanent argument in the text that stresses the divergent social and political roots of social protection and relies on a comparative and historically informed analysis. In this alternative framework, social protection is not an automatic, self-correcting mechanism but requires the mobilization of social movements, political capacity and ideological legitimation to be achieved (Berman, 2006). In a fundamental way, these distinct conceptual strategies demonstrate the ever present tension within his work between a penchant for bold, universalizing arguments and the concomitant concern for specifying institutional variation and complexity. By tracing these distinctive positions, I seek to demonstrate once again the formidable breadth and incisiveness of Polanyi's writing and to explore avenues whereby his analysis could be extended in fruitful ways.

In this chapter, I first address his argument about the nature of social protection: what it constitutes, who is protected, the agencies in charge of its delivery, and the social construction of "protection". I then proceed to a critical accounting of his argument regarding the origins of social protection: how it emerges, the social forces mobilized on its behalf, and its political/institutional foundations. I take particular care to delineate the contrasting conceptual frameworks Polanyi employed to address these questions, tracing first the "spontaneity " account that is most prominent in the narrative and then exploring an alternative schema rooted in a comparative-historical framework. Finally, I consider his broader insights about the intrinsic relationship between social protection and historical change.

The Contours of Social Protection

There is some ground to cover before tackling the essential question of the protective phase of the double movement. It will not come as a surprise to discover that Polanyi never offered a comprehensive account of what range of actions might constitute social protection; the range of social agencies that deliver it; or the way in which the whole notion of "protection" itself is socially, politically and ideologically constructed. None of these questions can be easily adjudicated without a more thorough explication, to which we now turn.

Defining social protection

Polanyi repeatedly posited that society needed to be protected against the market and he offers numerous examples (unemployment insurance, tariffs, central banking, pensions) of social protection in action. But at the same time, his predilection for a wide ranging exegesis means there is no single place in the book where he provides a conceptual overview of what social protection constitutes. The term "social protection" first needs to be distinguished from "embeddedness", a term which is equally associated with Polanyi. As noted in the previous chapter, the term "embeddedness" is used to describe the non-economic institutions and practices that are required for the structure and functioning of an economy. Social protection is conceived in broader terms as the social and political institutions that constrain the market, alleviate its harmful consequences and act as a countervailing power to the market, and ensure social and political stability (which might in part occur by embedding economic activity within institutional structures, political governance and cultural understandings) (Block and Somers, 2014).[2]

I would argue that he uses social protection in four interrelated ways. First, social protection is about limiting the speed by which the market penetrates existing domains of social and cultural life. In his discussion of enclosures, Polanyi emphasizes the Tudor state's stalwart intervention to "slow down the pace of change", which allowed people to "adjust themselves to changed conditions without fatally damaging their substance, human and economic, physical and moral" (GT, 37).[3] He similarly speaks of the rearguard action by the aristocracy to resist the commercialization of land until such time as the transformation became "socially bearable": "the squires were the first to make a stand in what proved to be a century's losing fight. Yet their resistance was not in vain; it averted ruin for several generations and allowed time for almost complete readjustment" (GT, 165). Tariffs play the same role in an internationalized economy, allowing workers, firms, industries, and entire nations sufficient breathing space to adapt to the vertiginous shocks of free trade. He does not detail the range of means by which such an objective could be ensured - providing assistance (material and otherwise) to those most affected by the process; subsidizing non-market alternatives; imposing restrictions on market actors that require them to limit either the pace or scope of interventions - but all accept the essential premise that some degree of economic efficiency is worth sacrificing for the sake of social stability and security. Polanyi is not necessarily suggesting that these developments are likely to lead to negative consequences over time – they might in fact be painful but necessary as he seems to suggest in his analysis of the enclosure movement – but he is articulating a broader moral argument that it is fundamentally unjust to subject a population to such ferocious upheaval and then expect them to adjust seamlessly to this fate (Block, 2003; Glasman, 1996; Hall and Lamont, 2013; Somers, 2008).

The second aspect of social protection is closely related to this issue as well. Because the insecurity of a market society poses such a dire threat – "annihilation", "acute social dislocation", "cultural devastation" are just a few of the perils that Polanyi highlights – a basic aim of social protection must be to shield citizens from this fate. Social protection should provide forms of security (adequate income, social rights, protection against rapacious employers, public housing) that safeguard an individual's vital powers and well-being and allow them to be "rescued from the grip of the laws of the market" (GT, 182). Yet this drive for security also has wider connotations. As highlighted in the previous chapter, he insists social protection might be necessary to protect the capitalist system itself from the market juggernaut:

> "it was a reaction against a dislocation which attacked the fabric of society, and which would have destroyed the very organization of production that the market had called into being…not human beings and natural resources only but also the organization of capitalistic production itself had to be sheltered from the devastating effects of a self-regulating market."
>
> (GT, 130, 132)

Capitalism, no less than the rest of society, requires a degree of stability that might entail redressing ruinous competition, imposing purposive limits on risk taking and speculation, stabilizing prices or injecting an element of long term calculation into the economic system itself (Streeck, 2009). In short, a market economy cannot function without a politically organized and regulated security predicated on the preservation of the common good.

Indeed, it is precisely because the market is unable to ensure critical resources on its own that social protection is deemed to be irreplaceable. Polanyi lucidly foreshadowed the contemporary literature on market failures, the fact that the actual benefits of a whole range of "public goods" – in the environment, health care, housing, education and transport – are not adequately priced by markets. "[T]he vigor and stamina of the population", he wrote:

> "the abundance of food supplies, the amount and character of defence materials, even the climate of the country which might suffer from the denudation of forests, from erosions and dust bowls, all of which, ultimately, depend upon the factor land, yet none of which respond to the supply and demand mechanism of the market."
>
> (GT, 184)

The value to society of public health, clean air, free libraries and wilderness far exceeds the profits that could reasonably be captured by market actors who would only take into account the benefits to themselves rather than the wider society (GT, 146). If left to the myopia of the market, society would under-invest in these public goods, so a third aspect of social protection must necessarily include the guarantee that the wider returns to society from these services will be realized. There is implicit in his work a notion of the common good, whereby one of the primary functions of social protection is to safeguard this against the predations of private interest (GT, 154).

Finally, there is also the implication that social protection should also include a concern to reduce the scope of the market altogether; that it requires the assiduous development of countervailing power within the state and civil society (Somers, 2008; Streeck, 2009). Polanyi presciently anticipated work by Asa Briggs, Gosta Esping Andersen and others that envisaged the welfare state as the exercise of political and social power to modify the play of market forces (Briggs, 1968; Andersen, 1990). Esping Andersen's notion of "decommodification", the formative role of social policy in allowing individuals to sustain themselves without recourse to the market, draws its inspiration directly from Polanyi (Andersen, 1990, 36–7). At the end of *The Great Transformation*, when he is contemplating the future circumstances in which the market system would no longer be self-regulating, Polanyi makes several references to a decommodification strategy whereby the core elements of production (land, labor and money) would be removed from the orbit of the market (GT, 251) (discussed more fully in Chapter 7).

It should be clear from the foregoing discussion that Polanyi, in the mirror image of his assertions about the universally deleterious consequences of a market society, primarily viewed social protection in positive terms, even if he recognized the possibility that "protection" might sometimes take on less appealing forms. As an example, Jane Humphries documented the way in which British social protection became synonymous with gendered paternalism, as legislation, such as the 1842 law banning British women from working below ground in collieries, attempted to shield women from the insecurities of market society by cocooning them within the "security" of the household

(Humphries, 1995). Even if this is not exhaustively treated in the text, he understood that social protection might well promote exclusionary and oppressive practices and be supported by any number of reactionary movements (Dale, 2010; Fraser, 2013; Silver, 2003). This highlights an important feature of social protection that Polanyi accepted but did not fully develop in his work: namely, that it is essential to register that similar policies of social protection might be enacted by states for quite distinct rationales (egalitarianism, paternalism, liberal individualism and the like), which are not normatively equivalent, and hence the political and ideological justifications for social protection will exert considerable influence on the actual character and evolution of these policies.

Agencies of social protection

The particular political or social agents that enact social protection is the next issue to address. The overwhelming thrust of the text is that this remains the primary province of the state. "Grave evils would be produced", he wrote, "unless the tendencies inherent in market institutions were checked by conscious social direction made effective through legislation" (GT, 129). Polanyi posits several reasons for this centrality. The state is envisioned as the institution that can best represent the general interest against the particularistic interests of the market: "the representation of which commonly falls to the persons in charge of the general interests of the community – under modern conditions, the governments of the day" (GT, 154). It is the only "social organ" that can recognize and redress the dangers engendered by the shortsightedness of market actors: "the trading classes had no organ to sense the dangers involved in the exploitation of the physical strength of the worker, the destruction of family life, the devastation of neighborhoods, the denudation of forests, the pollution of rivers…" (GT, 133). Only public policy has sufficient scope to cover all citizens in need of protection and only the government has the necessary power to bind all social actors to its dictates. Finally, it is the only social agency that has the capacity to regulate the rapidity of the transformation: "this role consists often in altering the rate of change, speeding it up or slowing it down as the case may be" (GT, 37).

Polanyi did acknowledge that social protection could also be delivered by associations within civil society.[4] The repeal of Speenhamland played a crucial role in this regard:

> "if Speenhamland had prevented the emergence of a working class, now the laboring poor were being forced into such a class by the pressure of an unfeeling mechanism. If under Speenhamland the people had been taken care of as none too precious beasts deserved to be, now they were expected to take care of themselves, with all the odds against them…The abolishment of Speenhamland was the true birthday of the modern

> working class, whose immediate self-interest destined them to become the protectors of society against the intrinsic dangers of a machine civilization."
> (GT, 83, 101)

In his discussion of the Owenite movement, he touches upon the extraordinary 19th-century proliferation of cooperative institutions, friendly societies, and mutual aid organizations that offered insulation from the ravages of the market (GT, 168–9). British friendly societies, which essentially acted as a non-profit social security system by providing workers with insurance in case of accidents, illness, burial expenses and unemployment, grew from several hundred thousand members in 1815 to over four million by 1872 (Thompson, 1993). Their ethos of mutual aid, which was founded on an abiding sense of solidarity and a desire to improve personal independence, served as the foundation of the working class culture from which trade unions emerged. The trade unions took up this burden in turn in the latter half of the century, providing their members with insurance against unemployment, sickness and accidents, as well as death benefits and old age pensions (Boyer, 1990). Given that the countermovement for social protection is drawn from all segments of society, the "breadth and depth" of the associational realm is arrayed as a general interest against narrow, sectional interest (GT, 154).

However, it would not be unfair to note that this critical relationship between the state and civic associations in the organization of social protection is not fully developed in his analysis. Polanyi appears to imply that if mutual self-help action is undertaken, then the state can (and will) delay its own implementation of political measures of social protection; but in actual fact, the groundswell of associational activity might be the consequence of the state's persistent and intentional refusal to offer adequate social protection in the first place. This was certainly the case in England in the aftermath of the passage of the New Poor Law in 1834: because the abolition of outdoor relief meant "protection" was available only in the despised workhouse, working class organizations had little choice but to rely on their own solidarity and mutuality since "calls upon the state" were going unheard. And to anticipate the discussion in the next section, these self-help initiatives were anything but *spontaneous*: they reflected hard graft, careful organization, persistent lobbying by workers faced with substantial material burdens. But the converse might be equally true: if the state totally monopolizes the provision of social protection, the emergence of associational initiatives could be severely dampened. Transformations in the wider political culture are a critical determinant of how associational activity and political power combine to generate momentum for social protection (Calhoun, 2012; Tilly, 1997).[5]

There is a broader theoretical lacuna at stake here as well. Notwithstanding his awareness of the differential consequences of the delivery of social protection, Polanyi does not fully explore how the provision of social protection, its relative scope and reach, and its fundamental basis for success will vary depending on which agency is charged with its delivery. As highlighted earlier, the primary rationale for the state is its ability to offer comprehensive coverage to all citizens, its power to bind all citizens to the program, and the administrative rationality that makes this possible.[6] Associations rely on a different set of mechanisms: the crucial ingredients in their successful delivery of social protection are the reciprocity, trust, and self-discipline of its membership and their ability to employ informal sanctions to ensure social coordination and cooperation. As such, distinct agents of social protection might develop particular affinities owing to these inherent characteristics: states certainly enjoy a comparative advantage vis a vis a strategy of slowing down the pace of marketization or the provision of public goods but associations might be better placed to offer forms of security that require greater flexibility and adaptive capacity.

It is worth appreciating once again what an extraordinarily complex entity the state is within Polanyi's framework and the extent to which the dynamic of disembedding/embedding is instantiated in its very structure (Dale, 2010). On the one hand, the state was indispensable to the creation of the self-regulating market and was compelled to safeguard (on behalf of a class interest) the operations of the market from incursions of the popular will. At the same time, the state was required (on behalf of the general interest) to safeguard society from the predations of the market economy by establishing a program of social protection. The state occupied a precarious balancing act in society: because these dual responsibilities were inevitably a matter of fierce political and ideological contestation, the state itself became a focal point of all the societal contradictions embodied in these contrary principles. Its successful action to further one often unintentionally undermined the tasks that it needed to accomplish the other, a point we will explore more fully in the following chapter.

The social construction of social protection

A final issue requires elaboration, namely the way in which social and political actors understand, and are willing to act on this perception, that the free market represents an ominous threat; without this recognition, it would be impossible for a countermovement to form or to demand protection. Polanyi's discussion of pauperism and the transitional period before industrialism is instructive in this regard, offering a cogent argument about the ways in which social change might be mystified and the need for a protective response consequently obscured.

His first observation was that major transformations in social life are rarely anticipated. "On the eve of the greatest industrial revolution in history", he writes, "no signs and portents were forthcoming. Capitalism arrived unannounced. No one had forecast the development of a machine industry; it came as a complete surprise" (GT, 89). Indeed, even when the massive transformation was underway, hardly anyone understood the ramifications of change. "But the contemporaries did not comprehend", wrote Polanyi, "the order for which they were preparing the way…The complicated economies of Speenhamland transcended the comprehension of even the most expert observers of the time…The pitfalls of the market system were not readily apparent" (GT, 81–2). In a similar vein, he commented:

> "The rise in rural pauperism was the first symptom of the impending upheaval. Yet nobody seemed to have thought so at the time…the ominous growth of rural pauperism was directly linked with the trend of general economic history. But this connection was still hardly perceptible."
>
> (GT, 89–90; see also 109–110)

The roots of this cognitive failure can be attributed in the first instance to the complexity of the transition period. The early signs of change were routinely misdiagnosed as symptoms of the inefficiencies of the old regime rather than as the growing pains of a new one:

> "The inexplicable increase in the number of the poor was almost generally put down to the method of Poor Law administration…The undeveloped condition of the market system concealed its inherent weaknesses. Neither the new wealth nor the new poverty was yet quite comprehensible."
>
> (GT, 89, 110)

The spatial and temporal complexity of the upheaval also contributed to the confusion. Polanyi emphasizes how the increased interdependency of the world economy was ignored as a critical factor: "the connection between rural poverty and the impact of world trade was anything but obvious. Contemporaries had no reason to link the number of the village poor with the development of commerce in the Seven Seas" (GT, 89).

The pace of change was so fast, and the scope of upheaval in social and economic life so encompassing, that comprehension became both an axiomatic preoccupation and a logical impossibility.[7] Indeed, despite the outpouring of contemporaneous analysis devoted to the subject, Polanyi wittily notes the plethora of clamorous rationalizations, many increasingly hare brained, offered in explanation (GT, 91). As discussed in Chapter 2, the presence of two mutually incompatible systems of social organization (Speenhamland and the market economy) created such extraordinary contradictions that the outline of the new system was indecipherable. "To later generations, nothing could have been more patent", observed Polanyi:

> "than the mutual incompatibility of institutions like the wage system and the 'right to live', or in other words, then the impossibility of a functioning capitalistic order as long as wages were subsidized from public funds.

But the contemporaries did not comprehend the order for which they were preparing the way."

(GT, 81)

At first glance, this last passage would seemingly demonstrate how his argument is once again overly reliant on the 1834 conjuncture; in other words, this problem of interpretation was seen to be the peculiar result of the dynamics of this transitional period and that henceforth the establishment of the self-regulating market underpinned a cognitive transformation which made the workings of the system more transparent and knowable. But I believe Polanyi sees this epistemological confusion as a ubiquitous predicament of the vertiginous social change of the 19th and early 20th centuries. Indeed, I would argue that he understands this mystification to be an endemic paradox of social life and that his particular misgivings about the liberal mindset – "whose minds habitually missed the true characteristics of the world they were living in" (GT, 202) – could easily be extended to include all social and political actors.

This assumption of perpetual bewilderment has direct consequences for the conception of social protection. Neither individuals nor groups immediately and intelligibly comprehend the extent or origins of their predicament. Polanyi acknowledged that individuals and groups not only misdiagnose their own circumstances, they often mistakenly support the wrong policies to alleviate their situation. Agrarian elites stuck with their paternalist predilections long after they had outlived their usefulness. Workers, confronted with the new insecurities of the market, took refuge in memories of earlier "golden ages", like the Luddites who contrasted the heartlessness of the mill owners with the security provided by the landed class. Indeed, as he laments, workers supported Speenhamland even though "that system which to all appearances supported them was in truth despoiling them, and that the 'right to live' was the sickness unto death" (GT 101). Nor did political ideology offer any useful shortcuts in solving this conundrum: he notes the "amazing congruence of the projects reflecting minds as different as those of the Quaker Bellers, the atheist Owen, and the utilitarian Bentham…their common illusions disclosed the same radical misunderstanding of pauperism in the nascent market economy" (GT, 110).

As incisive as this discussion is, the entire dynamic of social protection is subject to an intensive process of social, cultural and political contestation that Polanyi does not treat in any great depth. The very framing of a phenomenon as a social problem is a key moment in the genesis of group formation and collective action: for social movements, it represents the first step in the essential fusing of individual grievances into shared understandings, which are a prerequisite for shared allegiances and collective identity (Diani and Della Porta, 2003). Political institutions exert remarkable influence over popular conceptions of what it is that people require protection from, what the cause of this injury might be, and who should be held accountable for such a state of affairs. Once these narratives of justification and legitimation become entrenched as common sense over time, they exercise a formidable constraint on future possibilities of social protest and reform (Block and Somers, 2014).

Political elites engage in various strategies of obfuscation designed to either mitigate or enhance (depending on their specific interests at the time) public awareness of social problems: they can limit the flow of information to the public in order to make it more costly to obtain; they can manipulate the way citizens attempt to draw causal links between policy choices and consequential problems; they can diminish the public perception of government responsibility or culpability for these problems. This is also tantamount to deciding on the appropriate boundaries of social protection: the ability of individual citizens to claim the right to social protection and to have this entitlement recognized by state authorities.[8]

Despite his acute sensitivity to ideological matters, it is important to note that Polanyi did not extensively consider the extent to which the social recognition of a need for social protection can be transformed into a political and moral justification for it. The role of parliamentary committees and royal commissions of inquiry, which he mentions only in passing, is an exemplary case study of how this political process functioned in the 19th century (Somers and Block, 2005). During the critical period of marketization, the Whig governments established 41 such commissions in the years between 1832 and 1841: "one of the glories of the early Victorian age, they signaled a quickening of social conscience, a sensitiveness to distress, that had not been evident in any other period or any other country" (Thompson, 1993, 340). The Royal Commission on the Poor Law, which was formed in 1832 to investigate the existing system of poor relief, was quite consciously harnessed as a vehicle for the social construction of the problem of poverty. The commission called on rafts of expert witnesses and statisticians, interviewed local poor law administrators and scores of the genuine poor, and generated reams of documents; yet at the same time, its survey techniques were hopelessly biased, it relied heavily on selective instances of ineffective administration, and deliberately cherry picked whatever evidence would support its predetermined conviction that outdoor relief should be abolished (Blaug, 1963; Boyer, 1990).

As Block and Somers stress (2005, 2014), the Commission never confronted the popular belief that poverty resulted from unemployment, the introduction of new machinery, or the inefficient distribution of labor supply but rather attributed blame to individual immorality and indolence, as well as the outmoded practice of poor relief which contravened the "laws of nature". These commissions proved to be a battleground over the very nature of social protection: reformers utilized them to propose ambitious schemes of improvement while economic and social elites used their formidable political influence to obstruct change and water down proposals. They operated as a terrain of social consensus as well, utilized by political elites to handle and channel discontent from below, and, at the same time, to pressure recalcitrant economic and social elites to accept some measure of reform. Of course, this need not entail a direct chain of cause and effect in the policy field: as E. P. Thompson scornfully noted, the looming disaster of an Irish famine generated five parliamentary inquiries in as many years but failed abysmally to enact even a single effective policy to stem the calamity (Thompson, 1993).

In short, Polanyi fails to demonstrate the extent to which an ideology of social protection, as a mechanism of legitimation, is a necessary condition for any concerted program of social protection (Somers and Block, 2005, 2014). Such an ideology of social protection must not only assert that interference with the market can be countenanced on grounds of economic efficiency but it must offer a narrative predicated on social justice, equality, and security. It has to postulate a set of evaluative criteria that would dictate the proper scope and role of the market; the core protections and securities that would be offered by right to citizens; and the range of policies whereby these practices would be ensured. While there is a general appreciation in Polanyi's work that the case for political intervention, which he admitted "haunted the history of the market economy" (GT, 223), had to be continually rediscovered, I would argue that this overall reluctance to address the important question of an ideology of reform (beyond the invocations of the "general interest") can be traced to his "spontaneity" argument regarding the origins of social protection: if the implementation of these measures represented an inevitable response to dire societal needs, then an ideological foundation for social protection would be a superfluous, second order phenomena to investigate. This is the question, to which I now turn.

The Spontaneity of Social Protection

Given the centrality of social protection to his model of the double movement, it is not surprising that Polanyi devoted careful attention to the origins of social protection. This issue, he insisted, posed no great mystery:

> "for if market society was a threat to the human and natural components of the social fabric, what else would one expect than an urge on the part of a great variety of people to press for some sort of protection."
>
> (GT, 150)

Social protection represented "the manifestation of the weaknesses and perils inherent in a self-regulating market system"; without such protective measures, the market would have exterminated society (GT, 145). All sectors of society were therefore mobilized to confront this existential threat because of the "broader range of the vital social interests affected by the expanding market mechanism" (GT, 145). His explanatory framework is predicated on the encompassing approach discussed in the Introduction: the double movement constitutes an institutional system with two interlocking components – the self-regulating market and social protection – and the enactment of the self-regulating market therefore presupposes the concomitant development of social protection.

At the same time, Polanyi understood there were two competing explanations to his account of this process. First, there was the perspective of economic liberals who propagated an "anti-liberal conspiracy" to account for the onset of social protection. Because their dogmatic adherence to the market myth meant they could never envisage an endogenous collapse of the self-regulating system, liberals were compelled to argue that interference with the free market was the consequence of a planned intervention by an organized collectivist conspiracy. "Their whole social philosophy", he writes, "hinges on the idea that *laissez faire* was a natural development, while subsequent anti-*laissez faire* legislation was the result of a purposeful action on the part of opponents of liberal principles" (GT, 141). A second stance, espoused primarily by the Marxist tradition, posited a "class" interpretation, whereby protectionist measures such as agrarian tariffs were viewed as the result of the political power of reactionary landlords or factory legislation the outcome of collective agitation by the working class. In actual fact, Polanyi insisted these two accounts were virtually indistinguishable – "Upholding the view of opposing classes liberals and Marxists stood for identical propositions" (GT, 151) – because they denied the intrinsic relationship between the self-regulating market and social protection. I do not think it is going too far to claim that he believed that his wider argument about the centrality of the double movement would rise or fall on his ability to counter (both conceptually and empirically) these two viewpoints (GT, 141–2).

It is worth noting the distinct way Polanyi critiques each of these positions, which are presented over consecutive chapters of *The Great Transformation*. The demolition of the liberal case (in Chapter 12) is one of the most tightly organized sections of the book; indeed, it is one of the few places in the text where he resorts to a straightforward narrative and causal explanation, marshalling his arguments and empirical evidence in numeric progression. It is almost as if he recognized that the boldness of his claim, and its abiding importance to his own theoretical position, required him to engage in a more conventional style of social science argumentation in order to be fully persuasive. His brief against the Marxist position (in Chapter 13) does not have the same wealth of empirical detail and relies on different analytical and epistemological arguments but is equally central to his stance on the double movement. In the remainder of this section, I present a detailed account of his argument about the roots of social protection and his critique of the liberal and Marxist arguments and then critically review this argument. In the following section, I explore an alternative explanatory framework, inspired by an immanent argument within the book itself, arising out of the inadequacies of the original account. Finally, via an analysis of a single piece of social protective legislation from this era, I investigate the feasibility of integrating these divergent approaches into a unified Polanyian perspective.

Polanyi's "spontaneity" thesis

Polanyi's critique of the liberal argument turns the liberal's position on its head. "While *laissez faire* economy was the product of deliberate state action, subsequent restrictions on *laissez faire* started in a *spontaneous* way", he wrote. "*Laissez faire* was planned; planning was not" (GT, 141, my emphasis). In a related vein, he writes: "The legislative spearhead of the countermovement against a self-regulating market as it developed in the half century following 1860 turned out to be *spontaneous*, undirected by opinion, and actuated by a purely pragmatic opinion" (GT, 141, my emphasis). He goes on to reiterate the same point about the "practical character" of social protection over subsequent pages.

Polanyi claimed the liberal position was "a pure convention" and insisted "the testimony of the facts contradicts the liberal thesis decisively" (GT, 145). The *first* plank of his argument against the liberals was that the amazing diversity of policies enacted under the guise of social protection "would exclude the possibility of concerted action" and instead reinforced the idea that they sprung from a "purely practical and pragmatic nature". He cites the varied forms of legislation that were implemented: regulation of food and drink, inspection of utilities, restrictions on child labor, public health measures, public infrastructure improvements, wage setting, regulation of house prices, and establishment of public libraries. "Each of these Acts", he insisted, "dealt with some problem arising out of modern industrial conditions and was aimed at the safeguarding of some public interest against dangers inherent either in such conditions or, at any rate, in the market method of dealing with them" (GT, 146). *Second*, many of these policies were implemented with little advance notice or "*without consciousness* on the part of those engaged in the process of legislative rumination" (GT, ibid, my emphasis), given that the underlying motivation was the need to solve a pressing problem rather than a precipitous change of opinion or interests. Polanyi, for example, argues that workers' compensation, when first enacted in 1880 in Britain, was formulated according to the principle that employers owed no special responsibility to take care of the health of their workers, but by 1897, new legislation made employers specifically liable for the employees in their care even though no change of opinion or interest could be readily identified (GT, 146–7).

A *third* charge leveled against the liberal thesis was that protectionist legislation was promulgated in every country in Europe despite the fact that their political cultures, state structures and ruling ideologies were so disparate. "Victorian England and the Prussia of Bismarck were poles apart, and both were very much unlike the France of the Third Republic or the Empire of the Hapsburgs", wrote Polanyi. "Yet each of them passed through a period of free trade and *laissez faire*, followed by a period of antiliberal legislation in regard to public health, factory conditions, municipal trading, social insurance…and so on" (GT, 147). In each country, similar measures were supported by very different social and political alignments: "the supporting forces were in some cases violently reactionary and antisocialist as in Vienna, at other times 'radical imperialist' as in Birmingham, or of the purest liberal hue as with the Frenchman, Edouard Herriot, mayor of Lyons" (GT, 147–48). "All Western countries followed the same trend", he concluded, "irrespective of national mentality and history" (GT, 216). The only possible explanation for the nearly simultaneous passage of protective measures in countries with such divergent political and institutional contexts is that in each case the threat of the unregulated market was so calamitous that it made social protection inevitable.

Indeed, the *fourth* factor in his arsenal, was that even the most ardent supporters of *laissez-faire* endorsed these measures, a fact which he says is of "great theoretical and practical importance" (GT, 148). "No more conclusive proof could be offered of the inevitability of antiliberal or 'collectivist' methods under the conditions of modern industrial society", Polanyi argued, "than the fact that even economic liberals themselves regularly used such methods in decisively important fields of industrial organization" (GT, 148–9). He highlights the specific role of trade unions and business cartels – one devoted to raising wages, the other to raising prices – which, although acceptable under a strict interpretation of freedom of association and contract, was condemned by the supporters of *laissez-faire* as interference with the free competitive market. However, in order to safeguard the self-regulating aspects of the market, liberals were compelled to endorse trade union and anti-trust legislation.

The spontaneity thesis is also arrayed against the Marxist position. Polanyi is particularly keen to confront the contention that the composition of the counter-movement was largely determined by class position and political ideology. "At innumerable disconnected points", he wrote, "it [counter-movement] set in without any traceable links between the interests directly affected or any ideological conformity between them" (GT, 149). This is not to say that class is entirely absent from his own account, but rather that his concept of class diverges in important ways from the standard Marxist account. Polanyi clearly acknowledges that classes have distinct material interests and act strategically (in both the economic and political realms) in pursuit of those aims, but at the same time he insists that classes also stand for social interests that are wider than "mere class interests", the hallmark of "crude Marxism" in his eyes (GT, 153). "It appears reasonable", he argued, "to group our account of the protective movement not around class interests but around the social substances imperiled by the market" (GT, 162). Class is envisioned in terms of the broader social and cultural interests and relationships that constitute the lived experiences of groups. "Almost invariably professional status, safety, and security", he writes, "the form of a man's life, the breadth of his existence, the stability of his environment were in question… non-monetary interests were inseparable from monetary ones" (GT, 154). It is precisely because all segments of society were affected by the social distress induced by commodification that the countermovement encompassed the whole of society rather than merely being limited to narrow class based campaigns based on workplace exploitation (Burawoy, 2003; Silver, 2003).

From this starting point, Polanyi argues that classes pursued social protection on the basis of these wider social interests rather than material ones – "ultimately what made things happen were the interests of society as a whole" (GT, 161–2) – and that the "collectivist" measures enacted only rarely reflected the interests of a single class. Indeed, it is precisely because of the "social" construction of class interests that various classes joined together in cross-class counter-movements pressing for social protection. "Precisely because not the economic but the social interests of different cross sections of the population were threatened by the market" wrote Polanyi, "persons belonging to various economic strata *unconsciously* joined forces to meet the danger" (GT, 154–5, my emphasis).

But Polanyi wants to push this argument further. While he freely admits that class interests, in their wider connotation, play a key role in the inception of social protection – "Sectional interests are thus the natural vehicle of social and political change…only when one can point to the group or groups that effected a change is it explained *how* that change has taken place" (GT, 152) – he nevertheless insists that the agency of social classes is just a single piece of the puzzle. "Yet the ultimate cause is set by external forces, and it is for the mechanism of the change only that society relies on internal forces", wrote Polanyi. "The 'challenge' is to society as a whole; the 'response' comes through groups, sections, and classes. Mere class interests cannot offer, therefore, a satisfactory explanation for any long run process" (GT, 152–3). In other words, it is the structural imperative of the double movement, rooted in long-term historical trends, which is ultimately responsible for creating the possibilities for social change even if this is accomplished by distinct social forces, a discussion we will return to in the last section of this chapter.

Interrogating the spontaneity argument

Polanyi's spontaneity framework seamlessly intertwines two distinct types of explanation. On the one hand, he views social protection (as likewise the establishment of the free market) as a universal development that all nations, regardless of political or social circumstances, must eventually succumb to. "The great variety of forces in which the 'collectivist' countermovement appeared", he wrote:

> "was not due to any preference for socialism or nationalism on the part of concerted interests, but exclusively to the broader range of the vital

> social interests affected by the expanding market mechanism. This accounts for the all but universal reactions of predominantly practical character called forth by the expansion of that mechanism."
>
> (GT, 145)

Thus, there is little in these chapters about the diverse forms of unemployment insurance on offer or how old age pensions might have varied between countries; what Polanyi is most interested in demonstrating is not *variation* in social protection but rather its *universality*. Yet at the same time, the onset of social protection is articulated along the lines of an "encompassing" explanation: the underlying rationale for why all countries promulgate social protection is that once entwined in the self-regulating market system, social protection becomes a *fait accompli* given the survival of the economic and social fabric are at stake.

At first glance, it is the encompassing explanation that dominates these chapters and the overall tenor of his argument is presented in terms that are highly suggestive –as regards both language and concepts – of functionalist analysis (Burawoy, 2003; Dale, 2010.[9] For Arthur Stinchcombe, the hallmark of a functionalist explanation is the identification of a pressing social problem generated by tensions in a social system, which requires a solution, whereby the social arrangements that constitute such a solution are explained in terms of its functional benefits for the larger system at stake (Stinchcombe, 1968). In this case, social protection is seen as a solution arising out of the functional requirements of a modern capitalist society for social stability. Polanyi argued in this vein that "such measures simply responded to the needs of an industrial civilization with which market methods were unable to cope" (GT, 154; 146). A related postulate of functionalist argumentation is the claim of indispensability: that without the particular social arrangements in question, society itself might perish. "No society could stand the effects of such a system of crude fictions *even for the shortest stretch of time*", he wrote, "unless its human and natural substance as well as its business organization was protected against the ravages of this satanic mill" (GT, 73, my emphasis). At one point, his warning about the voraciousness of capitalism and the concomitant importance of social protection echoes the fate of Medea from Greek mythology when he states that without effective regulation "the market would have destroyed its own children" (GT, 192).

It is important to note that despite the repeated invocations of "society", Polanyi never offers any systematic account of what he means by this term (Burawoy, 2003; Dale, 2010; Fraser, 2013). Although he openly describes social protection as a "distinct organizing principle in society" he makes no effort to conceptualize society as a self-sustaining entity with dominant norms, values, beliefs, practices and mechanisms of control. This kind of rigorous framework is of course a hallmark of his analysis of the self-regulating market yet "society" escapes such critical scrutiny and this omission, as we shall see, undercuts his own position. While he was withering in his scorn for the liberal's belief about the trans-historical proclivity for the market, he predicates his spontaneity argument on an almost metaphysical belief in "society's" ability to recuperate, of social forces to spontaneously mobilize in defense of their interests, of the innate unity of society in the name of the common interest to be asserted even the most turbulent of times (Burawoy, 2003; Berman, 2006). While he delighted in demonstrating the foolishness of political economists for conceiving of the economy as an autonomous realm devoid of societal influence, Polanyi offers a kindred reification of society, where the drive for social protection is implied to have a timeless existence that stands outside of the human action that enables it. The juxtaposition as regards the respective origins of the strands of the double movement is quite striking: whereas the free market owed its existence to the *visible* (coercive) hand of the state, social protection relies on the *invisible* (benign) hand of society.

Perhaps the best way to illustrate the limits of this functional perspective is to delineate the core argument of the "spontaneity" framework. Polanyi's claim can be distilled to three interlocking propositions:

1 The self-regulating market poses such a grave threat to society that without immediate social protection society would collapse.
2 Because the free market threatens every sector of society, a broad, cross-class countermovement is therefore mobilized to call upon the state for social protection.
3 All states, regardless of political cultures or institutions, that are subject to the self-regulating system will implement social protection measures because the survival of society and the economic system itself is at stake.

If we examine his *first* supposition – without social protection the remorseless dynamic of capitalism would have extinguished society – there are several concerns to address. The first reflects my earlier objection to his doctrinal assertion of the primacy of the Year 1 of 1834, the point at which he argued the self-regulating market originated. As highlighted in previous chapters, many of the deleterious consequences attributed to the free market (cultural devastation, exhaustion of the social reproductive capacity of the working class, impoverishment) predated 1834 and similarly much of the so-called structural need for social protection could be traced not to the threat of *laissez-faire* but rather to the related processes of industrialization, urbanization, and class formation. This would seem to invalidate the elective affinity Polanyi postulates between the self-regulating market and social protection unless one accepts a definition of the self-regulating market that is so elastic as to become analytically meaningless.

Indeed, there is compelling evidence suggesting the countermovement for social protection arose well in advance of this period. Even though he stressed the evolution of mutual aid and trade unions after 1834, there is considerable scholarship that demonstrates associational activity to alleviate the harmful effects of the market was already well advanced by the mid-18th century (Calhoun, 2012; Thompson, 1966, 1993). In other European nations social protection was enacted well before the onset of the self-regulating system; by Polanyi's own reckoning, Germany passed factory legislation in 1853 even though a full-fledged free market did not exist in Germany until well after 1860. The historical record seems to weaken the presumption of an automatic correspondence between the free market and social protection given that the onset of the protective instinct predated the very inauguration of the self-regulating system.

The temporal ordering here is crucial. Polanyi insists that no society could survive "*even for the shortest stretch of time*" unless social protection was instituted yet the considerable time lag between the onset of *laissez-faire* and the implementation of protective measures in England belies such an assertion. Although legislation on working hours was passed in the 1840s, a great deal of social protection was enacted after 1860 with essential safeguards such as workmen's compensation (1897), old age pensions (1908) and unemployment insurance (1911) awaiting passage until, in the most extreme case, nearly eight decades after this so-called structural need arose. If we take Germany by comparison, Polanyi, who speaks of the "heyday of free trade" spreading throughout Europe, dates its inception of the self-regulating market in 1862 with a full panoply of social protection measures (protective tariffs, worker's compensation, social insurance) legislated by 1879, provoking the obvious question of what might explain why Germany's structural imperative for social protection was more insistent or had greater power to compel political action than England's.

It is a familiar handicap of functional explanations that the quantity or quality of a social problem, which is required to spark a systemic solution, is impossible to specify precisely. Even if we could determine the exact tipping point when the corrosive insecurity of marketization became so acute as to precipitate social protection, there is never any easy correspondence between a crisis in need of a solution and the social or political action required to resolve it. Political authorities might recognize the severity of the threat (as noted earlier, this is bound to be a matter of intense political and ideological contestation in the first place) yet there might be any number of compelling reasons why they might ultimately prefer inaction. Reform might damage the interests of economic elites with whom they have close links; they might calculate that their own political capacity to inaugurate such change is conspicuously lacking; they may fear that any change will be for the worse and that they will suffer the political fallout no matter the outcome, either for waiting too long to correct the problem or for failing to successfully overturn it. There might very well be structural forces that act to precipitate reform but a convincing explanation of this relationship requires us to carefully specify the specific mechanisms whereby structural inclinations are translated into action, which necessitates a different kind of account.

Functionalist reasoning is likewise implicated in the development of his *second* proposition, namely that a broad countermovement calling for social protection was the inevitable consequence of marketization. In several places, Polanyi highlights the way in which different social agents "*unconsciously* join forces" and similarly claims "yet *almost overnight*, the self-protection of society set in: factory laws and social legislation, and a political and industrial working class movement *sprang into being*" (GT, 154–55; 83, my emphasis). His emphasis on the "unconscious" roots of the countermovement – he speaks of the "half-unconscious stirrings" of the working class (GT, 167) – seems to imply a direct correspondence between the level of social distress and the frequency of collective action, a position typically associated with Durkheimian perspectives on social change (Smelser, 1962; Tilly, 1978). In this scenario, individual grievances emerge because of the disruptive rapidity and stress of social change and as frustrations and social tension accumulate; so too does protest. Collective action is viewed primarily as a series of unconscious, inchoate outbursts directly inspired by the strains unleashed by the social system. The contention that group formation and political coalitions spring into action overnight is consistent with this perspective, for it obliterates the complexities of motivation, emotion, custom, ideology, and political organization that make collective struggle such a difficult proposition to achieve in the first place (Burawoy, 2003; Calhoun, 1982, 2012). Class formation and mobilization is transformed into a seamless process whereby structural upheaval naturally coalesces into concerted action. There is a Polanyian corollary to the free rider problem at work here: individuals have little incentive to join in concerted action for political reform to pressure the state given that such movements are always spontaneously forthcoming by all segments of society, yet if this was the case, then how could the countermovement ever be mobilized in the first place. The spontaneity perspective finesses this dilemma through an aura of the inevitability of social protection, a perspective that is nearly indistinguishable from the naturalistic rhetoric raised by the ideologues of political economy in defense of the self-regulating market.

Both of these positions have been strongly challenged by the scholarship of social movements and labor history (Thompson, 1966; Tilly, 1995). Collective action is not the fusion of individual's unconscious desires but rather the conscious linkage of individuals and groups through shared values, solidarity and understandings.[10] Group formation is determined by pre-existing networks of solidarity, institutional resources, community resiliency and the capacity to solve collective action dilemmas, as well as by the possibilities and constraints that the wider political structure and culture imposes on all social actors. Not all social groups have an equal capacity for collective action or enjoy equal access to the state to press their demands (Calhoun, 2012). Nor do high levels of social distress automatically spark social mobilization and protest; in some instances, it might actually intensify powerlessness and a disbelief in the efficacy of collective action. The creation of British working class institutions and social movements, for example, was anything but spontaneous: it required concerted efforts to build and sustain these initiatives over nearly a century of formidable challenges, regular setbacks and defeats (Tilly, 1995). Within the framework of the "spontaneity" position, it is also difficult to appreciate how transformations in collective action might occur over time, and more importantly for Polanyi's own argument about the double movement, the way in which distinct patterns of marketization left their imprint on countermovements through the structuring of group resources, strategies and solidarity.

Polanyi's assertion concerning the cross-class constituency of the countermovement is also presented in distinctively functionalist terms. He summarizes this perspective:

> "Each class stood for interests wider than its own…the services to society performed by the landed, the middle and the working classes shaped the whole history of the nineteenth century. Their part was cut out for them by their being available for the discharge of various functions that derived from the total situation of society."
>
> (GT, 133, 152)

Each sector of society, for Polanyi, was allocated a distinct function and their ability to perform these key services for all of society accounts for their political influence and social standing. For the bourgeoisie, their interests:

> "ran on the whole parallel to the general interest in production and employment…Given the need of machine production for the establishment of a market system, the trading classes alone were in the position to take the lead in that early transformation. A new class of entrepreneurs came into being out of the remnants of older classes, in order to take charge of a development that was consonant with the interests of the community as a whole."
>
> (GT, 133)

The landed classes (aristocracy and peasants) served the societal interest by protecting the natural environment and also had "the task of safeguarding the martial qualities of the nation which continued to depend largely on men and soil" (GT, 133). The survival of the remnants of the feudal aristocracy throughout Europe, indeed their immense political and social influence that was all out of proportion to their numerical weight, was "explained by the vital protective function of these forces in retarding the mobilization of the land" (GT, 183, 185).[11] The working class, the repository of the "common human interest that had become homeless", was depicted (along with landed interests) as the "die hard defender of the social fabric"; they also were envisaged as a potential source of reform for they were "in the position to transcend the limits of a market society and to borrow solutions for the future" (GT, 155).

Even if one was inclined to pursue this line of reasoning, any number of issues would still need to be resolved. We would have to determine what the precise range of functions that were indispensable to the general interest of "society" might be, how these functions were assigned to key groups in society (and how this might change over time), the extent to which groups understood their core function and how this shaped their interests and collective action. However, Polanyi makes no effort to ground his functionalist argument in this sort of systematic approach. In his desire to jettison the economic determinism of Marxism, he ends up embracing a social determinism that was every bit as opaque.

Polanyi's *third* proposition, concerning the state's ubiquitous role in guaranteeing social protection, is equally plagued by this functionalist perspective. The attribution of the "unconscious" nature of social action is extended here to the realm of political deliberation: social protection is implemented, he says, "without any *consciousness* on the part of those engaged in the process of legislative rumination" (GT, 146, my emphasis). In the "purely practical nature" of social policy, problems emerge and are routinely corrected by state actors although the rationale underpinning their action is never entirely clear from Polanyi's analysis. What appears to be driving state actors towards social protection is not political machinations or ideology but rather the sheer elemental force of structural imperatives that they are powerless to ignore. "Objective reasons of a stringent nature", he maintains, "*forced the hands* of the legislators" (GT, 148, my emphasis). He further argues:

> "it could be shown that a closely similar change from *laissez faire* to 'collectivism' took place in various countries at a definite stage of their industrial development, pointing to the depth and independence of the underlying causes of the process so superficially credited by economic liberals to changing moods or sundry interests."
>
> (GT, 149–50)

State actors could no more overlook the threat of the permanent extinction of the workforce or the exhaustion of the land than they could their own electoral fortunes.

To substantiate his claim on the basis of a specific policy arena, Polanyi offers the case of the passage of workmen's compensation legislation in England. As noted earlier, he identified a profound shift in statutory coverage of workers owing to the considerable differences in legislation passed in 1880 and 1897 but denied this was in any way related to interest, ideology or political struggle. "Even in the settlement of one and the same problem as in the case of workmen's compensation", Polanyi wrote:

> "solutions switched over from individualistic to collectivistic, from liberal to anti-liberal, from *laissez faire* to interventionist forms without any change in the economic interest, the ideological influences or political forces in play, merely as the result of the increasing realization of the nature of the problem in question."
>
> (GT, 149)

In other words, as the costs of marketization became more oppressive, all social and political actors accepted the need for a more comprehensive reform.

Even if we leave aside any number of analytical questions that arise from such a functional perspective – for example, under what conditions do state actors come to such a propitious understanding of social problems or what might be the mechanism linking knowledge to action – the historical evidence appears to invalidate Polanyi's contentions. The 1897 Act, which was modeled on German legislation, established a fixed statutory scale of compensation for all injuries regardless of whether employer negligence was implicated; this compromise rewarded each side, with workers given the right to some payment while employers were able to insulate themselves by inserting a maximum liability claim into the statute. In actual fact, the real aim of the bill was to set discrete limits on employer liability, an outcome that was very much rooted in the changing fortunes of employment, party conflict and ideological battles (Lester, 2001).

In the last two decades of the 19th century, the structure of workplace relations in British manufacturing enterprises underwent significant transformation. After years of ceding competitive advantage to their European and American competitors in the critical industries (steel, chemicals and the like) that constituted the Second Industrial Revolution, British firms began to raise their levels of investment and reorganize their production systems to employ new forms of complex technology. This new regime substantially increased the likelihood of workplace injuries yet, in an era of intense competition, employers could ill afford the higher costs of a compensation scheme that failed to cap their potential liability and they lobbied fiercely for a maximum payout to be enshrined in statute. This contrast between injury and liability became the central contention in parliamentary debates over the legislation. As James Lester details, the Conservative government insisted there was no compelling need to improve workplace safety and maintained industrial accidents should be viewed as "nothing more than a cost of production", which made "compensation for accidents a charge upon their business, similar to the wear and tear of plant and machinery" (Lester, 2001, 474). This ideological standpoint, long ingrained within the language of political economy and diametrically opposed to a "protective" instinct, was forcefully opposed by the Liberal Party and by working class leaders who maintained the real issue was establishing safe workplace regimes that could prevent the question of liability from arising in the first place. They endorsed legislation to eliminate the common law defenses of employers and argued that, so long as employers had little material incentive to provide a safe workplace, worker's compensation would remain at best a partial solution. In the end, the 1897 Act passed because the Tories ideological stance was politically defeated not because of any unconscious working out of societal laws.[12]

Lastly, Polanyi's repeated use of the term countermovement suggests an additional explanation for the state's enactment of social protection. The obvious implication is that there is some intrinsic link between mobilization of the countermovement for social protection and the subsequent passage of legislation yet this causal link is imprecisely established. Even as he acknowledges the tremendous diversity of countermovements throughout Europe, he makes no attempt to investigate whether the onset of social protection could be traced in any direct way to the size, scope, tactics or militancy of the countermovement. Indeed, he never offers a specific example of a piece of legislation that was won by virtue of the countermovement's pressure nor do any of his comparative examples explore whether nations, which implemented social protection despite their divergent political cultures, state structures and ideologies, also had weak or vibrant countermovements calling upon the state for protection.[13] In his view, the countermovement acts as a powerful framing device for political elites, forcing them to take the needs and attitudes of ordinary citizens into consideration when making policy decisions. But, of course, state actors still have considerable room to maneuver for there might be plenty of occasions when calls upon the state for reform are ignored, repulsed or actively rejected on any number of grounds: political elites might be unwilling to commit scarce resources for reform, reject the idea of a pressing problem in the first place, lack the capacity to implement change, or indeed, augment their repressive capacity to forestall the ability of the countermovement to press its claims in the first place, as was the case with the Chartist movement and others in Europe. But the general tenor of this perspective would be to weaken the "unconscious" role of the state to mere rhetoric.

In summary, Polanyi's "spontaneity" framework is unable to offer a convincing explanation for any of the specific propositions that he put forward. The historical record would appear to invalidate the proposed automatic correspondence between the self-regulating market and social protection nor does he provide a persuasive account of how structural pressures are translated into political reform or social protest. Neither the composition, mobilization or efficacy of the countermovement is effectively detailed, nor are the complex political, social and ideological patterns underpinning social protection given their proper due. On the one hand, such a conclusion would seemingly leave the foundation of the double movement in some disarray given that it irretrievably flattens out the very dynamics of the protective phase. On the other, the question posed by Polanyi – of how to explain the ubiquity, diversity and pluralist constituency for social protection – still requires a more definitive explanation. As I elaborate more fully in the following section, there is an alternative framework embedded within the book that offers just such an interpretation.

The Politics of Social Protection

In defense of Polanyi, Fred Block and Margaret Somers argue the foregoing critique of his functionalist inclinations is entirely misplaced for it "misses what is most powerful and useful in Polanyi's argument: the way he moves back and forth between metaphor for meta-theory and a series of concrete causal arguments" (Block and Somers, 1984, 71; 2014). In order to successfully account for long run social change, Block and Somers argue that such explanations "must rest on analogies with familiar organic or mechanical processes" that are often the hallmark of functionalist analysis. However, rhetoric cannot stand alone and a proper argument requires that "specific causal arguments must be invoked to explain each step of the process; the analyst cannot rely on such assertions as that even systems mechanics require certain outcomes without giving concrete causal explanations of these developments" (1984, 72). They insist Polanyi did not allow the metaphor to substitute for analysis but instead offered a grounded historical and causal account of this process.

There are certainly compelling reasons why this line of defense might be persuasive. Close historical arguments of the kind marshalled by Polanyi in his attack on the liberal position are not usually associated with functionalism (Elster, 1986). He was adamant that his account was scrupulously based on the historical record, that he purposefully sought "quasi-experimental support" for his thesis. "Our own interpretation of the double movement is, we find, borne out by the evidence", he wrote.

> "For if market economy was a threat to the human and natural components of the social fabric, as we insisted, what else would one expect than an urge on the part of a great variety of people to press for some sort of protection? This was what we found."
>
> (GT, 150)

And he further boasts: "The testimony of the facts contradicts the liberal thesis decisively…Nothing could be more decisive than the evidence of history as to which of the two contending interpretations of the double movement was correct…" (GT, 145, 150). Of course, even if one took for granted the historical evidence that he gathered, it would still be possible to stipulate a different explanatory strategy than the "spontaneity" framework to account for these facts.

In many ways as well, Polanyi's emphasis on the blatant contradictions, reversals of fortune, and decisive turning points, which gave the 19th and 20th centuries their vertiginous character, would seem to weaken the thrust of a functionalist argument. In functionalist explanations, processes of social change are seen to generate pernicious effects that reduce the efficacy of existing social arrangements. Typically, these arrangements are then stabilized by some other mechanism, so that eventually an equilibrium is reached; however, in this "feedback loop", which often constitutes the core of the functional explanation, the stabilizing process in turn generates a new systemic tension requiring a new solution and so on (Stinchcombe, 1968). Although, as we shall see in the following chapter, there are elements of this sort of explanatory strategy in the book, in Polanyi's world-view, all institutional solutions *within the double movement* are ultimately self-defeating so long as the core dynamics of the double movement remain intact. The onset of social protection sets in motion a series of deep contradictions within the double movement system and a dynamic disequilibrium that sparked a series of systemic crises in economic, social and political life. Stability in the double movement was an everlasting ambition of political and social elites yet proved to be a fool's errand: the continuous interplay of social protection and *laissez-faire* could never achieve such a felicitous equilibrium but rather led to economic depression, political polarization, and exterminist wars and genocide as I recount in greater detail in Chapter 5.

But I do not believe his repeated use of functionalist reasoning can be so readily excused as mere metaphorical flourishes especially given its obvious centrality within the text. In any case, there is a more fundamental point to be addressed. Even if we accept that there might be good reasons for skepticism regarding the centrality of functionalism to his explanation of social protection, it is still incumbent to detail what his alternative causal framework regarding the origins of social protection might be and how it overrides the weight of the functionalist argument presented above. Given the centrality of the social protection phase to the double movement framework, this is an urgent task.

In this section, my emphasis grounds a different type of explanation embedded within the book that obviates the functionalist argument presented earlier. This interpretive framework revolves around a set of logically interrelated propositions that allow considerable scope for variation and institutional diversity. These are not quite posited as causal hypotheses but rather as a set of logical connections that detail the complex trajectory of social protection. Even though Polanyi does not fully explicate every single interrelationship within such a framework, it is precisely this sort of approach that made his work a veritable primer for scholars working in comparative political economy (see, for example, Hollingsworth and Boyer, 1997).

I would argue this immanent framework is premised on the following links:

1 Distinct patterns of marketization create distinct pathways to social protection;
2 Divergent effects of marketization lead to distinct patterns of collective action and countermovements calling for social protection;
3 Different patterns and effects of marketization also generate distinct political coalitions;
4 Different political coalitions and countermovements together produce distinct claim-making for social protectionist legislation;

5 Distinct claim-making, in conjunction with varied political, cultural and institutional contexts, generate distinct patterns of social protection;
6 Differential patterns of social protection legislation coalesce into distinct "regimes of social protection";
7 Different regimes of social protection, in attempting to regulate divergent patterns of marketization, generate distinct contradictions and crises.

Admittedly, this alternative perspective is obscured by the complex architecture of the narrative, by Polanyi's reluctance to systematically organize his concepts, and by the not-so-subterranean functionalism discussed above. He does not explore every single one of these links with the same care and attention and, as such, there are significant elisions in the way this approach is presented. These connections are not developed with the classic apparatus of social science explanation (causal hypotheses, sufficient and necessary conditions, and the like) to validate them but rather often consist of passing asides, suggestive hints, and the occasional tangent. What I am proposing herein is an interpretive framework, which although capable of generating causal hypotheses, functions more as a set of suggestive pathways than as causal explanations. It is designed to fulfill several purposes: to more closely integrate the primary dyad of embedding/disembedding within the social protection phase of the double movement; to highlight the extraordinary complexity of the origins of social protection that implicate social action at multiple levels and domains; and to emphasize the considerable variation in the way these links in the chain are accomplished by social and political agents operating under very different institutional and political constraints and with distinct motives and interests. In fact, the overarching implication of this alternative is to dispel the idea that there can ever be a single explanation for the rise of social protection: no single causal factor could possibly account for this extraordinary complexity.[14]

I trust the succeeding discussion will make it clear that this immanent framework is not the figment of a creative imagination, nor does it represent an egregious misreading of the book, but rather is premised on a forensic analysis of *The Great Transformation*. My rationale for these contrasting frameworks, in much the same way that Block and Somers suggested (they employ their own immanent critique in Block and Somers, 2014), is that Polanyi set himself very different tasks within the argument of the book and utilized different approaches to best address these questions. In order to demonstrate the presence of two competing societal principles at the core of the double movement, the dynamic of which he believes led so fatefully to the destructive spiral of world wars and genocide, it was incumbent on him to treat these phenomena in a holistic way as an integrated institutional pattern, hence the occasional use of encompassing explanations and functionalist argumentation. At the same time, he is all too aware of the fact that not all nations shared the same fate or experienced the ordeal of the double movement in the same manner; and, given his abiding interest in the interplay of structure and contingency, as well as the enduring perversity and paradoxes of historical change, he sought to explore diverse pathways and fundamental discontinuities in the origins of social protection.

These contrasting approaches are never explicitly presented by Polanyi as competing alternatives, nor at the same time, are they integrated into a single, overarching account. As such, they maintain an uneasy co-existence in the book, which is not entirely satisfactory given that these approaches can lead to very different kinds of conclusions, contradict the genuine insights of each other, and tend to become virtually indistinguishable in the narrative. In the last part of this section, I explore the efficacy of such a joint approach but first I outline the contours of this immanent alternative.

(1) Marketization and pathways to social protection

If we begin with the *first* strand, Polanyi acknowledged that the nature of social protection was inextricably linked to the specific arena of commodification that it was designed to combat. Rather than stressing the overarching structural imperative generated by the self-regulating market, the implication is that different patterns of commodification create particular types of harm that lead to diverse pathways to social protection (Burawoy, 2003; Fraser, 2013). This idea is transmitted via the very narrative structure, as Polanyi maps out in three successive chapters (Chapters 14–16: "Market and Man", "Market and Nature", "Market and Productive Organization") the myriad forms of social protection that emerged to ward off different onslaughts by the market: legislation to regulate working hours and social rights (pensions, unemployment insurance) to safeguard labor power; land laws, agrarian tariffs and pollution controls to protect natural resources and the culture of the countryside; central banking and monetary policy to ensure the organization of the capitalist market itself. "The competitive labor market hit the bearer of labor power, namely man", he wrote. "International free trade was primarily a threat to the largest industry dependent upon nature, namely agriculture. The gold standard imperiled productive organization, depending for their functioning on the relative movement of prices" (GT, 162). The particular dynamic of marketization exerts tremendous influence on the character of social protection that it is designed to combat. It is no surprise for Polanyi, given the unparalleled capacity of the gold standard to infiltrate every nook and cranny of social life around the globe, that the scope of monetary protectionism was particularly pervasive. "What the businessman, the organized worker, the housewife pondered", he wrote:

> "what the farmer who was planning his crop, the parents who were weighing their children's chances, the lovers who were waiting to get married, resolved in their minds when considering the favor of the times, was more directly determined by the monetary policy of the central bank than by any other single factor."
>
> (GT, 205)

As highlighted in Chapter 3, Polanyi did not devote sufficient attention to how the timing, pace, and sequence of commodification shaped the specific nature and scope of market penetration, but he did acknowledge their influence on the particular evolution of social protection. He recognized that different forms of commodification, which might occur in distinct historical eras, had divergent effects on the social and political construction of social protection. "While the perils threatening land and labor from the maelstrom of the market are fairly obvious", he wrote, "the dangers to business inherent in the monetary system are not as readily apprehended" (GT, 192). As an example, he suggested that social insurance became available on the Continent before England because of the distinct timing of industrialization and the onset of *laissez-faire* (GT, 206). Similarly, Polanyi chronicles how social protection in the United States followed a particular sequence owing to the specific character of commercialization and its ill effects: "monetary protectionism came first: the establishment of the Federal Reserve System, was intended to harmonize the needs of the gold standard with regional requirements: protectionism in respect to labor and land followed" (GT, 202). There is an implicit suggestion that the intensity of market integration will also exert a formidable influence – the more that a society is exposed to the vagaries of the market (the speed of global integration, levels of commercialization and privatization), the greater the range of social protective instruments required to alleviate the damage – and how nations are differentially integrated into the market economy will make variation in social protection inevitable (GT, 165).

Indeed, as I stressed in the previous chapter, there is no reason to believe that the process of commodification will affect every society in exactly the same manner. Some societies possess critical social, cultural and political arrangements and networks that allow their citizens and communities to survive relatively unscathed from the market onslaught (Hall and Lamont, 2013). "For any widespread form of change must affect the various parts of the community in different fashions", Polanyi wrote, "if for no other reason than that of differences of geographic location, and of economic and cultural equipment" (GT, 152). He stressed that the distinct social circumstances (nature of urbanization, fluidity of the class structure, and the like) that separated the European and English working classes contributed greatly to the divergent social consequences of marketization (GT, 98). Certainly, the scope of commodification and the vitality of pre-existing social arrangements relate directly to the issue highlighted earlier regarding the time lag involved in implementing social protection; the more resilient these social and cultural practices are in halting market penetration, the less incentive the state might have to pass social protective legislation. At the same time, we would also want to more closely identify the particular effects generated by the processes of market society and ask whether they lead to distinct routes to social protection. One might reasonably assume that arresting the deepening and extension of market imperialism might require a unique set of protective arrangements that differ in fundamental ways from those required to alleviate the corrosive impact of market society that led to the cultural obliteration of the working class. While it is true that Polanyi does not pursue any of these themes in a sustained fashion, his insistence on the institutional and social context of commodification offers a possible framework going forward (Fraser, 2013, 2018).

(2) Collective action, countermovements and social protection

As for the *second* link in the chain, given that divergent patterns of marketization generate different effects on society, they might also lead to distinct patterns of collective action on behalf of social protection. Jettisoning functionalist reasoning, Polanyi in this mode suggests that the nature of the countermovement (its constituency, tactics and efficacy) is the product of a complex interaction between social and economic transformations and the specific evolution of the public sphere. He appears to postulate a critical historical discontinuity in the development of collective action, between what is often termed "resistance" and what he calls a countermovement (in contemporary parlance a social movement), which harkens back as well to the distinction noted earlier between "springing into being" and the mobilization of a "legislative spearhead". "Yet simultaneously a countermovement was on foot", he wrote. "This was more than the usual defensive behavior of a society faced with change; it is a reaction against a dislocation which attacked the fabric of society" (GT, 145).

E. P. Thompson wrote about an 18th-century "rebellious traditional culture", where independent artisans, with traditions deeply rooted in the past, struggled futilely to avert the coming storm of industrialization that doomed their craft skills, livelihoods and way of life (Thompson, 1966, 1993). Tactics such as the Luddite sabotage of industrial machinery or food riots were hallmarks of this resistance phase. Polanyi emphasized that these protests were as much a matter of social justice as a response to sheer misery and hunger: resistance was intentionally directed against the repeal of traditional statutes that had protected workers against grain shortages or speculative price rises. Indeed, as Charles Tilly highlighted, food riots were not irrational protests but rather conscious political claim-making arising out of a deeply embedded moral economy: protestors carefully focused their wrath on specific individuals (grain dealers, wholesalers, speculators), often the leading wedge of commodification, whom they held responsible for the unjust practices and the decimation of their livelihoods (Tilly, 1997). Nevertheless, these protests tended to be dispersed and ephemeral and, as I noted in Chapter 2, an alternative to political economy never coalesced into a clear, well defined political platform or ideological program.

The emergent social movements of the early 19th century had different motivations, modes of organization and means of struggle to advance their goals: "The market system was more allergic to rioting than any other economic system we know", wrote Polanyi. "After 1797, rioting ceases to be a popular feature of London life, its place is gradually taken by meetings at which, at least in principle, the hands are counted which otherwise would be raining blows" (GT, 186). In this instance, Polanyi anticipates the work of Tilly who argued that the period from 1765 to 1835 in England witnessed a momentous transformation in the repertoires of contention featuring new forms of campaigning including public meetings, petition drives and demonstrations alongside a wider politicization of claim-making on holders of power and the closer association of popular politics to national affairs (Tilly, 1994, 2007).

This general process is developed in Polanyi's discussion of the social movement inspired by the leadership of Robert Owen, where he contrasts the defensive measures and "backward looking attitude" of the resistance exemplified by the Luddites with the progressive *esprit* of the Owenite movement (GT, 167–72). This movement was first and foremost directed against the onslaught of the factory system: it "represented the cravings of the common people, smitten by the coming of the factory, to discover a form of existence which would make man the master of the machine" and essentially "aimed at what would appear to us as a by-passing of capitalism" (GT, 167). Its scope was extensive, linking up divergent groups of workers and disadvantaged groups across the country; it served as a broad moral force that consciously strove to embody a sense of "spiritual inspiration": "there rarely was a less intellectualized social movement of a similar scope; the convictions of those engaged in it imbued even their seemingly most trivial activities with meaning…" (GT, 168). The movement was tactically innovative – "its wealth of forms and initiatives was unrivaled" – generating a number of pre-figurative associations (producer and consumer cooperatives, labor exchanges, system of barter currency) that laid the groundwork for the creation of a new society and served as the forerunner for the trade union and cooperative movements.

Polanyi is particularly insistent that what separated Owenism from other forms of opposition to marketization was its "social approach; it refused to accept the division of society into an economic and political sphere, and in effect, rejected political action on that account" (GT, 170). This insight allows him to more closely connect the concept of the countermovement back to his argument regarding the cultural devastation of the working class (disintegration of community life, insecurity of livelihoods, relations of solidarity) that was precipitated by the free market. It was precisely because the introduction of the market had such a pernicious effect on the character of the population that Owen intentionally sought to recreate this lost social and cultural heritage as a means of repairing the social substance of the working class. "The education of children and adults", he wrote, "provision for entertainment, dance, and music, and the general assumption of high moral and personal standards of old and young created the atmosphere in which a new status was attained by the industrial population as a whole" (GT, 170). And in contrast to the bleak picture that Polanyi presented about the cultural decimation wrought by marketization, now he emphasizes the remarkable recuperative powers of the working class: "Yet, a people, which, after the moral debasement of the Speenhamland period, still possessed the resilience required for a creative effort so imaginative and sustained, must have disposed of an almost boundless intellectual and emotional vigor" (GT, 169). Polanyi is signaling here the divergent emancipatory potential of social protection, whereby certain forms of social protection can be more or less successful in impacting on forms of social oppression and domination originating from the market (Fraser, 2013).

Polanyi accepts that the trajectories of the countermovements also had to be situated within the wider political culture. In regard to Chartism, he wrote "it is doubtful whether the emotional intensity, or even the extent of that movement, can be realized without some imaginative reference to the times" and highlighted how this movement (and the political counterattack that it precipitated) was tremendously influenced by the successive periods of revolutionary mobilization that had erupted across Europe since 1789 (GT, 172–3). Even if many of these insights are pursued in just a handful of pages, their cumulative effect is to dispel the functionalist reading of collective action as merely an unconscious outburst.

Nevertheless there are some additional considerations worth pursuing. Although he acknowledges the essential discontinuity between patterns of working class collective action, Polanyi's alternative framework does not fully explicate the reason for this transformation and in general, the causal impact of market society on the form, constituency and goals of the counter-movements is not pursued rigorously. Craig Calhoun, who identified a similar transition in working class struggles, emphasized that the roots of these earlier forms of protest (by whom he called "reactionary radicals" (Calhoun, 2012, 89) could be found within the local communities of solidarity that arose from the closely interconnected worlds of artisanal employment and domestic industry (Calhoun, 1982, 2012). He too argues that struggles in this era were primarily an attempt by craftsmen and household workers to defend traditional practices, rights and values that were under direct attack by the growth of the factory system and the complex interdependencies engendered by an expanding division of labor. However, the industrialization after 1820 (the major leap forward in factory construction took place in the years 1823–5 and 1832–4) not only grievously undermined the social foundations of this form of protest, it directly challenged the very efficacy of collective action as well. With the locus of economic change more and more directed by groups whose influence transcended local boundaries and sparked by transformations at the national level, community based struggles had neither the organizational expertise nor the ideological resources to combat these initiatives. As Calhoun stresses, their claim making was diametrically opposed to prevailing social and economic trends: "At the same time, this populist agitation was very radical, because it demanded things that could not be readily incorporated within the emerging framework of an industrial capitalist society" (Calhoun, 2012, 89). Given that their demands could not possibly be accommodated, it was no surprise that national movements such as Chartism emerged to take on this challenge, even if the evolution of that movement was itself the product of decades of political organizing at the local level.

It is this transition that also allows Calhoun to link changes in the evolution of the market economy to the significant differences between Owenism and Chartism, something that Polanyi never successfully integrates into his own analysis. The appeal of Owenism was directed primarily at artisans who sought greater autonomy and independence in the making and distribution of their products and the unemployed who had been displaced by marketization; their innovative policies, such as cooperative stores, financial institutions and joint stock companies, aimed at the socialization of the realm of exchange where their adherents most desired change and as such were based initially on local communities and networks. However, workers in large-scale factories faced a different set of material and organizational dilemmas and hence required a distinct collective strategy. An industrial form of cooperative production, despite Owen's ingenious experiments, proved difficult to sustain, given that the scale of organization and the financial resources required to implement such a scheme were onerous and because competitive pressures from the private sector severely impinged on the range and efficacy of alternative practice. Similarly, "factory workers had no autonomy to extend. They had bargaining positions to protect", argues Calhoun, and as such, trade unionism was seen as their most efficacious strategy (Calhoun, 1982, 122). Success in this arena in turn required a significant transformation at the national political level, which could only be accomplished by virtue of collective action organized at the class level; hence, Chartism drew its ranks from the emerging industrial workforce and its ethos aimed less at a partial transcendence of capitalism than the taming of its worst excesses. Even so, it is worth stressing that Polanyi's contention about the broad basis for the countermovement receives ample confirmation here as well given that the Chartists were not a movement defined primarily by class interests but instead sought to articulate a more encompassing vision as citizens demanding expansive social and legal rights (Somers, 1993, 2008).

(3) Political coalitions and social protection

The *third* link within the immanent framework is the supposition that distinct patterns of commodification (in conjunction with diverse forms of mobilization) also lead to a complex configuration of political coalitions lobbying for social protection. In order to flush out his contentions about the widespread social support for social protection, Polanyi offers a series of factors to account for these divergent patterns of coalition formation, which he asserts was "an everyday occurrence" (GT, 153). In the first place, he highlights the way in which transformations in market society, via its direct effects on class structure and social stratification, generated unique opportunities for political coalitions. In contrast to the pauperized state of a large proportion of the English working class, the social mobility of the lower classes was considerably more protean on the Continent, a feature that had important ramifications for the construction of cross-class alliances. “Yet not only had the recently emancipated peasant lout of the Continent a fair chance of rising into the middle classes of craftsmen and traders with their ancient cultural traditions”, wrote Polanyi, “but even the bourgeoisie, which socially towered above him, was politically in the same boat, being almost as removed from the ranks of the actual ruling class as he was himself” (GT, 174).

In England, he claimed the middle classes were seamlessly assimilated by the aristocracy into the top ranks of the social hierarchy and as such developed the necessary autonomy, confidence and class cohesion to pursue their interests unilaterally:

> “In England, the middle classes, whether squires and merchants as in the seventeenth century, or farmers and tradesman in the nineteenth, were strong enough to vindicate their rights alone, and not even in the near-revolutionary effort in 1832 did they look to laborers for support.”
>
> (GT, ibid)

The continental middle classes, on the other hand, had every incentive to persuade the working classes to enter into a devil’s bargain with them in favor of political rights and social protection:

> “Since 1830, if not since 1789, it was part of the Continental tradition that the working class would help to fight the battles of the bourgeoisie against feudalism, if only – as the saying ran – to be cheated by the middle classes of the fruits of victory.”
>
> (GT, ibid)

The fault lines imposed by marketization might have structurally conditioned the complex negotiation of political coalitions, but at the same time, social groups had substantial autonomy to construct alliances that furthered their interests.[15] The wider institutional context also mattered, with Polanyi emphasizing the way in which the greater time lag in industrialization on the continent meant that the drive for social protection was inextricably linked to either state unification (in Italy and Germany) or the creation of constitutional regimes (Belgium and France) (GT, 175). Because political elites required the support of the working classes for these political projects, they were compelled to offer social protection to the masses as the price for their commitment to these wider political imperatives.

Above all, because social reform required building bridges across various social interests, strategic action by elites, class actors and political entrepreneurs became paramount. While each sector of society experienced the travails of a market society in their own fashion – workers facing longer hours and sweatshops, the aristocracy the threat of cheap food, manufacturing interests the danger of unbridled competition and working class agitation – the success of the countermovement was directly tied to its capacity to mobilize as wide a constituency as possible for reform (GT, 152). The dilemma in this instance lies not in tracing the various motives for social protection but rather in explaining their success in achieving it. "The problem here was not so much why agrarians, manufacturers, or trade unionists wished to increase their incomes through protectionist action", wrote Polanyi, "but why they succeeded in doing so; not why businessmen and workers wished to establish monopolies for their wares, but why they attained their end…" (GT, 153). In an interesting passage from an earlier publication, he suggests that the answer to this question lie not in the "needs of society" or the "functions of classes" but rather with the strategic leadership of class actors:

> "It is not the force of their own interests that makes a group successful. Indeed, the secret of success lies rather in the measure in which the groups are able to represent –by including in their own – the interests of *others* than themselves. To achieve this inclusion, they will, in effect, often have to adapt their own interests to those of wider groups, which they aspire to lead."
>
> (quoted in Burawoy, 2003, 258)

While it is true that Polanyi did not explore the conditions in which interests become counter-hegemonic – by tracing the enabling conditions which underpinned such strategic acumen or by exploring the variety of representational tactics that could forge wider coalitions – these tentative musings on coalitional deliberations are quite distinct from the social determinism highlighted earlier that presumed the unconscious joining together of countermovement forces.

(4) Claim-making and social protection

The *fourth* strand in the alternative framework is the contention that different social movements and political coalitions together generate distinct "calls upon the state" for social protection. "Whether the source of the change", wrote Polanyi, "be war or trade, startling inventions or shifts in natural conditions, the various sections of society will stand for different methods of adjustment (including forcible ones) and adjust their interests in a different way from those of other groups to whom they may seek to give a lead…" (GT, 152). The social forces calling for a limit to working hours were by no means the same as those calling for an end to the commercialization of land; nor should we presume that the supporters of a more active welfare state were necessarily equivalent to those insisting on stricter tariff restrictions. Indeed, even within the same constituency, coalitions and movements could end up lobbying for policies that "point toward mutually exclusive solutions" (GT, 155). In England as an example, factory law reform was closely associated with countermovements in Yorkshire, while anti-poor law campaigns were particularly concentrated in Lancashire, as a result of profound differences between the regions in social and class relations, trade union organization and density of mutual aid societies (Hudson, 1992). This highlights the extraordinary political calculations and trade-offs within these diverse groupings as well as the way in which these divisions might generate political outcomes that are fatally destructive of the democratic process itself (a feature we will discuss more fully in the following chapter). It also helps to explain why the timing and implementation of protective legislation can vary considerably across national boundaries as a result of these ever shifting political and social calculations.

What he did not address fully was the possibility that social groups and coalitions might try to solve their problems by virtue of collective action that did not require any "call on the state". Abram de Swaan's work on the origins of public health offers great insight into this process. Although he ostensibly agrees with Polanyi that the drive for social protection was an all but universal instinct – "all major cities established a series of urban provisions, more or less at the same time and very much in the same manner" – he arrives at this conclusion by way of quite a different causal argument (de Swaan, 1988, 138). De Swaan maintained that the onset of systems of public hygiene was shaped primarily by *private* initiative: once the increasing interdependence and complexity of urban life made it impossible for middle class elites to isolate themselves spatially from the unsanitary practices of the "great unwashed" that created the potential for disease and ill health, they had every incentive to establish private service networks that provided healthy drinking water, garbage collection, and the removal of human waste to paying subscribers only. After a period of urgent political campaigns waged by reform groups and a difficult process of learning by municipal authorities, cities extended these private networks to poorer areas and provided the services as a public good financed through public taxation. Social protection therefore might very well arise from pathways that initially by-pass the state altogether even if the only way these privatized benefits can be extended to the entire population is through the political will to establish public goods.

This returns us to the question of whether there might be significant trade-offs between the associational or governmental delivery of social protection. As an example, Polanyi discusses the differences between the English and Continental delivery of social protection. "The Continental worker", wrote Polanyi, "achieved it [social protection] mainly by the help of legislation, while his British comrades relied more on voluntary association – trade unions - and their power to monopolize labor" (GT, 176). These divergent pathways exerted a profound influence on the character of collective action and political coalitions and generated distinct political and institutional variations: "while economically the difference between compulsory methods of protection – legislation versus unionism - can be easily overrated, politically its consequences were great" (GT, 176). In England, it was the trade unions that created the Labour Party, whose socialist politics remained narrowly sectional and trade unionist; in Europe, socialist parties created trade unions, whose goals were generally more radical and encompassing.

The particular form of social protection might also generate different bases of support and opposition. Elites can easily countenance associational security delivered through non-profits and charities especially if it requires fewer taxable revenues to be extracted from their own pocketbooks, yet they are likely to object to state redistribution or provision of collective goods that directly impinge on their material interests. Certainly, the scope of social protection will diverge as well: indeed, it was only with the growing complexity of the social world that so aptly characterized the 19th century, which required a higher level of organizational expertise, a greater ability to be properly discriminating in the delivery of services and the commitment of much greater financial resources, that the effectiveness of the traditional support systems of British associations was undermined thereby stimulating the politicization of social protection (Calhoun, 2012; Tilly, 1997). Despite the passing insight, these questions are not dealt with in any length in the narrative.

(5) Diversity of social protectionist legislation

The *fifth* proposition is that different forms of claim-making, in conjunction with variations in political culture and institutional context, will lead to distinct policies of social protection offered by states. Political mobilization has historically been closely associated with welfare state development and at the same time with particular forms of welfare regimes as well (Stephens, 1979). As an example, a comprehensive, universalistic welfare state typically has gone hand in hand with a centralized, encompassing trade union movement and nationwide, coordinated bargaining between social classes. It is clearly not his intention in the book to pursue these sorts of arguments in any depth – indeed, this is by far the least developed link within the alternative framework – but there is a glimmer of recognition that the nature and scope of mobilization does have an innate connection to the design of social protection. In this vein, he noted:

> "As long as the vote was restricted and only the few exerted political influence, interventionism was a much less urgent problem than it became when universal suffrage made the state the organ of the ruling million –the identical million, who, in the economic realm, had often to carry in bitterness the burden of the ruled."
>
> (GT, 206)

Polanyi acknowledged the reciprocal relation inherent in this process: namely, that the character of social protection also shaped the nature of collective action and group formation struggling for this very reform. "While land and labor were linked to definite, even though broad social strata, such as the workers or the peasantry", he wrote, "monetary protectionism was, to a greater extent, a national factor, often fusing diverse interests into a collective whole" (GT, 203). In his discussion of the political trajectories of the 1930s (discussed more fully in the following chapter), he implied that the precise form of social protection – which could take the form of German fascism, Soviet Communism, or the New Deal – could vary significantly depending upon the strength and mobilization of popular movements and the way in which this mobilization intersected with transformations in the political culture.

Polanyi was well aware of the remarkable diversity of social protection. He made numerous distinctions within the book between forms of protection in terms of their core dynamics and scope of activity. To give a single example, he argues that "[t]he integrating power of monetary policy surpassed by far that of the other kinds of protectionism, with their slow and cumbersome apparatus, for the influence of monetary protectionism was ever active and ever changing" (GT, 205). The precise delivery of social protection can vary considerably: he points out that while legislative acts were used to protect slum dwellers against urban improvements, in Europe statutes and administrative action were utilized (GT, 182).[16] He recognized that there was considerable variation in the capacity of states to enact social protection and specifically contrasts the gap between the states of the West and those of developing societies: "But if the organized states of Europe could protect themselves against the backwash of international free trade, the politically unorganized colonial peoples could not" (GT, 183). It was precisely this institutional diversity that contributed to the significant variation in the fortunes of nations:

> "If life in different countries was different, as had always been the case, the disparity now could be traced to a definite legislative and administrative acts of a protective intent, since conditions of production and labor were now mainly dependent on tariffs, taxation, and social laws."
> (GT, 204)

This political diversity has direct implications for the way in which the state's role in social protection should be conceived. Political elites and state actors are anything but "unconscious" reflections of structural forces but rather exercise a critical autonomy in defining social problems, shaping the demands of society for reform, formulating innovative policies and enacting measures, sometimes in advance of or even in opposition to social forces. Political reformers (of every ideological stripe) can use the government to maximize their opportunities, even changing the structural and institutional conditions under which they act. Nevertheless, political, economic and social structures define the circumstances within which they choose and establish the range of effective options and strategies they can adopt. The extent to which social protection is aligned with egalitarian and democratic objectives that privilege autonomy and self-determination will depend on the nature of political coalitions and the ability of reformers to offer an ideological narrative that justifies a countervailing power against the untrammeled market (Berman, 2006; Block and Somers, 2014; Fraser, 2013). Even if this alternative framework did not explicate these patterns and pathways in any systematic exposition, Polanyi did lay the groundwork for such an explanatory program (which was taken up by many political economists inspired by his work; see Hollingsworth and Boyer, 1997) within the terms of the double movement itself.

(6) Regimes of social protection

In the *sixth* link in the sequence, patterns of social protection can coalesce over time into a particular institutional nexus, or "regime" of social protection. Polanyi highlights the process whereby various measures of social protection, initially designed to redress different aspects of commodification, can become mutually reinforcing to the extent that each generates a community of interest binding distinct political coalitions and social classes to its measures.[17] Admittedly, he does not treat this question in any detailed manner yet there is one revealing passage that demonstrates the general perspective:

> "But once Corn laws and labor laws were in force…it would become difficult to remove the one without removing the other. Between agricultural and industrial tariffs, the relationship was even closer…The rising cost of living induced by corn laws invited the manufacturer's demand for protective tariffs…trade unions naturally insisted on higher wages to compensate for increased costs of living, and could not well object to such customs tariffs as permitted the employer to meet an inflated wage bill. But once the accountancy of social legislation had been based on a wage bill conditioned by tariffs, employees could not in fairness be expected to carry the burden of such legislation unless they were assured of continued protection."
>
> (GT, 204)

The state is not a passive actor in this process but rather a critical agent in managing the complex trade-offs between different protective measures, cementing the coalitions, creating political cohesion ("create parallel interests which were committed to its continuation" [GT, 204]), establishing institutional rules and rewards that raise the political and economic costs of exit from such a regime, and forming the new ideological common sense underpinning reform.

Of course, these regimes of social protection decay over time and practices that interlocked in a positive synergy in one period might manifest contradictory and destructive tendencies in another. As we will explore in the next chapter, Polanyi well understood that this politicization of social protection might create unintentional consequences for political stability once the state became a battleground for competing political forces and ideologies. However, while he was acutely aware of the contradictions generated by the market, what he did not explore in any depth was whether differences in the vulnerability of different regimes of protection to institutional failures (capacity shortfall, administrative fragmentation, bureaucratic inflexibility) or political failures (inability to achieve general consent for reform) might be rooted in the very nature of the double movement itself.

Finally, in the *seventh* link in the chain, these distinct "regimes of social protection" generate particular sorts of effects and changes within the self-regulating system itself, which lead to a series of social, economic and political contradictions and crises that threaten both the economy and the system of social protection alike. This dynamic takes center stage in the following chapter and will be discussed more fully therein.

The Factory Acts

Given that the two explanatory frameworks maintain a shifting, if not disquiet, truce within the book, I want to explore the possibility of whether an integrated Polanyian framework could be established. To this end, I focus on a brief discussion of a single case study of British social protection, namely the promulgation of regulations on factory conditions. As alluded to in the book, in the 1830s and 1840s, the British government passed a series of social protection measures, collectively referred to as the Factory Acts (1833, 1844, 1847), which set regulations on workplace conditions, the use of child labor, and the level of permissible working hours within establishments.

As Polanyi rightly notes, other European nations implemented similar measures so therefore an integrated approach needs to conceptualize the underlying social necessity for a healthy workforce and how this structural need might be expressed in terms of concrete social and political mechanisms that aided in the passage of social protection. In order to avoid the teleological reasoning that envisions social protection as merely the logical unfolding of some inherent societal logic, such an alternative would need to offer specific mechanisms whereby this social need becomes activated as a force for change. I would suggest two specific factors to explore: first, the extent to which considerations about the centrality of worker's social reproduction to the long term vitality of capitalism entered into the private calculations and public discourse of economic and political elites; second, the extent to which public debates about worker's protection actually reflected the "pressure of events", in other words, specific evidence of how political actors were induced into action by the pressing problems of marketization and industrialization. This willingness to intervene need not be accompanied in any way by a critique of the market system itself: social protection might very well be understood as the inevitable price to pay for living in a market society or as recognition that the cure for such social problems surpassed the capacity of individual capitalist actors and required the state's leading role.

If we focus on the British case, there is indeed considerable evidence that nearly all elements of British society – legislators, civic reformers, middle class elites, workers, evangelical campaigners, landed interests – viewed factory legislation as just this kind of social need. Many commentators argued that such an egregious interference with the freedom of the labor contract was nonetheless justified because the looming disaster of the exhaustion of the workforce posed such a pernicious threat to both economic growth and public order. Lord McCauley, speaking in the House of Commons, argued that the principle of the freedom of contract espoused by *laissez-faire* was unassailable and there could be no purely economic justification for such interference. However, he accepted that intervention was warranted if the social needs of the workers were at grave risk: "the principle of non-interference is one that cannot be applied with great restriction when the public health or the public morality is concerned" (Gray, 1996, 44). Victorian middle class reformers feared that social harmony was threatened by unregulated economic change and the social distress of the workers and insisted that unless the privileged classes were willing to accept such "improvements", the existing order was in danger of being overrun (Briggs, 1968). No matter the peculiar framing of the social problem, there was a broad political and social consensus that state action was paramount and no other possible solution likely to be as efficacious.

As we would expect, class interests and political machinations also played a vital role in the passage of this legislation. Polanyi believed the factory acts owed primarily to the action of "enlightened reactionaries", the landed aristocracy; in this instance, he is utilizing the appellation of "enlightened" as shorthand for the aristocracy's functional commitment to the long term defense of the land (GT, 165). However, what actually underpins their motivations in his analysis is a fusion of material interest and political opportunism.[18] Above all, the gentry feared that the political ascendancy of factory employers "would make the cry for cheap food irresistible, and thus, indirectly threaten to sap rents and tithes" and as a consequence, were motivated to support these measures by a "premonition of threatening pecuniary losses" (GT, 165–6). Landed interests were also acting strategically, for as Polanyi recognized, they reckoned that by engaging in such agitation with the working class, these same groups might be enlisted in their own coalition in defense of the Corn Laws and against free trade (although here it was an alliance between the workers and industrialists that took precedence).

However, there is a curious omission in his analysis in that he is unwilling to argue for the "enlightened" role of the bourgeoisie themselves. Although he mentioned the support that economic liberals offered on behalf of various social protective measures, it is notable that he limits his examples of this phenomena to a handful of cases, none of which could be remotely said to concern the quintessential areas of social protection (such as factory legislation, unemployment insurance and the like) that most directly impinged on manufacturing interests.[19] There is in fact considerable evidence to suggest that some employers within the leading textile sector were in favor of factory legislation and furthermore that this support was predicated on self-interest and intra-class dynamics rather than on any so-called "enlightened" vocation. Larger factory owners, with extensive capital investment in steam-powered machinery and a belief in the productive benefits of an educated and efficient workforce, had every reason to support restrictions on hours and child labor because this put their smaller competitors, who relied on child and sweated labor and thus faced a precipitous rise in labor costs and prices if such legislation was enacted, at a severe competitive disadvantage (Gray, 1996; Swenson, 2002).[20]

Factory reform offered additional economic advantages, for once the working day was shortened, employers had every incentive to increase the pace of production. Marx commented in this vein:

> "there cannot be the slightest doubt that the tendency that urges capital, so soon as a prolongation of the hours of labor is once and for all forbidden, to compensate itself by a systematic heightening of the intensity of labor, and to convert every improvement in machinery into a more perfect means of exhausting the worker, must so on lead to a state of things in which a reduction of the hours of labor will again be inevitable."
>
> (Marx, 1973, 422)

Indeed, in the aftermath of the Factory Acts, there was a noticeable burst of technological innovation in British firms as employers sought new ways to increase the levels of exploitation of their workforce (Berg, 1994).

If he somewhat overlooks the role of capital, Polanyi is particularly dismissive of the contributions of the working class in the passage of the Factory Acts. "The laboring people themselves were hardly a factor" he wrote, "in this great movement of which was, figuratively speaking, to allow them to survive the Middle Passage" (GT, 166). Indeed, he woefully underestimates the impact of working class agitation for reform. Factory legislation was bitterly opposed at every stage by many manufacturing interests and was sustained only by a popular insurgency that was intrinsically connected to a long line of associational, cooperative and trade union agitation against the market (Calhoun, 1982; Somers, 2008).

Polanyi did recognize that the changing fortunes of political alliances were critical in accounting for the enactment of social legislation, even if he did not offer either a rigorous conceptual or empirical account of the conditions under which these coalitional arrangements might coalesce more or less successfully. As noted earlier, one of the factors that he emphasized was the ability of class actors to "win support from outside their own membership" (GT, 152) yet it is not entirely clear from his analysis what the basis was for the English working class's ability to forge strategic partnerships with opposing classes at different periods of time and in pursuit of very different objectives (with landlords for the Factory Acts, employers for the Corn laws). However, this could be surmised as the consequence of a strongly class conscious actor employing a canny "divide and conquer" strategy, playing off one dominant group against the other; on the other, it might be viewed as the result of a weak, politically inept class being co-opted by their dominant coalitional partners.

Notwithstanding this omission, a Polanyian perspective is helpful in accounting for the success of the factory reform movement in uniting a diverse coalition with such competing motivations and interests. The campaign could rely on a concatenation of self-interest arising out of their unique experiences of marketization that was flexible enough to encompass gentry paternalism, working class moral economy, middle class reforming zeal and technological rationalism. It developed an ideological frame that fused moral, material, charitable and social control motives into a coherent whole. It forged a strategic alliance among groups who all saw the movement as a tactical means of achieving other, more important ends, and were willing to cooperate in the immediate term in order to improve their chances of securing their broader ambitions. In hindsight, factory reform seems almost overdetermined but this is a far cry from the structural imperative that lie at the core of the functionalist account highlighted earlier. Indeed, it was precisely because, as Polanyi noted, there were such broad cultural and social interests threatened by industrialization that the movement could depend on widespread material, ideological and political foundations and that this "call upon the state" took on such an irresistible momentum.

It was this broad support system that also gave state elites considerable flexibility and leverage to shape legislation in ways that clearly reflected the deliberate will and intention of political actors. The various pieces of legislation that constituted the factory acts were modified over time in response to both the evolving forms of industrialization and the changing fortunes of countermovement resistance and employer opposition; but at the same time they represented a distinct process of state learning. Various methods of regulation and enforcement were tried, tested and then either abandoned or reformulated after they proved ineffective or because of the intransigence of employers to restrictions on their managerial autonomy. In each case though, it is the conscious action of motivated political actors that drives the reform forward. Overtime, the Factory Acts joined with other pieces of social legislation and bureaucratic initiatives to create an institutional nexus of social protection that exercised a profound influence over social policy for the next century .

Social Protection and Social Change

There is a final theme that demonstrates the abiding importance of social protection to Polanyi's method and conceptual approach. One of his most enduring legacies was his emphasis on the centrality of institutions in the organization of social life: as a way of structuring economic activity, of shaping and constraining individual decision making, of constituting the social and political context for collective action and policy making. Social protection represented not only a set of concrete institutional rules and practices that accomplished these functions but also an organizing principle that was entrenched at the structural level. At the same time, this problematic of social protection was also inseparable from his moral and political concern regarding critical junctures and historical turning points. Although historical alternatives are always possible, the specific institutional design of social protection can very well generate regressive contradictions that circumscribe the range of choice in any particular conjuncture. Yet he equally acknowledged that even the best designed programs can sometimes run up against imposing structural constraints that have roots in social and economic transformations dating back centuries.

An illuminating discussion of these issues occurs in a brief, fascinating excursus in the appendix of the book where Polanyi compares two historical experiences of social protection, the Speenhamland system and the social protection regime established by the socialist government of Vienna from 1918 until 1933, which he experienced first hand (GT, 286–88) (Dale, 2010). The comparison serves to make a series of interrelated points, all of which confirm the salience of the alternative approach sketched earlier. *First*, he accepted that the rationale for implementing social protection varied considerably: "the attempt of Speenhamland to prevent the coming of market economy and the experiment of Vienna trying to transcend such an economy altogether" (GT, 287). *Second*, he understood there were distinct differences in the institutional design of these social protection regimes. In Chapter 2 we alluded to some of the problems that he highlighted regarding the Speenhamland system: faulty jurisdictional boundaries, haphazard eligibility rules, inadequate and indiscriminate financing, and perverse incentives that destroyed worker productivity and undermined the very aims of the program by driving wage levels well below subsistence levels. This is not to say these problems were in any way immutable but rather that solutions depended on a felicitous coincidence of complementary policies that were never forthcoming in the morass of contradictions that constituted the Speenhamland system. Polanyi speculated that the allowance scheme might have been efficacious if workers had been able to form trade unions, thereby producing a positive effect on wages, but the passage of the Anti-Combination Acts in 1799 eliminated this possibility, in the same way that the repeal of the Acts of Settlement in the period opened the door to a national labor market that all but doomed any effort to establish a national minimum wage (GT, 81, 289) (Somers and Block, 2005). The socialist municipality of Vienna, for its part, instituted a publicly funded unemployment insurance scheme, regulated rents and embarked on an ambitious program of public housing construction but its increase in social welfare expenditures were seen as an intolerably high burden on private accumulation, thereby driving liberals and employers into the arms of authoritarian reaction and dooming the experiment and Austrian democracy itself.

Third, Polanyi was acutely aware that these differences in design generated very different "cultural and moral effects". Whereas Speenhamland resulted in the traumatic degradation and cultural devastation of the English working class, the Vienna experience became:

> "one of the most spectacular cultural triumphs of Western history...[it] initiated an equally unexampled moral and intellectual rise in the condition of a highly developed industrial working class which, protected by the Vienna system, withstood the degrading effects of grave economic dislocation and achieved a level never surpassed by the masses of the people in any industrial society."
>
> (GT, 288)

Because of the truncated presentation, it is unclear whether Polanyi attributes this accomplishment to a superior institutional mix of policies, or to the tactical brilliance of its leadership, or to the social and moral capital of its population. But he emphasized that the specific temporal conjuncture set very different limits on what could be accomplished in each period. "The English village, in 1795, had to be sheltered from a dislocation caused by economic progress –a tremendous advance of urban manufactures", wrote Polanyi, "the industrial laboring class of Vienna, in 1918, had to be protected against the effects of economic retrogression, resulting from war, defeat and industrial chaos" (GT, 287).

In many ways, this extraordinary sensitivity to the possibilities of change and the dialectic of hope and despair (the Vienna experiment ended disastrously with the Nazi Anschluss in 1938) is one of the central features of the book and a critical conceptual, if not emotional, backdrop to the politics of social protection. However, it is not merely the immediate conjuncture that attracted his notice but rather the interplay of long term social and economic trends in setting the terrain of human agency and historical possibility, a theme that he returns to time and again in the book. It is not just the institutional design of social protection that encounters historically imposed limits, but also the success or failure of collective action itself. The success of class projects, argued Polanyi, is directly attributable to these wider forces:

> "instead of trying to explain developments that run counter to the general trend of the time by the (unexplained) influence of the reactionary

classes, we prefer to explain the influence of such classes by the fact that they, even though incidentally, stand for developments only seemingly contrary to the general interest of the community."

(GT, 184)

For example, the persistence of the Speenhamland grants, which retarded the rise in rural wages and prevented the dissolution of the traditional village, would not have been possible unless the squires "had assisted the country as a whole to meet the groundswell of the Industrial revolution" (GT, 185).

In his discussion of the Chartist movement, he fascinatingly implies their defeat, just like that of the traditional artisans before them, was directly attributable to the social context in which the struggle occurred and the prevailing direction of economic change. The political demands of the Chartists could only be fulfilled when market society had evolved to a certain point, in other words "only when the awful adjustments had been made":

> "Not before the working class had passed through the Hungry Forties and a docile generation had emerged to reap the benefits of the Golden Age of capitalism; not before an upper layer of skilled workers had developed their unions and parted company with the dark mass of poverty-stricken laborers; not before the workers had acquiesced in the system which the New Poor Law was meant to enforce upon them was their better-paid stratum allowed to participate in the nation's councils."
>
> (GT, 226)

Ellen Meiksins Wood makes a similar point: she argues that the Chartists were essentially a "backward looking movement" because they attempted to surmount the separation of the economic and political at the precise moment when the autonomy of the two spheres was becoming increasingly opaque. This is reminiscent of Calhoun, who as we observed earlier, suggested that "Chartism needs to be seen, in important ways, as an ending as much as a beginning" (Calhoun, 2012, 93). But she also wants to make a larger point, which is echoed in Polanyi's work, that successful reform under capitalism depends on the extent to which a transformative movement can be said to be in or out of synch with the prevailing winds of change. She maintains that the Chartists aptly demonstrate "the dramatic illusion that political strategies will prove inadequate to the fulfillment of their objectives, as well as short lived, to the extent that they are not commensurate in the prevailing social relations" (Wood, 1986, 121). Polanyi implies just this kind of relationship between historical context and successful collective action in the following passage: "Such groups are pushing that which is falling and holding onto that which, under its own steam, is moving their way. It may then seem as if they had originated the process of social change, while actually they were merely its beneficiaries, and may be even perverting the trend to make it serve their own aims" (GT, 28).

This dynamic might apply equally to nations and social institutions, whose fate is inextricably intertwined with the pace and direction of social change. "A nation may be handicapped in its struggle for survival", he wrote, "by the fact that its institutions, or some of them, belong to a type that happens to be on the downgrade – the gold standard in World War II was an instance of such an antiquated outfit. Countries, on the other hand, which, for reasons of their own, are opposed to the *status quo*, would be quick to discover the weaknesses of the existing institutional order and to anticipate the creation of institutions better adapted to their interests" (GT, 28). The quintessential case in point for Polanyi was Germany in the 1930s, where the Nazis achieved state power because of the precipitate collapse of the long-standing international system and then once in control charted a course that destroyed this very system. The process can also work in the opposite direction, where nations and social change are locked in a virtuous circle. Such a situation typified the relationship of the Atlantic sea-boarding nations (England, France, Holland, Portugal and Spain), who were able to capitalize on their fortuitous geographical location to gain great wealth during the Commercial Revolution and (for Holland and England especially) to establish a comparative advantage in the development of capitalist social relations (GT, 28).

Polanyi's musings about the complex relationship between social change, agency and historical fortunes are indeed provocative and no doubt were influenced by his own formative experiences and political engagements during this period (Berman, 2006; Dale, 2016; Polanyi-Levitt, 1990). This problematic of being "on the right side of history" was a key debate within European left politics in the early part of the twentieth century. From Trotsky's dismissive sneer that the Menshevik opposition should return to the "dustbin of history" in the immediate wake of the Bolshevik's insurrection in October 1917 to the hotly contested debates within social democracy about whether this seizure of power was in fact premature, it was an accepted wisdom of the left in this period that the fate of political alternatives was intimately intertwined with the possibilities and constraints imposed by the tide of history. Certainly, his speculation about the various historical detours and blind alleys of the double movement can be seen as a dialogue with these debates.

Yet there is also a critical difference between his approach and his erstwhile left compatriots that should be emphasized. For the prominent Marxists in this period, the discovery of societal laws was unquestionably an essential objective of their intellectual work. In each instance, political activism was inextricably fused with social theory, for this search for universal laws of development within capitalism had but a single aim: to illuminate the breadth of political opportunities for radical social change that these putative laws made possible. Trotsky, as an example, argued that it was precisely the "principle of backwardness" (a feature of his "law of combined and uneven development") which, under a favorable constellation of circumstances (an advanced level of productive forces, a highly organized and militant working class, a fragmented ruling class whose repressive capacity was severely impaired), allowed nations such as Russia to leap historical stages and achieve a revolutionary transition to capitalism that was hitherto denied to their more developed counterparts (Trotsky, 1977[1930]).

It should be stressed that the theoretical development of the double movement was never articulated with such transparent political ambitions. While the double movement is identified as the critical determinant of social change in the long 19th century, it is not at all clear that Polanyi envisaged it as a law-like regularity in history. Nor did he ever privilege any social or political actor as the prime beneficiary of the double movement; given the horrific ordeal society endured as a result of this phenomena, all he could offer was a quiet optimism that somehow a new way forward was emerging that would eliminate the specter of the double movement once and for all from history, a theme we will return to in Chapter 6.

Notes

1 The exception to be noted once again is Fred Block and Margaret Somers: not just in their earlier work (Block and Somers, 1984) but in a series of articles, they accorded considerable attention to the question of social protection (Block and Somers, 2003; Somers and Block, 2005). See also Berman, 2006; Burawoy, 2009; Dale 2010; Webster et al., 2008.

2 Nancy Fraser argues for an additional distinction-between social protection and emancipation. "Whereas social protection is opposed to exposure, emancipation is opposed to domination", she writes, "whereas protection claims to shield society from the disintegrative effects of unregulated markets, emancipation claims to expose oppressive relations within society and economy" (Fraser, 2013, 146). I think this is a telling criticism even if, as I signpost below and throughout the book, I also maintain that Polanyi's vision of the double movement is premised on an emancipatory stance that is not always acknowledged by his critics.

3 This same point had been made previously by R. H. Tawney in *The Agrarian Problem in the Sixteenth Century*: "On the whole one is inclined to regard the Government's intervention in this matter [enclosures] as resembling in its effects the attempts which were made at the same time to fix prices and wages. It retarded, though it could not check altogether, economic changes. It imposed a brake which somewhat eased the shock of sudden movements" (Tawney, 1922, 391).

4 An interesting omission within his analysis is the extent to which market actors themselves can engage in self-regulatory behaviour and forms of market embeddedness (through business associations, informal standard setting, monopolistic practices) in order to promote greater stability within market transactions.

5 In a justly famous paper, Charles Tilly highlighted the "parliamentarization of popular contention" in Britain in the eighteenth and nineteenth centuries (Tilly, 1997). He defines this process as the growing political influence over decisions and resources exercised by parliament and the centrality of Parliamentary struggles for political power within the wider political culture. As a result of this transformation (which was paralleled in other European nations), social movements and popular claim-making were henceforth more overtly directed to the central issues debated in parliament, which meant that the values, resources, and organizational strategies of popular movements were irrevocably shaped by, and indeed presupposed, this

formidable change in the character of the state itself. Tilly's wider conceptual claim is that conventional thinking that regards states and social movements as completely separate entities is flawed: "relations between claimants and objects of claims form not isolated pairs, but whole webs of relationship, the configurations of which (a) vary from one kind of claim to another, and (b) alter systematically as a consequence of interaction between broad structural changes and the course of struggle itself" (Tilly, 1997, 11–12).

6 The complex relationship between embedding/disembedding is also illustrated in the operation of social protection. In certain cases, the governmental institutions responsible for social protection might very well utilize *market* rather than *administrative* techniques to achieve their ends. In the case of the regulation of the international monetary system by central banks, Gallarotti argued than many of these so-called public institutions actually more closely resembled private firms: in the case of the Bank of England, he argues that its public functions of managing the government's accounts were perfectly in keeping with their private dictates as a joint stock company that enjoyed virtually unlimited autonomy from government oversight. "The British state", he wrote, "carried only limited control over and contact with the only viable agent for British monetary hegemony: the Bank of England. Aside from some informal overview functions, the British state had very little to do with the operations of the bank" (Gallarotti, 1995, 8). Indeed, in its protectionist role, the Bank of England employed a myriad of market techniques in order to mitigate the effects of the gold standard.

7 Charles Tilly also stresses this as an enduring feature: "Nineteenth century burghers, intellectuals and powerholders had good cause to worry about social change. They made serious, even desperate efforts, to understand what was happening to them" (Tilly, 1997, 11).

8 Of course, the geographical and territorial limits to this process have long been observed: while social protection was enjoyed by most citizens in Britain, authorities in their imperial outposts, such as Ireland and India, did not feel similarly compelled to offer protection to residents of these nations.

9 This predilection might also be viewed in terms of the enduring influence exercised by Marxism on Polanyi's work (Dale, 2010). G. A. Cohen argued functional explanation played a critical role in classical historical materialism (Cohen, 1978). The following quote from Capital, concerning the relentless dynamic of capitalism, reveals a similar perspective in terms that might have exercised an influence on Polanyi. Marx wrote: "But in its blind and measureless drive, its insatiable appetite for surplus labour, capital oversteps not only the moral but even the merely physical limits of the working day. It usurps the time for growth, development and healthy maintenance of the body. It steals the time required for the consumption of fresh air and sunlight...capital therefore takes no account of the health and the length of life of the worker unless society forces it to do so" (Marx, 1973, 375, 381).

10 This interpretation need not imply that grievances are unimportant or unrelated to group formation; indeed, Doug McAdam and his colleagues emphasize the critical mechanism of "suddenly imposed grievances" that dramatically heighten the political salience of particular concerns and thereby act as a stimulus for collective mobilization (McAdam et al., 2001).

11 There are obvious echoes here to the well-known thesis of Arno Mayer in *The Persistence of the Old Regime* (1978) yet they are actually making very different arguments. Polanyi goes on to maintain that the feudal aristocracy maintained its influence despite the fact that "they had shed the military, judicial, and administrative functions to which they owed their ascendancy (GT, 183). Mayer argues precisely the opposite case: even though their economic influence had waned

considerably, the continued political and social dominance of the aristocracy owed to their traditional influence within the military, judicial and administrative apparatus.

12 And to carry the point even further, there was some evidence as well that the 1897 Act, far from improving workplace safety, led to an even higher incidence of injury, which certainly contests the functional claim of Polanyi that social protection is promulgated in order to safeguard workers from the evils of the free market (Lester, 2001).

13 Charles Tilly admits that the historiography of popular protest "has not established that popular mobilization made a great difference to the courses or outcomes of these crises" (Tilly, 1997, 23–4). He argues that protest impacted in five principal ways: it compelled political elites to agree to bargain in the first place; altered the composition of political coalitions; led to realignments among elites; effected significant changes in the state's repressive apparatus; and transformed national patterns of political power). None of these factors are pursued in any rigorous fashion in Polanyi's analysis.

14 I need to be clear that what I am detailing in this section is what I believe to be Polanyi's strongest argument (as laid out in the text) about the roots of social protection but I am not at the same time stipulating that this argument represents a sufficient account of this process. As an example, Viviana Zelizer, in her study of the implementation of legislation protecting against child labor, emphasizes a cultural dynamic that created a new definition of children. As she notes, even the most energetic proponents of child labor laws were unwilling to outlaw all forms of child labor (child acting, working for family businesses, newspaper delivery). It was wider transformations in family life and in cultural attitudes about children and women, alongside the range of factors implicated in a Polanyian account, that produced the momentum for social protection (Zelizer, 2007).

15 However, what is not really dealt with in Polanyi's discussion is the extent to which these historically shifting class coalitions (as a result of the shifting class structures conditioned by specific patterns of marketization) can be said to exert a decisive influence on long term political trajectories (Halperin, 2004). In Barrington Moore's classic work *Social Origins of Dictatorship and Democracy*, class relations – in particular, the relationship between the commercial and landed classes, and the landed elites and peasantry – are the critical explanatory variable in accounting for the way in which nations organized political power in the modern world. In certain historical conditions, dominant class coalitions were overturned by revolution, which paved the way for either a gradual transition to democracy or the ascendancy of communist dictatorships (France versus Russia and China); in other countries (Germany and Japan), repressive dominant coalitions held onto power thereby providing a fertile soil for the growth of fascism (Moore, 1967). While Polanyi appreciated the importance of this constellation of class dynamics to the rise of fascism, he did not trace this in any comparative fashion. Nor did he specifically link transformations in the global political economy (particularly shifts in comparative advantage and trade flows) to the evolution of political coalitions and alignments, a curious omission which we will return to in the next chapter.

16 This of course has been one of the critical motifs of the comparative welfare state literature. The specific character of social protection will have profound consequences for institutional development and social relations: residual benefits which limit social protection to specific affected groups are typically meaner and reinforce wider patterns of social stratification and inequality than universal benefits which are available to all citizens and tend to promote greater solidarity and social consensus .

17 This insight was taken up by many writers in the welfare state literature who insisted that there might be a particular institutional design of the welfare state that could achieve a virtuous circle whereby groups that received benefits were empowered in ways that encouraged them to lobby even more forcefully for the welfare state that provided them (Esping Andersen, 1990).

18 This is very close to the analysis of Marx: see Elster, 1986 for an incisive reconstruction of Marx's argument.

19 The exception to this is his recognition of elite support for monetary protectionism. Polanyi writes: "It is important to realize that the ruling classes themselves lent their support to the management of the currency through the central bank. Such management was not, of course, regarded as an interference with the institution of the gold standard; on the contrary, it was part of the rules of the game under which the gold standard was supposed to function" (GT, 197).

20 Even so, manufacturing support for factory reform was anything but monolithic. It varied by the size of establishment, by location, by sector of industry, and even employers with identical economic profiles, might still exhibit very different attitudes to reform. Nor were political and economic aspirations so easily reconciled, for every employer had to choose between their (political) interest in preserving their managerial authority as opposed to their (economic) interest in undercutting their competitors (Gray, 1996). The reciprocal effect of factory legislation on capitalist interest formation and class solidarity should be highlighted as well. "One effect of the prolonged struggle over factory reform", commented Robertt Gray, "may, indeed, have been the creation of a more coherent 'manufacturing interest'" (Gray, 1996, 160). John Bowman made a similar point about the way in which struggles by coal workers unintentionally strengthened the organization of mine owners (Bowman, 1988).

Chapter 5

Contradictions and Crisis in the Double Movement

Once social protection became a critical requirement for the reproduction of civilization, a profound paradox was revealed that few at the time appreciated. "Inevitably, society took measures to protect itself", wrote Polanyi:

> "but whatever measures it took impaired the self-regulation of the market, disorganized industrial life, and thus endangered society in yet another way. It was this dilemma which forced the development of the market system into a definite groove and finally disrupted the social organization based upon it."
>
> (GT, 3–4)

His momentous task was to explain the unparalleled collapse of the entire global liberal order: "Nineteenth century civilization…disintegrated as the result of…the measures which society adopted in order not to be, in its turn, annihilated by the action of the self-regulating market (GT, 249). This precipitous demise began with the cataclysmic implosion of World War 1 and culminated in the ghastly triumph of Nazism in Germany in the 1930s. By any reasonable test of the historical imagination, these two events proved to be the decisive moments ("the origins of our times", which was the subtitle of the original edition) of the twentieth century, doing more to damage the foundations of Western civilization than any comparable development (Katznelson, 2003). What proved to be Polanyi's boldest stroke, and the animating focus of *The Great Transformation*, was his claim that both events could be traced to a single cause: the contradictory, crisis ridden evolution of the double movement.

To investigate the causes of Nazi Germany, Polanyi insisted, there was no choice but to return to the original scene of the crime, 19th-century England, and the birth of the self-regulating market. "For the origins of the cataclysm", he wrote, "we must turn to the rise and fall of market economy. In order to comprehend German fascism, we must revert to Ricardian England" (GT, 30). As we have previously seen, he argued that the establishment of a market economy and development of a market society generated such harmful effects

DOI: 10.4324/9781003133186-5

that a system of social protection was everywhere inaugurated to safeguard society. However, "it was in this attempt to stave off the entirely new dangers of the market mechanism that protective action conflicted fatally with the self-regulation of the system" (GT, 83). In essence, Polanyi is returning to the central dilemma of contestation *within* the double movement system itself: once it becomes internationalized, the entire world became subject to its dictates.

As I discuss in this chapter, Polanyi insisted that this clash of social principles within the double movement generated three primary contradictions: the *first* was the deleterious effect that social protection had on the system of private accumulation and profit-making and thus the vitality of the economy; the *second* resulted from the unintentional consequences of purposive action within the international system that undermined its effectiveness; the *third* was the social and political upheaval that arose from the mutual incompatibility of the core elements of the double movement. Once both market relations and social protection became internationalized after 1870 – truly the first era of globalization – he argued that the entire world became locked in the fatal embrace of the double movement that operated as a hidden "gear of social change" (GT, 237). The specific pathways that nations took to escape from the depths of economic and political crisis were, in the end, set by the dynamics of the double movement. "The conflict between the market and the elementary requirements of an organized social life", wrote Polanyi, "provided the century with its dynamics and produced the typical strains and stresses which ultimately destroyed that society" (GT, 249).[1] Both *World War I* –"the dissolution of the system of world economy which had been in progress since 1900 was responsible for the political tension that exploded in 1914" – and the *rise of fascism* – "in reality, the part played by fascism was determined by one factor: the condition of the market system" – could be traced to the "swift, silent current" of the contradictory course of the double movement over the course of the long 19th century (GT, 21; 217; 5).

One can genuinely applaud the breathtaking audacity of his historical and conceptual reach, his unerring instinct for the single, animating factor amid such a bewildering flood of temporality, and his insistence that establishing the proper causes of these events was essential to an understanding of the trajectory of modern society. Yet it is equally clear that such an imaginative leap imposes a heavy burden, conceptually and empirically, on any writer who has the extraordinary *chutzpah* to stake out such a claim. Polanyi created a causal edifice that, like every structure, is utterly dependent on the strength and reliability of each of its constituent parts. In order to prove an elective affinity between the double movement and historical change, he had to effectively demonstrate the following propositions: the double movement actually constituted a coherent international system that influenced the course of all nations; the clash between the component features of the double movement generated substantial tensions that seriously impaired the functioning of capitalism and the international system (albeit in different ways in different countries); over time, and in an explicable process, these contradictions accumulated and precipitated a widespread political and social crisis; this crisis owed primarily (although not necessarily exclusively) to the trajectory of the double movement; and therefore we can trace the fate of individual nations in this conjuncture by examining how they were differentially situated within the international system and double movement. Indeed, it is hardly an overstatement to say that the entire thrust of *The Great Transformation* is dedicated to proving the veracity of this causal chain and that the validity of the double movement as a conceptual and historical force rests on Polanyi's ability to support each of these contentions.

It is perhaps wise to reveal my punch line at the outset. As I discuss more fully throughout the chapter, notwithstanding this original contribution to the question of institutional change within capitalism, I am not persuaded that Polanyi adequately demonstrates all of these causal links: that all nations are equally embedded within the double movement system or that their fate in this epoch can be traced to their divergent roles within this system; that the contradictions of the double movement regime were the primary cause of the cataclysm of the Great War; or that his structural perspective offers a sufficient explanation for the distinct political pathways chosen in the interwar years. Despite these reservations, I readily acknowledge that his argument about the double movement and historical change constitutes an impressive accomplishment and, indeed, a *tour de force* of exposition that has few corollaries in the contemporary social sciences. As such, his audacious approach demands careful scrutiny and exploration.

The centrality of the contested oscillation within the double movement and its link to social change has rarely been acknowledged as an essential thread of his argument even if a number of scholars recently have attempted to extend and deepen his account (Dale, 2010; Fraser, 2013; Lacher, 2019; Streeck, 2016). The dynamic of contradiction and crisis in the double movement is an area where it can be argued that Polanyi was attempting to articulate an alternative to the Marxist tradition, and furthermore, where the opportunity of developing a distinct Polanyian conceptual framework of social change explicable across historical periods is most advanced.

The contradictions of the double movement and the fifty year crisis of the "long nineteenth century" (Arrighi, 1994)/"short twentieth century" (Hobsbawm, 1994) represent the logical culmination of his analysis of the double movement, and its central importance to his framework certainly warrants a comprehensive inquiry, which is my task in this chapter. I begin first with a discussion of the internationalization of the double movement: I explore the contours of the new international order, its qualitatively new social relations, the spread of social protection and the symbiotic relationship of the double movement to imperialism, and the wider causal links inherent within this institutional matrix. In the second section, I examine his notion of contradiction, with careful attention devoted to how contradictions engendered by the double movement emerge and their relationship to social change and crisis. In the third section, I offer a forensic examination of Polanyi's argument regarding the fundamental causal relationship between the double movement and the dramatic events of this epoch.

Internationalizing the Double Movement

In order for the double movement to play its formative historical role, Polanyi's first task was to convincingly demonstrate that it represented an institutional pattern to which all nations were subject. In other words, the double movement constituted an international system, with both *laissez-faire* and social protection spreading beyond their original English roots. He argued in this vein that 19th-century civilization rested on four institutions, incorporating a distinct spatial level (national/international) and cutting across both economic and political arenas: in the economic realm, there was the *self-regulating market* (national) and the *gold standard/free trade* (international); in the political realm, the *liberal state* (national) and the *balance of power* (international) (GT, 3). Henceforth, this institutional system constituted "the axis of the material existence of the human race" (GT, 18, 217).

Polanyi insisted the system functioned as a distinct social and political totality, with interlocking practices, rules of reproduction, and institutional processes that constrained and enabled social action. "The utopian springs of the dogma of *laissez faire* are but incompletely understood as long as they are viewed separately", claimed Polanyi.

> "The three tenets – competitive labor market, automatic gold standard, and international free trade - formed one whole. The sacrifices involved in achieving any one of them were useless, if not worse, unless the other two were equally secured. It was everything or nothing ...The expansion of the market system in the nineteenth century was synonymous with the simultaneous spreading of international free trade, competitive labor market, and gold standard; they belonged together."
>
> (GT, 138–9)

In this section, I review the specific components of the international market system and explore the new social relations that were inaugurated; discuss the internationalization of social protection and how this operated in the Polanyi schema as a process of imperialism; and finally, investigate the extent to which this new institutional matrix set the terrain for the fate of nations over the course of the 19th century.

The contours of the 19th-century system

If we begin with the constituent elements of the international system, the national component of the free market system, the *self-regulating market,* has been amply delineated in regard to England in previous chapters yet it must be openly stated that Polanyi makes only a perfunctory effort to demonstrate that the self-regulating system was similarly established in other nations. By the first quarter of the 19th century, there was no question that European economic development was indeed progressing along capitalist lines. The core nations of inner Europe (France, Germany, Netherlands, Belgium) had experienced proto-industrialization from the mid-18th century (with extensive craft industries organized along traditional workshop lines) and several regions (Alsace, Ruhr Valley, Rhineland, Saxony), in the first throes of capitalist industrialization, had full-fledged labor markets, capitalist agriculture, networks of entrepreneurs, and a sophisticated transport infrastructure underpinning emerging national markets (Pollard, 1981). Polanyi sketches the various historical stages of the commodification of land in Europe and offers an abbreviated synopsis of some of the key factors (industrialization, urbanization, the French Revolution, state legislation and regulation, expansion of surplus production to colonies) driving the process forward (GT, 179–81). But it should be noted that he makes no attempt to systematically explore the extent to which the onset of European industrialization and adoption of the self-regulating market owed to the same combination of factors (social, political, technological and ideological) as in England.

Polanyi acknowledged the massive "economic earthquake" of proletarianization, commercialization and proto-industrialization that irrevocably transformed the rural landscape of Europe throughout the entire 19th century. This development is an important predicate to his schema, as evidenced by his references to the "agrarian plight" and "all-round dislocation" that stimulated protective measures across Europe, even if he in no way discusses the elimination of traditional cultures of solidarity across the continent with the same attention to detail that he devoted to the case of Speenhamland. Once all the leading nations of Europe had embarked on the capitalist road, he insisted upon the decisive importance of the double movement in future development. "[T]he further expansion of the market economy took place under utterly new conditions", he wrote. "These conditions themselves were set by the 'double movement'" (GT, 214). The development of capitalist property relations, expansion of trade, adoption of the gold standard, and the like created the international system that henceforth acted as the stimulus for all other nations. "The change came suddenly", he wrote, "and this time simultaneously in all leading Western countries. While Germany repeated England's domestic development only after a lag of half a century, external events of world scope necessarily affect all trading countries alike" (GT 213).

Although he makes a passing reference to France and Prussia in this regard – "each of them passed through a period of free trade and *laissez faire* (GT, 147) – Polanyi offers no sustained evidence to demonstrate that they or other nations adopted the self-regulating system; in other words, that they had fully commodified the key factors of land, labor and money, established a competitive national market before the early 1870s when the international system is thought to have been inaugurated, and transplanted this framework to their international affairs via support for free trade policies. Indeed, there is ample evidence that suggests commodification was not far advanced in several European powers (Russia and Austria-Hungary in particular) nor was free trade ever as central to continental economic policy as in Britain (Mann, 1993). This is a curious omission given the paramount importance that he attributes to the self-regulating market:

> "It implies no less than that the balance of power, the gold standard, and the liberal state, those fundamentals of the evolution of the nineteenth century, were in the last resort, all shaped by one common matrix, the self-regulating market."
>
> (GT, 29–30)

Right from the outset, the potential danger to Polanyi's framework has to be acknowledged: unless he can persuasively demonstrate that all nations are embedded in the self-regulating system, then their subsequent adoption of social protection and the generation of contradictions – the next stages in the chain - risks becoming completely attenuated from the double movement itself. Furthermore, as highlighted in the previous chapter, the distinct dynamics of marketization in each nation would likely generate very different class formation and political coalitions, with unique consequences for the vitality of the liberal democratic regimes and hence for political crisis and upheaval (Moore, 1966; Luebbert, 1991).

The domestic political counterpart, the *liberal state*, encounters similar difficulties of exposition. In the first place, Polanyi nowhere offers a comprehensive definition of this component and it is not immediately apparent what purpose or function the liberal state represents in his system. His discussion implies a notion of the liberal state that is coterminous with liberal democracy, including protection from arbitrary authority of the state, parliamentary sovereignty, civil liberties and democratic institutions, which is dominated by a distinct set of class interests led by the bourgeoisie (GT, 185). However, frequent references to the state's safeguarding of market institutions and practices also suggests the term is equivalent to a minimalist state that imposes minor constraints on the private exercise of property rights and implicitly fosters and is guided by a belief in liberal ideology (GT, 136). He claims a direct correlation between the liberal state and the self-regulating market – "the liberal state was itself a creation of the self-regulating market"

(GT, 3) – but even for the case of England, this link is somewhat problematic, although much depends on one's definition and the impreciseness here gives ample leeway to posit such a relationship. While many of the constitutional and democratic characteristics of the British state predated the crucial 1834 conjuncture, the narrower interpretation of the liberal state as a non-interventionist regime gained greater force after the establishment of the self-regulating market as highlighted in Chapter 3.

Polanyi appears to rely quite heavily on the British case in constructing his ideal type. By 1860 the institutional separation of the economic and political spheres was well advanced in Britain. The British state, while safeguarding considerable political and civil freedoms, played a smaller role in the economy and society than in any other industrial society: it had far less day-to-day responsibility for management of the economy (even if state regulation, as noted earlier, was essential to guarantee self-regulation); it had abolished most tariffs; it had only tangential involvement in industrial relations; its welfare administration relied heavily on local discretion rather than centralized control (Woods, 2002). But it is certainly questionable how many of the other major European governments of the period fit this profile of the "liberal state" and Polanyi makes no effort to demonstrate that all nations followed this blueprint. Certainly, many nations (such as Germany, Russia and Austria-Hungary) featured authoritarian executive power, large scale civil administrations, substantial governmental involvement in economic affairs, weak legacies of democratic freedoms or constitutionalism, and the pre-eminence of aristocratic elements (Mann, 1993).[2] And as Arno Mayer masterfully detailed, the landed aristocratic elites still constituted the vast majority of cabinet seats, military officials, diplomats, and state bureaucrats across the states of Europe (Mayer, 1978).

The political component at the international level, the *balance-of-power*, was treated at some length at the end of Chapter 3, although there is an additional issue to address at this juncture. Earlier, I emphasized his argument that the balance of power, which in previous epochs had consisted of perpetual warfare, had in the 19th century produced a 100 years peace in large part because of the material instrumentality of *haute finance*, which substituted for the absence of a liberal international order with multilateral rules and institutions and collective problem solving. But there was also a more traditional political reading of this unprecedented peace that Polanyi entertained. Discussing the situation in the 1890s when *haute finance* was still in the ascendancy, he suggested another critical factor: "British and French interests differed in Africa; the British and the Russians were competing with one another in Asia…in spite of the Triple Alliance, there were still more than two independent powers to watch over one another jealously" (GT, 19). The implication is that the *strategic* elements of the balance of power system were instrumental: in classic fashion, so long as there was a third power that could align with one of the other parties, thereby ensuring that no single nation could ever impose its will unilaterally, this balancing act could survive (GT, 6). Indeed, a short while later, he concludes that it was precisely the disintegration of Europe into two hostile alliances that precipitated the collapse of the old balance of power order. Yet it is not immediately clear from his analysis how these tactical machinations relate to *haute finance*, which is essential in order to untangle the causal threads leading to the dissolution of peace. Were particular strategies within the alliance game enhanced or constrained by the pre-eminence of international finance? Can peace be achieved if only one of the two critical foundations is present or were both required to prevent the balance of power system from regressing back to its militarist roots? As we shall see, it is not entirely clear how the dynamics of this reconfigured power system were shaped by the processes of the double movement in such a fashion that war became inevitable.

Finally, we come to the economic factor at the international level, the *gold standard*, which receives the most sustained exposition in his schema. The gold standard, he argued, was "the accepted name for a system of international commodity money" (GT, 193) and represented the scaling up of the self-regulating market to the global plane. It created an international monetary system that promoted high capital mobility and underpinned the expansion of trade around the globe by enabling states with different currencies to freely exchange goods and services with each other.[3] Under the international gold standard, the value of a national currency was pegged to the price of gold; this established a fixed rate of exchange between gold and the currency, and consequently between their currency and all other gold standard currencies, which allowed any currency in the world to be freely exchanged with another. The value of national currencies:

> "derived from the certainty that their possession provided us with the means of possessing ourselves at any time of the commodity itself, gold. It followed that the national character of currencies was of no consequence, since they were but different tokens representing the same commodity."
>
> (GT, 196)

At the same time, the gold standard, which was adopted by most advanced nations by the 1870s, had an intrinsic relationship to trade and the balance of payments. Should a country run a persistent trade deficit, thereby devaluing its currency, gold would flow out of a country's reserves to pay off the overseas accounts and the domestic money supply would automatically contract, thereby lowering the level of economic activity; over time, this would drive domestic prices and wages down relative to world prices, thus increasing exports and reducing imports which would bring trade back into balance, thereby raising the value of the currency (GT, 193–5). Each country's paramount economic objective was to ensure gold convertibility, which mandated sound public financing and balanced budgets, and at the time there were no competing social or economic objectives (such as full employment) that could possibly challenge this staunch commitment (Eichengreen, 1992).

Several features of the gold standard are worth noting. This adjustment process was assumed by many to work automatically in a self-correcting manner – the balance of payments equilibrium rested on an involuntary adjustment of gold movements and currency prices – yet Polanyi argued this was a useful fiction. "To liberal economists the gold standard was a purely economic institution", he insisted, "they refused even to consider it as part of a social mechanism" (GT, 20). The gold standard could function only with the indispensable assistance of central banks and the government's unbreakable commitment to guaranteed convertibility and liquidity (GT, 137–8, 195–7). Although he insisted the gold standard led inexorably to deflationary policies and the wholesale disruption of "productive organization" (GT, 194), other writers have stressed the positive macro-economic effects of the gold standard for exchange rate and price stability that had beneficial impacts on domestic industry and international trade (Eichengreen, 1996; Frieden, 1992; Gallarotti, 1995). We will return to this question later in the chapter for these contrasting explanations would lead us to draw very different inferences about the supposed correlation between the crisis of the international system and the onset of war in 1914.

The Capitalist International and the State

The social relations of this new international system are worth delineating in greater detail. Polanyi insisted that this system enjoyed a "relative autonomy" from other spheres of influence and became "safeguarded by a type of sovereignty more jealous and absolute than anything known before" (GT, 202, 211). Indeed, in this new world, even national sovereignty itself seemed "an outcrop of parochial thinking":

> "With the international gold standard the most ambitious market scheme of all was put into effect, implying absolute independence of markets from national authorities. World trade now meant organization of life on the planet under a self-regulating market, comprising labor, land and money, with the gold standard as the guardian of this gargantuan automaton. Nations and peoples were mere puppets in a show utterly beyond their control."
>
> (GT, 203; 217)

Despite this epigram for disembedding, Polanyi was under no illusion that market relations could ever be purely autonomous, but rather were constituted by cross-cutting political and social forces. At the international level, political and economic power were completely interpenetrated: political power was necessary to first establish this international order and it derived considerable influence from the expansion of these relations as political prerogatives were now transmitted via the international market system.

Indeed, political supremacy was unquestionably linked to the dynamics of this new international order. Britain's fortuitous position as the world's first industrial power, as an example, was the foundation of its exceptional preeminence in the world political economy. It utilized its political power to facilitate commercial supremacy and this superiority in turn magnified its political domination. Eric Hobsbawm eloquently depicted the paramount role of Britain in the early 19th-century global economy:

> "An entire world economy was thus built on, or rather around, Britain, and this country therefore temporarily rose to a position of global influence and power unparalleled by any state of its relative size before or since…There was a moment in the world's history when Britain can be described, if we are not too pedantic, as its only workshop, its only massive importer and exporter, its only carrier, its only imperialist, almost its only investor; and for that reason its only naval power and the only one which had a genuine world policy. Much of this monopoly was simply due to the loneliness of the pioneer, monarch of all he surveys because of the absence of other surveyors."
>
> (Hobsbawm, 1990, 13)

Britain enjoyed disproportionate benefits from its participation in the world economy: it served as the primary clearinghouse for world finance and trade, sterling was the main international currency used in foreign trade and by governments for their foreign exchange reserves, and it dominated transport and energy distribution. Indeed, it was this unchallenged supremacy that gave it the leeway to promote the expansion of the world economy in ways that intentionally constrained its own autonomy. It condoned the transfer of advanced technology knowing full well that its rivals would be able to capitalize on their much lower wages to make spectacular productivity gains out of these new techniques; and it unilaterally opened up its domestic market via free trade even though its rivals conspicuously failed to return the favor at the cost of a spiraling trade deficit with its European neighbors (Pollard, 1981, 183–4). No doubt, Britain's colonial empire helped cushion the blow of these sacrifices but British economic and political elites were convinced the nation's prosperity was entirely intertwined with this leading role in the global economy.

Polanyi certainly appreciated this historically unprecedented role (GT, 14, 252). In a particularly revealing quote, he wrote:

> "International free trade involved no less an act of faith. Its implications were entirely extravagant. It meant that England would depend for her food supply upon overseas sources; would sacrifice her agriculture, if necessary, and enter on a new form of life under which she would be part

> and parcel of some vaguely conceived world unity of the future…and that the English nation would face the prospects of continuous industrial dislocations in the firm belief in its superior inventive and productive ability. However, it was believed that if only the grain of all the world could flow freely to Britain, then her factories would be able to undersell all the world. Again, the measure of the determination needed was set by the magnitude of the proposition and the vastness of the risks involved in complete acceptance."
>
> (GT, 138; see also 214)

Because interdependence represented such an audacious leap into the unknown, the only manner whereby this profound psychological barrier could be transcended was through the healing powers of liberal ideology. "No wonder that economic liberalism turned into a secular religion", he commented, "once the great perils of the venture were evident" (GT, 139).

Polanyi intimates the unprecedented development whereby state power could now be expanded not just by traditional political means rooted in national based sovereignty (military conquest and direct rule) but via the non-territorial material networks of the global economy (Gallagher and Robinson, 1953; Rosenberg, 2001). "We may safely neglect at this stage the distinction between political and economic power", he wrote:

> "between economic and political purposes on the part of governments; in effect, it was the characteristic of nation-states in this period that such a distinction had but little reality, for whatever their aims, the governments strove to achieve them through the use and increase of national power… The Pax Britannica held its sway sometimes by the ominous poise of heavy ship's cannon, but more frequently it prevailed by the timely pull of a thread in the international monetary network."
>
> (GT, 11, 14)

British political dominance was now transmitted by the informal networks of the international political economy and through the invisible threads of finance and exchange from which power was now derived.

Indeed, as we shall detail further in later sections, the dynamics of 19th-century internationalization greatly enhanced rather than reduced the centrality of the nation state within the global economy (Block, 2003; Somers and Block, 2021). "The constitutive importance of the currency in establishing the nation as the decisive economic and political unit of the time", he argued:

> "was as thoroughly overlooked by the writers of the liberal Enlightenment as the existence of history had been by their eighteenth century predecessors…while in imagination the nineteenth century was engaged

> in constructing the liberal utopia on a global scale, in reality it was delegating management of its affairs to national institutions, notably governments and central banks."
>
> (GT, 203)

Internationalization went hand in hand with political intervention: governments struggled mightily to mitigate the effects of the international economy and to equip their nations with the necessary prerequisites for success, and in so doing, transmitted the imperatives of domestic politics back into the international realm (GT, 215). States therefore became critical zones of contestation within the double movement: helping to constitute and sustain the international market regime, mediating the fluctuating effects of the market, and serving as a battleground for social forces attempting to shift the costs of participation in the double movement onto less powerful individuals, groups and nations.

Social protection and imperialism

In the wake of the creation of an international market system, social protection also became a ubiquitous feature of social life. Polanyi maintained the expansion of the international market system was unthinkable without the presence of protectionist institutions. Once again, he makes this symbiotic relationship apparent in several places in the text (GT, 198, 204–6, 214, 216–17):

> "The international gold standard could not be borne by the nations whom it was supposed to serve, unless they were secured against the dangers with which it threatened the communities adhering to it…These conditions themselves were set by the 'double movement'. The pattern of international trade which was now spreading at an accelerated rate was crossed by the introduction of protectionist institutions designed to check the all-round action of the market…From now onward the typical institutions of market economy could usually be introduced only if accompanied by protectionist measures…The supreme vehicle of the expansion of market economy, the gold standard, was thus usually accompanied by the simultaneous introduction of the typical protectionist policies of the age such as social legislation and customs tariffs."
>
> (GT, 198, 214)

Polanyi insisted all nations, regardless of specific national contexts, adopted welfare protection to redress marketization, central banking systems to mitigate the harsh effects of the gold standard, and tariffs to provide relief from the disruptive consequences of both the international monetary system and free trade (with the exception of Great Britain which largely remained a free trade regime until the war) (GT, 217). The inauguration of social protection was by no means antithetical to the continued diffusion of market relations for, as we shall see, one of the hallmarks of the so-called "protectionist" era was the uninterrupted expansion of trade and finance across the corners of the globe (GT, 204).

There are a number of points to highlight regarding this putative relationship. Although trade restrictions were indeed widespread, it is equally true that there was considerable variation in the extent to which nations utilized tariff controls, a point that Polanyi does not really elaborate at great length which impacts on his ability to draw a close correlation between these protective policies and subsequent policy responses to future crises (Eichengreen and Irwin, 2010). Nor did he investigate whether the timing and sequencing of social protection measures might owe to additional causal factors beyond the double movement. Certainly, the convulsive disruptions created by the Great Depression of 1873–86 played a role in stimulating tariff protection as did the growing militarization of states, whereby tariffs were viewed as an effective means of raising revenues to finance imperialist ambitions. John Hobson argues that a sufficient explanation of the shift to a protectionist regime must be explicitly multi-causal: "States raised tariffs partly as a response to developments within the state system, partly as a response to the needs of various economic groups, and partly as a response to the specific political, social and fiscal interests of the state" (Hobson, 1997, 11).

While there was some minimal international coordination and cooperation underpinning the international monetary system (Eichengreen, 1996) – for example, informal cooperation (aided by close social ties and ideological affinities) existed among national central bankers, which allowed them to harmonize various monetary policies – it should be emphasized that the "internationalization" of social protection in the Polanyi framework is simply an additive process of the adoption of national policies of social protection by all the advanced nations. While these measures might have shared similar objectives and elements, no multilateral and transnational structure of political cooperation existed; both the specific agencies and objects of social protection remained essentially nationally bounded in this time period (GT, 202–3). Indeed, as discussed more thoroughly below, it was the very absence of transnational cooperation that contributed to the demise of the double movement system (Evans, 2008).

What is fascinating is how Polanyi locates the internationalization of social protection within the overarching problematic of imperialism. As Fred Block and Margaret Somers astutely note: "In Polanyi's view, imperialism is the internationalist protectionist institution *par excellence*, in both its attempt to combat market strains and in its destructive impact" (Block and Somers, 1984, 60). The question of imperialism therefore became an integral motif of his framework of the double movement. Although he never specifically offered a definition of imperialism, his basic notion closely mirrors the conventional view that envisages it as the intentional use of state power for the promotion and attainment of private gain and profit. He characterizes imperialist intervention as the extraction of wealth and resources from foreign lands and the acquisition of overseas markets through brute military force and political coercion (GT, 207, 213–14). "Economic imperialism was mainly a struggle between the Powers for the privilege of extending their trade into politically unprotected markets", he wrote. "Governments lent support to their nationals engaged in business in backward countries. Trade and the flag were racing in one another's wake" (GT, 217). Imperialism constituted a structure of hierarchical power relations premised on domination and subordination that stood in stark contrast to the mutual exchanges among advanced nations that were the hallmark of economic interdependence. Its dire consequences – "unspeakable suffering", dependence, destruction of indigenous industries and economic development – reflected this unequal relationship.

His primary focus was to insist that the onset of imperialist strategies, which represented a clear historical break, was in fact sparked by the evolution of the double movement. In the earlier free market "anti-imperialist" phase (from 1780 until 1880), the "separation of politics and economics now spread into international affairs" and government policy intentionally "precluded the influence of private business interests on the conduct of foreign affairs" (GT, 213, 265). "Not only at home but also abroad", Polanyi commented in reference to British policy:

> "the principle of non-intervention of the state in the affairs of private business was maintained. The home government was not supposed to intervene in private trade, nor were foreign offices expected to regard private interests abroad otherwise than on broad national lines."
>
> (GT, 213)

The new bourgeoisie, united by their fierce attachment to free trade, were equally antagonistic to imperialist adventures and reckoned far flung colonies were a "political and financial liability" (GT, 212). "Anybody who talked colonies in the century between 1780 and 1880", he wrote, "was looked upon as an adherent of the *ancien regime.* The middle class denounced war as dynastic machinations and pandered to pacifism..." (GT, 212). It is only after 1880, and the onset of the protectionist era, that imperialism supposedly flourished and became a leading principle of the political strategies of the advanced nations.[4]

His explanation of this shift reveals the divergent ways in which he conceptualized imperialism as a response to separate moments within the double movement (GT, 213). In the first place, Polanyi explains the shift to imperialism as a function of the shifting dynamics of trade within the international economy that precipitated a transformation in state policies. "We submit that this change was due to the character of trade", he wrote:

> "which, under nineteenth century conditions, was no longer dependent for its scope and success upon direct power policy; and that the gradual

> return to business influence on foreign policy was due to the fact that international currency and credit system had created a new type of business interest transcending national frontiers."
>
> (GT, 265)

In the earlier anti-imperialist phase, there had been little direct investment abroad with the notable exception of speculative lending by financial capital (used mostly to finance government bonds or to invest in stock portfolios) but even this practice was deemed to be a matter of private not public concern. "No government thought it as worthy of support, "said Polanyi, "if its nationals engaged in the most risky job of loaning money to overseas governments of doubtful repute" (GT, 265).

The revival of imperialist policies was also the outcome of the changing composition of foreign trade, with a rapidly growing component given over to "non-speculative" investment (i.e. manufacturing exports and direct investment). As trade expanded and became more bilateral, this increase in interdependency led to the active promotion and protection of national economic interests abroad and greater meddling in the affairs of other governments. Because nations now conceived themselves as distinct entities in competition with other nation states, their economic interests presupposed an ongoing effort to manipulate markets in their own favor. Polanyi posits an indissoluble correlation between this rising tide of nationalism and capitalist internationalization: "Liberal nationalism was developing into national liberalism with its marked leanings toward protectionism and imperialism abroad, monopolistic conservatism at home…In truth, the new nationalism was the corollary of the new internationalism" (GT, 198).

Lastly, he attributes the transition to imperialism to the malign influence of the double movement, specifically the unintentional consequences that occurred from the rise of tariff protection erected across the advanced economies to mitigate the destabilizing forces of global competition. "The import tariffs of one country hampered the exports of another", he wrote, "and forced it to seek for markets in politically unprotected areas" (GT, 217). This precipitated a "scramble for foreign markets, colonies, zones of influence, and other forms of imperialist rivalry", which led to the intensification of political rivalry, rising militarization and a grievous weakening of the peace impulse that paved the ground for World War 1 (GT, 211). The unfettered access to colonial markets and resources also helped shield the imperial powers from the destabilizing outflows of the gold standard.

What stands out in his abbreviated analysis of the relationship between the double movement and imperialism is the fetish for periodization that marred some of his earlier analysis; indeed, his assertion of a definitive break between imperialism and anti-imperialism encounters difficulties of both an empirical and conceptual nature. In a passage that is indicative of the ambiguity of his formulation, Polanyi identifies what he believes is the critical dynamic:

> "herein we hold the key to the seeming paradox of imperialism-the economically inexplicable and therefore allegedly irrational refusal of countries to trade together indiscriminately, and their aiming instead at the acquisition of overseas and exotic markets. What made countries act in this manner was simply the fear of consequences similar to those which the powerless peoples were unable to avert."
>
> (GT, 214)

The implication of a zero-sum trade-off, where nations either freely traded with each other or else engaged in imperialist behavior, seems to be challenged by 19th-century developments. Even during the height of the protectionist era, nations increased their trade with each other: exports as a percentage of overall gross national product within the advanced industrial nations reached 9.4% in 1860, 10.9% in 1870, 12.5% in 1880, 12.6% in 1890 and finally leveled off at 14% in 1913 (Hobson, 1997). Furthermore, it was those nations that went furthest in implementing protectionist measures that witnessed the fastest rise in trade. And lastly, the overwhelming bulk of this export trade was concentrated between developed nations – 76% of total European exports in 1860 went to other European nations, a figure that remained remarkably consistent for over fifty years – which means this putative economic basis for imperialist expansion is noticeably weak.

Nor were *laissez-faire* policies by any means incompatible with colonial ambitions during the so-called "century of indifference" to empire. Imperialism, in regards to the intentional use of political means to open and sustain foreign markets, did not require the spur of social protection to become efficacious but rather was equally the product of what Gallagher and Robinson, in their justly famous article, dubbed "free trade imperialism" (Gallagher and Robinson, 1953). In this free trade period, the British government occupied or annexed innumerable territories in Asia and Africa. It repeatedly crushed with devastating military force and repression any indigenous economic development in India: placing direct limits on entrepreneurial activity, inhibiting capital investment and skills acquisition, forcing farmers to produce for foreign consumption, intensifying the hold of all the parasitical elements of Indian society that stifled endogenous development (Arrighi and Silver, 2003; Davis, 2001).[5] It actively utilized its political power to facilitate economic colonization in India including "direct governmental promotion of products required by British industry, government manipulation of tariffs to help British exporters, railway construction at high and guaranteed rates of interest to open the continental interior", all of which gave Britain the opportunity to recoup its declining trade deficit with the advanced nations via a large surplus of payments with India (Gallagher and Robinson, 1953, 4; Davis, 2001). What scholars, such as Mike Davis, have suggested is that Britain's free trade regime, if not the entire edifice of the world economy, which had been so dependent on the driving force of British accumulation, utterly hinged on this imperialist relation with the Asian periphery (Davis, 2001). The significance of this to the overall argument of the double movement cannot be underestimated: without this linchpin, Britain presumably would have been forced to abandon free trade, liquidity in the system would have been extinguished and the liberal world economy might very well have fragmented long before the 1920s as Polanyi argued.

The institutional matrix of the double movement

In postulating the historic centrality of the double movement, Polanyi insisted that the fate of nations was determined as much by their specific insertion into this international regime as by their peculiar set of domestic circumstances. "It will then be easy to see in what manner Germany and Russia, Great Britain and the United States, as power units", he wrote, "were helped or hampered by their underlying relation to the social process…While history was thus started on its course by an event external to all, the single nations reacted to the challenge according to whether they were bound" (GT, 29; 244). As highlighted in the Introduction, this methodological approach entails a specific analytical dilemma:

> "More broadly, the challenge is to establish a definition that effectively demonstrates that potentially major differences among cases in the critical juncture, in its timing or in other characteristics, in fact occurred in an analytically *equivalent* period - that is, that they represented *different* values on the *same variable.*"
>
> (Collier and Collier, 1991, 32)

Thus, in order to assert the causal significance of the double movement, it was essential that Polanyi convincingly demonstrate that all nations were embedded in the double movement system. Clearly, he believed this to be the case as evidenced by numerous statements to this effect: "by the turn of the century, the protectionist countermovement had created an analogous situation in all Western countries" (GT, 162); "All Western countries followed the same trend, irrespective of national mentality and history" (GT, 217); "Over the greater part of the world, civilization was of the same fabric… the singularly uniform pattern of history during this period" (GT, 209).

However, it is hard to avoid the conclusion that this supposition functioned more as a rhetorical assertion than as an empirically demonstrated proposition. Polanyi is a little too quick to discount local variation and inconsistencies in order to retain the analytical focus on the universalizing force of the double movement. As highlighted earlier, not every government in Europe fit the liberal state model or embraced free trade or had a fully functioning self-regulating market and market society. It is not entirely clear therefore what is required for a nation to become embedded within the international free market system: must a nation partake in *all four* components of the system (self-regulating market [free trade], gold standard, liberal state, balance of power) in order to be considered embedded within the system or did non-adherence to some components necessarily invalidate their incorporation within the international system (although how few components a nation could meet and still be regarded as part of the system is not easily resolved in his analysis). Polanyi does not explore whether a differential positioning within any of the four components had any explanatory significance whatsoever. To take a single case, Russia, as late as 1900, had only partly industrialized, and a competitive labor market was only partly established throughout the country; land had undergone commercialization relatively recently although this process was quite uneven and underdeveloped; its authoritarian system had begun to grant some political concessions but a liberal-democratic polity was far from a reality and social protection was still in its infancy. However, at the same time, it was a member of the gold standard club and was intimately embroiled within the balance of power system. The question therefore is whether Russia should be considered part of the double movement system, and while the answer from Polanyi's narrative is clearly in the affirmative, the rationale for this conclusion is less firmly established within the premises of his own model given that Russia is lacking in two (self-regulating system and liberal state) of the four critical elements of the 19th-century system.

What appears to be the defining feature of his argument is a nations' participation in the *international* aspects of the system, namely the gold standard and balance of power.[6] This seemingly implies a definitive hierarchy within the double movement system although a selection of different citations would illustrate quite different conclusions about which of these factors were the most important. No matter which element is given precedence, the entire question of a hierarchy creates a quandary for the overall framework. Given that it is unclear whether the causal influence of the international system would be less amplified if a nation is only partly embedded within the regime or if its protectionist institutions were underdeveloped, it would be equally difficult to investigate whether the impact of the systemic contradictions manifested by the international system (see below) would be more or less damaging depending on a nation's partial or complete insertion into this institutional nexus. For instance, we could not automatically presume that the political dilemmas that Polanyi insisted were a permanent feature of liberal states embedded within the double movement – social polarization, political paralysis and the like – will necessarily be characteristic of authoritarian governments or whether the social and class conflicts within these nations can be traced back to the interplay of the double movement itself.

Specifying the precise mechanisms whereby the tensions within the double movement system are transmitted to individual nations is also not so straightforward. As an example, it is a curious omission that he does not more closely trace the decisive impact of Britain's first transition to capitalism, which exerted a relentless pressure, as both *imperative* and *incentive,* on its European neighbours. The establishment of a market economy and industrial capitalism in Britain immediately reoriented the calculations of its international rivals and the subsequent dynamic of economic development in those countries (Wood, 2002; Lacher, 2006). Unless their economic elites adopted the most innovative production techniques and restructured their organizational strategies, they risked being swamped by the competitive élan of their British counterparts. States faced acute pressure to transform the institutional foundations of their economies along advanced capitalist lines and to improve the competitiveness of their national firms; their capacity to wage war was utterly dependent upon the revenue garnered from a strong economy and in this regard they operated at a severe disadvantage to their fully capitalist rival. In Germany, as an example, the competitive pressures emanating from Britain, which were transmitted through the transmission belts of the international market and power systems, acted as the motor for a state-led modernization program that grafted capitalist relations from above onto a pre-capitalist social context: subsidizing investment, rationalizing commercial regulations, abolishing feudal rights and consolidating markets in land and labor in order to forge a unified national market.

Even if he does not specify the demonstration effect of England, Polanyi generally implies that *laissez-faire* operated as a disciplinary force, subjecting all nations to the constraints of this particular development strategy. Of course, we still need to explain the precise mechanisms whereby the capitalist imperatives of the free market system were diffused across the globe and he highlights several such processes. Economic interdependence certainly made the advantages of participation and the costs of non-compliance increasingly transparent, with any failure to conform to the dominant system likely to result in declining economic fortunes and political fallout. He similarly emphasized the common institutional infrastructure that accompanied the formation of the international monetary system such as written constitutions, regulations on financial obligations, accountancy rules and court jurisdictions (GT, 205). And of course, the availability of protectionist institutions was critical: "From now onward the typical institutions of market economy could usually be introduced only if accompanied by protectionist measures" (GT, 214).

But there is also the implication that capitalism's totalizing logic locks in all subsequent development. Once the self-regulating system is entrenched, it becomes "catalyzed into a drive of uncompromising ferocity" whereby the other components of the international system had to be enacted if the practices of the free market were to be sustained (GT, 137). "Nothing less than a self-regulating market on a world scale could ensure the functioning of this stupendous mechanism", wrote Polanyi. "Unless the price of labor was dependent upon the cheapest grain available, there was no guarantee that the unprotected industries would not succumb in the grip of the voluntarily accepted task-master, gold" (GT, 138–9).[7] As we shall discuss below, this institutional nexus also had profound implications for the reproduction and survival of the double movement regime itself, for in such a densely intertwined relationship, failure in any single component of the system was bound to generate deleterious consequences for the remainder.

Contradictions and Crisis within the Double Movement

To summarize the discussion from the previous section, Polanyi maintains the internationalization of the double movement created an international system embodying two distinct social principles that generated durable interactions across various geographic domains (national and international), across various forms of sovereignty (market and political), and through the mediation of various institutional forces (national governments, market structures and corporate entities) and ideological mechanisms. In this framework, the double movement represented an extraordinarily complex, interconnected social order. Its reproduction depended on a perpetual contestation between economic, political and social actors representing divergent interests generated by the double movement itself, which meant that political and historical contingency was inscribed into its very operation. I argue this dynamic of institutional change is perhaps best captured by the expression "unstable equilibria", which Antonio Gramsci used to describe the balance of forces between dominant and subordinate groups (Gramsci, 1971[1929–35], 182). Not only were the outcomes of this continual oscillation impossible to predict in advance, it was the very nature of the double movement to generate systemic tensions and contradictions that threatened the very survival of the international system itself.

The idea that social systems and institutions generate contradictions that undermine their own efficient functioning has been a recurrent theme within the social sciences. Institutional orders might be organized in ways that undermine their own functioning or contain the seeds of their own demise; social action might actually preclude the realization of its own goals by paralyzing social learning or weakening supportive agency. As with the language used to depict market corrosion discussed in Chapter 3, there is a familiar vocabulary that is called upon to illustrate this tendency: undermining, subverting, destabilizing, self-defeating, cannibalizing, erode, deplete, impair, undercut, diminish, parasitical, incompatible, dysfunctional. Scholars across the social sciences have employed the notion of contradiction in numerous ways: the concepts of free riding and the tragedy of the commons; Albert Hirschman's perversity thesis that is weaponized by right ideologues as a cautionary tale for would-be reformers; Schumpeter on creative destruction which meant that "While capitalism delivers material prosperity, it is constitutionally unable to produce a stable social order".

But it is unquestionably within the Marxist tradition where the centrality of contradictions and crisis as a theory of institutional change is most pronounced. Marx argued, for example, that a persistent feature of capitalism was that market actors acted in ways that were individually rational yet proved to be disastrous in the aggregate. Employers sought to keep wages low for their own employees in order to secure higher profits, yet, at the same time, hoped other employers would pay their workers high wages since this created higher demand for their products; however, if all actors pursued their individual self-interest, the end result would be insufficient demand and slower economic growth (Marx, 1973). He similarly maintained that capitalism had an inherent tendency to undermine its own social and cultural foundations: such is the case with employers who insist on making their employees work dangerously long hours even if this imperils the health of their work force and therefore the very social reproduction needed to sustain their own profitability (Elster, 1986). The fundamental principle within Marxism, as summarized by Ellen Meiksins Wood, is: "Contradiction … is capitalism's basic operating principle in a way that is true of no other social form. It is the source, at one and the same, of both the capitalist system's unique dynamism and its constant self-subversion" (Wood, 2002, 278).[8]

Given his affinity with Marxism and his abiding fondness for the paradoxes and dilemmas of social life, it should come as no surprise that Polanyi demonstrated such a keen interest in the paramount role of contradiction, a term he uses throughout the text (GT, 80, 89, 195, 198, 217).[9] As noted earlier, this emphasis has not always been recognized as a central feature of his framework, which might in part be related to the competing language utilized by Polanyi to describe the problems generated by the double movement (Dale, 2008, 2010). The key chapter (Chapter 18) in which he constructs his argument about the crisis of the international system is entitled "Disruptive Strains" and he uses similar terms such as stress, tensions, pressure to describe the cracks in the international regime (GT, 201). While the term contradiction is often used as shorthand for problems generated by social systems, it arises from a different intellectual tradition (Marxism) than the related terms of stress and tension. This language owes its inspiration to the legacy of Durkheim and became an influential discourse (and one that was closely associated with structural-functionalist approaches) within American sociology in the post-war decades.[10] Such an approach however relies on static categories of social analysis and I would argue that when Polanyi seeks to capture the dynamic aspects of social change, it is the language and imagery of contradiction that takes center stage in his narrative.

Polanyi's approach to contradiction incorporates much of the familiar use of the term within Marxism, even if it is articulated in ways that remain true to his own analytical concerns. If we take his analysis of Speenhamland as a convenient means of summarizing his approach, he *first* utilizes contradiction to describe a fundamental clash between individual and collective rationality. Landlords, he argued, under Speenhamland had every incentive to lower wages given that the relief system made up any shortfall yet this resulted in a vicious cycle of wage cutting which drove wages below subsistence levels and thereby placed an intolerable burden on the entire system of social relief. *Second*, Polanyi focuses repeatedly on the way in which social action generates *countervailing* and *undermining* effects that tend to subvert the very conditions required for social action. In Speenhamland, the design of social protection was predicated on a high degree of local variability and discretion yet this heightened the purposive mobility of the poor, which subsequently overwhelmed the limited capacity of villages to fund adequate protection. *Third*, he envisages contradiction as any circumstance wherein social forces are in a permanent opposition, such that the satisfaction of one goal can only be accomplished at the expense of another; this *mutual incompatibility* exercises a permanent constraint on purposive action and makes an integrated policy or stable institutional regime much more difficult to achieve. He highlighted the "seeming contradiction of an almost miraculous increase in production accompanied by the near starvation of the masses", where the first process presupposed the existence of the latter and any government action to redress the abject poverty was likely to damage economic health.

Polanyi's most original contribution was to situate the concept of contradiction at the core of his framework of the double movement and historical change.[11] Contradictions are the crucial factor that not only impair the continued reproduction of the international system but also lead to its ultimate dissolution. To reiterate our earlier summary, the substantive burden of his argument is to demonstrate the following: that once the double movement is established as the critical institutional pattern to which all nations are subject, subsequent social change is largely the consequence of contradictions generated by the clash of the competing elements within the double movement; that neither a market-led nor political resolution of these contradictions will prove efficacious over time; and that the cumulative effect of these unresolved tensions is to generate a widespread political, economic and social crisis that eventually dooms the double movement system.

The contradictions of the double movement

If we begin with the *first* contradiction generated within the double movement system, Polanyi treats the dilemma between individual and collective rationality as an intrinsic feature of the double movement. This dynamic was typified by the ruinous competition engendered by the international trading system. All nations understood that their economic fortunes were irrevocably tied to the international economy, which mandated the greater competitiveness and export potential of their leading manufacturing firms. But equally, each nation was intent to shield its national industries and society from the "creative destruction" unleashed by such competition so tariff protection became an endemic feature of their policy portfolio. Of course, these twin aims produced the quintessential contradiction between individual and collective rationality: each nation was keen to ensure that its own capitalists were able to export as much as possible while simultaneously regulating the imports of other countries, which ultimately produced a beggar-thy-neighbor spiral that reduced the level of all nation's exports and thereby managed to replicate a slow-growth dynamic within the heart of the double movement (GT, 199).

Individual and collective interests also clashed when it came to ensuring the long-term security of the international system itself. This necessarily mandated that individual nations had to be prepared to act in ways that safeguarded the collective good of the international system even if it came at the expense of their own national interest. Such was the case when core nations, in order to guarantee the liquidity on which an international financial market rested or to facilitate adjustment, agreed to import goods, lend to deficit nations or impose few restrictions on capital mobility even though this might very well damage their own economies in the short run. In the 19th century, these commitments owed not to formal multi-lateral institutions but rather to informal cooperation and a willingness to operate with a flexible conception of long-term interests. So long as these understandings remained intact, the counter-cyclical nature of capital and goods flows tended to prevent serious crises (Eichengreen, 1996). However, once the dynamics of the double movement heightened economic nationalism, cooperation became harder to accomplish as national interests were prioritized at the expense of the long term viability of the international system itself. "The world continued to believe in internationalism and interdependence", Polanyi astutely recognized, "while acting on the impulses of nationalism and self-sufficiency" (GT, 198).

Actors within the double movement system were trapped within an ideological mindset that replicated this very contradiction. According to the precepts of the dominant 19th-century consensus, the compensating effects of the market were presumed to be automatic and universally efficacious: as an example, the efficient functioning of the gold standard presupposed that if one country depreciated its currency, or ran a balance-of-payments deficit, another nation within the international system would enjoy a payments surplus and a stronger currency. The possibility that the individually rational action of a single nation might worsen the circumstances of all was never seriously entertained, even though this often proved to be the case. A telling example of this dynamic was the way in which the advanced nations used the international system as a transmission belt to export their own difficulties and contradictions to the periphery. Within the gold standard, stability was often achieved by shifting the burden of adjustment onto nations outside the gold club; in order to avoid liquidity shortages and its attendant ills, it was individually rational for the core nations to relocate these costs to those nations that could least afford them (Eichengreen, 1996). Because the major powers were able to attract regular flows of inward capital, developing nations were forced to offer higher interest rates in order to divert finance to their shores but this in turn necessitated tighter credit for their domestic industries and hence slower economic growth and unemployment.

Polanyi well understood that there was an inherent peril of this enlightened selfishness, affecting all participants, strong and weak alike. There was always the risk that the weaknesses of the periphery, or precipitate action by a key country or social actor, would be redirected back to the center in an unanticipated feedback process or that these problems might be seamlessly translated via the international system into a calamitous instability for all. "An almost unbroken sequence of currency crises", he noted, "linked the indigent Balkans with the affluent United States through the elastic band of the international credit system" (GT, 24). The collective health of the international system was very much linked to the individual prosperity of even its weakest members.

The *second* form of contradiction, namely the inherent tendency of social action to undermine the very conditions upon which the survival of the system depends, was also an indisputable feature of the double movement. As discussed in Chapter 3, Polanyi believed that capitalism systematically degraded and destroyed its own foundations, which imperiled society and jeopardized the market system itself. He insisted the basic structure of the international market system –its global reach, its institutional pluralism, its political complexity - made it exceedingly difficult to coordinate the corrective measures to compensate for capitalism's tendency to generate structural problems of overcapacity, insufficient demand and the like. "Anarchistic sovereignty", he wrote, "was a hindrance to all effective forms of international co-operation" (GT, 253). This supposition closely mirrored the work of Keynes who had first argued that the tremendous expansion of the scope and liquidity of financial capital created significant coordination dilemmas for economic policymakers. Michael Mann makes a similar point that in the 19th century, in the absence of multilateral institutions that could cure the attendant ills of individual self-interest through inter-state cooperation, and given the dramatic uncertainty generated by such myopic calculations, all "actors were prone to make *systemic mistakes*" (Mann, 1993, 725, my emphasis). The consequence of this, as Polanyi detailed, was a litany of political miscalculation and intensification of political crisis.

A related example was the contradiction created by the interplay of economic and political power. Market imperatives were independent of the power of any single state yet at the same time they depended on the regular use of political intervention to secure these prerogatives. Yet the more the expansion of the market system required political means to flourish, the greater the likelihood that the contradictions of the political realm would be transmitted back into the international market system itself via the myriad links of interdependence. "Of course, none of these difficulties was supposed to arise under an allegedly self-regulating system", wrote Polanyi.

> "But the more often repayments were made only under the threat of armed intervention, the more often the trade routes were kept open only with the help of gunboats, the more often trade followed the flag, while the flag followed the needs of invading governments, the more patent it

> became that political instruments had to be used in order to maintain equilibrium in world economy."
>
> (GT, 208)

Political intervention not only undermined the material foundations of the system, it shattered its ideological precepts as well. The implication is that the international order could function only if it was shrouded by a veil of self-regulation that obscured the intrinsic political decision making that actually safeguarded the system (Somers, 2018). Once this aura of mystery was dispelled, the very autonomy of the market realm was undermined and became a permanent feature of political conflict and decision-making (GT, 197).

Easily, his most extended treatment of contradictions within the double movement came in his analysis of the *third* form of contradiction, namely the mutual incompatibility of the constituent elements of the double movement (Block, 2001; Block and Somers, 1984, 47–8; Dale, 2010; Fraser, 2013, 2018, 2021; Lacher, 1999, 2019). "Vital though such a countermovement was for the protection of society", Polanyi insisted, "in the last analysis it was *incompatible* with the self-regulation of the market, and thus, with the market system itself" (GT, 130, my emphasis). In the same vein, he claimed that all forms of social protection were "*incompatible* with the functioning of the economic system itself" (GT, 129, my emphasis).[12] The precise argument appears in identical formulations in numerous places in the text (GT, 177, 192, 216–8, 227, 230–1, 234). In each instance, Polanyi's contention is that although social protection is a prerequisite for a market economy – indeed, it could not possibly exist without it – it is ultimately detrimental to economic growth because it diminishes overall wealth, impairs the automatic adjustment of market actors, discourages investment and paralyzes business confidence. Given the irreconcilable differences between the opposing principles of social organization, the double movement system was therefore fatally compromised by an innate tendency for crisis.[13]

In a provocative encapsulation of this contradiction, he claimed:

> "For who could deny that government intervention in business may undermine confidence? Who could deny that unemployment would sometimes be less if it were not for out-of-work benefit provided by law? That private business is injured by the competition of public works? That deficit finance may endanger private investments...Who can doubt that factory laws, social insurance, municipal trading, health services, public utilities, tariffs, bounties and subsidies, cartels and trusts, embargoes on immigration, on capital movements, on imports....must have acted as so many hindrances to the functioning of the competitive system, protracting business depressions, aggravating unemployment, deepening financial slumps, diminishing trade, and damaging severely the self-regulating mechanism of the market."
>
> (GT, 143–4)

The narrative device of repetitive rhetorical questions, which is actually quite rare in the text, is worth highlighting. This passage comes in a section that is at first glance intended to deflect the traditional conservative charge that without the "ruinous interventions" of social protection the market economy would have been able to resolve its own difficulties (GT, 142–4). But, by stressing the interrogatory form, Polanyi also seems to be chiding those progressives who might be inclined to dismiss as malicious propaganda (for fear that this position represented an unconscious fealty to the very laissez-faire policies that they denounced) the notion that forms of social protection, trade union activity and political intervention generate detrimental effects on economic activity. But such an assertion would imply "that those institutions have entirely failed in their purpose, which was exactly that of interfering with the laws of supply and demand in respect to human labor, and removing it from the orbit of the market" (GT, 177). He was adamant that this focus was misplaced: given that a market economy could not possibly function without social protection, it was futile to lay the "blame" for these troubles on social protection. "No doubt some of the interventionist policies practiced by the municipality [Vienna] were incompatible with the mechanism of a market economy", he wrote. "But purely economic arguments did not exhaust an issue which was primarily social not economic" (GT, 287). In a capitalist social order that combined two opposing social principles, to the extent that social protection helped mediate the destructive effects of free trade and the gold standard, it would inevitably interfere with the functioning of these same processes (GT, 217).[14]

The dilemmas engendered by the incompatibility contradiction were formidable. Government intervention was implicated whenever the self-regulating aspects of the international market proved ineffective. "In the last resort, impaired self-regulation of the market led to political intervention", he wrote. "When the trade cycle failed to come round and restore employment, when imports failed to produce exports, when bank reserve regulations threatened business with a panic, when foreign debtors refused to pay, governments had to respond to the strain" (GT, 206). In case of the tensions created by the gold standard, he suggested a range of policy solutions:

> "if the balance of payment was threatened with illiquidity, reserves and foreign loans would tide over the difficulty; if an altogether new economic balance had to be created involving a fall in the domestic price level, the restriction of credit could be spread in the most rational fashion, eliminating the inefficient, and putting the burden on the efficient."
>
> (GT, 199)

Yet no matter the policy chosen, Polanyi delighted in illustrating the ways in which the self-defeating character of the double movement handicapped all forms of political intervention. As an example, he described the various permutations governments took to cure the problem of unemployment:

> "It is easy to see that all measures of economic policy which the banks may decide upon in order to create employment are limited by the exigencies of stable exchanges. The banks will not be able to expand or further extend credits to industry without appealing to the central bank which, on its part, will refuse to follow suit since the safety of the currency requires the opposite course...Under the gold standard -which we all the time assume to be in force - any governmental measure that caused a budgetary deficit might start a depreciation of the currency; if, on the other hand, unemployment was being fought by the expansion of bank credit, rising domestic prices would hit exports and affect the balance of payment in that way. In either case exchanges would slump and the country feel the pressure on its currency."
>
> (GT, 209–210)

Similarly, if a government tried to combat external economic shocks by raising interest rates, this merely slowed down economic growth and raised unemployment, all the while placing downward pressure on other nations to raise interest rates in defense of their own currency. Higher unemployment in turn made nations even more vulnerable to speculative attacks on their currency, which made it even more difficult for them to raise interest rates in the future. He concluded:

> "That in spite of these devices to mitigate the effects of deflation, the outcome was, nevertheless, again and again a complete disorganization of business and consequent mass unemployment, is the most powerful of all the indictments of the gold standard."
>
> (GT, 195)

In essence, the incompatibility contradiction meant that government intervention could best be likened to fighting a forest fire: even if a policy was successful in putting out one inferno, another would crop up in a different location, and then another, seemingly dooming all efforts to restore a healthy equilibrium. "The strains emanating from the market were thus shifting to and fro between market and the other institutional zones", Polanyi wrote:

> "sometimes affecting the working of the field of government, sometimes that of the gold standard or that of the balance-of-power system, as the case may be. Each field was comparatively independent of the others and tended toward an equilibrium of its own; whenever this balance was not achieved, the imbalance spread over into the other spheres."
>
> (GT, 211)

Some interventions sparked new problems, which required new solutions that merely served to displace the problem into the not-too-distant future, where yet another crisis might arise (Streeck, 2016). The never-ending battle to contain the spillover across the economic and political arenas of the double movement highlighted the futility of state action and created an irresistible momentum for crisis (Dale, 2010; Fraser, 2013; Streeck, 2016).

The political and social ramifications of the incompatibility contradiction were immense. The state became the very embodiment and crystallization of these contradictions. On the one hand, it organized capitalist accumulation in order to assist in the process of market adjustment; at the same time, it had to challenge the power of capital in order to compensate for its disruptive and disorganizing consequences.[15] Not surprisingly, the state was caught in a permanent schizophrenic condition, expected to achieve a healthy balance between these opposing dynamics, yet torn in opposite directions by their competing demands. In the last resort, Polanyi well understood that it was the state's responsibility to resolve these difficulties -"And whatever the market in question – labor, land or money – the strain would transcend the economic zone and the balance would have to be restored by political means" (GT, 218) – yet, the fundamental incompatibility of its goals meant that the efficacy of political intervention could only be imprecisely anticipated. Accordingly the state itself became not only a *site* of contradictions but a *producer* of them as well.

The state therefore represented a critical zone of contestation within the double movement. Polanyi did not idealize the state as the repository of social consensus or the arbiter of the collective class interest, occupying a position of benign neutrality from the heights of Olympian indifference; it was deeply implicated in both the resolution and forging of these contradictions.[16] In order to resolve the strains created by the double movement, the state had to engage in a series of complex trade-offs that enabled it to shift the burden of adjustment between various spheres: "if some external event weighed heavy on the country, its internal mechanism functioned in the same way, shifting the pressure from the economic to the political zone or vice versa" (GT, 215). This meant deciding which social groups and interests would face the brunt of adjustment and as a consequence, governments became a transmission belt for social and political conflict and the locus of significant efforts of political mobilization and lobbying by all social groups. The nation state's capacity to organize and channel this conflict became a crucial element in the evolution of the double movement.

Contradictions were also constituted and reproduced by social agency. All social groups could and did attempt to pressure the state to resolve the emerging tensions in ways that best suited their own interests and Polanyi clearly appreciated the ways in which class coalitions jockeyed for position to influence state policy. For instance, because strict adherence to the gold standard typically mandated deflationary effects (declining wages, reduced consumption and investment, unemployment) that central banking authorities could not entirely alleviate, democratic states consequently faced acute pressures from working class organizations to reorient economic policy in order to shift the costs onto other social actors. "Indeed, the great institutional significance of central banking", he insisted, "lay in the fact that monetary policy was thereby drawn into the sphere of politics" (GT, 197–8). Many governments concluded that the only feasible strategy of remaining within the gold standard club was to limit democratic participation and working class organization; so long as these were rudimentary, states had greater flexibility to impose the costs of adjustment created by adherence to the rules of the international market as they saw fit (GT, 209–10) (Eichengreen, 1996).[17]

Polanyi well understood the fundamental power asymmetry inherent in this process. State actors faced a structural incentive to privilege the views and interests of dominant economic elites (GT, 229) but it also sought to regulate capital in the name of the greater good; the paradox was how to prevent these protective measures from threatening profitability on behalf of the very growth that was a precondition for social protection in the first place (Kalecki, 1943). What this revealed was the crucial structural limits to reform in all capitalist democracies:

> "This is, ultimately, why the reform of capitalist economy by socialist parties is difficult even when they are determined not to interfere with the property system. For the mere possibility that they might decide to do so undermines that type of confidence which in the liberal economy is vital, namely, absolute confidence in the continuity of the titles to property."
> (GT, 234)

This dynamic also reinforced the prominence of the contradiction between the individual rationality and collective well-being of capitalists: even if the impact of social protection or governmental regulation on the profits of any one firm was bound to be minimal, so long as everyone acted as if the likelihood of damage was bound to be considerable, then this fear might be transformed into a self-fulfilling prophecy (Block, 1990).

Ultimately, contradictions were not dilemmas that could be solved or managed by improved strategies of reform. Given such an "unstable equilibrium", there was a strong likelihood that any lasting accord between the dialectical poles of the double movement could not be sustained for long and thus a pathological decay was inscribed within the double movement regime (Streeck, 2009; 2016; Streeck and Thelen, 2005). Crisis, in this Polanyian view, which was endogenous and systematic, entailed a total unravelling of the prevailing institutional system and its political and social support structures under the weight of these unresolved dilemmas. "No less than a complete destruction of the national institutions of nineteenth century society", he wrote, "accompanied the crisis in a great part of the world, and everywhere these institutions were changed and reformed almost out of recognition" (GT, 27–8). All nations within the double movement were eventually faced with the obsolescence of existing institutional arrangements and "an institutional deadlock which was essentially alike in a large number of countries" (GT, 238). "Systemic mistakes", to return to Michael Mann's felicitous phrase, became endemic (Mann, 1993).

Polanyi posited a number of mechanisms to account for the declining efficacy of these institutional processes. Because of the zero-sum dynamic highlighted earlier, *political* interventions to resolve contradictions encountered the perpetual dilemma of redressing one problem only at the cost of exacerbating another, which over time could only end in a political stalemate. Some policy trade-offs were politically unfeasible because their objectives were unattainable so long as the dictates of the international system were respected; others were socially unacceptable, either to elites who blocked particular solutions to the crisis or to the broader population who were no longer willing to countenance the costs of adjustments being made at their expense. The more politicized and transparent the decision-making to preserve the double movement became, the harder it was for state elites to offload the costs of adjustment onto any social group. The state's need to "impress upon the nation" the requirement for sacrifices to safeguard the international system became even more imperative as contradictions grew unchecked yet their ability to command such consent grew correspondingly weaker. The consequence of this Polanyian legitimation crisis was that "eventually the moment would come when both the economic and political systems were threatened by complete paralysis", which heightened the likelihood of authoritarian solutions to resolve the crisis (GT, 236).

Polanyi also recognized the distinct *historical* limits to any political strategy of adjustment, especially that some problems were simply irresolvable given the existing strategic repertoire. Referring to the unique circumstances of the 1920s when policy makers were unable to design the multilateral institutions that could have promoted the inter-state cooperation needed to avert a crisis, he wrote:

> "The only alternative to this disastrous condition of affairs was the establishment of an international order endowed with an organized power which could transcend national sovereignty. Such a course, however, was entirely beyond the horizon of the time. No country in Europe, not to mention the United States, would have submitted to such a system."[18]
>
> (GT, 22)

The same could be said for the overwhelming lack of an alternative policy to the rule of the gold standard: given the absence of any economic theory that could explain how to generate employment or utilize budget deficits to improve aggregate demand (as was the case with Keynesianism), it was not surprising that the entire focus of economic policy should be the safeguarding of budgetary stability as engendered by the gold standard (Eichengreen, 1996).

Lastly, in terms reminiscent of his discussion of Speenhamland highlighted in Chapter 2, Polanyi acknowledged that this unstoppable momentum for crisis also had critical *interpretive* and *ideological* roots (Block and Somers, 2014; Blyth, 2002). He captured this process in the following passage:

> "The true nature of the international system under which we were living was not realized until it failed. Hardly anyone understood the political function of the monetary system; the awful suddenness of the transformation thus took the world completely by surprise…Not even when the cataclysm was already upon them did their leaders see that behind the collapse of the international system there stood a long development within the most advanced countries which made that system anachronistic; in other words, the failure of market economy itself still escaped them."
>
> (GT, 20)

As long as a "dogmatic belief in the international gold standard continued to enlist men's stintless loyalties" (GT, 198), an alternative system was impossible to imagine: trapped within the ideological confines of the double movement, all social actors were doomed to repeat the mistakes of the past. In fact, both sides of the ideological spectrum were equally convinced of the futility of political intervention. While *laissez-faire* liberals, who believed in the self-correcting powers of the market, cautioned patience, communist parties similarly embraced a do-nothing stance because they were convinced that a massive economic collapse would hasten a revolutionary uprising. As discussed in the next section, such passivity essentially guaranteed that democratic institutions were extinguished.

The implication is that entrenched institutions might well have a life span that stretch beyond the point where they remain effective. "The secular tenets of social organization embracing the whole world", he wrote:

> "are not dislodged by the events of a decade…Its [*laissez faire*] spectacular failure in one field did not destroy its authority in all. Indeed, it partial eclipse may have even strengthened its hold since it enabled its defenders to argue that the incomplete application of its principles was the reason for every and any difficulty laid to its charge."[19]
>
> (GT, 143)

But the pull of ideology worked in the opposite direction as well. Once the normative underpinnings of the system vanished, an escalating spiral of crisis became inevitable.

Nevertheless, crises also represented moments of historical opportunity for they foreshadowed the genesis of new institutional arrangements and distinct emancipatory possibilities for social change. Amid the crisis, diverse combinations of political leadership, ideology and class coalitions competed to discover innovative solutions (GT, 22). Polanyi envisioned the dominant political experiments of the inter-war years – Stalinism, Fascism and Social Democracy – as constituent features of the same process (Berman, 2006). Each constituted a unique pathway out of the crisis of the *laissez-faire* system, the specific choice of which was determined by the peculiar national characteristics and unique historical trajectories of each country. "Yet from the point of view of market economy", he wrote, "these often radically different solutions merely represented given alternatives" (GT, 244).

Interrogating the contradictions argument

The centrality of contradictions within Polanyi's framework enabled him to capture the quintessentially dynamic elements of embedding/disembedding within the double movement in a manner that static institutional accounts could not match. This represented a formidable accomplishment yet there are aspects of this perspective that warrant further reflection. In the first instance, there is an ongoing tension within his account regarding the divergent efficacy of market and political methods in the resolution of contradictions that encapsulates the dialectic of market disembedding and political embedding identified in previous chapters. On the one hand, it would be fair to say that the overwhelming thrust of his argument is that political redress must ultimately be implicated: in circumstances in which self-regulation of the market proved ineffective – "when the trade cycle failed to come round and restore unemployment, when imports failed to produce exports… (GT, 206)" – the visible hand of the state was required to restore the equilibrium. And given that a social protective element is virtually instantaneous in Polanyi's framework –after all this is precisely what he claimed allowed the reach of the international market to be extended so effortlessly – the efficacy of market-led adjustment must be considerably lessened and political intervention virtually inevitable. "Less and less could markets be described as autonomous and automatic mechanisms of competing atoms", once social protection was initiated (GT, 218).

Yet, the very rhetorical construction of his argument returns us to the contested relationship between the internal components of the double movement. In several passages, Polanyi appears to implicitly accept that the automatism of the market is not entirely fictitious: "When the trade cycle failed to come around and restore employment, when imports failed to produce exports"; "each field was completely independent of the others and tended toward an equilibrium of its own" (GT, 211). In other words, on some occasions, and up to a certain point (neither of which is specified in any detail), the trade cycle does come around, exports and payments do balance, financial outflows are countered by trade inflows, compensating effects are indeed efficacious, and an equilibrium can be reached before contradictions fester and crisis becomes ineluctable (GT, 211) (Eichengreen, 1996). Counterbalancing market mechanisms might equally emerge to correct for the mutual incompatibility contradiction (Brenner, 2006).

Even if labor's bargaining strength is enhanced by full employment, corporatist bargaining, or shop floor militancy, this need not automatically lead to an economic downturn. There might very well be countertendencies that return profitability and productivity to normal, if not higher, levels rather than to depression and slow growth. Higher capacity utilization and sales might occur, or firms could be encouraged to substitute capital for labor, thereby increasing technological innovation and improving labor-saving productivity, or they could ratchet up levels of exploitation. Likewise, businesses have ample opportunity to circumvent worker's institutional strength or onerous social protection by simply investing in areas where the regulatory regime is minimal and workers are unable to oppose its prerogatives. Of course, these various equilibria, as has already been noted, are perilously ephemeral: there is considerable uncertainty about how quickly market actors can mobilize technological or organizational innovations (or even if they see them as desirable); and market solutions might very well generate additional contradictions that require political intervention. But the general point to reiterate is that the conditions under which the autonomy of the market leads automatically to either malevolent or beneficial consequences needs to be more carefully specified.

Even in circumstances where Polanyi insisted that social protection was an absolute prerequisite, there was still a prominent role for market-led adjustment. For example, whenever there was an outflow of gold associated with an external shock in confidence as opposed to a fall in exports or rise in foreign interest rates, he stressed the burden of adjustment would fall on monetary authorities and a defense of the gold standard would be undertaken regardless of the scale of domestic difficulties that such action might precipitate. "Social dislocation", he argued, "was avoided with the help of credit movements; economic imbalance was righted by financial measures" (GT, 206). The Bank of England's role as lender of last resort and orchestrator of inter-state co-operation to facilitate the unimpaired movement of goods and capital took on a singular importance in these circumstances (Arrighi and Silver, 2003). As Barry Eichengreen has shown, even in circumstances when there was a momentary decline in financial confidence and the corresponding risk of capital flight intensified, short term capital often flowed toward Britain even in the absence of any official government intervention. Because market actors could reasonably assume that the Bank of England's unshakeable commitment to gold convertibility meant that it would do whatever was necessary to prop up the gold standard, financial markets responded in the same direction in anticipation of official action and in order to secure the windfall capital gains that would result from governmental efforts to protect the rate of exchange, thereby minimizing the need for government intervention in the first place (Eichengreen, 1996, 31; Block and Somers, 2014). In other words, market adjustments could, under certain circumstances, relieve state actors of the burden of adjustment and could stabilize the dislocations associated with the maintenance of an international monetary regime (Krippner, 2011).

Admittedly, in this instance, it is the very predictability and credibility of social protection itself that allows market forces to be involved in the adjustment process, a fact that certainly confirms the salience of the double movement itself, but at the same time, this oscillation between market and political mechanisms is not so easily calculated within the double movement framework. Polanyi does not discuss in any systematic fashion the conditions under which the "relative autonomy" of the market is impaired, the point at which its compensatory mechanisms, which are at the heart of capitalism's very dynamism, prove ineffective in regulating their own destructive consequences thereby necessitating the rescue mission of the state, or the way each of these moments might diverge depending upon the precise market structures, systems of accumulation, and institutional structures of each nation.[20] Unless one could stipulate the precise mechanisms and circumstances of these forces of market failure, which Robert Brenner has succinctly named the "malign hand" of the market, or specify the conditions (for each component of the international market system) whereby remedial action by market actors fails to bring about the necessary adjustment, the salience of the contradictions perspective in accounting for social change is bound to have far richer *descriptive* rather than *explanatory* power (Brenner, 2006, 25; Panitch and Gindin, 2012). This is not to say that such an account is unfeasible within the overall schema of the double movement – again, it is a mark of Polanyi's achievement that the very question is so acutely posed – merely that it does not appear in his own analysis.

Similar reservations could also be lodged regarding his articulation of the *political* resolution of contradictions within the double movement. What Polanyi somewhat downplays is the possibility that states might be able to intervene in ways that contain crisis and lead to new developments; in other words, notwithstanding the centrality of crisis within his framework, he does not explain in any compelling fashion how crises are contingent in terms of both their duration and resolution (Panitch and Gindin, 2012). He does not engage in any rigorous exposition of the scope or diversity of state policies used to combat the contradictions of the international system. He does not utilize a historical-comparative case study approach to investigate whether problems were more effectively remedied in some nations more than others; or discuss the various combination and sequences of policies that proved most efficacious in each instance; or detail the various institutional or ideological mechanisms that were usefully harnessed in this regard.[21] Nor does he fully explore the range of "state failures", analogous to the "market failures" highlighted earlier, whereby political intervention might exacerbate the contradictions. Given these limitations, there is a hint of a teleological perspective when he stipulates the inevitable collapse of the double movement system.

As for his overarching emphasis on the incompatibility contradiction, there is considerable empirical evidence that validates Polanyi' contention that the imposition of various forms of social protection might have pernicious effects on economic activity (Marglin and Schor, 1990; Streeck, 2009). Yet what is missing from his discussion is a fuller appreciation of the ways in which the competing elements of the double movement might also generate mutually *beneficial* consequences. Social protection, as has been well noted in the contemporary literature on political economy, might be perfectly conducive to economic efficiency and growth (Block, 1990; Block, 2003; Hollingsworth and Boyer, 1997). Higher levels of education, health care, infrastructural improvements, public goods delivery, income redistribution and the like can directly improve the competitiveness of national firms and strengthen the domestic market; indeed, states that do not offer these benefits simply shift the burden onto private actors thereby weakening firm profitability and competitiveness. As highlighted earlier in Chapter 4, many measures of social protection, such as unemployment insurance, reductions in working hours and pensions, act as "beneficial constraints" that can generate positive economic effects (especially for productivity growth and profitability) because they make it harder for low wage producers to succeed and thus give their high wage, capital intensive competitors the upper hand (Streeck, 1997). There is a rare acknowledgement of this dynamic, when Polanyi emphasized the efficacious macro-economic role of central banks in spreading the costs of adjustment, owing to the instabilities of the gold standard throughout the entire economy (via interest rates and currency policies that affected all economic actors not merely those in specific disadvantaged positions) so that only the most inefficient firms ended up being liquidated (GT, 199).

Nor does he fully delineate how various social protective measures influence different components of the international system (financial mobility, investment, trade, and the like) in distinct ways and with varying damage to the market's equilibrium mechanisms or to economic vitality. This obviously represents quite a challenge to any analytical framework as Wolfgang Streeck rightly suggests: "Since the economic functions of social institutions are often latent and unintended, or cannot be directly intended at all, and in fact are frequently contradictory and dialectical, telling productive from counter-productive constraints in advance may often than not be difficult or impossible". But he also argues that "while distinguishing between benevolent and malevolent constraints will for intrinsic reasons always be difficult, this does not mean that more focused empirical research could not uncover important differences and similarities, or generate useful analytical concepts, typologies, or even theories" (Streeck, 1997, 211, 216). By properly differentiating between the normal resolution of contradictions via either market adjustment or efficacious political action from instances where tensions cannot be so easily contained, it might be possible to construct an explanation of how contradictions begin to intensify, accumulate over time and across various social domains, and foreclose certain policy options that make stability in the system impossible to maintain (Streeck, 2009; Fraser, 2013). In other words, as Leo Panitch and Sam Gindin suggest: "[W]e need to ask not just *why* crises occur, but why some crises are *distinct*: why they last so long, are marked by persistent economic uncertainty, and produce significant political and social change" (Panitch and Gindin, 2012, 5).

Admittedly, it would represent a formidable analytical and empirical task to systematically incorporate political and economic antecedents into a framework that was sensitive to comparative and historical variation or that could account for the conditions under which contradictions lead inexorably to crisis. But it is not unfair to argue that Polanyi's analysis does not accomplish these tasks. Indeed his repeated pronouncements about the incompatibility of social protection (or democracy for that matter) to the healthy functioning of a market economy would seemingly point us in a different direction. It is because political and social interference with the self-steering mechanisms of the market has the potential to generate such harmful consequences for economic and political life that there appears to be an unstoppable momentum pushing the double movement towards crisis and historical transformation. Yet, the paradox for his historical reconstruction should be apparent: if there is no automatic breakdown of the mutual coexistence of the double movement, if contradictions might be cured by either market action or political redress, if some measure of stability could be achieved within the "unstable equilibrium" of the double movement, then the gear of history need not inevitably lead to cataclysm. And consequently, the assertion of a direct causal link between the double movement and the crises of the long 19th century would be considerably weakened.

The 'Origins of Our Times'

This last section considers Polanyi's historical claim that the crisis of the double movement was the driving force behind the key transformations of the twentieth century. There is an important issue to clarify at the outset. As noted earlier, he clearly envisioned this entire period, 1879–1929, as an unbroken period of social change in which the unfolding dynamics of the double movement constituted the "singularly uniform pattern of history during this period" (GT, 209). In this sense, this epoch meets the challenge, espoused earlier by David and Ruth Collier, of stipulating that the various events that occurred throughout the era across multiple locations and moments were part of an "analytically equivalent period". However, within this conjuncture, there are two separate cases/outcomes to consider – World War I and the rise of Fascism – both of which, Polanyi argued, could be traced to the contradictory development of the double movement. "In reality, the post war obstacles to peace and stability", he insisted, "derived from the same sources from which the Great War itself had sprung" (GT, 21). This is not to suggest that either of these outcomes can be traced to the same precise combination of factors, only that in his analysis it is the double movement that constitutes the critical motor of change for both events.

The road to the "Great War"

Polanyi's argument about the core relationship of the double movement to the implosion of the Great War can be quickly summarized. As contradictions within the international system festered, a series of destabilizing shocks became manifest. The widespread use of tariff protection throughout the advanced nations acted as a relentless drag on economic growth, leading to rising unemployment and deflation (GT, 198). As the world economy dissolved into colonial rivalry and heightened competition for foreign markets, economic nationalism intensified and "the ability of *haute finance* to avert the spread of wars was diminishing rapidly" (GT, 19; 211). The balance of power was similarly vulnerable once the world economy unraveled. "As long as the gold standard and what became at best its corollary – constitutional regimes – were in operation", he wrote, "the balance of power was a vehicle of peace" (GT, 252). He claimed that the establishment of two distinct power alliances arrayed against one another meant that the "peace interest" of the balance-of – power system no longer functioned. With both the economic and political foundations of peace increasingly unstable, the entire foundation of the international system on which 19th-century civilization rested was on the verge of disintegration (GT, 227). As with any structural argument, Polanyi is not suggesting the deterioration of the double movement led directly to the events that sparked the war but rather that once the international system on which peace depended had collapsed, a crisis of some sort was inevitable even though no one could have predicted the epic conflagration that resulted.

Despite its obvious significance to his overarching framework, Polanyi surprisingly devoted very little attention to the case of the Great War. While the bulk of the first chapter is ostensibly devoted to the events leading up to this cataclysm, in actual fact, it is almost entirely given over to the discussion of the hundred years' peace, and it is not until the very last page of the chapter that he even addresses the decline of the international system and the downward spiral into conflict. His next chapter deals with the interwar years and the rise of Fascism and one waits in vain for him to return to this topic in later chapters of the book.

Indeed, what is actually more revealing is the way in which he fails to logically extend the implications of his own argument. If we take the case of the collapse of the "peace interest", one would reasonably expect that his explanation would closely parallel his prior contention about the success of *haute finance*: in other words, there should be an intrinsic link between the conditions under which finance capital was able to guarantee peace and those that subsequently undermined the peace interest. As summarized in Chapter 3, Polanyi insisted that *haute finance* had secured peace because: it had an unparalleled "amphibious capacity" to bridge both national politics and the international economy and to insinuate its imperatives down to all domestic actors; it dominated the material resources that all governments required for economic growth and utilized this to extract a *quid pro quo* for peace; it possessed unique structural knowledge that made them indispensable confidants of state leaders; and its "iron grip" over financial administration enabled them to recast imperialist rivalries into peaceful pursuits. If war now had become inevitable, it is only logical to assume therefore that the efficacy of *haute finance* must have dissipated in some way. We can suggest a number of tentative hypotheses: perhaps governments were able to secure other sources of funding via tariffs and other mechanisms thereby negating the leverage of finance capital; or the social and institutional coherence of *haute finance* might have splintered, owing to greater social differentiation or through the middle classes' assimilation into the ranks of the aristocracy; or its political influence was impaired by the spread of nationalist sentiments within European societies and governments (Mayer, 1978).

The point to stress is that Polanyi does not engage in this kind of analysis at all. His sole reference is contained in a single juxtaposition on the last page of the opening chapter. He initially proclaims that "[i]n the nineties *haute finance* was at its peak and peace seemed more secure than ever" but only a few sentences later, he concludes "[t]he ability of *haute finance* to avert the spread of wars was diminishing rapidly" (GT, 19). But there is no sustained analysis that stipulates the mechanisms underpinning the demise of the pacific capabilities of financial capital during this interim period or the extent to which the double movement was necessarily implicated in this process.

What also goes completely unmentioned in the book is the rise of an alternative "peace interest" in the shape of transnational working class solidarity. Even as the European bourgeoisie cravenly abandoned the ideals of the Enlightenment and liberal democracy, a new international based on a principled commitment to pacifism and anti-militarism challenged the headlong descent into war (Bronner, 1990). Within Polanyi's own conceptual framework, the rise of a working class peace faction poses an interesting paradox. If the middle classes had a nascent interest in peace because of the rise of the new international economy, in what way did the emergence of a working class peace interest reflect transformations in the world market during its imperialist/protectionist epoch? This is never properly discussed in his narrative.

The implication appears to be that once growing inter-imperialist rivalries severed the automatic correspondence between the middle classes and peace, and economic nationalism began to dominate as a result of the contradictory dynamics of the double movement, militarism metastasized into a favored instrument of domestic politics among the major powers and the scope for political and military co-operation was substantially narrowed. But this causal relationship is not systematically pursued in any respect either and one would need further elaboration of whether the putative role of the double movement could actually account for these developments in any case. If we take the case of German militarism, Polanyi insisted that Germany under Bismarck had been the "chief beneficiary" of the peace interest because peace was thought to serve its national interest; however, once the gold standard was embraced and tariff protection enacted, colonial expansion, heightened economic competition, and militarism better suited its economic and political ambitions and the peace standard became represented by free trade Britain (GT, 18–19). Yet it is doubtful whether this oscillation between aggressive nationalism and pacifism can be traced to an intensified commercial rivalry between the major powers: if anything, the German and British economies became even more interdependent (Britain was Germany's largest trading partner) in the years preceding 1914 which should have made military conflict even more unlikely under his scenario where the peace interest was said to grow whenever "the investment habit had taken root" (GT, 14; Mann, 1993). Indeed, he does not attempt to demonstrate, for either Germany or any of the major powers, how its particular insertion into the matrix of the double movement conditioned its political transition to a rejuvenated militarism.

I am not implying that such a relationship is impossible to establish merely that Polanyi relied on rhetorical assertions rather than sustained analysis in order to demonstrate such an association. Certainly, German militarism was conditioned by its particular pathway to industrialization that made its national capitalism more territorial and nationalist oriented than many of its European counterparts, which gave it an incentive to contemplate territorial annexations and economic hegemony on the continent that other European powers never entertained. There is no doubt that the moral and ideological collapse of liberalism in the decades preceding the war was strongly influenced by the rise of economic nationalism but German militarism also represented a conscious strategy to deflect and weaken the perceived political menace from the left (Bronner, 1990). Kaiser Wilhelm emboldened his chancellor to "first cow the socialists, behead them and make them harmless, with a bloodbath if necessary, and then make war abroad". But, at the same time, it is doubtful whether a structural explanation would have much success in accounting for the unstable power dynamics within European monarchies or the rise of warlike sentiments among the aristocratic elites that dominated European foreign policy decision making, factors which other authors have suggested played a key role in the trajectory towards war (Mann, 1993; Mayer, 1978).

Nor does Polanyi adequately demonstrate the salience of the double movement in accounting for the realignment of diplomatic strategies within the balance-of-power system. There is no doubt that political and military alliances leading up to the war were primarily concerned with carving up the spoils of colonial adventures, but at the same time, he does not fully explore how economic interests and diplomatic ambitions became inextricably linked. Cain and Hopkins, as an example, postulated that given Britain's abiding need to safeguard their investments and holdings in India – the linchpin of its entire free trade regime – it made perfect sense for Britain to reach an agreement with the main European power with vital interests in East Asia, at the time represented by Russia, yet this could only be accomplished via a further agreement brokered with France (Cain and Hopkins, 2000). Such an alliance might have placed Britain on a collision course with Germany, but in this instance, inter-imperialist antagonism served as the foundation for political cooperation rather than conflict as all three countries – Britain, France and Russia – fought the war as allies. The contradictions of the double movement did not lead automatically to war any more than tariffs precluded economic interdependence in a global economy. Indeed, Michael Mann suggested the direction of causality lay in the opposite direction: "But economic rivalry was more product than cause of geopolitical rivalry. Military and political power actions persuaded capitalists, more than vice versa, into imperialism...Even where nationalist economic rivalry was significant, it rarely fueled actual warmongering among capitalists" (Mann, 1993, 780).

Lurking behind this discussion of the political-international roots of the crisis is his related claim that the collapse of the world economy was of paramount importance in the road to war. "The dissolution of the system of world economy which had been in progress since 1900", Polanyi insisted, "was responsible for the political tension that exploded in 1914" (GT, 21). The clear implication in the text is the institutional foundations of the international market system suffered an irreversible breakdown, although what is never made explicit is precisely the conditions under which these tensions inevitably matured into crisis. The operation of the gold standard, as an example, routinely generated any number of economic difficulties (unemployment, balance of payments deficits and the like) and in the *interwar* years he maintains that its ultimate breakdown was presaged by the destruction of national currencies, severe swings in exchange rates, payments deficits and trade flows, massive credit crises, inflationary spirals, beggar-thy-neighbor tariff spirals, and a precipitous loss of credibility; in short, a series of political failures could not avert a deepening economic paralysis. Unfortunately, he offers no conclusive evidence that any of these problems were acute in the years immediately preceding the Great War nor does he, as noted earlier, systematically explore the political and economic breakdowns that failed to resolve the tensions before conflict erupted.

In actual fact, this proposition is diametrically opposed to the prevailing views of many economic historians who have characterized the period 1879–1914 as an unprecedented "golden age" of monetary relations that created the foundation for economic growth (Eichengreen, 1992, 1996; Gallarotti, 1995). In their view, this era featured a remarkable stability of exchange rates and parity of core currencies; upward growth in export strength of national economies; few balance of payments problems; high capital mobility and abundant investment; and long term price stability at relatively low levels of inflation. The 19th-century gold standard, which Gallarotti characterized as a "well-functioning and desirable international monetary regime", was sustained by ample public and private forms of cooperation that smoothed over adjustments and by the widespread confidence in the credibility of the system (Gallarotti, 1995, 19). In the wider *fin-de-siècle* culture, capitalism appeared to many observers to have developed a renewed social and technological vigor which underpinned significant cultural, social and political accomplishments (Bronner, 1990).

Eichengreen also attributes this market stability, which he pointedly contrasts to the persistent instability of the inter-war years, to the very dynamic of market insulation that Polanyi emphasized. So long as macro-economic policy making was largely insulated from popular accountability and removed from the debates of everyday political life, and elite belief in the credibility of the political commitment to the gold standard and sound credit was ensured, then the gold standard system remained essentially stable (Eichengreen, 1996, 4, 31). While this is a crucial component of his interpretation of the inter-war crisis, it must be stressed that he does not actually make this argument for the pre-1914 era even though many European nations, far from being liberal states as assumed in his institutional framework, were authoritarian regimes where economic policy was largely shielded from mass pressure. It was certainly the case that many of these institutional bulwarks were being undermined by long term developments. Transnational cooperation among monetary authorities shattered under the pressure of nationalist rivalries and persistent demands for the right to vote brought class struggle to the fore of political competition across many nations (Halperin, 2004). But the crisis of the liberal order that Polanyi speaks of appears to have been caused by the effects of the war rather than vice versa. It was the Great War that irrevocably shattered the illusion of cooperation and credibility that the old order rested upon.[22]

These omissions and limitations directly affect his related case about the rise of fascism. As we discuss below, Polanyi believed the central paradox of the interwar years was the inexplicable resurrection of the *laissez-faire* system. Yet this constitutes a proper dilemma only if the effects of the first iteration of the double movement system had proven so dire that any return to such a bankrupt system would have been accepted by all parties as an exceptionally foolhardy venture. Unless he could demonstrate conclusively that the collapse of the double movement system was instrumental in the onset of war, then the subsequent claim would become much harder to establish. Again to reiterate, this is not to say that a correlation between the double movement and the Great War could not have been better established as the foregoing discussion has alluded, only that his analysis does not make such a connection explicit. Without such a link, the demise of the system would appear to have been the consequence of the exogenous shock of the war itself rather than the endogenous evolution of the double movement.

The Rise of Fascism and the Double Movement

Polanyi's explanation for the rise of fascism throughout Europe similarly stressed the evolution of the double movement as the primary gear of social change.[23] "The appearance of such a movement in the industrial countries of the globe, and even in a number of slightly industrialized ones", wrote Polanyi:

> "should never have been ascribed to local causes, national mentalities, or historical backgrounds as was so consistently done by contemporaries. Fascism had as little to do with the Great War as with the Versailles Treaty, with Junker militarism as with the Italian temperament."
>
> (GT, 237)

As he detailed, fascist movements emerged in both defeated and victorious nations, in countries with contrasting political cultures and distinct historical traditions. "In fact, there was no type of background – of religious, cultural or national tradition – that made a country immune to fascism", he wrote, "once the conditions for its emergence were given" (GT, 238). The only factor that could possibly account for the remarkable vitality of the fascist movement was the collapse of the world economy and the contradictions of the double movement.

Polanyi's starting point was the deeply conservative "return to the past", namely the reestablishment of *laissez-faire* in the midst of the extraordinary political and social upheavals that spread through Europe in the aftermath of the war. "It became, in effect, the spearhead of a heroic attempt", he wrote, "to restore world trade, remove all avoidable hindrances to the mobility of labor, and reconstruct stable exchanges" (GT, 231). The restoration of the gold standard took priority for both economic and political reasons. Because so many national economies had disintegrated after the war – a period that featured bankrupt currencies, hyper-inflation, budget shortfalls and disorganized trade – it became the accepted wisdom that only a return to sound money and credit principles as exemplified by the gold standard could put economies back on a stable footing. Political elites similarly accepted the premise that a felicitous reconstruction of the balance of power and an invigorated "peace interest", already weakened by the punitive prescriptions of Versailles, could only be accomplished if free trade and international financial mobility were restored, both of which mandated the return of the gold standard (GT, 22). By 1926 the gold standard had been reinstated throughout the advanced world as the linchpin of international monetary relations.

But the return to the gold standard proved to be "a factor of incalculable integrating and disintegrating force" that undermined the double movement order and severely worsened the crisis: "there was hardly an internal crisis in Europe that did not reach its climax on an issue of external economy" (GT, 23). Normal market adjustment mechanisms proved inadequate as weaker nations, especially those on the periphery of the world economy routinely plagued with destabilizing trade swings, were buffeted by persistent economic shocks. Despite attempts to foster transnational cooperation, the coordination of expansionary monetary and fiscal policies was seriously impaired by the lingering resentment generated by oppressive war debts and reparation payments. Charles Kindleberger emphasizes, as did Polanyi, the:

> "absence of a benevolent hegemon –a dominant economic power able and willing to take the worst cases of small powers and the operation of the international system into account by stabilizing the flow of spending and by acting as the lender and consumer of last resort."
>
> (Kindleberger, 1986)

Great Britain, the former hegemon, lacked the resources while the rising power, the United States, had ample funds to assume this responsibility but it lacked the political will. Without the stabilizing financial flows ensured by such coordination, nations faced wide fluctuations in their currencies and gold reserves, forcing many to raise interest rates and tighten credit in a futile effort to defend their precarious financial infrastructure, which depressed production and trade and led to chronic balance of payments deficits. It was the very simultaneity and connectivity of the international financial architecture that meant the symptoms of crisis were now seamlessly transmitted by the threads of interdependence back to the core nations (Eichengreen, 1996).

Indeed, the interventions required to keep the international economy afloat became increasingly tortuous. Polanyi highlights the dramatic expansion of credit and debt utilized by the major powers to "maintain a semblance of unity in a dissolving economic system"; "balance of payments, budgets, exchanges were made to balance artificially in a number of countries with the help of a supposedly all-powerful credit mechanism" (GT, 232). Debts created on political grounds as the result of reparation demands were now eased by loans granted solely on political criteria to enable nations to make reparation payments. "When by the early 1930s, world trade was down to a trickle, international short term lending attained an unheard-of-degree of mobility", wrote Polanyi. "As long as the mechanism of international capital movements and short term credits functioned, no disequilibrium of actual trade was too great to be overcome by methods of bookkeeping" (GT, 206). This massive shell game papered over the widening imbalance between the stronger and weaker nations – to "shift the burden of incompletely stabilized economies of eastern Europe, first to the shoulders of the Western victors, second from there to the even broader shoulders of the United States of America" (GT, 232) – so that American financial surpluses could finance European current account deficits (the United States became the world's largest lender by the end of the 1920s). Yet once the Great Depression of 1929 paralyzed America, the shocks spread throughout the international economy, thereby plunging all into a deep crisis.

The destructive force of the incompatibility contradiction was in full evidence once government intervention again became the fulcrum of political economy. In order to shelter themselves against the ever-changing fortunes of the international economy, nations erected the full panoply of protectionist measures including import quotas, bi-lateral trade treaties, controls on capital exports, and exchange equalization. "While the intent was the freeing of trade, the effect was its strangulation", wrote Polanyi. "Instead of gaining access to the markets of the world, the governments, by their own acts, were barring their countries from any international nexus, and ever increasing sacrifices were needed to keep even a trickle of trade flowing" (GT, 27). Beggar-thy-neighbor policies had the unintentional effect of sharply contracting overall trade and effective demand across the international economy, precipitating mass unemployment and stagnating growth (Eichengreen, 1992). Increased public expenditures on social protection also generated higher deficits that led to a devalued currency and higher levels of taxation, which antagonized the middle classes that had been pauperized and traumatized by the vertiginous swings in finance that marked the era. In the intervening years after the war, many European governments, anxious to defuse the radicalization unleashed by the Russian Revolution, granted rights to mass suffrage, promoted ambitious welfare state measures, and encouraged unionization as a means of ensuring labor peace. A revitalized labor movement won real wage increases, often in excess of normal productivity gains, and in some cases a rise in labor's share of the national income; this squeezed business profits and discouraged investment, thereby intensifying the economic crisis even further.

This dynamic proved particularly detrimental to the gold standard. Its credibility hinged on its enshrinement as the unquestioned priority of economic policy and its ideological allure as the abiding "faith of the age" (GT, 25) (Block and Somers, 2014). Yet, an empowered working class pressured its political allies for the restoration of employment as the critical economic priority. Once economic policy became a keenly contested feature of domestic politics, the credibility of the gold standard was fatally eroded (Eichengreen, 1996). Financial investors could no longer guarantee that monetary authorities, when forced to choose between defense of the gold standard and measures to reduce unemployment, would automatically choose in favor of gold; even the slightest suspicion that a state might introduce expansionary measures now led to rapid capital flight and disinvestment of a nation's currency in order to avoid the losses that would entail should the currency devalue, which of course such action tended to precipitate as a self-fulfilling prophecy. "As long as the vote was restricted and only the few exerted political influence", wrote Polanyi:

> "interventionism was a much less urgent problem than it became when universal suffrage made the state the organ of the ruling million – the identical million who, in the economic realm, had often to carry in bitterness the burden of the ruled."
>
> (GT, 206)

As a result, destabilizing capital movements drastically expanded and domestic decision-making took on unparalleled significance internationally. "But such awareness was inseparable from the recognition that the foundations of the currency might depend upon political factors outside the national boundaries", he wrote:

> "Thus the social *bouleversement* which shook confidence in the inherent stability of the monetary medium shattered also the naïve concept of financial sovereignty in an interdependent economy. Henceforth, internal crises associated with the currency would tend to raise grave external issues."
>
> (GT, 24–5)

Where a sound currency became the "pivot of national politics", the straightjacket of the gold standard instantiated a deflationary logic within the strategic options of every government. "During the twenties…questions of social organization had to be wholly subordinated to the needs of the restoration of the currency", wrote Polanyi. "Deflation was the primary need; domestic institutions had to adjust as best they might" (GT, 233). All political leaders were faced with an unenviable trade-off between protecting their currency and thereby intensifying unemployment or safeguarding social protection and thereby weakening investment (which ultimately produced unemployment in any case). "In other words, there had to be", he bluntly stated, "either a cut in the social services or a fall in the exchanges" (GT, 228). He describes how one European labor government after another was forced to abandon office on the horns of this perverse dilemma: cutting social services or wages was an anathema, if not political suicide, yet abandoning the gold standard was equally deemed an unthinkable sacrilege (GT, 227–30).

This political paralysis precipitated a widespread social polarization and a generalizable political crisis. "In the final phase of the fall of the market economy", he claimed, "the conflict of class forces entered decisively" (GT, 219). The stark choice between employment or currency was ferociously contested along class lines. The working classes, battered by unemployment and falling wages, mobilized against employers who embraced the economic crisis as a means of disciplining the workers. "But what the laws of the market could not force upon reluctant wage earners", wrote Polanyi, "the foreign exchange mechanism most effectively performed" (GT, 230). Each class entrenched itself within its respective strongholds – the workers in parliament where their numbers had greater weight, employers in industry where they controlled decision making - and used these arenas to zealously attack the prerogatives of their adversaries (GT, 235).

"Under conditions such as these the routine conflict of interests between employers and employees took on an ominous character", argued Polanyi. "While a divergence of economic interests would normally end in compromise, *the separation of the economic and political spheres* in society tended to invest such clashes with grave consequences to the community" (GT, 235). On the one hand, "the undeniable fact that the working classes were in the position to force possibly ruinous interventions" had the potential to spark widespread panic and provoke a breakdown of the market economy (GT, 190). On the other hand, liberal economic elites, with the demonstration effect of the Russian Revolution firmly ensconced in their imagination, feared that worker's demands would eventually lead to a flagrant disregard for property rights and abandonment of the market system altogether. This led many to support the total exclusion of the working class from public life and the curtailment of democratic freedoms and institutions. Yet this proved to be a fatal error: the "stubbornness with which economic liberals, for a critical decade, had in the service of deflationary policies, supported authoritarian intervention, mainly resulted in a decisive weakening of the democratic forces which might have averted the catastrophe" (GT, 233–4). The rise of authoritarianism and the decline of liberal democracy, a pervasive feature of the epoch, was the direct consequence of the crisis of the market economy.

By the time Britain abandoned the gold standard in September 1931, the conditions were ripe for a "world revolution" – the rise of fascism as a world historical actor. "If ever there was a political movement", Polanyi wrote, "that responded to the needs of an objective situation and was not a result of fortuitous causes it was fascism" (GT, 237). Indeed, it was the evolution of this profound economic and political crisis that conditioned the political trajectory of fascism. He framed the causal relationship as follows:

> "During the period 1917–23 governments occasionally sought fascist help to help restore law and order: no more was needed to set the market system going. Fascism remained undeveloped. In the period 1924–29, when the restoration of the market system seemed ensured, fascism faded out as a political force altogether. After 1930 market economy was in general crisis. Within a few years fascism was a world power."
>
> (GT, 242)

Polanyi postulated an elective affinity between the institutional breakdown of the world economy and the prominence of fascist movements because he believed fascism represented a possible "escape route" from the stalemate of political economy. "Eventually the moment would come when the both the economic and political systems were threatened by complete paralysis", he wrote. "Fear would grip the people and leadership would be thrust upon those who offered an easy way out at whatever ultimate price. The time was ripe for the fascist solution" (GT, 236). The fascist solution to the impasse proposed reform of the market economy via the elimination of all democratic institutions, both in the industrial and in the political realms (GT, 237). To safeguard the efficient functioning of the market, fascist governments outlawed trade unions and working class parties and at the same time formed mandatory producer associations tied to corporatist plans laid down by the central state. Authoritarian (and soon to become totalitarian) dictatorships replaced liberal states, state intervention (featuring abandonment of the gold standard, deficit spending, public job creation, social welfare) superseded liberal orthodoxy, and in the international realm, autarchy was preferred to interdependence in order to foster maximum flexibility in the military-strategic arena. But fascism, as Polanyi well understood, was also a totalizing phenomenon that "radiated into almost every field of human activity whether political-economic, cultural, philosophic, artistic or religious" (GT, 239–40). It constituted a "political religion" with acolytes encouraged to spread the fascist gospel by joining and capturing a diverse range of civil society organizations and promised a program of social engineering that would systematically remake society (Berman, 2006).

Of course, the fascist solution to the crisis of the market economy could only be guaranteed if they were able to make the transition from political movement to state power, which in actual fact was restricted to only a handful of nations. Although Polanyi does not engage in any systematic comparison of these cases, he does offer some suggestive hints to account for the fascist's successful seizure of power in Germany, Italy and elsewhere. This, he argued, was related not to the size of the movement but rather to the influence it was able to exercise among economic and social elites:

> "Though usually aiming at a mass following, its potential strength was reckoned not by the numbers of its adherents but by the influence of the persons in high position whose good will the fascist leaders possessed and whose influence in the community could be counted upon to shelter them from the consequences of an abortive revolt, thus taking the risks out of revolution…Hitler was eventually put in power by the feudalist clique around President Hindenberg, just as Mussolini and Primo de Rivera were ushered into office by their respective sovereigns. Yet Hitler had a vast movement to support him; Mussolini had a small one; Primo de Rivera had none."
>
> (GT, 238)

In each case, the fascist ascension to power was manipulated through the tacit approval of government authorities and elites. This still begs the question of why these elites were so keen to see fascists enter government, to which Polanyi suggests several possible explanations. Some elites were influenced by the spread of various ideological movements – irrationalist philosophies, racist discourses, social Darwinism, an emphasis on martial discipline - that tilled the ideational soil in which fascism could prosper (GT, 238). There was also a blatant class calculation as well. Business leaders, whom he claimed had "an almost instantaneous emotional reaction" in favor of fascism, proved willing to countenance the brutal repression of their working class adversaries, little expecting that this coercion would then be unleashed against them in the economic field (GT, 239). Indeed, it was the weak attachment of the European elites to democratic institutions and principles that proved decisive in the fascist takeover. "If a 'revolutionary situation' is characterized by the psychological and moral disintegration of all forces of resistance", he wrote:

> "to the point where a handful of scantily armed rebels were enabled to storm the supposedly impregnable strongholds of *reaction*, then the 'fascist situation' was its complete parallel except for the fact that here the bulwarks of *democracy and constitutional liberties* were stormed and their defenses found wanting in the same spectacular fashion."
>
> (GT, 239)

Polanyi also marveled at the tactical ingenuity of fascist movements, their chameleon-like ability to be all things to all people, their bounty of "charismatic leadership". They derived an extra advantage when they were able to couple this ideological and tactical flexibility with a manipulation of the nationalist question, the festering sore left over from the poorly conceived peace: "the nascent fascist movement put itself almost everywhere into the service of the national issue; it could hardly have survived without this 'pick-up' job" (GT, 241). He also implied that the favorable structural opportunity that the fascists enjoyed required a particular interpretive framework that accepted the time was ripe for radical change. "Thus Germany, once defeated, was in the position to recognize the hidden shortcomings of the nineteenth century order", he wrote, "and to employ this knowledge to speed the destruction of that order. A kind of sinister intellectual superiority accrued to those of her statesman in the thirties who turned their minds to the task of disruption, which often extended to the development of new methods of finance, trade, war, and social organization…"(GT, 29).

Interrogating the roots of Fascism

Polanyi's argument concerning the centrality of the double movement to the rise of fascism represented the logical culmination, both theoretically and substantively, of *The Great Transformation*, and is a tour de force of narrative brilliance and explanatory ambition. As such, a close scrutiny of the conceptual and empirical foundations of his framework is certainly warranted. He believed that any persuasive explanation had to accomplish two tasks: first, it had to account for the presence of fascist movements across so many nations with such diverse historical, political and social characteristics; and second, it had to be able to explain the rise and fall in the fortunes of this movement during the inter-war years, specifically its evolution from marginalized movement to world power. Polanyi insisted that explanations rooted in specific historical or national factors were unable to answer both of these questions satisfactorily – in actual fact, these kind of accounts rarely framed the question in these terms whatsoever – but that his argument stressing the double movement offered distinct advantages. It could explain the first because the economic, political and social crisis, stimulated by the breakdown of the world economy, subjected all countries to the same development thereby creating a structural predilection for the emergence of these fascist movements; and for the second, he insisted fascism was "a social force that waxed and waned according to the objective situation" (GT, 239). Furthermore, he was convinced that the historical record and cross-national comparisons firmly validated these conclusions.

If we take the case of German fascism, there is no question that the historical record confirms much of his account. David Abraham's incisive work on the Weimar years, *The Collapse of the Weimar Republic*, highlights many of the same critical themes as Polanyi. He too envisages the crisis of liberal democracy and rise of fascism in Germany as having roots "in the political, ideological and social structures of Germany before the Great War" and suggested that the "Weimar era was the last act in the drama of Germany's nineteenth century" (Abraham, 1986, xlv–xlvi). Abraham traces how the inter-war economy was buffeted by the turbulence in the world economy leading to high unemployment and an agricultural crisis. He argues that organized labor's wage and social policy achievements paralyzed the German economy and gave its capitalists a rational incentive to roll back these gains. These contradictions generated seemingly intractable divisions within and between classes resulting in widespread class polarization and politicization of class struggle.[24] Each class attempted to harness the economic crisis to their own political advantage: workers to extend their economic gains into broader political and social rights, capital to restore profitability by dismantling labor's advantages altogether. These deep social cleavages undermined the social cohesion and trust that democracy requires in order to function effectively (Berman, 2006). It also contributed to the growing incoherence and continuous narrowing of public policy decision-making as Weimar officials found it impossible to reconcile class conflict and at the same time solve the pressing economic problems within the confines of the existing democratic order. The result, suggests Abraham in terms reminiscent of Polanyi's framework, was a "catastrophic equilibrium that opened the door to extra-systemic solutions" (Abraham, 1986, 274).

Despite this mutual affinity, Abraham's work also reveals some of the limits of Polanyi's approach. As he points out, by the fall of 1932, in advance of Hitler's succession, the worst of the economic crisis had passed and the Nazi's were in electoral decline so their eventual triumph hardly seems preordained. Polanyi tries to anticipate just this sort of parry: "Hitler claimed he had saved Germany from Bolshevism. But could it not be shown that the flood of unemployment which preceded his chancellorship had ebbed away before his rise to power?" (GT, 190). For Polanyi, this merely strengthened his fundamental claim that the collapse of the institutional order of the 19th century meant that the only actors that could possibly succeed were those such as the fascists who were prepared to destroy the old order. Yet this assumption has a fundamental flaw. If the crisis in the world economy had created a structural opening for political groups, such as fascists, which were devoted to the downfall of the international system, there was another German political group during this period that was equally committed to the destruction of the old order and who presumably should have been able to enjoy the fruits of such an opening as well. But whereas Polanyi rightly noted the fascist's tactical acumen, the German Communist party demonstrated a seemingly limitless, if not suicidal, capacity for political errors (of tactics, strategic alliances and, most critically, of analysis) (Bronner, 1990). There is no compelling reason why we should automatically attribute their failure, and by comparison the Nazi's success, directly to the structural conditions facing both groups. Yet this is essentially the tack he takes in the book: he insists that any repeat of the Bolshevik revolution in the West was an impossibility, because the structural conditions that led to this were inapplicable to the West (GT, 234). But Polanyi here is conflating the structural opportunity for movement mobilization with the likelihood of a movement seizing state power, which cannot be ascribed directly to these structural predispositions. His abiding appreciation of the political, ideological and strategic flexibility of fascist movements was not matched with an equal reckoning of the left's abject failures of social learning during the same period (Berman, 2006).[25]

Even if his overall account of the structural foundations of fascism remains compelling, the actual explanation of how fascist movements were transformed into fascist governments has a distinctly *ad hoc* feel. An explanation that implicated the double movement as the key causal force would need to begin with a comparative perspective that detailed the extent to which governments differentially implemented tariff and trade restrictions or draconian foreign exchange controls; the relative size of public spending for social protection; the scope of unionization and the strength of labor parties; the shifting fortunes of political coalitions; and the depths of economic downturn and the timing and vitality of recovery. As Polanyi recognized, countries that stayed on gold were far more likely to restrict trade and implement additional protectionist measures in order to strengthen balance of payments and stem gold outflows yet conversely, those that abandoned gold earlier were able to free up monetary policy and avoid prolonged slumps (Eichengreen and Irwin, 2011). But what he did not explore in any systematic fashion was the extent to which these institutional contexts and choices impacted on economic growth in a way that made it easier to resolve political stalemate and social polarization. Each of these features, which varied considerably across the advanced world, would necessarily intensify or weaken the putative structural predilection of the double movement to lead to fascism.

Ultimately, what is missing from his analysis is a more sustained explanation of how this structural potential was ultimately resolved in all nations by *political* means; in other words, the success or failure of political movements (and the specific ideological/political pathways they espoused) depended in the last instance on the decisive importance of political factors such as party ideologies and coalitional strategies (Berman, 2006). The intransigence of German elites to countenance any compromise that would have preserved the democratic system was essentially a political choice to abandon democracy (GT, 257). Once they deemed that the costs of maintaining liberal democracy were too high, elites convinced themselves that the only feasible solution to their economic bind was a dismantling of the political system. But equally, it was the tactical blunders, ideological inflexibility and strategic ineptitude, especially as regards its inability to form a durable progressive coalition or to offer a common reform program that broke with the straightjacket of liberal orthodoxy, of the ruling German Social Democratic party that "helped to bring about precisely what it sought to avoid" (Bronner, 1990, 52; Berman, 2006). A blind attachment to outworn formulas of social change based on class struggle and historical materialism meant the SPD became, in Mark Blyth's felicitous phrase, "mass forces for political inaction", which doomed them to political irrelevancy. "There was no *economic* way", concluded Abraham, "because there was neither *political* will nor an alternative political economy" (Abraham, 1986, xvi). Of course, these abject political failures owed to contingent historical accidents as well as to long-standing antecedents rooted in the specific context of German history and ideological struggles within the socialist movement where the potential for achieving meaningful reform within capitalism was grievously underestimated, leaving no other way out of political and social paralysis than Fascism (Berman, 2006).

By marginalizing these political concerns in favor of a structural determinism, Polanyi also weakens the salience of his approach to other comparative episodes. One empirical anomaly to note is the case of Sweden, which in the interwar years was ferociously buffeted by the turbulence in the world economy: unemployment skyrocketed, high wage growth fueled a decline in profits and economic growth, and fierce class polarization marked the political scene. Yet, despite fitting nearly all the crucial "structural" requirements, fascism remained stillborn in Sweden. Gregory Luebbert attributed this to the fortuitous political alliance constructed between the urban working class and the middle peasantry under the auspices of the Swedish social democratic party (Luebbert, 1991). Through efficacious political bargaining and social pacts that elicited shared compromises on behalf of economic growth, the Swedish government was able to avoid conventional deflationary policies, won peasant support for democracy (in some countries where fascism took state power, it was the peasantry that constituted the mass base for fascism), and steered a social democratic route between liberal democracies and fascism, a trajectory that is somewhat underdeveloped by Polanyi in his analysis.

The case of Italy also bears mentioning because it too demonstrates the difficulty of establishing a close correlation between the structural imperative of the double movement and fascism. This example would appear to only weakly fit his schema given that Italian fascism became a mass movement as early as 1921 and took state power in 1924, years before the full crisis of the world economy exploded. Polanyi's rebuttal to this is interesting for the explicit distinction he makes between fascism and authoritarianism:

> "Until then [1929] fascism had hardly been more than a trait in Italy's authoritarian government, which otherwise differed but little from those of a more traditional type. It now emerged as an alternative solution of the problem of an industrial society."
>
> (GT, 243)

Although he is correct that Italian fascism's "social engineering" phase greatly accelerated after 1929, there are two reservations that can be lodged against this assertion. In the first place, scholars have claimed that many of the roots of the fascist state could be found in the pre-1929 period (Morgan, 1995). Mussolini's famous dictum – "everything within the state, nothing outside the state, nothing against the state" – was uttered in 1925 and signaled the growing totalitarian nature of his government: the depiction of the state as an ethical authority and the embodiment of moral values; the total subordination of the individual to the dictates of the state; the growing corporatization of economic life; the colonization of life worlds and culture to construct a broader basis of consent for the fascist regime (Morgan, 1995, 80; De Grazia, 1981). It is doubtful whether the putative characterization of this government as authoritarian (which I associate with the suppression of political opposition, police repression, and the elimination of independent media) rather than fascist accurately captures the complexity of the Italian case.

Sheri Berman, whose work emphasizes the ideological evolution and coalitional strategies of political parties, hints at a more fundamental disagreement with Polanyi. "But the fact that the precise nature of political battles and their outcomes varied greatly from country to country", she writes, "shows that one needs to go beyond structural changes and cross-national exogenous shocks and examine local political contexts and local political actors to get the full story" (Berman, 2006, 11). In this view, structural crises can never constitute a sufficient explanation for the specific form and content of political action. All material circumstances and political pressures must be *interpreted* by social actors in ways that are conditioned by ideological and political struggles within political parties, which is what accounts for the variation across nations. But at the same time, she is keen to illuminate the close similarities between such wildly different political ideologies such as fascism and social democracy in terms of their common project to protect society from the malign market – both stressed full employment as a policy goal and promised improved social welfare measures; both recognized corporatist institutions were essential for economic management and stressed the state's paramount role in economic planning; both presented themselves as representatives of the 'people's' interests – although this would seemingly take us back to Polanyi's initial insight about the centrality of the double movement, in that they essentially represented different variables of the same process.

Conclusion

If Polanyi's argument linking the double movement to the cataclysms of the 20th century still requires amendment to be fully persuasive, it is not to fault his historical imagination or conceptual framework but rather because I believe his primary ambition – to uncover the single causal factor illuminating the social change of the long 19th century – may be ultimately unrealizable. In this regard, I have been especially persuaded by the formidable work of Charles Tilly, a self-confessed "recovering structuralist", who suggested in a widely influential broadside on the study of revolution (followed thereafter by jeremiads in other prominent fields in sociology), that the pursuit of a single, over-arching model of revolution which could somehow explain all known examples of this phenomenon was a fool's errand.[26] Even the most ingenious of analytical approaches, he insisted, was doomed to failure because it was looking for answers that could not be supplied. "I am arguing that regularities in political life are broad, indeed trans-historical, but do not operate in the form of recurrent structures and processes at a large scale", argued Tilly.

> "They consist of recurrent causes which in different circumstances and sequences compound into highly variable but nonetheless explicable effects…The test of a good theory is therefore not so much to identify similarities among instances as to account systematically and parsimoniously for their variation."
>
> (Tilly, 1995, 1601)

Despite offering the building blocks for such an analytical framework of the double movement, it should be clear by this point that I do not believe that Polanyi's account actually offered this kind of explanation.

Even if I have found fault with his specific historical analysis, the wider point he stipulates –namely, that the social order of capitalist democracy (as encompassed in the double movement problematic) is structurally and endemically prone to crisis – remains a formidable insight (Fraser, 2013, 2018; Streeck, 2011, 2016). If we are to carry the ideas of the double movement forward into an analysis of contemporary political economy, this recognition of the durable boundary struggles between the opposing poles of the double movement will be our lodestar but, at the same time, it will be necessary to jettison the idea that the double movement can ever be the singular phenomena that he vouchsafed. As I have argued in the previous chapters, it is the very analytical complexity of his approach that offers such rich material for constructing an alternative perspective on the double movement that emphasizes the interplay of social processes across historical periods and comparative cases. Of course, this would require a separate book to elaborate in any systematic way but it is important in the present volume to explore whether the dynamic that he so imaginatively identified in his work is still relevant at present and investigate whether the insights of the double movement can be utilized to illuminate the contours of the core processes of our present market society. It is to this task that we now turn to in Chapter 6.

Notes

1 Michael Mann, in his magisterial study *The Sources of Social Power* (Mann, 1993), offers an analysis that is remarkably similar to the account given by Polanyi. He locates similar culprits of social change: "a predominantly diffused capitalism and the authoritative nation state became the principal restructurers of Western society" (Mann, 1993, 737). And like Polanyi, he argued that these two factors were inextricably intertwined in a single institutional system: "Thus, civilization during this period came as near to a single general developmental process as any ever has" (Mann, 1993, 737–8). Yet, at the same time, Mann distances himself from his insistence that the double movement was the critical event: "It is a basic tenet of my work that societies are not systems. There is no ultimately determining structure to our entire social experience" (Mann, 1993, 736).

2 Nor is it clear whether the order of causation (from self-regulating market to liberalism) is the same as hypothesized by Polanyi. In Germany, for instance, it was an authoritarian state, admittedly one undergoing limited democratization, that inaugurated the process of capitalist development from above, and while this did indeed create subsequent pressures for democracy, liberalism as a political system was still considerably underdeveloped across the continent.

3 Jeffrey Frieden interestingly argued that the gold standard could actually be considered as much a tenet of social protection as a component of the free market system: "Indeed, there is some good reason to regard an international monetary regime as a public good…some generally agreed rules of the game…are needed to provide the stability necessary for international trade and payments" (Frieden, 1992, 209). And it is even more curious when we consider that the paramount instrument of monetary protectionism, central banks, were often little more than private banking institutions pursuing market goals through market mechanisms (Gallarotti, 1995).

4 This proposition of a qualitative shift in imperialism was a staple of both late Victorian ideology and Marxism (see Gallagher and Robinson, 1953, for an extended discussion).

5 This policy was an atavistic repetition of the British government's colonial policy in Ireland . In the late 16th century, England launched a capitalist colonization of Ireland that represented an early forerunner of market fundamentalism. It presupposed the complete restructuring of Irish land holdings along capitalist lines that replicated the English commercial model, which entailed the expropriation of indigenous landholders in favor of English and Scottish settlers who incorporated

the latest capitalist innovations. Polanyi seriously underestimates the extent to which imperialism was a permanent feature of English capitalist development.

6 The gold standard, as an example, is posited as the central priority in several passages: "of these institutions, the gold standard proved crucial; its failure was the proximate cause of the catastrophe. By the time it failed, most of the other institutions had been sacrificed in a vain effort to save it" (GT, 3; see also 192, 217). Yet, he also emphasizes the primacy of the balance of power system: "Power had precedence over profit. However closely their relations interpenetrated, ultimately it was war that laid down the law to business" (GT, 12).

7 These economic mechanisms were also duplicated at the political level. In Britain, the entire program of reform under *laissez-faire* was predicated on the cognate belief that legislation must ultimately follow along self-reinforcing lines. Polanyi wrote: "Thus the Anti-Corn Law Bill of 1846 was the corollary of Peel's Bank Act of 1844, and both assumed a laboring class which, since the Poor Law Amendment Act of 1834, was forced to give their best under the threat of hunger, so that wages were regulated by the price of grain. The three great measures formed a coherent whole" (GT, 138). Polanyi does not explore whether this same nexus was a common feature of social development in the rest of 19th-century Europe.

8 Any number of scholars inspired by Marxism have placed contradictions at the center of their analysis, including James O'Connor with the second contradiction of capitalism (O'Connor, 1988) and Jurgen Habermas on legitimation crises (Habermas, 1973). Among contemporary scholars, Nancy Fraser traces the transformation of fictitious commodities that has undermined the very conditions that capitalism needs for its own survival. Speaking of the clash between commodification and nature, she writes: "simultaneously, needing and rubbishing nature, capitalism is a cannibal that devours its own vital organs, like a serpent that eats its own tail" (Fraser, 2021, 101). She employs the same vivid metaphor in numerous other papers (Fraser, 2015, 159, 165; 2020, 9).

9 Hannes Lacher acknowledges the centrality of contradiction to Polanyi's argument in GT but he insists that Polanyi consciously developed this position against Marxism: "an attempt to conceptualize and operationalize its dynamics and contradictions in a non-Marxist foundation" (Lacher, 2019, 697).

10 As an example, Neil Smelser used the same phrase "disruptive strains" to characterize one of the key stages in his model of collective action (Smelser, 1962). Gareth Dale also fascinatingly traces how Polanyi's close study of the work of Ferdinand Tonnies in the 1930s influenced his thinking in this regard (Dale, 2010).

11 Block and Somers, following on from their "always embedded economy" stance discussed in Chapter 3, argue that this thesis of "impairment" offers a misguided perspective on Polanyi's work. Block writes: "Even by the logic of [Polanyi's] own argument, there can never be a self-regulating market system, so the idea of impairing its functioning is an absurdity" (Block, 2003, 297). In the same way that I argued their neglect of the processes of disembedding was not helpful in reconstructing the argument of the double movement, I would similarly maintain that the central narrative arc of his book, namely the interconnection between the self-regulating market and the rise of Fascism, is inexplicable without the centrality of contradictions to his argument.

12 It is worth noting the influence of Polanyi's argument on future scholars. In his seminal text, *Contradictions of the Welfare State*, Claus Offe makes an equivalent formulation: "capitalism cannot co-exist *with*, neither can it exist, *without* the welfare state" (Offe, 1984, 153).

13 Polanyi's discussion about the mutual incompatibility contradiction stresses a similar dynamic stipulated by proponents of the "profit squeeze", who argued that

the slowdown in Western economies in the 1970s could be traced to the malign effects of working class strength and welfare state growth on profitability and productivity (Marglin and Schor, 1990).

14 Charles Lindblom, in "The Market as Prison", makes very much the same point: "[T]he standard formulation of one of our economic problems is that union pressure on wages causes inflation or restriction of job opportunities in the immediately affected industrial firm. *Given* a market system, that is probably true. But let me suggest the other possible formulation: given the inevitable and understandable desire of workers to increase their share of national income, a market system will produce inflation or unemployment. The second proposition is no less true than the first" (Lindblom, 1984, 9).

15 This very dynamic – often characterized as the conflict between accumulation and legitimation – was the central focus of the remarkable body of work on state theory from the 1970s onward as exemplified by Fred Block, Jurgen Habermas, Claus Offe, Nicos Poulantzas, and others. For a useful summary of these debates, see Carnoy, 1984 or Pierson, 1996.

16 For an opposing view that emphasizes Polanyi's neglect of the class biases of the state, see Halperin, 2004.

17 Some scholars have suggested that imperialism was one solution to this dilemma. Once states reduced democratic associationalism, it still required a strategy whereby working class groups could be integrated into the social order so as to minimize their potential for social unrest. Incorporating workers into the national polity through nationalist rhetoric and militarism was seen as a low cost solution but of course the intensification of chauvinistic hatreds engendered by such imperialism served to undermine the foundations of the international system itself (Mann, 1993). Polanyi surprisingly took little note of this dynamic in the text.

18 This is essentially the argument made by Charles Kindleberger in his influential study of the Great Depression (Kindleberger, 1986). In the absence of public policy autonomy at the level of the continent or international economy, and given the inability of any national government to exercise the necessary leadership by stabilizing spending and acting as a lender of last resort (the UK no longer possessed the capacity, and the US refused the role), it was inevitable that the contagion of the financial crisis could not be contained thereby transforming it into a wider social and political catastrophe.

19 Keynes made a related point: "The nineteenth century relied on the future permanence of its own happy experiences and disregarded the warning of past misfortunes" (quoted in DeCecco, 1978, 39).

20 In one passage, Polanyi implies that self-regulation was more likely to be efficacious in circumstances where nations were on an equal footing within the international economy: "In none of these cases could processes of economic self-healing be relied upon...But this would have required that the countries should be more or less equal participants in a system of a world division of labor, which emphatically was not the case" (GT, 207). But this point is not followed up in any meaningful way.

21 Many of the writers in state theory that succeeded Polanyi attempted to explicate the conditions under which the state might successfully achieve this equilibrium. Claus Offe, as an example, stressed the importance of institutional design: of constructing an effective administrative separation of accumulation and welfare tasks in order to minimize rivalries and keep mutual encroachment to a minimum; of making decision making more transparent in order to better anticipate side effects; and of establishing a widespread capacity for democratic deliberation that provided greater reflexivity of previous policy outcomes (Offe, 1992).

22 This is essentially the substance of Gallarotti's analysis as well who writes: "The regime proved only as strong as the norms upon which it was founded. When this classical liberal consensus withered away with the coming of World War I, so too was the regime doomed" (Gallarotti, 1995, 13).

23 Although my focus is solely on the development of his argument in *The Great Transformation*, Polanyi wrote many other articles on fascism; for a comprehensive review of his contribution, see Dale, 2010; Millett, 2021.

24 One of the hallmarks of Abraham's book is his painstaking delineation of the shifting intra- and inter-class alignments that resulted from the ever changing fortunes of the international economy: between large estate owners and middle farmers, between the dynamic, capital intensive, export oriented industrialists (who initially supported the Weimar social policies) and older, labor-intensive, domestic oriented industrialists and between capital and labor. See also Berman, 2006, Halperin, 2004.

25 Gareth Dale traces the ways in which Polanyi's political engagements during the inter war years, encompassing communism, guild socialism, Christian radicalism and social democracy, impacted on his intellectual framework (Dale, 2010, 2016).

26 Instead, Tilly argued for a research strategy predicated on uncovering the recurrent pattern of social mechanisms, which he pursued for contentious action (McAdam, Tarrow and Tilly, 2001), collective violence (Tilly, 2003), inequality (Tilly, 1998) and democratization (Tilly, 2006).

Chapter 6

The Double Movement in the Contemporary Era

Polanyi was convinced the era of the double movement had reached its decisive apogee as a result of the cataclysm of the Second World War. "In retrospect our age will be credited with having seen the end of the self-regulating market", he proclaimed. "The restoration of the past is as impossible as the transferring of our troubles to another planet" (GT, 142; 250–1). All the absolutes of *laissez-faire* civilization imploded in the face of the unprecedented horrors of war. Policy makers could no longer take refuge in the psychic security of the free market and finally accepted the necessity for a truce between society and economy that would banish self-regulation forever. "Within the nations we are witnessing a development", he predicted, "under which the economic system ceases to lay down the law to society and the primacy of society over that system is secured" (GT, 251). In the last chapter of *The Great Transformation*, Polanyi engaged in philosophical and political speculation about the contours of the future regime, already contained within the interstices of the old order, but there was little question that he accepted that the future shape of capitalist democracy had been irrevocably transformed. Indeed, he presciently anticipated many of the political developments of the post-war era (the growth of the United Nations, the development of transnational institutions such as the World Bank and the International Monetary Fund [IMF]) as the following passage aptly demonstrates: "The only alternative to this disastrous condition of affairs was the establishment of an international order endowed with an organized power which would transcend national sovereignty. Such a course, however, was entirely beyond the horizon of the time. No country in Europe, not to mention the United States, would have submitted to such a system" (GT, 22).

"It cannot be denied", admitted Block and Somers, "that, however great a thinker, Polanyi was very much a failed prophet" (Block and Somers, 2014, 218) given that he failed to anticipate the possibility of a resurgent market fundamentalism. However, paradoxically, I would argue that much of the impetus for the renewed appreciation of his corpus in academic and political life in recent years can be directly traced to this dilemma. If a new market utopian project had indeed resurfaced, then who better than Polanyi to help us make sense of this new self-regulating system. And at the same time, if

DOI: 10.4324/9781003133186-6

indeed the return of *laissez-faire* demonstrated the validity of a double movement cycle, then would not an optimistic interpretation promise the eventual return of the countermovement and the ascendancy of social protection?

There are a number of analytical questions that must be addressed in order to explore these questions. First, we need to more precisely delineate the post war system and its neoliberal successor and ask whether it can be properly understood as a renewed iteration of the double movement. Did the post war period represent an era of Polanyian social protection (Ruggie, 1982; Berman, 2006; Marglin and Schor, 1990) or a renewed project of disembedding and self-regulation (Halperin, 2004; Lacher, 1999, 2019). In other words, did it represent a fulfillment of Polanyi's vision or a "negation of all that Polanyi hoped and wrote for" (Lacher, 1999, 344)? Is our current interregnum of globalization and neoliberalism an avaricious repeat of the 19th-century self-regulating market or is it a hybrid system combining elements of both dominant social principles of market and social protection? In adjudicating these questions, we return not only to the question of the balance of power within these periods but also how we understand transitions from one era to another. In the first section of this chapter, I explore these questions with a stylized overview of the past seven decades of political economy from a double movement standpoint that stresses the dynamic, dialectical intersection at the heart of the double movement.

Second, if we are indeed in a new double movement conjuncture, to what extent can the expanded framework sketched earlier offer a useful heuristic to explain the contours of the neoliberal period? Obviously, it would require a separate book to do justice to this question –to explore whether the explanatory framework Polanyi used to account for the origin of the self-regulating market in the 19th-century was equally relevant to the establishment of neoliberalism; to trace the extension and deepening of market imperatives and their destructive consequences; to identify the political and social agencies for social protection; to explore the destabilizing contradictions and crisis tendencies confronting all political and economic elites – so, given obvious space limitations, I have chosen instead to focus on two themes that can illuminate the benefits of a Polanyian framework. In this second section, I first explore the profound social and political consequences of neoliberalism, with specific attention to the interaction of insecurity and inequality (as exemplified in the work of Polanyi and Thomas Piketty); and second, the relationship of the double movement to the rise of right-wing populism. Finally, in the concluding section, I turn to the question of crisis and the future of the double movement. Is neoliberalism's demise imminent, as has been predicted repeatedly over the past two decades, or is its unexpected resilience and instability the paradox to be answered? In the last section, we explore the crises and contradictions of the present era and probe the tendentious question of what comes next for the double movement.

The Return of the Double Movement

As previously highlighted, one of the critical questions implied by Polanyi's work is whether the double movement actually constitutes a permanent feature of social change throughout capitalist history. Even if we are willing to discount his flawed prediction about the demise of the double movement as an understandable bout of hopeful optimism in the aftermath of the horrors of World War II, any presumption that the double movement is a cyclical regularity in history would need to demonstrate a number of propositions. First, we need to identify that there is a discrete cycle that can be ascertained: in other words, a social phenomenon (the double movement) can be clearly specified and demonstrated to have repeatedly occurred across separate historical periods. Second, we should be able to identify the starting and end points of these cycles and offer a rationale for the timing and duration of these particular critical junctures. This is not so straightforward, as it implies a capacity to adjudicate which of the leading social principles are in the ascendancy even if the interrelationship between embedding and disembedding remains the primary focus of attention. Third, the driving force(s) underpinning each cycle can be readily identified, in terms of the intensity and direction of change, the motivations and strategies of key actors, and the internal evolution of the cycle whereby one phase systematically leads into the succeeding one. However, it should be stressed that, even if one accepts the notion of an trans-historical cycle of the double movement, there need not be any presumption that every recurrence of the phenomena will necessarily be the same; the duration, trajectory and outcomes of cycles can vary considerably depending upon different circumstances and distinct historical sequences.

While Polanyi viewed the mutually constitutive components of the double movement (self-regulating market, market society, countermovement, clash of social principles) as a singular, dynamic system, it is also true that he appears to treat these contrasting principles of social organization as distinct temporal stages in which the balance of power within the double movement can oscillate, and one of the social principles can dominate. His book posits two distinct occurrences of the double movement. Using his timetable, the onset of the self-regulating market and development of a market society lasted from 1834 to 1875, roughly tracking the high water mark of the laissez-faire period. He dates the full establishment of a social protection period from 1875 until 1914 (even if countermovements and the social protective instinct were present in the earlier era). The period 1914–1944 contained an attenuated free market experiment (1919–1929) and a transitional social protection period where the influence of liberal orthodoxy was not completely extinguished and nations experimented with diverse forms of social protection (1929–1939). If we were to extend this chronology beyond the period of Polanyi's own analysis in *The Great Transformation*, then it is necessary to adjudicate the contours of two successive historical periods: the post war era from 1945 until 1980 and the neoliberal era from 1980 to the present.[1] It is to an analysis of these periods that we now turn, although I want to register a preliminary caution at the outset: the following sections are not intended as a comprehensive account of either period but rather to demonstrate the affinities to the Polanyian framework presented earlier.

Embedded Liberalism

The unparalleled cataclysm of the Great Depression and World War II left a deep psychological scar on economic policymakers and political elites who wanted at all costs to avoid the mass unemployment and political instability of the inter-war years. The so-called "Golden Age" system from 1945–1980 represented a conscious repudiation (institutionally and ideologically) of 19th-century *laissez-faire* and the economic nationalism of the inter-war years (Berman, 2006; Blyth, 2002; Helleiner, 1994; Marglin and Schor, 1990; Piketty, 2014; Ruggie, 1982). Policymakers were convinced that in order to avoid the scourge of mass unemployment and the political cataclysm of the 1930s, markets had to be reined in to promote social stability and states' capacity to direct economic development considerably augmented in order to safeguard society and the market system itself. "Unchecked markets were now viewed as dangerous, societal interests were now viewed as trumping private prerogatives; and states were seen as having the right – indeed the duty- to intervene in the economy and society to protect a 'common' or 'public' interest", argues Sheri Berman:

> "After 1945, in other words, people began to perceive states as the guardian of society, and economic imperatives were often forced to take a back seat to social aims. The result was the reconciliation of things long viewed as incompatible: a well-functioning capitalist system, democracy, and social stability."
>
> (Berman, 2006, 12)

In a justly famous article, John Ruggie, explicitly building upon Polanyi's framework, argued that the post-war era could be best understood as a system of what he termed "embedded liberalism" (Ruggie, 1982). This institutional order, conceived at the Bretton Woods conference in 1944, linked domestic interventionism with a new international monetary and financial order featuring stable exchange rates, limits on destabilizing capital flows, selective tariffs, and newly designed institutions (International Monetary Fund, the World Bank, and the like) that promoted economic development and provided assistance to developing nations.

The Golden Age created a virtuous circle at the heart of the market economy that promoted economic growth, prosperity, equality and social opportunity (Marglin and Schor, 1990). Massive increases in labor productivity in tandem with strong trade unions guaranteed higher wages, which became translated into higher consumption and tax revenues, which in turn enabled the provision of higher quality public goods (education, health care, housing, transport) that dramatically improved living standards and well-being. "A strong case can be made", argue Jacob Hacker and Paul Pierson, "that the twentieth century witnessed greater progress on key dimensions of social well-being than did all the centuries of human experience before it combined" (Hacker and Pierson, 2016, 56). With expanded social safety nets, economic security was increasingly seen as a social right (Somers, 2008) and a broad class compromise helped create a partial decommodification of social life (Offe, 1984). Inequality in the advanced nations fell for four consecutive decades as a result of real wage increases for workers and higher tax burdens on the wealthy. A greater share of national income went to labor rather than capital, middle-class livelihoods were extended to a growing portion of the population, and social mobility was considerably enhanced. Colin Crouch emphasized the formidable political transformation at the heart of the post war bargain:

> "Ordinary people were increasingly able to determine their collective fate through electoral processes. They built mass parties that could represent their interests in government. Business recognized limits to its power and answered to democratically legitimated governments. *Markets were subordinated to politics not the other way around.*"
>
> (Crouch, 2005, my emphasis)

Of course, different states chose distinct pathways within this new institutional order, but this general model represented the political consensus cutting across ideologies encompassing social democracy, liberalism and Christian Democracy, all of which agreed, albeit for differing reasons, that market forces needed to be moderated on behalf of social stability. Not surprisingly, decades of uninterrupted growth, material prosperity and strong social safety nets became entrenched as the common wisdom and shaped expectations of what a modern capitalist society should look like, with deeply rooted popular perceptions of continuous economic progress and upward mobility viewed as a basic right of democratic citizenship (Somers, 2008; Streeck, 2014).

However, even in this era, the forces of disembedding were hardly quiescent (Lacher, 1999). Market relations were extended, intensified and deepened during the post war years. Revolutionary transformations in information, communications and transport technologies enabled production and distribution to be internationalized into globally integrated networks of production. Commodification vastly expanded in the developing world featuring: widespread proletarianization and the establishment of a global division of labor; dispossession of the peasantry and elimination of customary institutions; and commercialization of arable lands. An invigorated ethos of consumption and materialism became prominent cultural markers of the period throughout the advanced world. Hannes Lacher is prominent among Polanyi scholars in rejecting the idea of the post war era as a period of embedding but rather insists that it represented a prodigious expansion and deepening of market imperatives. It:

> "neither banished the profit motive from the center of the organization of material life, nor did it render markets into a mere accessory of economic life...welfare capitalism was not a 'society without markets' but a society in which the logic of the market had penetrated to the very core of social arrangements."
>
> (Lacher, 1999, 325)[2]

This is a salutary reminder but the false binary it implies -that only when disembedding is completely eliminated and the market totally subjugated to democratic oversight can we truly be said to have entered an embedding stage of the double movement- is not instructive in terms of reconstructing the double movement (Block and Somers, 2021). Such a dichotomous position discounts the formidable accomplishments of the Golden Age for well-being, equality and social justice and flattens the complex, dialectical relationship of the double movement that I have been emphasizing throughout.

Nevertheless, even if one wants to posit the historical significance of the Golden Age, it is still incumbent to explain its relative short duration and the subsequent transition to neoliberalism. The most compelling explanation confirms the Polanyian insight of historical change presented earlier in Chapter 2, where transitions to new periods of the double movement represent discontinuous events that contain the seeds of their own destruction (Blyth, 2002; Streeck, 2009). Michal Kalecki, in a ground-breaking article published in 1943, presciently identified the core contradiction that would destabilize and undermine the institutional order of the Golden Age (Kalecki, 1943). Sustained full employment (alongside trade union strength and collective bargaining) pushed up wages and enhanced worker's ability to move jobs. Thus, in order to retain their skilled workers, firms had no choice but to pay higher wages but the only way to do this and still remain profitable was to raise prices. But replicating the classic contradiction of individual/collective rationality, if all businesses opted for this strategy, it would spark an inflationary spiral. This in turn lowered the value of any future wage increases, thereby sparking labor conflict and lowering investment, which exacerbated the basic contradiction. Governments attempted multiple fixes to these structural tendencies, prominent among them a generous monetary policy that enabled wages to grow faster than productivity or profitability, which preserved social peace and employment but at the cost of rampant inflation (Streeck, 2014).

With labor's share of national income steadily increasing and managerial discipline sharply curtailed, the only way to restore business confidence was a set of policy initiatives that subsequently became enshrined as neoliberalism:

reinstating managerial discipline, destroying inflation, increasing returns to investment and restoring price stability as the key marker of economic policy.[3] The pathway to neoliberalism in this framework was a conscious effort by capital to reduce the countervailing power of labor and their ability to resist business interests. In short, the collapse of the Golden Age and triumph of neoliberalism represented a project of class power, a political response by market and political actors to the democratic gains of the subordinate classes that weakened class discipline and curtailed profitability (Blyth, 2002; Hacker and Pierson, 2010; Harvey, 2005; Panitch and Gindin, 2012; Slobodian, 2018).[4] Not surprisingly, the opening stages of the new cycle began with pitched battles against organized labor – the PATCO strike in the United States and the 1984 Miners Strike in the UK were illustrative examples – followed by a precipitous rise in interest rates to well over 20%, owing to the shock therapy imposed by Federal Reserve chair Paul Volcker that tamed inflation but at the expense of high unemployment, which in effect marked the dismantling of Golden Age social protections.

At the height of the Golden Age, the Polanyian promise of a capitalism that guaranteed economic prosperity, equality and social stability appeared to have become an enviable reality. But, it proved chimerical and this has prompted numerous scholars to reconsider the epoch. Piketty has suggested that the post war era was a historical anomaly, the product of a set of fortuitous circumstances that are unlikely to be repeated, before the fundamental dynamics of capitalism inevitably reasserted themselves (Piketty, 2014). This has long been the position of many Marxist scholars who have long argued that social democratic reforms to tame capitalism are illusory and bound to be short-lived (Lacher, 1999; Panith and Gindin, 2010). In a fundamental sense, this takes us back to the paradox raised earlier: why do all capitalist states, despite quite different historical and institutional legacies, and with the foreknowledge that previous experiments with *laissez-faire* resulted in social upheaval and political cataclysm, repeatedly return to solutions that privilege market freedom and the reproduction of class inequality? There must be something inherent to capitalism as a social order that continually promotes this solution to problems of capital accumulation and profitability, which is to what we now turn.

The return of laissez-faire

As scholars have observed, neoliberalism is an umbrella term that carries widely differing meanings.[5] Peter Hall and William Sewell argue for four such distinct ways in which neoliberalism is formulated: as a policy paradigm, political ideology, economic theory, and social imaginary (Hall and Sewell, 2013). I do not have the space here to discuss each of these permutations and, in any case, my primary interest is to enquire whether the onset of neoliberalism can be understood within the framework of the double movement.

Although there are certainly important differences between the 19th-century self-regulating market and its 20th-century successor – the weight of finance in the global economy, the unprecedented role of inter-state cooperation and crisis containment, the reintroduction of capitalist social relations into the former Soviet bloc nations – it is the similarities that are particularly striking. The internationalization of capitalist imperatives; the accelerated speed of everyday social life; the interdependencies of fate whereby a New York hedge fund manager and a cotton farmer in Karnataka are both shaped by the unpredictable forces of climate change; the mobilization of state power on behalf of class interests: all of these are as much hallmarks of the 20th/21st-century iteration of the double movement as they were in the 19th century. However, unlike the 19th and 20th centuries, when capitalism co-existed with other social formations (slavery, serfdom, mercantilism, state socialism), capitalism as an institutional order is now nearly universal with no challengers in sight. "As it extricated itself from the social democratic regime imposed on it after 1945", emphasized Wolfgang Streeck, " it [capitalism] became *more like itself*, revealing in the course of its development, its 'true nature', or its 'essence'…In the neoliberal era…capitalism became progressively *more capitalist*" (Streeck, 2010, 33).

Indeed, the drive to subject greater and greater areas of social, political and cultural life to the dictates and imperatives of the market takes center stage in a Polanyian lens of the present era (Harvey, 2005; Sewell, 2008; Streeck, 2016). We live in an era where it appears as if every social entity is in danger of being monetized as a commodity to be bought and sold on a market. The creation of new fictitious commodities has escalated at a furious pace, whereby the genome, the information commons, knowledge, social reproduction (via global care chains and adoption) and even nature (via carbon offsets, emission permits, environmental derivatives) are all at risk of being converted into valuable assets and forms of capital (Burawoy, 2010). There have equally been significant transformations in the original three fictitious commodities of labor, land and money, which is where the dynamics of neoliberalism most closely approximate a second coming of the self-regulating market, as safeguards against full commodification has been eradicated in multiple Polanyian crisis zones (Fraser, 2013, 2014; Streeck, 2016). A new wave of proletarianization in developing societies has created a new global proletariat in China, India, Bangladesh, Indonesia and urban areas across the globe, but at the same time, there has been a destructive wave of decommodification as more and more workers are shuffled into the informal sector or, even worse, into bonded labor, a modern form of slavery (Bales, 2000). "Increasingly, exploitation is a privilege", insists Michael Burawoy, "rather than a curse" (Burawoy, 2010, 308).

In the advanced world, a new world of precarious work confronts all workers: constant job restructuring and the decline of good paying jobs, loss of job security, stagnant wages (especially for those with only a high school education), vertiginous fluctuations in income and livelihoods, demands for greater flexibility, free lancing and short term contracts. As Richard Sennett insists, this drive for flexibility is incompatible with the development of genuine capacities for productive work and stable professional and craft identities (Sennett, 1998). Workers face a relentless pressure to upgrade their human capital and marketable skills, to adopt an entrepreneurial orientation and a viable market identity that can win them their next temporary position (Azmanova, 2020; Standing, 2015). The pace of work has dramatically intensified (owing to corporate downsizing, price competition within product markets, and outsourcing) with workers facing longer hours, irregular shifts, unpaid overtime, weekend work, a destabilizing eradication of the work/leisure divide that ties workers to their workplace 24/7, all of which has undermined family life and led to profound caring deficits (developments that have been exacerbated under pandemic conditions of remote working).

The commodification of land/nature has been deepened and intensified as well. In a process reminiscent of the English enclosure movements, there has been a renewed effort in Latin America, South America and Asia to take back the commons, with peasant small holdings expropriated and private property rights created which has transformed petty commodity producers into landless laborers (mirrored in the United States by the disappearance of the family farm as a result of agro-business). Rain forests have been appropriated and cleared for the benefit of large agro-producers through the creation of special enterprise zones. Farming has been gradually drawn into the wider orbit of global capital circuits with international corporations dominating seed development, fertilizers, machinery and food production and with rural households brought into export production and integrated into the vertiginous world of commodity price movements and competition. Water and energy sources have been privatized and even more extraordinary has been the diffusion of commodification to the realm of bio-diversity (Shiva, 2001). Transnational corporations have sought to establish property rights by patenting products, such as seeds, spices, grains, trees, that have been the common heritage of communities for thousands of years. Although firms have offered to exchange quite substantial material rewards to local groups in payment for this commercial use, by transforming bio-diversity into a commodity that can be bought and sold like any other, they are willing to treat it as a bounty that can be "mined" like any extractive good without concerns for sustainability or community well-being. Lastly, the rapid expansion of extreme weather events (wildfires, flooding, landslides) across the globe is evidence that climate change has reached a critical stage and that our current model of capitalist growth is unsustainable.

As highlighted in Chapter 1, the massive growth in fictitious money capital (derivatives, collateralized debt obligations, credit swaps, and the like) that galvanized the 2008 financial crisis was limited only by the feverish imagination of their financial alchemists. The unprecedented expansion of debt in the United States via home ownership, credit cards, borrowing off home equity, what Crouch called "Privatized Keynesianism" (Crouch, 2009), enabled Americans to maintain their living standards and personal consumption but it also left them far more vulnerable to the volatility of the market (Krippner, 2011). More broadly, financialization has become the linchpin of the global expansion of production and new forms of innovation and accumulation but at the same time, the disproportionate weight of the financial sector has given it an outsized importance in disseminating market imperatives and contradictions throughout the entire capitalist institutional order. "The turn to finance allowed the state to avoid a series of economic, social and political dilemmas that confronted policy makers beginning in the late 1960s and 1970s", argues Greta Krippner, "paradoxically preparing the ground for our own era of financial manias, panics and crashes three decades later" (Krippner, 2011, 2). Indeed, as we discuss more fully below, each of these fictitious commodities has become an important zone of crisis in the modern political economy (Burawoy, 2010; Fraser, 2013, 2014, 2018; Streeck, 2016).

Democratic capitalist states have overseen a massive increase in the importance of markets in regulating economic life via relaxation of capital controls, deregulation of financial markets, free trade agreements, structural adjustment programs, privatization, and welfare state cuts. As an illustrative case, European integration, from the creation of the internal market to the inception of the euro, has been predicated on core tenets of liberalization that enabled the free movement of goods, services, capital and labor which substantially enhanced the power and autonomy of market actors. Numerous scholars have argued that the fiscal and monetary straightjacket of the euro has actually functioned like a modern day equivalent of the 19th-century gold standard, enforcing financial discipline and mandating draconian austerity that dismantled social protections within member states that received bailouts (Blyth, 2015; Hopkin, 2020; Offe, 2015; Woodruff, 2016). In the Eurozone crisis of 2015, the Greek ruling party, Syriza, was presented with a poisoned choice: either default on their debts, withdraw from the euro, and thus be forced to impose harsh austerity measures; or they could accept a bailout from the European Central Bank (ECB) and IMF, stay in the Eurozone but with the price of imposing sharp cuts in pensions, unemployment benefits, housing subsidies, and government spending. As Mark Blyth wryly noted, it was deflation and austerity all the way down (Blyth, 2015). However, five years later during the pandemic emergency, the ECB was willing to do whatever was required to avoid deepening the recession -cutting interest rates, bailing out overleveraged banks, expanding credit, directly subsidizing member states with trade deficits- but this schizophrenic response simply created a paralyzing deadlock between competing social principles (market orthodoxy vs social protection) which produced unresolvable contradictions at the heart of the European project since the Euro still gave nations with trade deficits no other adjustment mechanism than deflation (Woodruff, 2016). "It is fair to conclude that the Euro has rendered European democratic capitalism *more capitalist* and *less democratic*", argues Claus Offe in distinct Polanyian language. "It has been instrumental in the transformation of markets being embedded in states to states being embedded within (financial) markets and rather defenselessly exposed to their contingencies" (Offe, 2015, 43, my emphasis).

The state itself has been subject to these very processes of marketization in a way that has transformed the contested relationship at the heart of capitalist democracy. The extension of cost benefit analyses to political decision making across a range of policy arenas (university funding, hospital siting, environmental regulations, the price of school lunches); the scourge of subcontracting to private firms; the rise of public-private partnerships; a belief in the superiority of market allocation that circumscribes an active role of the state: all of these profoundly remade the state along neoliberal lines with matters once the purview of democratic oversight now hived off to private actors. The internationalization of the state meant governments were now required to manage their national policies in such a way as to safeguard the ongoing health and maintenance of the international market system even if this might conflict with their own domestic political needs (Gindin and Panitch, 2012). A related political dynamic is the displacement of political decisions from the national level, where they still remain subject to popular pressure, to the international level, where they can be insulated from all types of democratic scrutiny (Crouch, 2005; Hopkin, 2020; Slobodian, 2018; Streeck, 2011). A telling example of neoliberalism's anti-democratic politics is the profound democratic deficit at the heart of the European polity. The weakness of the European Parliament and the lack of democratic accountability of an unelected European Commission and ECB have fueled a deep, abiding sense of disenfranchisement and lack of social trust among European citizens especially since the European institutions with the greatest impact on the daily life of its citizens are those most removed from democratic accountability (Offe, 2015). This process represents an intentional shrinking of the range of political choices that are responsive to ordinary voter needs and preferences; decisions about who will bear the brunt of social suffering imposed by market forces and who in turn will benefit from social protection is less a matter of democratic debate and deliberation than a delegation of power to unelected officials.[6]

If the evidence that neoliberalism instituted a new period of disembedding seems conclusive, this does not mean that the forces of social protection and embedding have become completely denuded. One of the striking features of political life in this latest iteration of the double movement is the stubborn persistence of social protection throughout advanced societies (Hacker and Pierson, 2016; Pierson, 1994). In 1980, at the onset of the neoliberal era, the average Organisation for Economic Co-operation and Development (OECD) country devoted 14.5% of its GDP to social spending; four decades later, the average had grown to 20%. France, as an example, underwent considerable liberalization (privatization, downsizing, labor market flexibility, internationalization), but it still managed to introduce new, more generous welfare policies such as early retirement and higher unemployment payments; while it was still plagued by many of the detrimental consequences of the neoliberal era – disastrous levels of youth unemployment, especially within immigrant communities, declining job security, income volatility – the resilience of its social safety net substantially mitigated negative effects on social well-being (Hall and Sewell, 2013). Even as it unleashed market imperatives, the European Union (EU) also promulgated substantial environmental, social and labor protections in its Social Europe program. In the United States, Democratic administrations have expanded health care coverage, provided direct cash payments to families with children, offered subsidies for housing and child care, all of which have reduced poverty and social inequality, and as of this writing, the Biden government is proposing a trillion dollar extension of the social safety net that would include funding for elder care, paid leave and medical leave, universal pre-K, affordable child care and free community college. In the developing world, a broad range of innovative policies have been massively successful in curbing poverty, inequality and infant mortality and promoting social mobility. Cash transfers to the poor, such as the Bolsa Família in Brazil and Opportunidades in Mexico, have expanded access to health care and education for hundreds of millions.[7]

The World of Insecurity and Inequality

A Polanyian account of the contemporary era must of course reckon with the consequences for social justice and well-being that the neoliberal cycle has generated. As detailed in Chapter 3, Polanyi argued that subjecting all of social life to the untrammeled dictates of the market acted as an immense *insecurity* generator: it eroded trust, solidarity and altruism; atomized communities; led to moral debasement and the collapse of personal character; and created severe injuries that were often hidden from sight. The bewildering pace of change, the disorienting interdependency of social life, the fact that social and economic transformations proved largely incomprehensible to the average citizen: all of these were hallmarks of how insecurity became enshrined as a permanent feature of social and economic life. Albena Azmanova has acknowledged that one of the dominant features of contemporary capitalism is the "universalization of insecurity, which is now afflicting the majority of the population, almost irrespective of employment type and income level" (Azmanova, 2020, 2). In this section, I want to review the contemporary parameters of insecurity and explore the extent to which a Polanyian framework is useful in understanding our current predicament. But I equally want to explore the impact of *inequality*, a factor Polanyi only highlighted in passing, but which has become an urgent matter of political and academic debate ever since the publication of Piketty's *Capital in the Twenty-First Century* in 2014 (Piketty, 2014), which became an important touchstone for scholarly debate, political discourse and activism around the globe.[8] In the same manner in which Polanyi argued that insecurity was a structural feature of a market society, the central claim in Piketty's magisterial work is that inequality is a permanent dynamic within capitalist history. I want to address the ways in which Polanyi and Piketty's analysis overlaps and how a focus on both insecurity and inequality offers a salutary framework for analyzing the contemporary epoch.[9]

Insecure times

Whereas in the post war Golden Age, economic risks were borne collectively through public programs and benefits, in our insecure times, risks in many advanced societies are routinely shifted onto individuals and their families as a consequence of the shifting world of work highlighted previously (Hacker, 2006; Vail et al., 1999). Job loss, catastrophic illness, work injuries, housing insecurity, inadequate retirement income: all of these heighten economic insecurity and vulnerability to shocks across multiple domains (health, employment, family, income/wealth) that persist and accumulate over time (Hacker et al., 2013). Some individuals might possess valuable buffers that enable them to withstand these shocks – financial resources, flexible work patterns, back up caring arrangements and the like – but others might have to resort to further commodification (converting a spare room into an Airbnb rental; using their free time to work for a ride share firm) in order to stave off disaster.[10] Far too many Americans are one pay check away from being homeless, one serious illness away from medical bankruptcy, one job loss away from a precipitous decline in their living standards. Marketization generates contrasting classes of "losers": those who can adjust to being rendered economically obsolete by finding a new job or relocating to an area where there is a better labor market (even if this option is sharply circumscribed by family and caring responsibilities); versus those who fail to adapt and are unable to recover, in part because of circumstances beyond their control such as the decimation of the very forms of social protection (job retraining, continuing education, child care subsidies) that might have assisted such efficacious adaptation (Offe, 2015).

Nor are the middle classes immune from these vertiginous tendencies either. Two earners have become an absolute necessity to maintain family living standards, but this creates unbearable pressure from having to juggle work, caring responsibilities, tutoring, logistical and financial support for their children's creative and sporting activities, alongside their own personal happiness and interests. Of course, families with means can partly redress these tensions by harnessing domestic commodification – hiring nannies or child minders, eating prepared meals or at restaurants, outsourcing cleaning, gardening and home repairs to commercial services – but this merely relocates the dictates of market imperatives to another area of social life (and shifts the risks of commodification onto the backs of the low paid workers they indirectly or directly employ). All told, this pathological insecurity has generated higher levels of stress, strains on family life, deteriorating physical and mental well-being, even before the added anxieties and crises fostered by the pandemic became an everyday feature of social life.

The emotional residue of this perpetual insecurity can be profoundly disorienting. Bone weary exhaustion and debilitating stress is the inevitable result of the constant improvisation required to make ends meet to pay the rent or to put food on the table or to find someone to babysit young children in case of a work or medical emergency. Anxiety and fear becomes commonplace when people have to worry about when these next shocks might occur, whether their kids will grow up with the same opportunities to pursue the life projects they value, or even if the looming ecological unpredictability (climate change disasters, future pandemics and the like) will lead to a catastrophic future. These palpable emotional states are co-joined with a growing awareness that our fate is impacted by decisions and actions of other social actors at a great distance from us, which people are powerless to affect.

This ever present insecurity creates a perpetual need for people to become adaptive and resilient, emotional states that have been elevated to the "status of a public virtue and civic responsibility" (Streeck, 2016, 43), even though, as Polanyi well understood, there is a finite amount of adaptability that any community or individual can withstand. Hall and Michele Lamont speak of "social resiliency", the capacity of groups or communities to "sustain and advance their interests in the face of challenges to it" (Hall and Lamont, 2013, 2). Of course, given that failure in this regard is often regarded as a socially harmful personal deficiency, it is not surprising that those who lack the strategic resources or capacity to adjust will convert their anger and frustration at this ever present insecurity into a toxic political rage machine as we discuss more fully in the following section. But there is an even more important paradox to register about this matter of social resiliency. "The more resilience individuals manage to develop at the micro-level of everyday life", argues Streeck, "the less demand there will be for collective action at the macro-level of everyday life to contain the uncertainties produced by market forces, a demand that neoliberalism could and would not fill" (Streeck, 2016, 40). In other words, once the burden of adaptation and resiliency is shifted onto individuals, the responsibility of political actors to tame the insecurity of the market can be conveniently overlooked.

This willful ignorance and neglect is most injurious when considering the most extreme form of insecurity, what Ann Case and Angus Deaton have called the "deaths of despair", which have plagued white, working class Americans in the last two decades (Case and Deaton, 2020). In 1999 middle aged whites with a high school diploma averaged 601 deaths per 100,000 people (a figure that had fallen steadily for decades); by 2013 this toll had risen to 736 deaths (by comparison, deaths among working class Canadians of the same age had fallen steadily for several decades, to 247 per 100,000 people), an increase in mortality rates totally unprecedented for peacetime. They identified three main causes of death – alcoholism, suicides and drug addiction (primarily opioid use) – but also highlighted the ill health, mental distress and family instability experienced within these communities. These deaths, they insisted, "reflect a long-term, and slowly unfolding loss of a way of life for the white, less educated, working class" (Case and Deaton, 2020, 146). Communities blighted by job loss and bleak job prospects, disinvestment, hospital and school closures, the flight of young people from rural areas, social isolation and loneliness, has meant the slow, steady undermining of all aspects of people's lives. Unmoored from collective organizations and institutions, socially disconnected, the normal routines and traditions of working class life have been decimated with the concomitant loss of dignity and self-respect. These deaths, which have been largely ignored in political discourse and cultural representations, represent the exact sort of "hidden injuries" that Polanyi lambasted – a failure not just of the political imagination but of social recognition as well.[11]

The age of inequality

In the Piketty world view, capitalism has a structural tendency for wealth to accumulate in the hands of a tiny few. If the market economy is left to operate according to its own dictates, inequality is the inevitable consequence, which exerts a detrimental effect on the rest of society. His famous algebraic expression of this dynamic, $r>g$, represented his claim that the return on capital tends to grow at a faster rate than economic growth, which he argues has been a tendency for nearly all of capitalist history (Piketty, 2014). To illustrate its contemporary manifestation, Piketty marshals a series of eye opening data that illustrates the obscene wealth gaps within and between countries. In the United States, where the wealth gap is most pronounced, the top 1% share of national income nearly doubled from 11% in 1980 to 20% in 2015. The bottom 50% share of national income fell from 20% in 1980 to 13% in 2015. The poorest 40% of Americans own a mere 0.3% of assets and wealth, while the top 20% own 84%. The picture at the global level is even more inegalitarian:

> "The wealthiest 0.1% of people on the planet, some 4.5 million out of an adult population of 4.5 billion, apparently possess fortunes on the order of ten million euros on average, or nearly 200 times the average global wealth of 60,000 euros per adult, amounting in aggregate to nearly 20% of total wealth. The wealthiest 1% -45 million people out of 4.5 billion- have about 3 million euros on average…This is about 50 times the size of the average global fortune, or 50% of total global wealth in aggregate."
>
> (Piketty, 2014, 438)

The ten richest billionaires in the world have a combined wealth greater than the bottom 50% of the global populace.

There is a tension within Piketty's work that parallels our earlier discussion, which argued the double movement was both a structural regularity and a politically contingent project within the capitalist social order. On the one hand, he seems to imply that r>g is an abstract law at the heart of capitalism but, at the same time, he insists very much like Polanyi that capitalism is a historical institutional order and inequality, therefore, is the specific outcome of political, social and cultural arrangements that are characteristic of each inequality regime. "The history of the distribution of wealth has always been deeply political", Piketty writes:

> "and it cannot be reduced to purely economic mechanisms…the history of inequality is shaped by the way economic, social and political citizens view what is just and what is not, as well as by the relative power of these actors and the collective choices that result…How this history plays out depends on how societies view inequalities and what kind of policies and institutions they adopt to measure and transform them."
>
> (Piketty, 2014, 20, 35)

In the same way that Polanyi saw the creation of free markets as the direct exercise of political power, Piketty insists inequality is a conscious policy decision that implicates intentional choices across a range of domains and institutions: corporate governance that privileges shareholders and designs outrageous compensation packages to reward so-called super-managers; policies that reduce marginal tax rates or permit widespread tax evasion by the rich (in 2018 the world's richest man, Elon Musk, paid a grand total of $8,410 in federal income taxes); cultural norms and narratives (the plethora of high-profile dramas such as *Succession* and *Billions* profiling the uber-rich; the outsized attention given to the annual *Forbes* ranking of the world's wealthiest people); alongside educational systems, political regulations and immigration policies.

Although not a focus of either author, the specific relationship between inequality and insecurity is worth highlighting. Once money becomes the dominant arbiter of worth, or the primary determinant of life chances, or begins to crowd out other non-market interests and incentives, commodification (as the genesis of insecurity) can exacerbate inequality. Lamont and Pierson stress this very relationship:

> "In the context of rising economic inequality, commodification can play a significant role in spreading that inequality to other domains. By gradually magnifying the implications of these income disparities for life chances and well-being, commodification processes can greatly intensify the long term implications of purely economic inequality."
>
> (Lamont and Pierson, 2019, 9)

The transformation of higher education in the United States is an illustrative case of this process. David Grusky and his colleagues, building upon the work of Charles Tilly and his concept of "opportunity hoarding" (Tilly, 1994), stress the deep penetration of what they call "opportunity markets" into all aspects of education that enable wealthier parents to buy elite education and other desirable outcomes for their kids (Grusky et al., 2019). Well-off parents commit substantial resources to high quality pre-schools, after-school and summer skills training, and college coaching, what Grusky and his colleagues describe as a "direct form of money laundering", in order to develop an impressive personal portfolio for their children and a supportive mentoring network.[12] With tuition fees astronomically high, the ability to pay sharply circumscribes educational opportunity, which means economic advantages become self-reinforcing over time. Of the 38 top ranked universities in America, students who came from the top 1% of family income distribution made up the same proportion of the student body as the bottom 60%; but, then again, less than half of low income students even attend any college at all. Given that college attendance has become a prerequisite for entry into the middle class and because returns to education continue to accrue, children without access to higher education will enjoy significantly less social mobility. But it should also be highlighted that the inequity of opportunity markets carries over to everyday life at university, which is no less stratified by class than any other social institution, where working class students face significant stigmatization, atrophied social networks and, all too frequently, a bewildering college experience.

While there is no question that Piketty is far more interested in tracing the historical trajectory of inequality across multiple societies and time periods than he is in documenting its harmful consequences, his argument parallels Polanyi's own treatment of the corrosiveness of the market. Using a similar kind of Polanyian language of contradictions as discussed in the previous chapter, Piketty argues that inequality is the "principal destabilizing force" under capitalism (Piketty, 2014, 571). It can lead to vast differences in resources that have "consequences for lifestyle choices, housing, vacation opportunities, and money to spend on projects, children, and so on are considerable" (ibid, 256). It's not just that the wealthy live in bigger houses, can satisfy nearly any medical or educational needs, can travel as often and as widely as they like, or even have an army of assistants looking after their every need (caring, cooking, cleaning, transport). Their wealth gives them greater freedom to pursue whatever life project they value without any encumbrance whereas the poor and working class suffer diminished social mobility, opportunity, if not freedom itself.

This yawning gap in capabilities represents an acute threat to democracy. Inequality, Piketty argues, is "politically incompatible with meritocratic values and principles of social justice fundamental to modern democratic society" (Piketty, 2014). The wealthy possess the economic and social resources to dominate political life and policy making and to promote their own private interest as equivalent to the common good while those who lack economic resources or social standing will not be seen or treated as civic equals no matter the formal democratic equality promised. Democratic legitimacy will become fatally weakened under such conditions of unequal hierarchies and oligarchic power once citizens lose faith in the ability of political actors to intervene in markets on behalf of collective interests. Not surprisingly, Piketty emphasizes the way in which inequality not only breeds anger and resentment against an unfair system that appears to be rigged against the average person but also a xenophobic nationalism that scapegoats the less fortunate, which frays social solidarity and makes social cooperation impossible to achieve (Piketty, 2014). Inequality therefore grievously undermines the very social trust and social cooperation that democratic governance and legitimacy requires. Capitalism itself is also at risk given that inequality has led to greater financial instability, stagnation in the purchasing power of the lower and middle classes, and the subsequent downturn in economic fortunes as growing numbers of households are saddled with mountains of debt (Piketty, 2014, 297).

But Piketty and other scholars (Milanovic, 2019; Therborn, 2013) also enlist a fundamental moral critique against inequality. Declining life expectancy, ill health, restricted life chances makes inequality an urgent issue of fundamental human dignity. Millions of children in the developing world die before their fifth birthday every single day from preventable causes; air pollution cuts short the life spans of billions of people across the globe and extreme weather events, owing to climate change threaten the most vulnerable; in every country, the pandemic ravaged the poor and working class, who did not have the luxury to conduct their work remotely and who were more likely to live in crowded housing. In summary, inequality represents a diminishment of personhood and human freedom and hence is one of the most profound threats to human rights in political life today.

Countermovements and ideology

To summarize Polanyi's argument about the countermovement discussed in Chapter 4, he insisted that a wide range of social interests was threatened by the untrammeled free market. "Precisely because not the economic but the social interests of different cross sectors of the population were threatened by the market", he wrote, "persons belonging to various economic strata unconsciously joined forces to meet the danger" (GT, 154–5). Because of the systematic undermining of social life and community as a result of the commercialization and commodification of the past four decades, numerous scholars within the Polanyian tradition have maintained that there is a broad movement to protect human and natural spheres from market dictates (Burawoy, 2010; Evans, 2008; Fraser, 2018, 2021; Silver, 2003; Webster et al., 2008). Robert Wade captured this received wisdom:

> "Conventional responses to the crisis suggest that we have entered the second leg of Polanyi's 'double movement', the recurrent pattern in capitalism whereby…a regime of free markets and increasing commodification generates such suffering and displacement as to prompt attempts to impose greater regulation of markets and decommodification."
>
> (Wade, 2008, 6)

On the other hand, although she emphasizes the importance of "boundary struggles" against the market across multiple domains of social life, Nancy Fraser nevertheless insists the current era throws up a profound paradox. "A curious disjuncture – while today's crisis appears to follow a Polanyian structural logic, grounded in the dynamics of fictitious commodification", she writes, "it is not manifest in a Polanyian political logic, figured by the double movement" (Fraser, 2013, 121). How do we square these contrasting accounts, both from within the same intellectual tradition, and responding to the same contemporary developments?

There is no question that resistance to neoliberal marketization is ubiquitous across every site of commodification and throughout the globe.[13] In the arena of nature, there have been landless peasant movements against deforestation of the Amazon on behalf of cattle production, indigenous protests to prevent pipeline construction in North America or bio-piracy in Africa, campaigns to safeguard water rights or to block extractive developments in pristine wilderness, all of which have faced police brutality and violence from privately sponsored goon squads. From the Green New Deal to Extinction rebellion, movements for a more sustainable future and an expeditious response to climate change are gaining political momentum. In the world of work and the social sphere, groups like the Indignados in Spain have protested against austerity policies, skyrocketing youth unemployment, housing evictions, with innovative protest repertoires and broad popular support. Trade unions have promoted living wage campaigns and cross national solidarity to combat capital flight and students and charitable organizations have formed anti-sweatshop campaigns. Each of these could be added to easily – in fact, Gareth Dale wittily catalogued the various political campaigns and social movements that scholars have nominated as potential counter-movements (Dale, 2010, 215–20), although this might also be the consequence of the analytical inconsistencies in the very concept of the countermovement noted earlier in Chapter 4.[14] There is a species of wishful thinking, if not an unwarranted Polanyian optimism, in the ubiquitous search for the one, true countermovement that might prefigure the inevitable return of the protective phase of the double movement and the long predicted demise of neoliberalism.

At the same time, scholars have highlighted the limitations of the current crop of countermovements in constituting a countervailing power to neoliberal hegemony (Evans, 2008; Azamanova, 2020). "Why, despite apparently favorable conditions", laments Fraser, "is there no counter-hegemonic project aimed at protecting society and nature from neoliberalism" (Fraser, 2013, 121–2). By "counter-hegemonic", Fraser is arguing for several interrelated deficiencies. These movements are said to be far too temporary or ephemeral in their existence and effects; they lack a broad vision for social reform or a strategic vision for social change; as localized struggles, they are unable to scale up into a critical mass or coalesce into a wider political challenge that is commensurate with the scale of the institutional order they are trying to overcome (Evans, 2008). Even more critically, they have not articulated a comprehensive critique of neoliberalism that links their own struggles to the systemic, interlocking crises of the present era. Fraser insists in this vein: "Only by addressing *all* major features of these crises…and by discussing the connections among them can we build a counter-hegemonic bloc that backs a common project and possesses the political heft to pursue it effectively" (Fraser, 2021, 96). The missing piece in her view is that countermovements fail to recognize all of their present woes can be traced back to the same original sin of *capitalism*. If taming the market's worst excesses has become nearly an impossible task, then "anti-capitalism, therefore, could – indeed, *should* – become the central organizing motif of a new common sense" (Fraser, 2021, 87).

In a fundamental sense, Fraser is right to acknowledge small struggles, as invaluable as they might be in constraining the market and offering some important measure of protection against its ravages, only rarely become "great transformations". But I think this is problematic for several reasons. It misinterprets the nature of social change within the double movement: previous iterations in the 19th and 20th centuries did not have a single leading counter-hegemonic movement that led to the establishment of a period of social protection (even if trade unions and social democratic parties were first among equals). Nor should we assume movements that stop short of calling for the abolition of capitalism or refuse to see themselves through this frame are somehow unworthy of the rubric countermovement. Even if local struggles against market predations never reach a critical mass or scale up to a national, never mind global level, their fundamental values of self-management, solidarity and equality contain a political imaginary of universality, an implied common sense and solidaristic struggle against the voracious market.

What is also slightly puzzling about these calls for a "counter-hegemonic movement" is that the past two decades witnessed the birth and evolution of an entity that seemingly offered just this sort of strategic orientation, namely the World Social Forum (WSF). Founded two decades ago in 2001 as a direct counterpart to the annual gathering of global elites in Davos, Switzerland, the WSF represents a remarkable feat of transnational social cooperation with annual meetings (alongside regional forums and issue forums) held in Brazil, India, Tunisia, Montreal, attracting hundreds of thousands of social movement activists, trade unionists, policy makers and left intellectuals. It was conceived as a meeting place for activists and organizers from communities around the globe that had been most battered by the destructive forces of the market as a way to exchange information, disseminate best practice about repertoires of struggle, discuss possible strategies for reform, and as a space for solidarity, inspiration and the political imagination, which its slogan "Another world is possible" boldly affirmed. Activists who had been disappointed that the early anti-globalization protests in Seattle in 1999 and elsewhere had failed to develop a common agenda for a global alliance against neoliberalism, were now able to present and debate a diverse range of non-market alternatives, such as sustainable farming, innovative taxation, social economy, participatory budgeting, basic income, livable cities and the like. The meetings were democratically organized, featured consensual decision making, and consciously stressed the importance of embedding distinct strands of progressive politics (environmentalism, anti-racism, peace, feminism, trade unionism) representing distinct constituencies and boundary struggles into a common agenda and coalition. And by intentionally restricting the participation of political parties of every political stripe, they successfully managed to avoid the internecine battles between left groups over ideological pieties that so often paralyzed initiatives like this in the past.

Of course, there were growing pains and substantive criticisms of its evolution. Some activists wanted the WSF to take more overt stances on pressing political issues (such as the Iraq War or climate change); others felt its anti-hierarchical decision making had led to a lack of accountability among its founding organizers; many early supporters believed it had disintegrated into a mere debating forum rather than an organization with the capacity and power to press for consequential action within the political arena, which they saw as a necessary prerequisite for establishing durable alternative institutions and policies (Whitaker, 2020). There is no question that any potential counter-hegemonic political formation would encounter similar trade-offs, dilemmas and hard choices of organization, decision making and strategy but, if ever there was an organization and movement capable of constituting a countervailing power against neoliberal hegemony, it would be the WSF, yet even its most dedicated admirers would acknowledge its obvious limitations in this regard. Despite all its attendant flaws, and the oppositional forces it has provoked, neoliberalism has proven far more resilient than even its most fervent opponents would have imagined.

If we switch our focus to the terrain of inequality, the quintessential counter-movement against inequality in the Piketty sense was Occupy Wall Street, which began with the mass occupation of Zuccotti Park in lower Manhattan in September 2011 and featured many of the same strengths and limitations as noted above. There is no question that the movement galvanized inequality into discussions of social justice in the United States (and the multiple countries where activists copied this protest repertoire) and brought an issue that had hitherto been relegated to the margins of American life back onto the political agenda. Numerous cities and states adopted a $15 minimum living wage; resolving the ballooning student debt crisis ($1.7 trillion in outstanding debt) became an urgent matter for policy makers; and taxing the 1%, a term launched by the Occupy protests, is now openly supported as accepted wisdom by the majority of the Democratic Party. But perhaps its most enduring accomplishment was the widespread resonance of the movement's slogan, "We are the 99%", which caught the zeitgeist in popular culture in a way that was unprecedented. This is not to suggest that the protests managed to avoid the limits of other countermovements: it was riven with internal disagreements, many early followers were dissuaded from further participation by its cacophonous, contentious general assemblies or felt excluded by the full time, 24/7 commitment demanded by its activists. The movement explicitly resisted developing a pragmatic program or making alliances with political parties and, after several months, it abruptly faded into historical memory. While it galvanized an entire new generation of activists who were inspired by its example, it has yet to spawn any future successors.

Notwithstanding that his book sales undoubtedly benefited from this protest wave, it would be fair to say that Piketty is less interested in discussing the social and political forces arrayed against neoliberal inequality than he is in detailing the ideological and institutional bulwarks that sustain it. In his latest volume, *Capital and Ideology*, his focus is on the dominant ideational mechanisms whereby social inequality is inscribed as a common sense across a range of distinct inequality regimes such as Mughal India, West Indian slave colonies, post-Soviet republics, 19th-century liberalism and capitalist democracies. "[A]n inequality regime can persist only through a complex combination of coercion and consent", he writes. "The social model championed by the dominant groups must elicit from a population (or a significant portion of it) a minimum level of adhesion" (Piketty, 2020, 60). What is fascinating is how closely the ideological mechanisms he emphasizes mirror those that Polanyi employed to explain the ascendancy of the self-regulating market. For example, there is the universalizing gambit paired with the futility thesis: the claim that "existing disparities benefit not only the poor but also society as a whole, and that any attempt to alter the existing order of things will cause great pain" (Piketty, 2020, 7).

But Piketty's primary focus rests with the mechanism of legitimation. "Every human society must justify its inequalities", he argues, "unless reasons for these are found, the whole political and social edifice stands in danger of collapse" (Piketty, 2020, 1). These justifications will vary significantly across inequality regimes –functionalism for tertiary (feudal) societies; social stability for proprietarian (19th-century liberal) regimes – but it is his discussion of the ideological legitimation of inequality in present day capitalist democracy that I want to focus on. Piketty initially highlights the habits of mind and heart of the neoliberal individual: sovereign, empowered, free to choose among the life projects they value the most, a fervent conviction that social outcomes are the consequence of individual attributes and free choices not structural determinants, a willingness to embrace risks and value an entrepreneurial spirit. He approvingly quotes from Michael Young's dystopian fable, *The Rise of the Meritocracy*, to demonstrate the gravitational attraction of merit based rationales for the wealthy:

> "If the rich and powerful were encouraged by the general culture to believe that they had fully deserved all they had, how arrogant they would become, and, if they were convinced it was all for the common good, how ruthless in pursuing their own advantage."
>
> (Young, 1948, 89)

Indeed, in liberal capitalism, merit is the most blatant and widespread justification for inequality (Sandel, 2020). "It is hardly surprising", argues Piketty, "that the winners in such a society would wish to describe the social hierarchy in this way and sometimes they succeed in convincing some of the losers" (Piketty, 2020, 265).[15]

The astronomical rise in compensation among super-managers, corporate executives and hedge funders is often justified by their supposed technological innovations, productivity gains and managerial prowess but Piketty ridicules these claims as a "pure ideological construct" (Piketty, 2020, 331). His riposte is worth quoting at length:

> "No one doubts that it is important in society to have entrepreneurs, inventors and innovations…no matter how justified inequalities of wealth may be initially, fortunes can grow and perpetuate themselves beyond all reasonable limits and beyond any possible rational justification in terms of social utility…A person who has good ideas at the age of forty will not necessarily still be having them at ninety, nor are his children sure to have any. Yet, the wealth remains…"
>
> (Piketty, 2020, 443–4)

If inequality breeds a sense of entitlement among the winners, it generates a common sense of resentment among those left behind, who are told they only have themselves to blame for their lack of entrepreneurial vigor and their inability to get ahead (the political consequences of which we will explore in the following section).

But, beyond these ideological factors, there is also an epistemological challenge that his broader research project is intended to surmount. The average citizen is unconcerned with inequality not only because of ideological blinders but because of the profound information/cognitive deficits about the nature of the phenomena itself. As Piketty comments:

> "For this half of the population, the very notions of wealth and capital are relatively abstract. For millions of people, 'wealth' amounts to little more than a few weeks wages in a checking account or low interest

> savings account, a car and a few pieces of furniture. The inescapable reality is this: wealth is so concentrated that a large segment of society is virtually unaware of its existence, so that some people imagine that it belongs to surreal or mysterious entities."
>
> (Piketty, 2014, 259)

Other scholars have found that individuals routinely underestimate inequality, both in terms of the staggering amount controlled by the rich as well as by the persistent economic disadvantage faced by the less fortunate (Son Hing et al., 2019, 111). In these circumstances, it should come as no surprise that when asked in a 2020 Pew Research Center opinion poll to rank social problems, only 1% of Americans listed inequality as their top priority, even though 70% in the same poll favored higher taxes on the wealthy.

What's admirable about Piketty's project is his Enlightenment style optimism that this myopia can be cured by the very kinds of data collection and presentation that he has devoted his career to. If only citizens fully understood just how bad things really were, the "force of the better argument" would persuade them to take collective action to redress it, be it the global wealth tax he espouses or other egalitarian measures (repairing the social safety net, high quality public goods, and the like). But it is not unfair to say that he does not explore in any rigorous way the mechanisms whereby greater knowledge can lead to efficacious political action, an oversight that seems very reminiscent of Polanyi's spontaneity account of the counter-movement. Other scholars have argued that heightened inequality might actually generate psychological mechanisms that lead people to legitimate and rationalize greater disparities (Ridgeway, 2017; Son Hing et al., 2019). Indeed, Azmanova maintains that the indignation sparked by the Occupy style protests were a:

> "symptom not of the crisis of capitalism but rather of its unfailing good health. This is the case because remonstrations against inequality present the matter of capitalism's numerous and grave failures as issues that can be easily tackled with a dose of redistributive policies and strengthened oversight. Thus, what appears to be a radical challenge to neoliberal capitalism is instead a reinforcement of it."
>
> (Azmanova, 2020, 7)

Persistent inequality does not automatically lead to calls for greater redistribution or ameliorative measures; indeed, as we shall discuss more fully in the next section, it is the very Americans who would benefit most from an expansion of health coverage through Obamacare who voted for politicians who sought to abolish it.

But there is an additional paradox to highlight in this regard. Henry Farrell, in an astute commentary on Piketty's proposal for a global wealth tax, noted the dilemma at the core of his work: "if we could get to the point where the political balance of forces were favorable enough to implement such a policy, then the counter tendency to this long run structural force would have already been overcome by countervailing power" (Farrell, 2015). Piketty agrees that it is very unlikely that such a "utopian ideal" would be legislated anytime soon (Piketty, 2020, 471) and, as with Polanyi, there is a tension at the heart of his project between the nature of capitalist outcomes as structural imperative or contingent political project. Although there are some interesting reflections on the changing class composition of what he calls the "Brahmin" social democratic left (from a working class base to an urban, professional, highly educated constituency), the conditions under which a political project to tame inequality might be feasible are not exhaustively discussed. Indeed, it is an open question whether the political, social and ideological forces at present are capable of reversing the core dynamics of capitalist inequality, or for that matter, the dominant neoliberal paradigm that is perpetuating it, a theme we will return to in the conclusion to this chapter.

The Rise of Right-Wing Populism

It is inarguable that the countermovement, which has had the most widespread influence and achieved the most in terms of concrete political ambitions and political power, has been the rise of right-wing populism. Although Rogers Brubaker rightly notes that the term "populism" lumps together quite disparate political projects on the left and right, for the purpose of this section, my focus is on the populist right (Brubaker, 2017).[16] I am including within this broad, encompassing term political leaders such as Donald Trump, Jair Bolsanaro and Narendra Modi; the triumph of illiberal, authoritarian leaders in Hungary and Poland; a surge in support for populist right parties across Europe in France, Netherlands, Austria and Scandinavia; as well as political movements such as the Tea Party in the United States and the Brexit referendum in Britain. Populism could well be regarded in a Polanyian lens as a "protectionist movement" directed against the volatility of the market, the uncertainties of global interdependence, the fast changing nature of cultural and demographic change but also as a specific reaction to the political economy of insecurity and inequality discussed above (Hopkin, 2020). As highlighted in Chapter 3, at the heart of Polanyi's analysis of the double movement, is a recognition that what makes capitalism distinct as a social order is the process of fictitious commodities but as Eric Lonergan and Blyth astutely observe:

> "Labor is the only commodity capable of generating a social reaction to movements in its price…the more that you try to treat wages as a price, as just another cost to minimize, the greater the social reaction against market exchange it provokes."
>
> (Lonergan and Blyth, 2020, 69–70)

Polanyi well understood that demands for protection against the market could take on both progressive and reactionary political forms – in the 1930s, New Deal liberalism, Swedish social democracy, German fascism and Soviet communism were all prominent – and right-wing populism looks to be one of the dominant pathways in the contemporary era.

In this section, I begin with an overview of the contours of populism and identify some affinities that it shared with the rise of authoritarian movements that Polanyi chronicled. I then explore the reasons for its success from a Polanyian standpoint and finally discuss the Brexit referendum as an illustrative case of the dynamics of populism.

The populist temptation

In documenting the rise of reactionary movements in the 20th century, Polanyi detailed a series of phenomena which he believed not only explained their ascendancy but also characterized the contradictory nature of their political formation: "the spread of irrationalist philosophies, racialist esthetics, anticapitalist demagogy, heterodox currency views, criticism of the party system, widespread disparagement of the 'regime' or whatever was the name given to the customary democratic set up" (GT, 235). As a taxonomy of contemporary populism, this is an extraordinarily prescient portrait as the select overview below should hopefully demonstrate although Brubaker's caution that "populism is a matter of degree, not a sharply bounded phenomenon that is either present or absent" (Brubaker, 2017, 362) is worth keeping in mind.

If we first examine the theme of "irrationalist philosophies", there is no question that our era is dominated by the spread of disinformation and what Zeynep Tufekci calls "weaponized ignorance" diffused by digital platforms, social media and right-wing networks such as Fox News. The business model of digital platforms is predicated on keeping people glued to their screens for as long as possible (thereby maximizing advertising revenue) and their dominant algorithm "aligns incentives with those who stoke outrage, spread misinformation, and appeal to people's existing biases and preferences" (Tufekci, 2018). The public sphere has unfortunately become an echo chamber and epistemic bubble rather than a domain of deliberation and public reasoning. Conspiracy theories have flourished in the present period as exemplified by QAnon, the belief that the American government is controlled by a global cabal of Satan worshipping paedophiles who run a global child sex trafficking ring, which has taken hold among 15% of Americans. This minority is equally persuaded that Covid-19 vaccination is a plot to implant microchips in their blood; or that the Deep State is controlled by anonymous global elites (typically assumed to be of the Jewish faith); or that Trump actually won the 2020 election (attested to by over 60% of Republicans, 75% of QAnoners and 29% of all Americans).

These theories are not simply the result of faulty cognitive reasoning – they afflict the educated as well as the uneducated – but rather are a feature of widespread social mistrust and political polarization that provide fertile ground for populism. "Conspiracy theories are thus not a curious addition to populist rhetoric", insists Jan-Werner Muller, "they are rooted in and emerge from the very logic of populism itself" (Muller, 2016, 32). Like other ideologies, conspiracies offer a simplifying account and provide psychic security to the dissonant complexity of everyday life; they represent a crusading faith that cannot be disconfirmed in any conventional manner. A belief in demonstrably false things has become ever more central to group identities with group belonging and conformity far more alluring than reason based claims and paranoid delusions routinely asserted as factual reality. In such an environment, it is difficult to see how the normal procedures of democratic life, which require reasoned deliberation and debate, can be sustained against the relentless drumbeat of "fake news". But the deliberate manufacture and diffusion of falsehoods, as an example the "Big Lie" propagated by Trump and his followers that the 2020 election was rigged and he actually won, is also an intentional means of subverting future democratic processes by making truth/reality/facts essentially contested topics. And, tragically, this fervent attachment to disinformation in the midst of a pandemic has convinced millions to forego life-saving vaccinations, leading to the unnecessary deaths of hundreds of thousands in the United States.

"*Racialist esthetics*" are unquestionably implicated in the populist temperament as well. Numerous scholars have demonstrated a high correlation between racial animosity/racial resentment (measured by a belief that racial minorities do not face persistent discrimination or lack of opportunity) and the resurgence of the Tea Party and a propensity to vote for Trump (Tesler, 2016). In Europe, 60% of the Alternative für Deutschland (the right-wing German party) supporters; 36% of National Front supporters in France; and nearly half of the Party for Freedom in the Netherlands, agreed in a survey that "their people's culture is superior to others". It can also be exhibited by the demonization of immigrants or by the embrace of racialized zero-sum thinking (if "they" are doing well then I must be losing out) (McGhee, 2020). Above all, there is the exclusionary rhetoric of the "people" that Brubaker argues is the epitome of the populist persuasion: "The core element of the populist repertoire is the claim to speak and act in the name of 'the people'… populism involves the claim to speak and act in the name of the people *and against the elite*" (Brubaker, 2017, 362).[17] Elites, in this world view, are depicted as insulated from the everyday struggles of ordinary people; as culturally diverse, urban cosmopolitans with little attachment to the local solidarities of community and nation. Muller stresses a similar process: "Populists claim that they, *and only they*, represent the people…for a political actor or movement to be populist, it must claim that a *part* of the people *is* the people- and that only the populist authentically identifies and represents this real or true people" (Muller, 2016, 19, 22). But he also argues that the assertion to speak on behalf of "the people" is not just a political but a moral claim that enables populist leaders to ascribe specific boundaries to who should be included or excluded in the name of "the people".

Muller insists this process of populist legitimation entails a fundamental threat to democracy. The contention that a leader or political movement possesses a unique moral monopoly to speak on behalf of the people implies that its political opponents can therefore be castigated as illegitimate, or labelled as "enemies of the people" who warrant imprisonment as the ubiquitous chants of "lock her up" at Trump rallies clearly welcomed. This relates directly to the inherent danger of Trump's post-election obstructionism and incessant "big lie" rhetoric. Once a populist leader is forced to confront his own political demise, the rhetoric of the one true leader of "the people" leads seamlessly to an embrace of doing whatever is necessary to stay in power, even at the risk of the destruction of democracy itself. It is important to acknowledge the ways in which this process of legitimation of the "people" is heavily racialized. The American right's frenetic obsession with Barack Obama's birth certificate is a telling illustration of this process: the clear intent of this contrived controversy was to assert that Obama was an illegitimate president, a fundamentally un-American figure with customs that were supposedly antithetical to traditional American values, who had usurped his office under false pretences. At its most extreme, the populists' moral monopoly of "the people" can be virtually indistinguishable from the most virulent racist tropes. Tucker Carlson, the host of the most successful Fox News program, recently warned in overtly white supremacist language that "an unrelenting stream of immigration" was being perpetrated because the Biden administration sought "to change the racial mix of the country… To reduce the political power of people whose ancestors lived here…the great replacement: the replacement of legacy Americans with more obedient people from faraway countries".

If we consider "*heterodox currency views*", a favorite of Polanyi's own analysis, Bitcoin mania and cryptocurrency craze has been touted as a radical, decentralized alternative to fiat money, but in effect functions as a classic Ponzi scheme where so long as new investors can be coaxed in and old investors persuaded not to cash out, the illusion of a stable, viable currency can be sustained. In a perfect analogy, one commentator likened this speculative frenzy to "Wily E Coyote running off a cliff. He can keep going until the moment he realizes there's no ground beneath him. When he does, he falls, and it's a long long way down". But its combustible fluctuations in value alongside the heightened risk of outright fraud, owing to the lack of government-backed security or regulation, makes it highly unlikely to serve as a routine medium of exchange. As if to prove the general point, the stock price of Dogecoin, created in 2013 as a satirical prank of cryptocurrencies like Bitcoin, suddenly escalated in early 2021 as the result of an off-handed tweet by Tesla founder Musk, rising in value by over 400% in a single week and topping up at more than $50 billion in value by the end of April 2021, which was higher than the market capitalization of Ford Motors.

Lastly, "*widespread disparagement of the regime*" is also a prominent hallmark of the populist era. The symptoms of democratic dissatisfaction in capitalist democracies are everywhere to be seen: shrinking membership in political parties, declining turnout, electoral volatility, fracturing class alignments, less support (especially among the young) for democratic institutions, distrust of politicians and disdain for politics in general and a deep political polarization that has seeped into civil society (Mair, 2013). There is a pervasive sense that politics no longer serves the interests of the average citizen but has been captured by corrupt, incompetent political elites whose education and professional backgrounds separate them from the interests of the average citizen. Indeed, the most common *political* explanation for the rise of populism implicates two interrelated factors: the narrowing of available political options where voters are said to no longer have a real choice between competing visions of social justice; and the convergence of both center-left and center-right parties around neoliberal ideas and policies, which prevented them from articulating a compelling political vision that challenged neoliberal hegemony or constrained its most egregious consequences (Berman, 2016; Hopkin, 2020; Mudge, 2018).

While this argument certainly offers a compelling structural account of the political dynamics that conditioned the rise of populism, my enthusiasm is tempered by a closer consideration of the distinct national conditions that impact on this claim. Given the headlong descent of the Republican Party into anti-democratic authoritarianism, not to mention its regressive stances across a wide range of policy issues from reproductive rights to inequality to climate change, the differences between the two main American political parties on grounds of social justice have never been starker. Perhaps the main exculpatory factor in case of the Democratic Party's failure to pass even more consequential progressive legislation lies not with their supposed neoliberal proclivities but with the sclerotic nature of the American political system (the disproportionate representation of white, rural voters in the Senate, the filibuster, gerrymandering, as well as an illegitimately constituted Supreme Court) that has blocked popular Democratic presidents from passing overwhelmingly popular legislation. In the case of the British system, Jonathan Hopkin offers the case of the Labour Party's electoral conundrum that forced it into a "Faustian bargain" with the financial sector and neoliberal policies (Hopkin, 2020). Because the party wanted to implement a modest redistributive agenda but feared that even the merest whisper of tax increases or higher spending would spook the markets and prove electorally unfeasible, they chose to give financial actors free rein and then used the extra resources they could garner via sustained economic growth for social policy measures such as a reduction in child poverty and greater funding of public services especially in education and health care. In both the American and British cases, despite preventing a global meltdown and another great depression through massive financial stimulus in 2009–10, the Gordon Brown and Obama governments, like other governments of that period, received no political credit whatsoever for their bold action and instead, their political opponents lambasted them for their profligate habits and used their deficit spending as justification for a round of harsh austerity cuts that merely spurred support for populist outsiders.

Explaining the rise of populism

There are generally two schools of thought that attempt to explain the rise of populism (Berman, 2021; Brubaker, 2017; Gidron and Hall, 2017; Hopkin, 2020). The first stresses the structural economic transformations (economic decline, globalization, financial crises, neoliberal austerity) that produce greater insecurity, uncertainty and anxiety, which create a fertile ground for political upheaval. The second emphasizes cultural factors such as racial resentment, status anxiety, fear of demographic change, increasing cultural diversity that creates an angry, fearful populace who are easy marks for authoritarian demagogues proposing simple answers and a return to an idealized past. However, Gidron and Hall stress the need for a more dynamic explanatory strategy: "As social science often does, it presents economic and cultural actions as competing explanations of a phenomenon…We need better frameworks for understanding how the two types of developments might combine to generate the discontent underlying support for radical parties" (Gidron and Hall, 2017, 1029). A Polanyian interpretation is an attempt to explore these factors in tandem, by bridging structural accounts that privilege broader economic and political transformations, with the intermediary social processes that produce cultural effects and emotional states that enhance the propensity for political extremism.

To briefly summarize the discussion in the previous chapter, Polanyi believed the rise of authoritarianism was a particular kind of escape route from the political and economic stalemate that paralyzed advanced societies in the inter-war years. "If ever there was a political movement that responded to the needs of an *objective situation*", he insisted, "and was not a result of fortuitous causes, it was fascism" (GT, 237). In this structural perspective, the rise of populism should be seen as the consequence of a common set of factors that have produced similar outcomes across advanced societies despite very different political institutions and political cultures. Hopkin, who draws on Polanyi for his own work on the rise of anti-system politics, elegantly captures this structuralist persuasion:

> "It is a simple matter of causal logic that the simultaneous rise of anti-systemic movements of such radically different ends can only be convincingly explained by factors that they have in common, rather than those that differ between them. The failures of the neoliberal economy and its

> severe consequences for society generate the kind of anger that fuels anti-system voting but that anger needs to be interpreted and mobilized in order for political change to happen."
>
> (Hopkin, 2020, 12)[18]

Although the success of populism (as with authoritarianism in the interwar era) cannot be read off this structural predilection, I have followed Polanyi's lead in emphasizing the formative effects of the 2008 financial crisis, given that great economic crises, particularly financial crises that lead to deep recessions, always provide fertile ground for political extremism. A detailed research project exploring this link across multiple historical periods concluded:

> "Politics takes a hard right turn following financial crises...this pattern is visible in the data both before and after World War II...the gains of extreme right wing parties was particularly pronounced after the global crisis of the 1920s/1930s and after 2008."
>
> (Funke et al., 2016, 232)

As discussed earlier, stagnating incomes and wages, higher unemployment, and austerity led to greater economic hardships and distress that prepared the ground for the right's ascendancy. But, populist anger has to be activated by political agents and harnessed to specific political causes and it is in this sense that Brubaker usefully highlights the importance of "crisis" as an interpretive frame and rhetorical device for populist politics (Brubaker, 2017). Crisis is intentionally employed by populist leaders as a rationale for why more radical policies are required as a matter of urgency, which simultaneously heightens attention on the worthy victims deserving protection as well as on those whose social suffering can be conveniently overlooked.

However, it is when crisis becomes inscribed into everyday life, as we discussed earlier in terms of the rampant diffusion of insecurity, that cultural grievances become a permanent feature of social and political life. This state of affairs can galvanize a series of emotional states – anxiety, uncertainty, anger, powerlessness, resentment, nostalgia – that can be commonly found across very different social and cultural contexts (Inglehart and Norris, 2016). I want to briefly explore how certain emotional trajectories create an "elective affinity" for particular kinds of populist politics but there are a few caveats to register beforehand. These different emotional states are not separate, free-floating phenomenon that can be analyzed schematically but rather are overlapping, mutually constitutive and reinforcing. Likewise, these cultural forces do not, in and of themselves, constitute a sufficient explanation for populism. As Blyth notes, "such factors characterize what's there, they don't explain it. The problem is that you cannot explain a cultural change by reference to a cultural change" (Blyth, 2018). It is precisely to avoid this kind of circular reasoning that a Polanyian framework is careful to emphasize the interactive dynamic across multiple levels of analysis, from structural transformations (neoliberalism) to social processes (market corrosion) to social effects (insecurity) to cultural forces (grievances and emotional states).

As previously highlighted, uncertainty and anxiety are ubiquitous features of our new insecure world but I want to address the specific character of status anxiety that numerous commentators have stressed in their analysis of populism (Gidron and Hall, 2017; Hochshild, 2016; Ridgeway, 2017). Neoliberal ideas tend to promote market inspired hierarchies of worth (merit, entrepreneurship, competition) that people use to evaluate their lives and which shape their expectations for the future. As Cecelia Ridgeway argues: "people care about status quite as intensely as they do about money and power. Loss of social standing – or the perception of it- can inspire anger and resentment" (Ridgeway, 2017). In middle class calculations, this especially takes the shape of what Barbara Ehrenreich called "fear of falling" – a pervasive anxiety that economic and cultural transformations could jettison them down the status hierarchy. A related process worth noting is social marginalization: the belief that a social group is being unfairly treated as unworthy or undeserving of critical attention and assistance; or it no longer commands the traditional standards of respect and recognition it has typically enjoyed; or their everyday circumstances in relative comparison to others have been severely eroded. Status anxiety is often combined with nostalgia, the conviction that life was better off in the past for people like themselves.

Populism appeals to nearly all these emotional registers. Trump's slogan, forever emblazoned on his ubiquitous red cap, proclaimed "Make America Great Again" and support for populist politics is often highest among those who agree that life was appreciably better in the past (some 60% of National Front supporters, as opposed to about 40% of French citizens in general, agreed with this sentiment). Populists are likely to propose simple diagnostic interpretations of what's gone wrong or who's to blame and revel in quick fixes to complex problems. They often promise to reinstate traditional hierarchies of value and target social protection to supporters who have been most affected by status reversals. In Hungary, as an example, the Orbán government provided development subsidies to rural areas, promised job guarantees to supporters, and offered generous tax breaks for family welfare (Offe, 2015). They accord supporters with symbolic badges of respect or denounce their opponents in ways that signal their appreciation and valuing of the "people's" innate qualities. Despite the obvious differences in income and social standing that would normally have set him apart from his supporters, Trump demonstrated a unique genius, be it through his bluster, bullying, mockery, or norm breaking, which convinced his supporters he was on their side, he was one of "the people" too. What made them willing to countenance his ethical lapses, his adultery, mendacity, sexual misconduct, his corruption and self-dealing, his penchant for stiffing small businesses, any of which would have been fatal if committed by another politician, was his performative belonging and outspoken tribal affiliation.

Anger and resentment – the "offspring of fear" in Martha Nussbaum's pithy formulation (Nussbaum, 2018) – are related emotional states that also pave the ground for populist appeals. Anger can take numerous forms: resentment at the continuous hardships people are forced to endure; feeling that the rules of the game are rigged against them and their children will face even more limited opportunities in the future; discontent that the meaningful choices that most impact their lives are being decided by elites beyond their control; or sheer exhaustion at having to prove themselves resilient and able to bear whatever shocks are thrown at them. A widespread sense of unfairness that fuelled populist gains was the popular anger in the aftermath of the 2008 financial crisis that the perpetrators who nearly crashed the world economy not only escaped jail time but were rewarded with million dollar bonuses and golden handshakes while ordinary people ended up footing the bill for the entire fiasco through higher taxes on their stagnant or falling wages.

Even while moral outrage can sometimes be the spur for political action to resolve an egregious injustice, powerlessness is often the flip side of private anger. A heightened sense of vulnerability, an abiding conviction that life is spiralling out of their control, a feeling of being left behind that they cannot shake. These emotional states can find resonance in any number of populist appeals. Powerlessness makes people prone to appeals to "take back control" (the Brexit slogan) or to leaders who display an unshakeable conviction in their own infallibility no matter the amount of disconfirming evidence. Politicians who specialize in scapegoating or demonization of others who can be blamed for their fate (especially if it serves to distract from their own culpability), be it faceless European bureaucrats, hapless immigrants, secretive globalists, or self-serving, out-of-touch, corrupt elites, appeal to anger's base instinct for revenge and retribution.

While it is important to avoid condescending or dismissive critiques of these emotionally fuelled grievances or to fail to take ordinary people at their word regarding the legitimate harm and injuries they have endured, this does not automatically imply that their emotionally crafted justifications for populist action should be accepted at face value, especially when they are predicated on misinformation and wilful ignorance (Muller, 2016). People who demonstrated against Obamacare while carrying signs reading "keep your government hands off my Medicare" or who expressed anger at rural hospital closures even though they voted for politicians who vetoed the very expansion of Medicare (via Obamacare) that would have guaranteed funding that kept these institutions alive might not be shameless hypocrites – a charge that could easily be levelled at the populist leaders who knowingly manufactured these outrages – but their misplaced anger demonstrates the intrinsic limits of first-hand experience in producing a privileged understanding of social change. Nor is it quite so straightforward to attribute moral equivalence between various forms of anger. The performative outrage of Covid-19 denialists at community meetings to protest mask wearing ordinances or vaccine mandates does not deserve to be accorded the same moral standing as the righteous anger of the vaccinated directed against the unvaccinated for endangering their fellow citizens and neglecting a vital civic duty. Finally, it is important to register that support for populist politics as a result of these emotional states does not imply that this is the only political pathway that such emotions can lead to; nor is there any guarantee that populists in power will translate their appeals into policies which actually alleviate the social suffering that gave rise to their popularity in the first place.[19]

The paradoxes of Brexit

If ever there was a case study that demonstrated not only the utility of a Polanyian framework but also his abiding fascination with paradoxes, it would be the Brexit referendum of 2016. Conceived by Prime Minister David Cameron as a way to fend off a hard right, anti-European faction within his own Conservative party, Brexit ended up becoming a massive tactical blunder (leading in the short run to the demise of Cameron's own political career) and a historically unprecedented act of self-harm. Even though the Remain position was supported by the entire British establishment, including nearly all major political parties, business associations, trade unions, and the most prominent Leave supporters entertained little faith in their success, the Leave position, which mandated that Britain withdraw from Europe, shocked the country with its extraordinary, unexpected victory. Nigel Farage, the leader of the UKIP Party and one of the Leave campaign's most prominent supporters, claimed, in classic populist rhetoric, that it represented "a victory for the real people", which automatically consigned the 48% who voted Remain as unworthy members of their own political community.

But Brexit reflected deep fault lines within Britain that Polanyi would have clearly recognized. Decades of an economic model predicated on an open economy that maximized exposure of its leading sectors to global markets left its citizens' economic fortunes increasingly vulnerable to market forces with all its attendant insecurity as highlighted above (increasing household debt, job volatility, declining social mobility). In the aftermath of the 2008 financial crisis, inequality grew considerably not only between individual households but between regions: economic growth was heavily concentrated in London and the Southeast while the declining industrial heartlands of northern England, south Wales and western Scotland all suffered income losses, stagnating wages and labor productivity and lower business investment. To make matters worse, these de-industrializing areas were also hit the hardest by austerity policies implemented by the incoming 2010 Tory government, which mandated deep cuts to housing benefits, council tax allowances, child and disability benefits and the arts alongside reductions in key social services (schools, libraries, hospitals and health clinics). In short, Brexit can be seen quite clearly as a protest vote against chronic economic insecurity and social distress (Hopkin, 2020).

However, there is no question that in advance of the referendum, few British voters cared very much or ever gave much thought to Europe as a political concern. They were largely ill informed about its intimate workings, and the Tory right's incessant warnings about the heavy-handed, regulation-mad European super-state never achieved any political weight until the announcement of the referendum instantaneously heightened its salience among the British public. But it was the nature of the binary choice on offer, either Remain or Leave, that transformed a vote on Europe into a protest vote reflecting widespread political discontent and mistrust.[20] With the entire British establishment united in favour of Remain, Leave voters took the opportunity to land "a free flying kick at the well upholstered bums" of political elites (O'Toole, 2019, 204). If the supposed anti-democratic nature of Europe had barely registered among voters, the main slogan of the Leave campaign, "Take Back Control", certainly resonated among citizens who had been buffeted by rising inequality and economic insecurity that was largely ascribed to market forces beyond Britain's control, and who were disenchanted by the perpetual inability of British governments (of both main parties) to cushion them from social and economic upheaval.

Brexit certainly demonstrated the dilemma of employing measures of direct democracy such as national referendums in an era of widespread disinformation and polarization. The campaign was marred by unprecedented political mendacity and disinformation. Take the leader of the Leave's campaign, Boris Johnson, at the time the former Mayor of London, who infamously boasted that £350 million a week would be diverted from Brussels and returned to the NHS if their side triumphed, a brazen falsehood that was widely disparaged yet was endlessly repeated in the press and which came on the heels of another outright lie that the NHS had been placed in such a perilous state because it had been grievously crippled by the "health tourism" of European migrants (in fact, it was the Tories' own cuts that undermined the health service). Not to be outdone, Farage contributed an outrageous poster campaign that portrayed an endless stream of refugees entering Britain with the slogan "Breaking Point" alongside thinly veiled threats that if Turkey was admitted into the EU, the country would be "swamped", the all too familiar term utilized by anti-immigrant nationalists and the right-wing press, by millions of Muslims. When business leaders, economists, banking analysts all insisted that Brexit would create unparalleled economic damage, senior Tory minister Michael Gove boasted that the "people have had enough of experts", a pointed confirmation of the pervasive distrust and perpetual gaslighting permeating British political life.[21]

If Brexit proved to be an anti-establishment protest, Jonathan Hopkin offers a useful summary of its broader socio-economic roots that lends credence to the claim it also represented a Polanyian countermovement in response to the wider insertion of market dynamics into British social life (Hopkin, 2020, 140–45). Leave voters could be differentiated by income, education, age and geography, all of which are excellent social indicators of exposure to economic insecurity. The lower the income or subjective well-being, alongside the pessimistic conviction that British life had declined in the period since the financial crisis, the higher the support for Leave. Leave voting was highly correlated with economic change, with low skilled, low income workers, who had been most affected by economic decline, material distress and austerity, voting in the majority for Leave (the anomaly of Scottish working class voters, who faced similar socio-economic profiles, yet voted overwhelmingly for Remain, will be addressed below). This was especially true if a working class area, such as those in northern England, had experienced a downward shift in income and house prices over a prolonged period of time or suffered from heightened exposure to global competition. Among voters with only a secondary education, 78% voted Leave as opposed to only 26% of university graduates. Age mattered as well, with 61% of over-65s supporting Leave, while young people, even though they too faced considerable economic insecurity, voted overwhelmingly for Remain. Unquestionably, Brexit was fuelled by anxiety, insecurity, a loss of status and a growing sense of powerlessness. "It counters their sense of powerlessness" argues Fintan O'Toole, "with a moment of real power – Brexit is, after all, a very big thing to do" (O'Toole, 2019, 153).

However, as O'Toole insisted, it proved to be a grievous act of self-harm. Abolishing the so-called "Brussels red tape", the mantra of the Tory hard right, meant, in actual practice, dismantling the very environmental, labor and social protections that had partly constrained the market forces which caused such economic distress in the first place. Similarly, in the category of "biting your nose to spite your face", working class proponents of Brexit ignored repeated warnings that the greatest damage from a European exit would befall their own regions because they would face the costs of reduced access to European markets and depended the most on EU structural funds. These same voters then paradoxically re-elected electoral majorities in 2017 and 2019 from the very party that had served as an architect of their economic misery in the past decade.[22] It remains a perplexing conundrum that in a nation so sensitively attuned to class distinctions, if not resentments, working class voters nevertheless gave such fervent support to a political campaign that was midwifed by the unholy trinity of Farage, a supercilious, City fat cat, Jacob Rees-Mogg, a snooty, desiccated *faux* aristocrat, and Johnson, a well-heeled *parvenu* playing the role of the bumbling man of the people, none of whom had the slightest affinity with the working class that they were supposedly representing. Indeed, what seemed so improbable was that the Leave coalition was made up of a coalition between disadvantaged working class voters from de-industrializing cities in the North and Wales and well-off rural and suburban Conservative voters who had prospered in recent decades.

A partial explanation of this puzzle implicates the key cultural factors that other authors have stressed in accounting for the rise of populism; in the case of Brexit, these were primarily the issue of immigration and English national identity. In numerous opinion surveys, immigration was quite high on the list of voter preferences in the years preceding the referendum, with Leave voters far more likely (by 47% to 16%) to consider immigration a top priority for governmental action (Hopkin, 2020). Freedom of movement enjoyed by all European citizens was the special culprit in the Leave worldview and Brexit panic for it was routinely asserted that unchecked migration threatened job losses, wage declines and intensified pressure on scarce social services, such as health care and housing. There was a strong correlation between the propensity to vote Leave, especially among older voters, and a rapid increase in migration over a short period of time (even if the actual number of migrants remained small in comparison to population figures), the kind of rupture in habitation that Polanyi highlighted, where fear of change, cultural diversity, a loss of status were all galvanized by the spectre of immigration.

As with the economic consequences of Brexit, Leave voters who emphasized the pernicious effects of immigration were forced to overlook several inconvenient facts: migration actually proved a net contribution to the national income; it had only a small, negligible effect on wages and employment; and, rather than a drain on public services, migrants provided essential staff, especially in the beleaguered health sector. This crucial paradox was highlighted by numerous commentators: namely, the areas that were most likely to vote Leave were actually those which had the *lowest* levels of migration and therefore were the *least* likely to have everyday interactions with people of different races, ethnicities or national origins (high immigration areas, such as metropolitan areas throughout the country, voted overwhelmingly to Remain) (Hopkin, 2020).[23] It is hard to resist the conclusion that receptiveness to racist, xenophobic attitudes towards immigrants, which economic distress might well have helped convert into convenient scapegoats for their anger, contributed to populist support in these areas. Even if immigration became a useful foil and an emotional projection for voters to express their general discontent, it is interesting yet again how the actual culprits to blame for cuts to vital social services and public spending – Conservative politicians who supported a decade of austerity – once again escaped scot-free from this critical scrutiny. It is precisely this combination of displacement, wilful ignorance and emotional projection that enabled the Leave campaign to mobilize and manipulate this generalizable anxiety into an anti-establishment groundswell.

Lastly, O'Toole, in his marvellous essay on Brexit, *Heroic Failure*, persuasively argues that the referendum represented a crisis of the political system and national identity (O'Toole, 2018). In the decades before the vote, there had been a marked increase among English voters who, when asked whether they saw themselves more as English, British or both, expressed a clear preference for an English identity. This was particularly marked in specific regions of the country such as the Northeast (where 70% identified with an English identity) or the Northwest, East Midlands and Yorkshire (where the figure was 66%), in sharp contrast to Londoners, where only 33% preferred an English identity (Institute for Public Policy Research, 2016). Not surprisingly, people who felt a strong attachment to an English identity were far more likely to support Brexit, even it if meant the breakup of the United Kingdom (which also addresses the puzzle of why working class Scottish voters, who shared a similar socio-economic profile as their northern English counterparts and had suffered similar levels of economic insecurity and social distress, nonetheless voted by large majorities for Remain because they saw the referendum as the product of a resurgent English nationalism).

What constituted this English identity was not so straightforward but followed common elements identified in other populist movements – a nostalgia for an idealized past, a sense of lost status, a sentimental attachment to the heroic days of Empire, a resentment of Sottish and Welsh political independence – but it also was shaped by the particular idiosyncratic convolutions of both "Greatness" and "Britishness" that had afflicted the British polity for decades. Indeed, O'Toole argues that Brexit was the culmination of an internal political crisis of legitimacy and belonging that had been festering for decades. "The very word Brexit contains a literally unspoken truth", he writes.

> "It does not include or even allude to Europe. It is British exit that is the point, not what it is exiting *from*. The tautologous slogan Leave Means Leave is similarly (if unintentionally honest): the meaning is in the leaving, not in what is being left or how."
>
> (O'Toole, 2019, 242)

Brexit, in this regard, represented an unconscious projection of the deep, unresolved contradictions of an archaic British political system struggling with modernity onto the European polity: the unravelling of an imagined community and a sense of national belonging under the centrifugal pressures of regional inequalities and competing power centers. Indeed, the irony and final paradox of Brexit was that instead of meaningful reform, which would have instituted new forms of pluralistic power sharing and countervailing bulwarks against the aggrandizement of centralized Westminster control, the referendum merely enabled an overly centralized state that only begrudgingly acknowledged alternative sources of countervailing authority to reassert unquestioned control.

The Beginning of the End or the End of the Beginning

The Polanyian insight we have repeatedly emphasized throughout the book – the double movement is both a structural regularity within capitalism and a politically contingent project – logically implies a critical scrutiny of the staying power of neoliberalism and whether a double movement successor might be on the horizon. But in asking what's next for the double movement, we are obliged to pose three additional questions. First, is the crisis of neoliberalism so severe that it is widely discredited (by both elites and the general population)? That is, do people attribute the primary ills of the current era to neoliberalism and do they believe solutions to repair these faults will only make matters worse? Second, are there potential alternatives to neoliberalism with clear reform agendas that would be successful in redressing these ills? Third, can proponents of these alternatives assemble a winning political coalition that can overcome political, institutional and social obstacles to its adoption and can this new program be accepted as a new common sense.

This might seem an insurmountable set of conditions but it is worth stressing that the triumph of neoliberalism four decades ago managed to meet every single one of them, even though just a decade earlier, it had been consigned to the political wilderness (Block and Somers, 2014; Hall and Sewell, 2013). The post war model was widely seen, even by its strongest supporters, to be seriously malfunctioning with piecemeal solutions only temporarily displacing problems. Neoliberalism was an ideological successor in waiting: it relied on a familiar repertoire of policies and stratagems (even if it took a wilful act of historical amnesia to purge the memory of liberalism's previous track record of economic and political catastrophe); its analysis of Golden age contradictions appeared an accurate interpretation ("In short, Keynesianism did not fit the facts, monetarism did, and that is why it won the day" (Blyth, 2015, 201). It assembled a political coalition largely through the capture of adherents within existing Conservative parties but then extended its political hegemony across ideological lines and across political systems to become the unchallenged political-economic project of the 21st century. The question I want to entertain in this brief conclusion is whether any potential successor to neoliberalism would be able to offer affirmative answers to any or all of these dilemmas.

But, some preliminary caveats arising from our analysis of Polanyi's own work should be highlighted. First, as he well acknowledged, there are always multiple political pathways out of crisis and it is not so straightforward to adjudicate the future trajectory of any of them or if and when any of them might achieve dominance. Second, the fact that solutions to a crisis might be required does not necessarily mean they will be forthcoming nor is there any guarantee, even if they are discovered, that they will prove efficacious. Crises do not automatically lead to fatal collapse nor do they always lead to renewal and reconstruction either. It's no wonder –and I am unable to resist the siren call myself- academics are so fond of quoting Gramsci's famous epigram in this regard: "The crisis consists precisely in the fact that the old is dying and the new cannot be born; in this interregnum, a great variety of morbid symptoms appear". Lastly, as we discussed earlier in Chapter 4, Polanyi insisted our ability to accurately perceive the contours of crisis was critically impaired by the dynamics of the double movement. The rapidity of social change, its spatial complexity, the complex intertwining of political and economic factors, all contributed to make transitional periods particularly opaque to the understanding of all social agents. This is no less true of academics attempting to speculate about our current period so my tentative thoughts in this section should necessarily be seen as preliminary and provisional.

If we begin with the first question, whether neoliberalism is in a pervasive state of crisis, nearly every commentator writing about the current period, notwithstanding their ideological bent, highlights the exact same set of systemic disorders and pathologies afflicting the neoliberal model (Mazzucato, 2012; Kuttner, 2018).[24] These include: stagnating growth rates; rising inequality and insecurity; corporate short termism and malfeasance; uprooting of communities and habitations as a result of relentless commodification; ecological devastation and climate change; global pandemics; oligarchic power; and widespread political mistrust and cynicism. "The case for radical change is thus overwhelming", concludes Mariana Mazzucato, who, by no stretch of the imagination, can be deemed a political radical (Mazzucato, 2012, 23). It is precisely this broad consensus, encompassing diverse political philosophies, about the ubiquity of the overlapping crises which leads Streeck to emphasize the complexity of this transitional period:

> "The diversity of theories on what all agree is a severe crisis of capitalism and capitalist society is an indication of contemporary capitalism having entered a period of deep *indeterminacy*- a period in which unexpected things *can* happen at any time and knowledgeable observers can legitimately disagree on what *will* happen."
>
> (Streeck, 2016, 12)

It is not unfair to group Fraser and Streeck on the more pessimistic side of this debate, given their contention that capitalism is marked by a pervasive instability and disequilibrium. Fraser attributes the flashpoints of crisis to the destabilizing and undermining transformations of fictitious commodities that have decimated non-market arenas in ways that are mutually reinforcing and interactive. She believes capitalism's multiple disorders and debilitating pathologies will continue to metastasize, outstripping the capacity of political and social actors to cure them, and leading inexorably to a demand for deep structural change. Streeck similarly likens governments to forest firefighters, implementing temporary measures to entrenched problems that merely generate new problems and dysfunctions, requiring additional stopgap solutions, which turn out to be as short lived and self-defeating as previous ones did. "Too many frailties have become simultaneously acute", he maintains, "while too many remedies have been exhausted or destroyed" (Streeck, 2016, 13). He envisions capitalism entering a slow, prolonged period of *social entropy*:

> "My image of the demise of capitalism…is one of a long drawn out death by a thousand cuts, over an extended period of time, the extent of which will be uncertain and possibly surprising. Perhaps the best metaphor for what we are likely seeing is aging: the continuous accumulation of small, and increasingly, not so small dysfunctions, none of them deadly as such, but most of them beyond repair…As time passes, the parts of the whole will less and less fit together; the elements of the system will be more and more out of joint; frictions of all kinds will multiply; unanticipated consequences will spread, along ever more twisted and unpredictable lines of causation; equilibrium will become the exception instead of the rule –until in the end something new will emerge, out of a myriad of provisional fixes invented on-the-go to cope with the proliferating daily disasters produced by a society in chronic disorder".
>
> (Streeck, 2014, 52)

There is a close affinity here with Polanyi's own warning that the delegitimation of an institutional order does not happen overnight. "The secular tenets of social organization embracing the whole world are not dislodged by events of a decade", he argued. "It's spectacular failure in one field did not destroy its authority in all" (GT, 143).

At the opposite end of the spectrum, the economic historian Adam Tooze also warns we are witnessing the comprehensive crisis of the neoliberal era – "The year 2020 exposed the risks and weaknesses of the market-driven global system like never before. It's hard to avoid the sense that a turning point has been reached" – but the implications he draws from this conclusion veer significantly from Fraser and Streeck (Tooze, 2021). He believes the normal claims of neoliberal hegemony – the self-healing powers of the market, the market's infallible allocative efficiencies, the need for a minimal state that keeps government intervention in markets to a minimum – have been completely jettisoned, if not discredited, in the aftermath of the pandemic crisis, conclusively demonstrating the salience of Polanyi's insight that a market economy cannot survive without the full power of the state. Case in point was the prompt, decisive state action (supported by governments of differing ideological stripes and enthusiastically endorsed by the guardians of neoliberal orthodoxy, the IMF and World Bank) that averted a complete collapse of the global economy. OECD nations issued $18 trillion in new debt, a figure completely unprecedented in peacetime, through a series of new, bold innovations in financial wizardry including central bank swaps and quantitative easing. However, as Erza Klein astutely recognized:

> "the most revealing part of the response was what didn't happen. Bond vigilantes didn't send markets into a tailspin. Interest rates didn't skyrocket. And there is no evidence of a hyperinflation spiral. Private investment didn't plummet…The decades of doomsday predictions of

> what would happen if the government should spend huge amounts of money without paying for it – they didn't materialize."
>
> (Klein, 2021)

For Leo Panitch and Sam Gindin, this development is a telling illustration of a much broader political process of "failure containment" (Panitch and Gindin, 2012). Since the 1990s the United States has understood that the trade-off for allowing volatile financial markets to flourish was that states had to be prepared to contain the inevitable crises that these same markets galvanized. From the 2008 financial crisis to the 2020 global pandemic, states have therefore facilitated historically unprecedented forms of social cooperation and collective obligations among central bankers, Treasury officials, private banks, and other key political and economic actors, to limit the spread and effects of these crises. For Panitch and Gindin, this represents an exceptional form of social learning by capitalist elites, who are willing to abandon the neoliberal playbook and do whatever is necessary to preserve the global capitalist order. For Tooze, it demonstrated a fundamental paradox: although these initiatives were intended to rescue the old system of neoliberalism rather than create the foundations for a new one, this very exercise of political power is persuasive evidence that a post-neoliberal transition is already underway, even if the contours of the new system cannot yet be precisely discerned.

Even more importantly, the effective response to the pandemic demonstrated the political capacity to solve huge, pressing social problems had not atrophied nor was it fated to create harmful side effects. The power to tackle seemingly intractable problems is not a question of capacity per se but rather one of *political will*: if political elites were as committed to utilizing this capacity for democratic, egalitarian ends as they have been to safeguard the market economy, there is no telling the kind of accomplishments that might ensue (Tooze, 2021). It is fascinating how this optimistic perspective has captured the imagination of so many commentators. The former Labour leader, Ed Miliband, entitled his recent manifesto, *Go Big!*, while Mazzucato subtitled her book "a moonshot guide to changing capitalism" (Miliband, 2021; Mazzucato, 2021). Their ambitious blueprints call for a radically different politics and identify critical questions – what should be the critical rights guaranteed by citizenship; how can we reduce the power of markets and strengthen non-market arenas and values; how do we rebalance the relationship between the economy and market on behalf of social justice and economic security; how do we cure caring deficits and solve climate change – that are directly inspired by a Polanyian framework. And as we shall explore more fully in the next chapter, many of the specific proposals they espouse, such as enhanced public goods, new forms of economic security, basic income and a Green New Deal, are component features of what I call a decommodification strategy (Vail, 2010).

In an important sense, this recognition returns us to the framework of embedded liberalism. Ruggie insisted the post war international arrangements were "not simply emanates of the underlying distribution of state power but represent a fusion of power and *legitimate social purpose*" (Ruggie, 1982, my emphasis). There have been renewed calls for an Embedded Liberalism 2.0 that would recreate the economic dynamism and social stability of the post war era (Helleiner, 2020). It would empower a new international architecture whose social purpose would be greater equality and social justice, predicated on a new set of values such as well-being, capabilities, equality over the life course, an equitable sharing of risks, mutual responsibility and ecological stewardship. It would employ global public goods (poverty alleviation, climate change, pandemics, security), international labor standards, global tax minimums and Tobin transaction taxes (on air travel, carbon emissions, financial transactions), which would require (and hopefully inspire) the design and diffusion of new forms of social cooperation and power sharing. And, like the earlier post war accord, it is the very breadth of the overlapping crises which offers hope that it could mobilize support from across diverse constituencies even if the critical work of establishing a widely agreed common program would undoubtedly mandate considerable bargaining and trade-offs.

One can be reasonably sceptical about the likelihood of this scenario – the challenges of achieving these objectives at even the European level have proven immensely difficult so an embryonic international order along these principles would certainly raise even more obstacles- while still signposting the formidable evidence of the Golden Age as proof that a future egalitarian capitalist order can be achieved. Tony Judt's wistful encouragement for a critical historical imagination seems even more imperative at present:

> "Rather than seek to restore a language of optimistic progress, we should begin by reacquainting ourselves with the recent past…The first task of radical dissenters today is to remind their audience of the achievements of the twentieth century along with the likely consequences of our heedless rush to dismantle them."
>
> (Judt, 2010, 96)

Indeed, it is something of a paradox that while neoliberal proponents proudly look to the past for inspiration, no matter the inconveniences that the historical record might entail, social democrats only rarely trumpet the salutary lessons of their own 'trentes glorieuses' (Konzcal, 2020 is a notable exception).

In Chapter 4, I explored how Polanyi insisted successful reform under capitalism depended on the extent to which projects could be said to be in or out of synch with the prevailing winds of historical change; that they had to be "commensurate with the prevailing social relations" in order to become successful. Even if no one can predict which potential successor to neoliberalism might eventually triumph – embedded liberalism 2.0, anti-capitalism, decommodification, authoritarian populism, social entropy – in an encouraging Polanyian outlook, the very nature of the interpenetrated crises offers the prospect of a countermovement that could unite the competing interests of climate change campaigners, feminists, trade unions, landless peasants, farmers, human rights activists, basic income proponents and many others. But it is equally true that if we seek to understand our present era, let alone try to predict the future, it is perhaps wise to stop focusing on what our current predicament has in common with the double movement cycles of the past and instead investigate the conditions under which the double movement itself might be transcended, which is the theme of our concluding chapter to which we now turn.

Notes

1 Thomas Piketty in his magisterial work *Capital in the Twenty-First Century* (Piketty, 2014) argues for a long term cycle of inequality regimes that maps exactly onto Polanyi's framework. In fact, Part 3 of *Capital and Ideology* (2020), which discusses the post war and neoliberal epochs, is entitled "The Great Transformation of the 20th Century", in direct homage to Polanyi.

2 Lacher insists that the post war period of embedded liberalism represented the negation of Polanyi's vision of the double movement and more importantly, gave a clear indication of his socialist inclinations. "*The Great Transformation* is best understood", he argues, "as an effort to demonstrate the historical *impossibility of social democracy*" (Lacher, 2019, 205). For an incisive survey of the complex nature of Polanyi's political influences, which encompassed Marxism, Communism, guild socialism, social democracy and Christian socialism, see Dale, 2010.

3 This was a dynamic that Polanyi understood very well as we traced in Chapter 3: "This is ultimately why the reform of capitalist economy by socialist parties is difficult even when they are determined not to interfere with the property system. For the mere possibility that they might decide to do so undermines that type of confidence in which liberal economy is vital, namely absolute confidence in the continuity of titles to property" (GT, 234).

4 Beyond the central role of social power and contradictions, scholars have enlisted additional explanatory factors to account for the return of *laissez-faire* in the 1980s, which essentially rely on the same set of explanations Polanyi used to account for the origins of the self-regulating market. Ideology takes center stage in many accounts, similarly emphasizing its crusading zeal, its long march through political life, the social and political networks that propagated its message, and the intellectual transformation that undermined the foundations of the postwar era (Block and Somers, 2014; Blyth, 2002; Hall and Sewell, 2013). Others stress the central role of the state and political power in freeing up capital (Fourcade and Babb, 2002; Harvey, 2005). What we lack at present is a comprehensive Polanyian account of the origins of neoliberalism that could link all five factors –technology, social power, the state, ideology and contradictions- into an integrated account that traced how these distinct factors formed a set of elective affinities that created a groundswell for the transition.

5 I am focusing on neoliberalism because of its obvious connection to the discussion of the double movement but this does not mean that every significant political

economic development in the past four decades should be subsumed under this analytical category. Globalization, post-industrialism, the knowledge economy, technological revolutions are phenomena that overlap with neoliberalism, and have certainly been impacted by it, but they require separate explanatory frameworks.

6 Even if it is not directly the result of neoliberalism, the deformation of American democracy as evidenced by the mutation of the Republican Party into an anti-democratic, proto-authoritarian organization needs to be acknowledged. They have refused to accept electoral outcomes (fully 70% of Republicans believe the Biden election in 2020 was illegitimate) and proven willing to subvert them via nullification or insurrection as evidenced by the January 6, 2021 invasion of Congress that threatened harm to members of congress and the Vice President. They have implemented countless voter suppression policies, demonstrated a willingness to countenance violence as an acceptable tactic to achieve political goals, and demonized political opponents as imminent threats to democracy. In such a climate of polarization, all political disagreements become transformed into existential threats, which makes democratic deliberation on pressing social problems an impossibility not to mention crowding out the space for the innovative problem solving and experimentalism that is so urgently required. American political instability, therefore, represents a serious global risk: if its commitment to multilateral institutions, or capacity to mobilize political cooperation can no longer be guaranteed, which none of its allies believe to be the case if a Trumpist party is in charge, then pressing problems of climate change, future pandemics and financial crises will be harder to avert.

7 It is worth highlighting the anomaly of China in this regard. Although its transition out of state socialism overlapped with the triumph of neoliberalism, China, unlike Russia, managed to avoid the destructive shock therapy transition modeled along neoliberal precepts (rapid privatization of enterprises, which were forced to withstand competitive markets; elimination of price controls; elimination of social subsidies) that led to a massive collapse of GDP and social well-being in Russia (Weber, 2020). In fact, since 1980 China's GDP has increased fiftyfold, incomes have risen by some 70%, sparking the growth of a middle class and a historically unprecedented reduction of poverty, with over 600 million lifted out of destitution in just three decades.

8 Although my primary emphasis is on Piketty's work, his scholarship was part of a groundswell of academic work on inequality that included Atkinson, 2015; Pickett and Wilkinson, 2009; Stiglitz, 2013; Therborn, 2013.

9 Piketty's intellectual affinities with Polanyi are considerable. He too is contemptuous of academic specializations, lamenting what he called "foolish disciplinary squabbles". The bold queries, the historical and intellectual puzzles that capture his intellectual imagination feel like a direct descendant to Polanyi's work. So too does his commitment to understanding capitalism as a historical social order or his vivid narrative style and incisive moral polemic. But it is also worth noting that whereas Polanyi was the quintessential iconoclastic scholar toiling in solitary obscurity (at least in his writing of *The Great Transformation*), Piketty has collaborated with a team of international colleagues who have painstakingly assembled over several decades a historical data set designed to overcome methodological difficulties that plagued attempts to chronicle inequality as a historical phenomenon.

10 The advance of this market imperialism can be quite insidious. As soon as your home, car, skills become potential commodities that can fetch a market price, and the opportunity cost for not using them for such purposes increases, the hyper-commercialization of everyday life and the transformation of individuals into "daily capitalists" becomes relentless (Milanovic, 2019, 191).

11 A corollary to this development can be observed in India, where sharply rising debt burdens of farmers, owing to their insertion into the global economy has led to a wave of farmer suicides throughout rural areas.

12 It is well recognized that low income children with attractive secondary school grades and test scores often fail to apply to the most selective colleges because they have either not heard of them or because they are convinced that they could never be admitted. Disadvantaged kids lack parents with direct knowledge of university life and do not possess knowledgeable peer groups or school counsellors that are embedded in a wider social network who can provide them with high quality advice and mentoring (Grusky et al., 2019).

13 Beverley Silver (see also Burawoy, 2010) contrasts what she calls Polanyi type struggles against commodification and Marx type struggles against exploitation (Silver, 2003). Both of these are in evidence in the movements discussed herein.

14 Dale argues in this vein: "The countermovement does make sense but as a heuristic that refers to the way in which, when the self-regulating market undermines the security of their livelihoods, human beings look to political ideas and organizations that claim to defend society against market excesses. If given any more determinative content than that, for example when used to imply that these ideas and organizations actually do 'rally' society against the market, the concept tends to collapse under its own weight; it comes to function, if you will, as a bad abstraction" (Dale, 2010, 220).

15 Piketty's understated, deadpan comic timing can be appreciated throughout this discussion. In one passage where he is presenting the eye opening data that Harvard graduates make on average nearly half a million dollars a year, he dryly comments: "such a finding does not seem entirely compatible with selection based solely on merit" (Piketty, 2014, 485).

16 There have been left populist movements in advanced industrial societies – the Gilets Jaunes in France is a recent manifestation – and left populist parties (Five Star in Italy, Podemos in Spain, Melenchon's Left Alliance in France or the Varoufakis/Lafontaine List in the European Parliament) but, at present, this tendency remains politically marginal in comparison to their right-wing counterparts. The notable exception to this tendency is in Latin and South America where left populists have formed governments in Mexico, Venezuela, Bolivia and Peru. Clearly, these left populists share little in common with the xenophobia and authoritarianism of Trump and Oban but at the same time, Jonathan Hopkin argues that they are both symptomatic of what he calls "anti-system politics" given that they all demand fundamental changes to the political and economic system (Hopkin, 2020). I agree wholeheartedly with Hopkin that the term "populism" has "inescapably acquired a heavily pejorative connotation, undermining serious and systematic analysis" (Hopkin, 2020, 6), but I am using the term, albeit with a narrower focus on the right-wing variant, because of this widespread use.

17 Post-war social democrats put forth their own progressive version of "the people" that stressed their capacity for self-government, self-determination and self-improvement which would underpin a participatory and deliberative democracy (Berman, 2006).

18 Hopkin stresses the importance of not just asking why populism might have arisen but also the conditions under which it is more likely to succeed and argues that the success of a reactionary movement cannot be read off an objective situation but requires activation by political and ideological actors. He offers a fascinating excursus, implicating the nature of welfare states, electoral systems, party formation, migratory flows and exposure to global markets to account for the different forms and outcomes of populist movements (Hopkin, 2020).

19 For an incisive review of what populists do once they are in power, see Muller, 2016, chapter 2.
20 Muller argues that the blunt instrument of a referendum is by design incapable of promoting democratic politics: "A referendum isn't meant to start an open-ended process of deliberation among active citizens to generate a range of well-considered popular judgments; rather the referendum serves to ratify what the populist leader has already discovered to be the general populist interest as a matter of identity…" (Muller, 2016, 29).
21 Shortly after the vote, Tory minister David Davis insisted that "There will be no downside to Brexit, only a considerable upside", which even at the time, seemed like an overly optimistic discounting of potential obstacles but, now in hindsight, appears a case of wilful ignorance. British newspapers in the fall of 2021 all feature headlines warning of labour shortages across multiple sectors (transport, health, hospitality, farming) – not entirely surprising given that 1.3 million people left the country after the final agreement – that are leading to massive energy shortages and empty supermarket shelves.
22 This paradox reflects the long term shift of working class support from Labour to the Conservatives. In 1997, 59% of Tony Blair's voters were working class. By 2019, Boris Johnson won the working class by 44–33%.
23 This is not an uncommon pattern. In Germany, the right-wing party Alternative für Deutschland, which championed a virulently anti-immigrant platform, gained its greatest political support in poorer areas of the country, such as the regions of the former East Germany, which had no migration to speak of.
24 For the opposing view, Azmanova insists "no such crisis has taken place. What are commonly seen as its manifestations –from the rise of populism to the upsurge of precarious employment and slacking of growth – are, rather, the 'growing pains' in a process of transforming capitalism from the neoliberal mode to the precarity form" (Azmanova, 2020, 2).

Chapter 7

Transcending the Double Movement

There is no question that Polanyi's fundamental approach – his emphasis on the complexity of social change, the dilemmas and crises that arise from the coexistence of competing principles of the double movement, the enduring critique of a market society and its devastating social and cultural consequences – leads inexorably to a consideration of future alternatives to the double movement, which is the theme of this concluding chapter. As highlighted in Chapter 5, he well understood that the 1930s conjuncture, which witnessed the rise of several distinct political alternatives (Fascism, communism, social democracy), had demonstrated that there are always multiple pathways out of crisis, each of which will be constrained and facilitated by the international economy, social struggle, political capacity and the social imagination. Certainly, the current crisis in all its manifestations – widespread unemployment, the precipitous decline of social safety nets, caring deficits, pernicious insecurity and inequality, ecological devastation, the hollowing-out of democracy, the decline of political legitimacy not to mention the successive crises of the 2008 financial crisis and the Covid-19 pandemic – invites the consideration of social transformative projects that have hitherto not been on the political agenda (Panitch and Gindin, 2010).

Indeed, Polanyian inspired calls for a new political/economic/social transformation have resounded across the ideological spectrum. Pope Francis in his October 2020 encyclical, "Fratelli Tutti" (Brothers and Sisters All), issued an urgent demand for a "torrent of moral energy" on behalf of a new campaign for human renewal and the common good: "I hope that this time of danger will free us from operating on automatic pilot, shake our sleepy consciences and allow a humanist and ecological conversation that puts an end to the idolatry of money and places human life and dignity at the centre". A manifesto signed by some 3,000 scholars from 600 universities across the globe, openly used the language of "decommodification" – the organizing principle of this chapter – to highlight pathways out of the current crisis. "The crisis also shows that work must not be treated as a commodity", they argued, "that market mechanisms alone cannot be left in charge of the choices that affect our communities most deeply… Decommodifying work means preserving certain sections from the laws of the

DOI: 10.4324/9781003133186-7

so-called free market; it also means ensuring that all people have access to work and the dignity it brings". Even the house journal of capitalist elites, *The Financial Times*, got in on the act in an editorial on April 4, 2020: "Radical reforms – reversing the prevailing policy direction of the last four decades – will need to be put on the table. Governments will have to accept a more active role in the economy. They must see public services as investments rather than liabilities and look for ways to make labour markets less insecure. Redistribution will again be on the agenda".

However, it is worth reiterating that the strengths of the Polanyian framework as we have articulated throughout this book lie primarily in its diagnostic acumen rather than strategic insight. Polanyi did not focus exhaustively on the specific political/institutional contexts or political-economic strategies that were most efficacious in resolving crises nor did he devote any sustained attention to the obstacles and dilemmas of social reform. While it is true that much of the contemporary debate about macro-level solutions to the political and economic crisis –new forms of Keynesian counter-cyclical stimulus, tackling global inequality, global coordination to address climate change- operates on grounds that were not necessarily central to his account of the double movement, there have been some innovative contributions to imagining a Polanyian pathway on behalf of a reconstructed political economy that fuse his analytical and moral concerns (Block, 2006, 2011; Fraser, 2013, 2014, 2018; Hopkin, 2020; Somers, 2008). As we shall discuss more fully below, there are a number of general principles for social reform that he emphasizes – the prescriptive power of institutions and civil society to act as a countervailing power to the market, the importance of understanding economic prosperity on wider grounds than merely GDP growth, the reversal of commodification and the scourge of insecurity – it is also the case that there is no straightforward Polanyian road map for reform even if his framework is, as we shall detail below, premised on a fierce emancipatory critique.

A critical social science, however, must do more than illuminate the terrain of social suffering or stake a moral claim against insecurity and oppression. It has to propose feasible and desirable pathways that can surmount the social and economic order that is generating these harms (Wright, 2010). In this chapter, my particular emphasis is on a reformulation of the idea of *decommodification*, which I argue below is closest in spirit to a Polanyian pathway for an egalitarian and emancipatory alternative beyond the double movement.[1] In the first section of the chapter, I trace the roots of this perspective within Polanyi's own writings and explore his considerable influence on the paradigmatic account of decommodification by Gosta Esping-Andersen. I argue that a renewed emphasis on decommodification requires an expanded conceptual reconstruction that can take into account the pervasive extension of commodification in recent decades that has been amply documented in the previous chapter (for a fuller explication of the rationale for this enhanced perspective, see Vail, 2010). In the second section, I offer a detailed account of this expanded framework; explore why each of its component features should be central to a Polanyian egalitarian agenda; and detail the institutional and political dilemmas that impact on their realization. In the final section, I explore the political complexity of this reform program and ask whether it constitutes a feasible route beyond the double movement.

Transcending the Double Movement

In terms of the transcendence of the double movement, I highlight three themes in this section: Polanyi's philosophical musings in the last chapter of what he called "freedom in a complex society"; the centrality of Aristotle to his own more nuanced understanding of the nature of economic activity; and his tentative thoughts on how market imperatives might be overcome in a post-double movement society. As discussed earlier in Chapter 3, Polanyi acknowledged that markets play an indispensable role in promoting freedoms that "we prize highly. Freedom of conscience, freedom of speech, freedom of meeting, freedom of association, freedom to choose one's own job-we cherish them for their own sake" (Polanyi, 1947, 75). But in a complex society, he insisted, markets not only enlarge the space of individual freedom, they can reduce it as well and tracing this logic is revealing of the ways in which he conceives of not just freedom but the nature of emancipation as well (GT, chapter 21).

In the first instance, Polanyi clearly envisages *complex freedom* not merely as the absence of arbitrary interference with individual autonomy but within the wider context of the social, political and cultural forces that impede human flourishing (Block and Somers, 2014, chapter 8).[2] Forms of "unfreedom" such as unemployment, destitution, ill health, systematic discrimination and intolerance, workplace authority, insecurity (all of the hallmarks of the "perversion of cruelty" (GT, 224) of marketization) constitute "brutal restrictions" (GT, 258) on individual liberty and self-development, with the potential for freedom sharply circumscribed, and only the "comfortable classes" able to enjoy the full measure of security (GT, 254). Freedom achieved "at the cost of justice and security" (GT, 254–5) represented an impoverished form of autonomy. "It appears that the means of maintaining freedom", he wrote, "are themselves adulterating and destroying it" (GT, 254). For security to be guaranteed for all, the scope of freedom had to be conceived as a "prescriptive right extending far beyond the narrow confines of the political sphere into the intimate organization of society itself" (GT, 256), where life chances are firmly grounded in social rights as a condition of citizenship rather than prior determinants or as the outcome of market interactions (Somers, 2008).

Indeed, at the very heart of his notion of social protection (echoed in critical social policy writings on the welfare state (Hacker, 2006) is the belief that both freedom and security must be predicated on the principles of shared fate, mutual responsibility and the common good. The flourishing of human capacities does not require the liberation of the individual from the social; rather it is achievable only through social interaction and recognition of our mutual interdependence and collective obligations (Sayer, 2011). Polanyi writes in this vein:

> "Any decent individual could imagine himself free from all responsibility for acts of compulsion on the part of a State which he, personally, rejected; or for economic suffering in society from which he, personally, had not benefitted. He was 'paying his way', was 'in nobody's debt', and was unentangled in the evil of power and economic value. His lack of responsibility for them seemed so evident that he denied their reality in the name of his freedom."
>
> (GT, 258)

Once social bonds are constructed according to the opt-out principle of contractual freedom rather than reciprocity and mutual obligation, then neither a flourishing society nor a market economy (which depends on these relations) can exist. In a complex society, creating the necessary social foundation in which freedom can properly flourish requires an acceptance of greater individual responsibility for one another, a recognition that we are inextricably tied to wider communities of fate.[3]

In these circumstances, individuals must be compelled to take responsibility for private actions that produce wider public consequences; individual choices that reduce the freedom or flourishing of others might necessarily trigger constraints on self-interest and market liberty in order to safeguard greater security and freedom for all (GT, 254) (Satz, 2010). Restraining an individual's ability to work long hours (by banning overtime or through statutory limits on working hours) could limit individual autonomy, but it also provides a wider redistribution of work opportunities, as well as offering the potential for a reallocation of caring work that enhances security and emancipation for all. Compelling individuals to wear a mask during the pandemic or insisting vaccination as a legitimate condition for various activities (attending a sporting event or concert, entering a store, going to university) was not an infringement of individual freedom but rather a necessary recognition of our shared fate and responsibilities. French President Emmanuel Macron, defending his *pass sanitaire*, consciously echoed Polanyian language: "It's about citizenship. Freedom only exists if the freedom of everyone is protected…it's worth nothing if by exercising our freedom, we contaminate our brother, neighbour, friends, parents or someone we come across at an event. Then freedom becomes irresponsibility".

There are Weberian echoes in his frank acknowledgement that a *complex freedom* also necessitates a renewed appreciation of the positive aspects of *democratic coercion* and compulsion exercised by the state. "No society is possible in which power and compulsion are absent", Polanyi wrote, "nor a world in which force has no function" (GT, 257). An essential prerequisite for democratic legitimacy is the capacity to make collectively binding choices that limit opportunistic behaviour and encourage mutually beneficial action and social cooperation that acts as a "countervailing force to the market" (Somers, 2008, 43; Offe, 1996). Jacob Hacker and Paul Pierson argue in this vein:

> "Government works because it can force people to do things. Government is effective because it limits freedom…without its ability to compel behaviour, it would not just be powerless to protect our liberties; it would cease to be a vehicle for achieving many of our most important shared ends…"
>
> (Hacker and Pierson, 2016, 1)

As Margaret Somers astutely notes, the conception of the market as a sphere of freedom rather than coercion is a sleight of hand – what she terms an "alchemy of misrecognition" – whereby the everyday compulsions, arbitrary exercise of power and domination in the market, not to mention the political engineering that created a market economy in the first place, are obscured and mystified (Somers, 2018).

As Polanyi well understood, the market ideology that identified liberty as equivalent to non-interference with self-interest was actually an assertion of privilege and hierarchy rather than autonomy and ignored the true significance of freedom in a complex society. "That the freedom to exploit one's fellows", he wrote:

> "or the freedom to make inordinate gains without commensurate service to the community, the freedom to keep technological inventions from being used for the public benefit, or the freedom to profit from public calamities secretly engineered for private advantage, may disappear, together with the free market, is all to the good."
>
> (Polanyi, 1968, 74–5)

In the last paragraph of *The Great Transformation*, Polanyi presents an almost spiritual case for this notion of complex freedom:

> "Resignation was ever the fount of man's strength and new hope. Man accepted the reality of death and built the meaning of his bodily life upon it. He resigned himself to the truth that he had a soul to lose and that there was worse than death, and founded his freedom upon it. He resigns himself, in our time, to the reality of society which means the end of that freedom. But, again, life springs from ultimate resignation. Uncomplaining acceptance of the reality of society gives man indomitable courage and strength to remove all removable injustice and unfreedom. As long as

> he is true to his task of creating more abundant freedom for all, he need not fear that either power or planning will turn against him and destroy the freedom he is building by their instrumentality. This is the meaning of freedom in a complex society; it gives us all the certainty that we need."
>
> (GT, 258B)

Somers brilliantly illuminates the implications of this moving passage when she insists that Polanyi "truly believes the non-contractual relations of reciprocity, solidarity and redistribution are not only necessary characteristics of a robust civil society; he also stipulates that they are on the same existential plane as death and freedom" (Somers, 2008, 117).

As we elaborate more fully in the next section, these philosophical ruminations about complex freedom underpin the Polanyian inspired programs of decommodification discussed below (Konzcal, 2020). The success of boundary protections against market predation hinges on the ability to foreclose market actions that privilege individual aggrandizement as opposed to collective security, social reproduction and human flourishing. Recasting social protection to safeguard against a more encompassing market dependency will require a welfare state that prioritizes the development of capabilities and social solidarity. Open source software, a hallmark of decommodified circuits, is typically rooted in licensing protocols that combine maximum freedom (products are freely available to anyone, anywhere in the world) with concomitant restrictions on this free use (users must abide by conventions that forbid privatization); as James Boyle astutely notes, "some of the theorists of the commons do not see restrictions on use as anathematic to the goal of freedom; indeed, they see the successful commons as defined by its restraints" (Boyle, 2009, 66).

A *second* point of intervention is Polanyi's illuminating characterization of Aristotle's distinction between "production for gain" and "production for use" as "probably the most prophetic pointer ever made in the realm of the social sciences" (GT, 53). "In denouncing the principle of production for gain 'as not natural to man'", he wrote, "as boundless and limitless, Aristotle was, in effect, aiming at the crucial point, namely the divorcedness of a separate economic motive from the social relations in which these limitations inhered" (GT, 54). Under the pernicious influence of the economistic fallacy, market institutions are reified as habitual, unchangeable features of modern life, exchange value dominates use value, economic activity is subordinated to money making, private enrichment and competitive acquisition, and relative scarcity substitutes for general needs and the common good. Aristotle – and clearly Polanyi is using him as a convenient foil for his own beliefs − instead argued that the fundamental purpose of economic activity should be to enable people to pursue the good life broadly understood: to live well, to cultivate friendships and enjoy family life, to participate in political affairs and artistic endeavours. What was required was to transform the market society into an institutional domain that enhanced human creativity not exploitation and fostered well-being rather than self-interest. As we discussed in Chapter 3, he used these insights to critique prevailing visions of economic prosperity that conspicuously ignored human suffering and countenanced unfeasible levels of insecurity; he suggested that models of economic growth had to be predicated on social stability, sustainability and well-being, a perspective with considerable appeal in the 21st century (Stiglitz et al., 2010; Hall and Lamont, 2013).

Third, his incisive critique of commodification contains perhaps his most sustained thinking about the necessity for transcending the market system. In the Polanyian logic of the double movement, the core dynamic of a market society mandates the continual spread of market relations into more and more social domains, whereby market imperatives corrupt non-market norms and precepts, subjecting greater swathes of the population to market dependency and subordination. In the face of this relentless juggernaut, and, given the structural imperative for market actors to disengage from social obligations, moral embedding and institutional constraints, Polanyi understood only too well that efforts to entrench alternative pathways to growth and prosperity always faced an uphill battle to become institutionalized as a new common sense. Because he sought to reconfigure market society in such a way that markets would be subordinated to the wider needs of society in order to become a "useful but subordinate trait in a free society" (GT, 234), this led him to ponder the question of whether any escape from the destructive tendencies of the double movement ultimately depended upon finding appropriate ways of "transcending" the market altogether. Not surprisingly, he offered a handful of epigrammatic statements about this general problematic: "Socialism is, essentially, the tendency inherent in an industrial civilization to transcend the self-regulating market by consciously subordinating it to democratic society" (GT, 234); "a development under which the economic system ceases to lay down the law to society and the primacy of society over that system is secured" (GT, 251); "market institutions were checked by conscious social direction made effective through legislation" (GT, 129). However, given his overarching rationale for *The Great Transformation*, it is not surprising that these thoughts never approached any level of specificity.[4]

Indeed, these provisional formulations raise just as many questions as they answer. Any progressive political economy that attempted to gradually "transcend the market" by subordinating it to democratic, social direction would need to accomplish several thorny tasks (GT, 25, 177, 234). It would be required to: reorient incentives for production and exchange away from profit maximization and self-interest towards reciprocity, fairness and sustainability; establish limits on the rights of market actors to dispose of their property as they see fit; weaken the forces of destructive competition and acquisitiveness while still preserving the capacity for innovation; lessen market dependency and forms of market compulsion that reduce well-being and human flourishing; and provide the necessary public goods that ensure basic needs and share risks across the population. As scholars attempting to develop feasible alternatives to the market have long argued, finding ways to achieve these goals is not so straightforward nor is it immediately apparent how they can be achieved without impairing the very dynamism of the market economy (Wright, 2010) or entrenching forms of social protection that perpetuate other forms of social oppression and domination (Fraser, 2013).

Although Polanyi optimistically predicted the demise of the double movement, he was equally clear that this development would by no means constitute the end of markets altogether: "[T]he end of market society means in no way the absence of markets" (GT, 252). He anticipated a new era where the fiction of self-regulation would be once and for all banished even if he recognized that no modern economy could dispense with markets altogether. Markets possess both clear economic benefits (allocative efficiency, unique incentive mechanisms for innovation, decentralized coordination of information) as well as wider social and political advantages (support for the rule of law, development of civil society, dissolution of hierarchies, personal freedom); for Polanyi, it was the fanatical drive for self-regulation, as opposed to markets themselves, that produced such destructive outcomes. And certainly, in the decades since the publication of his masterpiece, all putative systemic alternatives to the market economy have been utterly discredited by the verdict of history. "No one believes that markets should be the only way goods and services are distributed", writes Erik Olin Wright in a concise summary of this new conventional wisdom, "and equally, virtually no one today believes that a complex economy can function without some presence of markets" (Wright, 1998, xi). This Polanyian brief for a hybrid political economy, whose precise contours could vary, depending upon the balance of power between markets, states and civil society, is the broad consensus of many progressive reformers and academics that have relied on these insights for their research exploring the variation within and between capitalist societies (Hollingsworth and Boyer, 1997; Hall and Soskice, 2001). And it remains the quintessential element of social democratic reforms that seek to contain and modify the most destructive aspects of capitalism.

Nevertheless, beyond this partial rapprochement with the market, he also envisaged the possibility of reversing the process of commodification that transformed vital social spheres into "fictitious commodities". If these core domains were returned to their original non-market status, the scope of the market would be correspondingly reduced and its attendant pressures considerably lessened. As a prime example, he highlighted the necessity for uncoupling labor from the market:

> "To take labor out of the market means a transformation as radical as was the establishment of a competitive labor market. The wage contract ceases to be a private contract except on subordinate and accessory

> points. Not only conditions in the factory, hours of work, and modalities of contract, but the basic wage itself, are determined outside the market."
>
> (GT, 251)

Polanyi insisted on the fundamental right of every individual to a job and claimed the primary objective of economic policy should be the avoidance of the profound social, cultural and physical degradation that resulted from mass unemployment (GT, 256).

It was these speculative musings that directly inspired Esping-Andersen's influential work on decommodification (Esping-Andersen, 1990). Esping-Andersen argued decommodification is the extent to which individuals are able to maintain a livelihood without recourse to the market: "the readiness to enable individuals and families to uphold a socially acceptable standard of living independent of market participation" (Esping-Andersen, 1990, 37). His original perspective focused on how individuals mitigated the perils of labor commodification – "In any case, the concept of decommodification has relevance only for individuals already fully and irreversibly inserted in the wage relationship" (Esping-Andersen, 1999, 45) – through social protection via housing subsidies, unemployment benefits, health insurance and pensions provided by a universalist welfare state.[5] His rationale for a decommodifying social policy closely follows the outlines of the Polanyi argument stated above. He highlights the way in which the commodification of workers treats them as mere objects, easily replaced, atomized and forced to bear the brunt of the vagaries of competition and the business cycle and yet workers are not commodities like all others. "It is possible to withhold washing machines from the market until the price is agreeable", argues Esping-Andersen in distinctively Polanyian terms, "but labor is unable to withhold itself for long without recourse to alternative means of subsistence" (Esping-Andersen, 1990, 37). He returns to Polanyi when discussing the foundational requirement for social protection in the world of laissez faire: "Decommodification is therefore…as Polanyi argued, necessary for system survival. It is also a precondition for a tolerable level of individual welfare and security" (Esping-Andersen, 1990, ibid).

In recent years, a handful of scholars have begun to use the term decommodification to capture the dynamism of recent developments in the current era. In a survey of the diverse universe of what he calls "anti-systemic" movements, Immanuel Wallerstein emphasized the benefits of such a framework:

> "The third component has to be the establishment of interim, middle range goals that seem to move in the right direction. I would suggest that one of the most useful –substantively, politically, psychologically- is the attempt to move towards selective, but ever widening decommodification."
>
> (Wallerstein, 2002, 38)

Some have highlighted the "decommodifying effects" offered by fair trade (Fridell, 2007) or anti-privatization campaigns (Bond, 2000) while others have explicitly acknowledged Polanyi's unique contribution to the renewed attention to decommodification (Dale, 2010; Konzcal, 2020; Kuttner, 2018; Raynolds, et. al., 2007). However, for the most part, these writers have not offered an alternative conceptual framework that advances beyond the paradigmatic account by Esping-Andersen.

The "analytical parsimony" of Esping-Andersen's model unquestionably offered a handy comparative tool for evaluating the progressive potential of welfare states yet I believe that an appreciation of our rapidly changing market societies suggests the need for a more expansive framework for decommodification that goes beyond his primary focus on labor commodification (Vail, 2010). Such a wider definition rooted in a Polanyian analysis would enable us to take account of a world in which the market juggernaut has expanded far beyond the familiar trinity of land, labor and money commodification emphasized by Polanyi; where the corrosive elements of the market have generated a maelstrom of destruction uprooting communities, making individual livelihoods more insecure, and weakening non-market values and practices; and where the resurgent market economy acts, in David Graeber's apt phrase, as a powerful leveling force of "social amnesia" (Graeber, 2002, 79). An expanded analytical framework would incorporate processes that challenge and limit the scope of commodification by fencing-off non-market spheres from market encroachments. It would include initiatives that attempt to reverse the destructive aspects of the market by increasing the provision of public goods and by enhancing social protection. It would embrace measures that promote democratic control over the market by creating non-commodified economic circuits that are politically and socially embedded and grounded in a logic predicated on social needs rather than profit. It would include efforts to undermine the grip of market hegemony by increasing the transparency of the market and revealing its true social costs and consequences. In short, decommodification is any political, social or cultural process that reduces the scope and influence of the market in everyday life.[6]

As detailed in the following section, there are any number of real world initiatives that could be considered component features of a decommodification program: fair trade, ethical consumption, open source software, cultural commons, public goods, social enterprises, micro-credit, mutual aid, global labor standards, social investment, working time reduction, basic income. Indeed, the very plurality of decommodification initiatives constitutes an implicit rebuke to the universalistic pretensions of market fundamentalism; across a wide variety of social, cultural and political domains, vibrant decommodified alternatives already operate as a profound cognitive and emotional counterweight to the colonizing logic of the market. It also ratifies an abiding element of Polanyian pragmatism that recognized the powerful demonstration effect of practical programs, which, he insisted, have the "advantage, decisive in politics, of representing the possible...." (GT, 251).

In this same pragmatic spirit, referencing our earlier discussion in Chapter 3 regarding the complex dynamics of market/non-market, embedding/disembedding, it is worth noting at the outset that some decommodification initiatives might intentionally deploy market processes to advance their overall objectives. Fair Trade coffee groups use the familiar commercial repertoire of niche marketing, branding and standardization to increase consumer demand for their products. Open source software developers rely on a creative reworking of copyright (the General Public License, *copyleft*, which gives people the right to use, modify and redistribute programs and code but only if the original distribution rules are maintained) to sustain their activities (Boyle, 2009). Conditional cash transfers that offer direct cash payments to the poor in return for keeping their kids in school or participating in regular health checks, relies on the poor's ability to solve their own problems without imposing the paternalistic surveillance of the traditional welfare state; but at the same time, they are influenced by "recognizably neo-liberal elements, including the valorization of market efficacy, individual choice, and autonomy" (Ferguson, 2009, 174).[7] Swedish social democrats combined their social protection measures (unemployment insurance, generous pensions, health security) with an active labor market policy that promoted the greater flexibility and portability of labor power as a commodity. In none of these does the partial appropriation of market practices in any way invalidate the original egalitarian intent of the programs or weaken their decommodified standing. Indeed, this "commodifying effect" is likely to be a feature of decommodification initiatives that are at present only speculative. Philippe van Parijs, one of the leading proponents of a basic income, highlights precisely this dynamic:

> "Consequently, BI [Basic Income] can be said to increase the commodification of people, in the sense that it fosters participation in the labor market for a greater proportion of people and a longer portion of their lives, while at the same time decreasing the commodification of people by making them less dependent on the labor market for their subsistence. This is a paradox not a contradiction. Indeed, the fundamental reason why I find BI such a good proposal is precisely that it contributes to commodification in the former sense while contributing to decommodification in the latter."
>
> (Van Parijs, 2006, 206–7)

Conversely, market actors can utilize non-market practices with "decommodifying effects" in order to increase profitability and market dominance. Leading commercial firms (such as IBM and Hewlett-Packard) routinely hire out their programmers to work full time on open source projects because they calculate that improvements in free software will rebound to their own interest. Microsoft's donation of its operating system to Indian states that had previously utilized the free Linux system was an act of corporate generosity calculated to establish a future commercial beachhead by binding them to a proprietary standard. Hotel chains and restaurants regularly woo customers by picking up the tab for free services (drinks, spas, entertainment) because they believe it will inspire better brand loyalty in the future. The preeminent role of gifts within the digital economy obfuscates the real nature of the exchange which results in the creation of a new fictitious commodity of personal data that is seemingly given away for free rather than appropriated (Fourcade and Kluttz, 2020).

In conclusion, I argue that decommodification should constitute a central feature of an egalitarian and emancipatory agenda predicated on Polanyian insights.[8] By calling for social, political and moral limits to the market, a decommodification agenda would not only reduce our individual and collective dependency on the market (for livelihoods, social status, emotional sustenance), it would lessen our societal subjection to market discipline and its attendant uncertainties and insecurities. Decommodification could generate wider social benefits by ensuring basic needs, enhancing individual capacities and capabilities, and autonomy and self-realization. It will promote social cooperation and collaboration, deepen social solidarity, and improve our social capacity for collective decision making. It is to a fuller account of this project that we now turn.

Decommodification and Egalitarian Political Economy

The five processes of decommodification explored in this expanded framework are as follows: boundary protection, enhanced public goods provision, decommodified economic circuits, a revitalized social protection and market transparency.[9] For each category, I explain the rationale for its insertion into a decommodification framework, explore why it is critical to egalitarian and emancipatory objectives, detail the analytical and social complexity of its delivery, and highlight the various strategic and institutional dilemmas that constrain its efficacy.

Boundary Protection

Any question of reducing the scope and reach of the market begins necessarily with a consideration of the arenas of social, cultural and political life that need to be shielded from the incursions of the market. Historically, markets have always been subject to limits on their scope, the goods that can be legally exchanged, and social and political actors routinely mobilize around these boundary locations to foreclose market activity. As highlighted in the previous chapter, recent decades have witnessed a "second enclosure" movement, a renewed attempt by market actors to colonize non-market spheres such as the biosphere, indigenous knowledge, education, the information commons, culture, and the public sphere (Boyle, 2009; Harvey, 2005). Market actors have established property rights over the genome and biosphere; they have incorporated market ways of thinking and calculation (best exemplified by the ubiquity of cost-benefit analysis) into the public domain; they have extended copyright and other proprietary restrictions on the flow of information and creativity. Few social domains have been able to resist this market onslaught, which has generated pernicious effects in many of these realms. Bio-prospecting of plants, seeds and even genetic material has trampled traditional social ties and forms of economic activity and accelerated the decline of agricultural bio-diversity. The privatization of public services has reduced access to basic needs, weakened the ethos of public service, hollowed out the efficacy of local government services, and fatally damaged a societal ability to articulate and pursue a common interest (Marquand, 2004; Sandel, 2012). Complex systems of social coordination and cooperation that have persisted for centuries, such as common resource pooling systems (in irrigation, forestry, water) have been undermined by a rush to grant private property rights (and it must be added as well by harmful state intrusion).

Across numerous social and cultural spheres, the corrosive effect of this untrammeled commodification has placed the issue of boundary protection (and implicitly the moral limits of markets) firmly on the decommodification agenda. From an emancipatory standpoint of complex freedom, the argument for boundary protection lies in the recognition that the introduction of markets might well weaken social cooperation as well as crowd out the feasibility and efficacy of choosing non-market preferences which people might otherwise value highly (Sandel, 2012; Satz, 2010). When child labor is a widespread practice, adult wages are likely to be ratcheted down to the point where poor parents think they have little choice but to countenance sending their kids to work. Once expensive fast passes give people the right to bypass lengthy lines at a popular fairground, the fundamental norm of fairness underpinning the social process of queuing will be undermined, thereby making it harder for people to interact in everyday life as equal citizens. In these instances, limiting access to market options might actually empower individual autonomy and enhance citizenship by increasing the likelihood of social cooperation on the basis of equality (Somers, 2008). And as a general rule, when the introduction of markets can be demonstrated to reduce self-governance and the capacity to participate in civil society and the public sphere, a strong case for boundary prevention or strong regulation is enhanced. Lastly, following on from our earlier discussion of the pernicious effects of a rise in insecurity that place unfeasible demands for flexibility and constant adaptation to market dictates, boundary demarcation has the potential to safeguard community and promote human flourishing.

Preventing market predations can be accomplished by various processes of boundary protection. *First*, non-market domains could be fenced-off in ways that proscribe strict limits on the market's field of action (Klein, 2002; Marquand, 2004). This might encompass a moratorium or outright ban on patents that establish property rights over the genome, body and biosphere; elimination of user fees or access charges in non-market arenas that reduce participation in these domains; as well as the general outlawing of the price mechanism in various social spheres such as education, health care, and access to basic services and resources. *Second*, following on from Polanyi's incisive discussion (see Chapter 4) of how the Tudor state attempted to reduce the pace of enclosures in a "socially bearable" manner (GT, 37), it could regulate the pace of change more closely in order to shield citizens from market volatility and disruption to long established community relations. As an example, non-profit housing associations and community land trusts can inhibit the destructive consequences of private housing speculation by insisting on long term leases and by placing restrictive covenants that limit both speedy turnaround sales and outsized gains resulting from external increases in value. A *third* process would forestall market action by positively safeguarding areas through taking them into public or community ownership, such as the establishment of community land or conservation trusts that preclude future commercial development. *Fourth*, boundary protection might also entail a positive valuation and support for non-market domains, such as processes and policies that generate popular support for their preservation, or stipulate a right for individuals to not be excluded from access or enjoyment of these spheres. Policies in this vein might include greater support for parental leave and child care, government subsidies for social economy service delivery, a requirement for social impact statements, and fully funded public options (Somers, 2008). Finally, boundary protection could include foreclosing exit options for market actors from social and political obligations. As Wolfgang Streeck stresses, capitalists are "agile, creative, and unpredictable actors endowed with superior knowledge and resources" and are able to "enjoy a permanent first mover advantage and are usually one or more steps ahead" (Streeck, 2016, 207) so social and political oversight will require a combination of creativity, coercion and adaptive capacity that can anticipate and adjust to "systemic bad faith" on the part of market actors.

This notion of boundary protection revisits several thorny issues raised in earlier chapters. This category essentially constitutes a debate about what precisely constitutes a non-market arena, what are the boundary relations across the market and non-market spheres and what the consequences of these boundary interactions will be. What lies outside the market can encompass a diverse range of social, cultural and political arenas such as the state, the associational sector, the public domain of citizenship, the household and mutual aid, private life, religion, the social economy, ecological commons and the cultural realm, not to mention the remnants of social formations from previous epochs such as slavery or feudalism (bonded servitude) that still persist. Each of these realms possess distinct logics, decision rules, cultures, core values, functions, rules of reproduction, and adaptive capabilities to fend off the market. As an example, a non-market arena that functions as a "commons" (an information commons such as the internet or an environmental commons such as a wilderness or a regional biosphere) has a specific governance structure that guides access to the resources and use of this sphere, it has distinct coordination rules and social sanctions that shape interactions, it features particular sorts of reciprocal arrangements and gift exchanges, all of which would differ greatly from another non-market realm such as the household. This institutional diversity makes it more difficult to specify what constitutes the non-market arena and, more to the point, it highlights that not every protection of a non-market arena automatically contributes to wider egalitarian and democratic outcomes (Fraser, 2013; Block and Somers, 2014).

The dynamics and consequences of boundary interactions need to be interrogated as well. The implicit thrust of arguments for boundary protection takes us back to the question of market corrosion raised in Chapter 3 and whether the market represents a distinct logic and set of operating principles (profit maximization, self-interest, competition, capital accumulation, private ownership) that intrinsically clash with and corrode non-market spheres. As we saw then, the "corrosion thesis" can take many different forms: it might be the assertion that some areas of social life should remain "inalienable" (should not be transferred or sold to others) because it will jeopardize human flourishing; or does violence to the very conception and value that people attribute to the goods in question; or that various spheres of social life – the body, family life, child rearing, education, sexuality, citizenship, and the like – require insulation from the market because their core values and practices are incommensurate with the market. However, as we suggested, these boundary relations and interactions do not *automatically* corrode the values and practices of the non-market arena. "Just because care is paid by a wage doesn't mean that it isn't motivated by love as well as money", writes Nancy Folbre. "A great deal of caring labor is provided through the market. Day care workers, home healthcare workers, teachers and nurses, among others, often develop loving personal relationships with the people they take care of" (Folbre, 2001, xii). The mere exchange of money in a social relation does not make it inherently degrading or destructive of human flourishing: most struggling musicians would gladly accept a regular wage and would not presume that their creative integrity had been sullied by the coin. Equally, even if Polanyi downplayed the emancipatory role of markets, commodification might improve the likelihood of realizing core progressive values: the ability to sell one's labor power can be a truly emancipatory moment for those trapped in bonded labor; the marketization of gay and lesbian identities can confer a wider social acceptance of alternative lifestyles; Mexican families who receive cash stipends for each child that regularly attends classes and health care check-ups have notably improved their education and health outcomes and reduced child labor (Chasin, 2000; Bales, 2000). The reverse process is no less true. As highlighted in our discussion of embeddedness in Chapter 3, market activity is routinely entangled with and constrained by social norms, emotions, institutional rules, and political regulations.

Do these complexities in any way undermine the case for boundary protection? To reiterate the broader point stressed previously, boundary protection is likely to be contingent and will have to be evaluated on a emancipatory pragmatism where either ring-fencing the market or permitting market incursions has to be judged on the basis of what is most likely to generate egalitarian and democratic outcomes (Satz, 2010; Zelizer, 2005). Viviana Zelizer, who has been sharply critical of the commodifying/decommodifying perspective, echoes this perspective:

> "We should stop agonizing over whether or not money corrupts but instead analyze what combinations of economic activity and intimate relations produce happier, more just, and more productive lives. It is not just the mingling that should concern us but how the mingling works."
>
> (Zelizer, 2005, 298)

Such an arrangement will always be temporary and highly fluid, shifting according to future changes in technology, the drive by market entrepreneurs to discover new profit centers, the efficacy of government regulation, and the shifting balance of power within these boundary struggles (Fraser, 2013). But at the same time, this pluralistic stance need not preclude an affirmation of the positive benefits of decommodification. The fact that the market is not automatically corrosive does not imply that it never is for there are ample cases to illustrate this general principle. Once we accept this basic proposition, then what is required is a more careful delineation of the conditions that make corrosion more or less likely as well as a closer specification of the sphere that is being corroded given that the putative case for boundary protection is surely weakened if the social relations under threat are organized along inegalitarian and oppressive lines as in some non-market realms. Such a project is beyond the space limitations of this chapter but remains an urgent intellectual task for the future.

Public Goods Provision

Public goods have always been a prominent feature of market societies, a domain of social needs and the common good that for Polanyi represented a vital counterweight to market hegemony. The ubiquity of public goods in contemporary life can be best comprehended by a partial accounting of those goods currently on offer in most advanced societies: national security, good governance, internet, public health, sanitation, caring activities, neighborhood safety, parks, recreation centers, libraries, municipal water supplies, public spaces, traffic and street lights, public education, roads, public broadcasting, clean air. There is a taken-for-granted quality about nearly all of these examples, an implicit recognition that a complex modern society could not function properly unless these goods were readily available. But of course the key questions are what makes these goods and services *public* goods, to what extent they can (or should be) be safeguarded from private interests, the conditions under which they can be extended to additional areas of social life, and why they remain central to egalitarian ambitions.

Public goods meet two unique conditions. First, they are goods and services where one person's consumption of the good does not reduce the availability or possibility of another's consumption; my consumption of knowledge does not reduce the overall stock of knowledge available to others.[10] Second, it is impossible to prevent people from using/consuming a public good even if they played no role whatsoever in the production of the good; I cannot be prevented from attending a street fair even if I did nothing to help get it organized. Many public goods, such as public parks, public streets, open access scientific research, and free software, also function as a commons: although there could be informal rules and norms that guide conduct within the arena, they are readily accessible to any member of the public and no one in the community needs the permission of anyone else to use them. As such public goods constitute an important dimension of individual freedom and a platform for social cooperation (Benkler, 2006).

Public goods are central to a decommodification strategy for several reasons. In the *first* place, as Polanyi rightly stressed, they represent a unique form of social provisioning of activities that are essential to social life. Public goods arise from the fundamental need to alleviate the harmful side effects generated by the complexity and interdependence of modern life where the solutions to these ills are most efficiently undertaken by public not private action. If sewers and waste treatment are provided as private services (as indeed they once were) rather than as public goods, they would likely cover only a small percentage of the population with the ability to pay even though such an arrangement might generate widespread harm given that contagious epidemics (created by poor sanitation in untreated areas) are likely to spread everywhere irrespective of class endowments. Indeed, if left to the market economy, the provision of public goods would be far below the optimal level. Market actors often have little incentive to provide these services because it might be too difficult to parcel up or impose charges for a good (street lights and libraries come to mind in this respect); it might not be possible to charge enough for the good to ensure a substantial profit stream; or it could be too hard to exclude people from consumption of the good in question.

Second, public goods are an implicit recognition of the valuable benefits to society of the social infrastructure that is not fully valued by market forces but which nevertheless is crucial for the vitality of community and social reproduction. In the arena of public transport as an example, private firms can cream off the rewards of the most profitable routes but often prove unwilling to support services that are infrequently utilized (even if they remain vital to sustaining networks of social cooperation), which is why so many governments have treated this sphere as a key foundation of social solidarity and provided these services as necessary public goods. Libraries, playgrounds, athletic fields, community gardens are all tangible places that facilitate friendships, mutual support, and cooperation across social classes and groups (Klinenberg, 2018). Child care could reasonably be deemed a public good on several grounds. Individuals who devote relatively little time, emotional labor or resources to child rearing are essentially free riding on parental labor given that they will likely enjoy the benefits of this social reproduction via pensions and health care paid for by the grown up, tax paying children. Likewise, children are more likely to become productive, responsible citizens, all things being equal, if their childcare is first rate and child care might well help to ameliorate gender inequalities. As a result, there should be greater public support (child care subsidies, tax relief, after school services and the like) and public acknowledgement of the centrality of this activity (Folbre, 2001). In essence, public goods not only represent an implicit critique of market ideology that insists private action is sufficient to achieve the public interest but they also constitute a positive assertion of the basic needs and social objectives that are required for an inclusive and egalitarian society, which should therefore be provided as a matter of fundamental social right on grounds of equity and fairness rather than private calculation (Somers, 2008).[11]

Third, public goods might be instrumental in the development of an inclusive citizenship and broader political and civic skills. When people opt for private services (private schools, private police, private health care, private leisure facilities, private pensions), they often prove less willing to fund public goods, the quality of public services subsequently worsens, thereby weakening the very rationale for these goods and creating a vicious spiral of decline that grievously corrodes the public's trust of government services and damages the very possibility of cultivating a shared sense of community upon which a democratic citizenship is founded. As Michael Sandel argues, once the sphere of public goods –schools, playgrounds, parks, swimming pools, community centers- ceases to become a place where citizens from all social and economic backgrounds encounter one another, it becomes increasingly difficult to sustain a common civic life. He insists that a "politics of the common good", a widespread recognition of a shared moral and citizenship obligation to help rebuild the infrastructure of civic life, is an essential prerequisite for the vitality of the public sphere (Sandel, 2012; Klinenberg, 2018).[12]

But a citizenship right necessarily implicates the question of how people can exercise these rights through public goods in the first place. A decommodification strategy relying on public goods provision would make these goods truly "public" by encouraging new forms of co-production that explicitly involve civic associations, non-profit groups, and a broad range of stakeholders in the design, production and maintenance of these goods and services (Ostrom, 1990; Siriani, 2009). These chains of social cooperation, by harnessing the contributions of diverse individuals, can lead to improved innovations in service delivery as well as the development of the problem solving capacities of the broader citizenry, who then could be enlisted in much broader forms of deliberative and participatory decision making to solve increasingly complex social problems. Public goods in this regard should be envisioned as a vital realm of civic engagement and empowerment. As numerous authors have detailed, participation in the information commons/ open source software has created durable forms of social cooperation, enhanced valuable participatory skills and inculcated egalitarian norms (Benkler, 2006; Kelty, 2008). Similarly, the incorporation of an active participatory element within the National Trust in the UK (via the "Going Local" program which has turned over the running of several properties to local communities) has transformed the organization from a heritage industry reliant on huge palaces, stuffy tearooms and overpriced gift shops that were largely the province of the white middle classes into a vibrant social enterprise and community meeting place that is restoring a genuine sense of belonging and community pride.

It is because of these strong "decommodifying effects" that the sustenance and extension of public goods constitutes an important category in this expanded framework. However, there is a permanent oscillation between public and private goods, an ever-changing dynamic that occurs as the outcome of political battles, technological changes, and ideological contestation. Many public goods (such as libraries, public sanitation, public transport, fire departments) first originated as private goods before being absorbed into the public domain after hard fought political and social campaigns and concerted state action.[13] In recent decades, the reverse has been the case as countless public goods have been captured as lucrative profit centers under the scourge of privatization. In future decades, services that are currently produced as private goods, such as air travel, energy production, broadband and information infrastructure, might well be seen as fertile ground for conversion into public goods as the result of persistent market failures, poor allocation of resources or a greater desire for public control of such valuable activities.

Within this tug of war, the pendulum can swing towards public goods in several ways. Some public goods enjoy the unique advantage of positive scale returns, where the greater the use of a good, the more value that is accrued by the good in question. As an example, the more people who use an open source journal to publish their research or the larger the readership, the more prestige the journal acquires. Aidan Hollis and Thomas Pogge's ingenious proposal for a health impact fund, which would establish an alternative patent regime for pharmaceuticals, is predicated on the power of scale returns to crowd out proprietary options. Their scheme, devoted to the eradication of infectious diseases caused by poverty and inequality, is designed to operate as a public good. Any innovations that a private firm discovered from their research would be rewarded not through monopoly copyrights, but rather in proportion to its impact on reducing the global disease burden. The greater the efficacy of the cure, the more money they would receive. Under this arrangement, companies would have every incentive to encourage and support efforts by cheap generic producers (already well established in Brazil, India, South Africa) to copy its drugs because this would multiply the overall number of people who could potentially be cured (Hollis and Pogge, 2008).[14] Dean Baker has proposed an innovative mechanism for creating public goods in the cultural sector of the United States (where creative industries are dominated by commercialism and copyright) whereby individuals would be able to deduct a small portion of their taxes to donate to a non-profit arts or media group of their own choosing; in return, those arts groups who receiving funding under the program would agree to place their creative outputs in the public domain for a clearly specified period rather than under private copyright (Baker, 2003).

One of the primary constraints on the provision of public goods is that their creation typically encounters significant collective action problems. Because public goods cannot exclude people who have not contributed to the production of the good in question, there is an incentive for people to free ride which leads to the dilemma of how the good can then be produced in the first place. State action acts as a shortcut in this respect because it provides the goods as core public services funded through taxation. But there might also be incentive structures for other public goods where small numbers of contributors (with a plethora of motivations including self-interest, status, solidarity, community) can work cooperatively to provide the good. Open source software is the quintessential case of this new social configuration: a small critical mass of unpaid volunteers, with motivations spanning geek appeal, status and self-interest, have collaborated on the creation of innovative information tools that can be freely disseminated (Benkler, 2006; Kelty, 2008). The organization of a neighborhood watch group, facilitated by greater feelings of collective efficacy stimulated by previous participation in community associations or by home ownership (a proxy for stable social interactions over time and material incentives), might also be the product of similar small group dynamics (Sampson et al., 1997). Public/private partnerships, enlisting the participation of charities and non-profits, might assume the operation and administration of public goods (such as the Central Park Conservancy) in order to solicit philanthropic contributions for capital improvements, staffing and regular maintenance. The provision of new public goods, such as community toilets in rural areas that lack access to proper sanitation facilities or public playgrounds in disadvantaged urban neighborhoods, might engage an efficacious mix of purposive action, with NGOs providing the necessary social entrepreneurship and community training to deliver the services while receiving ample inter-governmental funding for their efforts. The sustenance of public goods then depends on a felicitous combination of informal institutional arrangements, solidaristic behavior and a cohesive social and political alliance.

However, state action and social coordination might both prove more difficult to achieve once the scale of action increases dramatically. A microcredit association that wants to expand access to financial resources to greater segments of a population is unlikely to have the capital requirements to accomplish this goal but might resist aligning with commercial banking interests for fear of watering down their original ethos. Similarly, supplying community toilets beyond a few villages to an entire region in India would tax the organizational and material capacity of most non-profit associations (if not many state governments) and might impact negatively on any cooperative, egalitarian group structure. One of the hallmarks of global interdependence is that many of the most urgent challenges faced by nation states can only be achieved through the provision of *global* public goods such as international financial stability, infectious disease control, sustainable energy policies, and biodiversity preservation. None of these can be achieved by a single state yet securing the cooperation of more than 150 separate nations for trade agreements, or human rights standards, or climate change reform, has proven to be exceedingly problematic (Kaul, et al., 2003).

Indeed, even hybrid state-society projects face real difficulties in trying to manage scale. One of the more interesting speculative decommodification projects is the proposal for a global reconstruction fund that could be funded (estimates of the annual intake range from $30–70 billion) through specially earmarked taxes on currency transactions, carbon emissions or air travel. In one sense, the political feasibility of this program, even if it has only just become a feature of everyday political discourse, is not particularly forbidding: the collection of revenue could be linked to the accomplishment of a widely desired end (reducing pollution, greenhouse gases, financial volatility); free riding could be minimized without too much difficulty; and even inequities stemming from the origins of the problem (richer nations have much greater responsibility for climate change than developing ones) could be alleviated through a sliding tax scale. Where the real challenge lies is in the realm of social coordination and cooperation. States would require agreement on any number of potentially divisive issues: to which nations would the funds be disbursed; who would actually control the monies; to which public goods would the funds be committed; how would progress be monitored and evaluated and by whom? None of these dilemmas are irresolvable but they would require a capacity for democratic deliberation and social cooperation that is hitherto underdeveloped at either the national or transnational level.

Socially Embedded, Decommodified Circuits

In this section, the focus is on establishing decommodified economic circuits within existing market sectors (production, exchange, investment, allocation of credit, ownership) where the social organization and practices of the circuit constitutes an alternative logic to prevailing market processes. One might reasonably suggest that there are already numerous examples of such circuits within contemporary market societies. Commons-based peer production, the hallmark of open source software and open science research, is a cooperative production enterprise, featuring decentralized collaboration that produces non-proprietary information goods without the need for price signals, managerial commands or monetary incentives to spark contributions (Benkler, 2006). Social economy enterprises (producer cooperatives, housing associations, environmental conservation firms, health care providers) produce goods and services that have clearly stated social objectives, are organized on a not-for profit basis (surpluses are either reinvested or redistributed within the community) and operate independently of both the market and state (Wright, 2010). In autonomous public spaces in cities throughout Europe, alternative social centers (often originating as squats of abandoned or derelict buildings) have been established by cultural activists with a diverse program of activities (cinemas, theaters, studios, community arts training and the like) that are conceived as a radical alternative to the dominant forms of cultural production and exchange.

Under fair trade, farmers are guaranteed a floor price above the world commodity price (enabling them to earn a living wage that better insulates them from the dizzying fluctuations of the international market), trading relations between participating farmers and fair trade groups are conducted according to mutual respect and reciprocal obligations rather than economic calculation and exploitation, farmers typically are compelled to form democratically-run cooperatives and receive a social premium that is exclusively devoted to non-market ends (housing, schools, health clinics) and consumer demand and purchasing power for their products are explicitly used to promote these ethical objectives (Fridell, 2007; Jaffee, 2007). Even more speculative proposals, such as pension reform, are predicated on a similar set of principles: the huge capital pools represented by pension funds across the leading industrial societies, rather than being organized according to narrow investment criteria and short term returns, could be used to underwrite any number of social objectives, including investment in key social needs and sustainable development, funding a European wide basic income, or even the establishment of a global pension scheme (Blackburn, 2007).

So what then is the social logic underpinning these alternative circuits? The very nature of these alternative circuits begs the question of what makes fair trade "fair", what makes the social economy "social", what makes ethical consumption "ethical"? In each instance, the qualifying adjective represents an unspoken assertion that this circuit can be differentiated in some significant way from core capitalist principles and can enhance egalitarian and emancipatory aims. Like Polanyi, numerous scholars have offered epigrammatic formulations of this approach. Diane Elson talks of "socializing markets", of embedding "market transactions in egalitarian social relations so that they can serve democratically agreed social ends" (Elson, 2000, 69). Andre Gorz suggests a non-reformist reform logic is "one which does not base its validity and its right to exist on capitalist needs, criteria and rationales" (Gorz, 1967, 7). Ellen Meiksins Wood argues that "democracy needs to be reconceived not simply as a political category but as an economic one… I have in mind democracy as an economic regulator, the driving mechanism of the economy" (Wood, 1995, 290) But these general pronouncements, while helpful in articulating an overarching philosophy, do not really get to the heart of the matter; they speak to what is desired rather than spell out how this can be accomplished in practice.

For a social logic to take effect, decommodified circuits have to be grounded in the very workings of the market economy in order to restructure its imperatives and constituent practices. "It means to root a bias to greater equality and inclusion in the organized logic of economic growth and technological innovation rather than making it rest on retrospective redistribution through tax and transfer", Roberto Unger suggests. "It means to demarcate the market economy by innovating in the arrangements that define it, rather than merely to regulate it in its present form or to compensate for its inequalities through after-the-fact transfers" (Unger, 2006, 21). Therefore, a socially embedded, decommodified circuit is any form of economic activity (broadly defined) that influences and reorients the motivations, incentives, interests, values, priorities, and behaviour of economic actors to promote human flourishing and egalitarian objectives rather than market rationality (even if these activities could occur within existing market relations and not challenge the very nature of these relations).[15]

Fair trade, in this regard, represents an alternative circuit because: its floor price transforms the incentives and behaviour of farmers, persuading those who would otherwise flee subsistence agriculture for overcrowded cities to remain on the land and to form democratic cooperatives; it shifts priorities and values by ensuring a long term economic security that serves as a springboard for producers to diversify incomes, improve their organizational capacity and generate valuable non-market ends; and it requires consumers to shift their own interests by purchasing products based not on price but on ethical concerns. Similarly, open source software changes incentives in a way that promotes non-market collaboration and solves collection action problems that enhance social coordination and production; it privileges autonomy, creativity and freedom as core values of its social interactions and relations; it's ethic of open sharing of information production and exchange stands in stark contrast to proprietary monopolies. As Yochai Benkler argues, the creation of these decommodified information circuits represents a formidable constraint on market imperialism:

> "If we are indeed seeing the emergence of a substantial component of non-market production at the very core of our economic engine…then

> this change suggests a genuine limit on the extent of the market. Such a limit, *growing from within the very market that it limits*, in its most advanced loci, would represent a genuine shift in direction from what appeared to be the ever-increasing global reach of the market economy and society in the past half-century."
>
> (Benkler, 2006, 18–19, my emphasis)

Even if we accept the possibility of establishing decommodified circuits, the singularity of the market domain and the ubiquity of market rationality – of profit maximization, competition, private interest, allocative efficiency, capital accumulation – still inform the incentives, interests, values and behavior of all economic agents within capitalism. This does not automatically negate the important decommodifying effects of these alternative circuits but it does highlight the fact that decommodification initiatives will indubitably face the same constraints, to which all economic actors in a market system are subject. All decommodification projects must confront the perpetual dilemma of cooptation and defection back to the market as a consequence of the relentless pressures of market imperatives. Once campaigners and non-profit associations proved the viability of micro-credit, it was not long before the finance industry rushed into the sector seeking a profitable niche market yet their predatory practices and discourse of free market competition have threatened the entire legitimacy and popularity of the non-profit sector. The Mondragon workers cooperative in the Basque region of Spain, which has traditionally featured employee participation and representation on director's boards and maintained egalitarian wage policies, believed the only way it could remain competitive in a global market was to outsource some of their operations to firms abroad yet the workers in these firms have not been included within the cooperative's participatory/egalitarian umbrella which has threatened worker solidarity across the entire organization. Likewise, fair trade products are only viable so long as they can compete against their commercial rivals and attract sufficient market share; social economy enterprises, such as cooperative production or finance, must similarly attract sufficient capital and generate adequate profits in order to sustain themselves within their specific market segment.

We also need to pragmatically evaluate the scope and material weight of these decommodified circuits within their specific market sectors in order to estimate their overall capacity to fulfill egalitarian objectives. Fair trade is a cautionary tale in this regard (Jaffee, 2007; Raynolds et al., 2000). While the market for all fair traded goods has grown to nearly $12 billion in sales worldwide, when contrasted to the 2020 net sales of $550 billion of the world's largest firm, Walmart, it looks quite puny by comparison. Even though nearly 1.6 million farmers and workers are now enrolled in fair trade schemes, the vast majority of rural workers still toil in subsistence based circumstances and their livelihoods remain vulnerable to the vertiginous upheavals of global commodity markets. For many fair trade commodities, there is insufficient demand from Western consumers to warrant bringing in more farmers into these schemes – indeed, coffee producers are only able to sell a third of their output at the fair trade price – nor are the social and political conditions for cooperative arrangements always propitious. Even more to the point, fair trade impacts on only a small fraction of the commodity chain of their products; most transnational trade circuits (for coffee, this would include transport, roasting plants, packaging, distribution, marketing and retail) are organized along standard market lines, with the bulk of wealth transmitted and earned along the value chain captured by economic elites. Given these circumstances, the potential contribution to egalitarian outcomes from fair trade would appear at best modest and the same could reasonably be argued for other decommodified circuits such as microfinance, barter systems and the social economy, which (unlike their open source counterparts that now make up 75 percent of the world's web servers and browsers) have yet to achieve a significant weight within capitalist economies.

In recognition of these limits, decommodification proponents have suggested that it is not simply the establishment of these circuits but rather their progressive diffusion and extension over time that will be consequential. This returns us to the problematic highlighted in Chapter 3, whereby decommodification is a process that gradually undermines the scope and depth of capitalist relations in such a way that over time market institutions become less capitalistic in character than before (Wright, 2010). The dilemma in this regard is whether decommodified circuits can grow to the extent that they begin to crowd-out or discipline market actors; to over time act as a countervailing mechanism (in conjunction with more traditional methods such as regulation and redistribution) to ameliorate the harmful aspects of markets. A larger and more sustainable demand for fair trade, as an example, might be enhanced by government subsidies and purchasing power or through the coordinated effort of civil society organizations (universities, churches, trade unions) to harness their member's buying power. The success of these efforts might persuade firms to adopt fair trade lines of their own thereby boosting significantly the overall scope of the fair trade circuit. In order to capture a greater portion of income along the commodity chain for direct producers, the fair trade base price could be substantially increased, retailers of fair trade products could be required to return a higher percentage of the retail price directly to farmer's organizations, and a minimum equity stake in Northern fair trade firms could be extended to all participants (Fridell, 2007; Jaffee, 2007).

Of course the precise conditions under which one could envisage a transitional strategy for social transformation based on decommodified circuits would need to be carefully stipulated. Is there something intrinsic to the structure and functioning of some market sectors that makes non-market production and exchange more feasible? Is it easier to reorient ownership relations and property rights than it is to restructure the pricing mechanism?

Are there particular social and political strategies that could be enlisted on behalf of this evolution? At what point would the weight of these decommodified circuits constitute a tipping point (comparable to the similar transition to a capitalist economy discussed in Chapter 2) that prefigured the end of market society? A fuller discussion of these questions is beyond the scope of the present chapter.

Rethinking Social Protection

This category returns us to the familiar territory of Polanyi's conception of social protection (as discussed in Chapter 4) as well to its formative influence on Esping-Andersen's model of decommodification. As discussed earlier, this account of decommodification centered on the extent to which individuals were able to sustain livelihoods without recourse to the market. "To understand the concept, decommodification should not be confused with the complete eradication of labor as a commodity", cautioned Esping-Andersen. "It is not an issue of all or nothing, rather the concept refers to the degree to which individuals, or families, can uphold a socially acceptable living independently of market participation" (Esping-Andersen, 1990, 37). In his original formulation, he focused on the provisions of the welfare state –pensions, unemployment insurance, health care, public housing, and the like- and whether any restrictions on access or rights to these services were imposed, which enabled him to construct a typology of welfare regimes based on the extent to which they incorporated a decommodifying effect. In later work, Esping-Andersen turned to the changing social structure of risks, arguing that significant transformations in family and household arrangements, labor markets and work life, technological advances, migration, and economic restructuring had created a new set of gendered risks (single parenthood, job insecurity, skills mismatch, income volatility). This insecurity was far more unpredictable and varied much more over the life course than ever before, plagued a more heterogeneous population, and had begun to outstrip the administrative capacity of the welfare state to deliver efficacious solutions (Esping-Andersen, 2009).

In Esping-Andersen's view, these developments mandated the need for a fundamental rethink of the social safety net. Radical reforms within social protection were required such as basic income, asset predistribution, baby bonds, reduction of work hours, paid parental leave, universal pre-K education, subsidies for child care and elder care, living wages and lifelong education and skills development that enhanced capabilities, ensured economic security and sought to intervene in the very social and political arrangements that structured the distribution of life chances and opportunities (Unger, 2006). These innovations would be funded by a variety of creative tax measures (a ban on tax havens, global minimum tax, global transaction taxes, national wealth fund) and would be delivered by a plurality of institutional agents beyond the state (non-profit groups, public-private partnerships, community trusts, social enterprises). They would be purposively designed to maximize citizen uptake by easing access, eliminating onerous, Kafkaesque eligibility rules, and lessening arcane bureaucratic requirements that lessened participation.

In a fundamental sense, the reconsideration of this wider orbit of social risks takes us back to the question of market dependency raised earlier as well as the issue of an emancipatory autonomy highlighted in the discussion on complex freedom. As noted, Esping-Andersen closely mirrored Polanyi in emphasizing the dependency created by labor market commodification: "The main springs of modern social policy lie in the process by which both human needs and labor power become commodities and, hence, our wellbeing came to depend on our relation to the cash nexus" (Esping-Andersen, 1990, 35). Unquestionably, the loss of a job or the perilous income volatility associated with today's insecure labor market, remains a grave threat to livelihoods and well-being. Yet the realm of necessity that constitutes paid work also deeply shapes and influences the terrain of non-work – how much leisure time we are fortunate to enjoy, how much time we can devote to caring activities, the limits of our physical and emotional strength after our work has drawn to a close, whether our work provides us with sufficient material resources for a dignified life – and this market dependency can be a catalyst for additional forms of insecurity that people have little control over.

Once we consider dependency in this wider connotation as being subject to the will of others – and of being in perpetual uncertainty regarding whether such interference will ever be forthcoming- then market dependency must be envisaged as operating beyond the domain of the labor market. The privatization of the commons or commodification of the biosphere not only impacts on those individuals whose livelihoods are predicated on these arenas, it also represents an unwarranted intrusion that can destroy communal solidarity and create massive insecurity. Many forms of work do not equip individuals with the opportunity for self-development that would enable them to participate fully within their community. In all market systems, individual livelihoods and the ability to pursue desired life projects are profoundly influenced by the choices and actions of market actors such as banks, corporations and consumers. Market dependency therefore should be conceived as a social relation and, as such, weakening this dependency must operate at the level of the entire market society. "Capitalism is unjust and undemocratic not because of this or that imperfection in relation to equality or freedom", argue Leo Panitch and Sam Gindin, "but because at its core it involves the control by some of the use and development of the potential of others…" (Panitch and Gindin, 2010, 6). It is for this reason that more radical innovations for social protection intentionally mirror Polanyi's concern for a security that enhances autonomy and develops human capabilities. The freedom from paid work, the freedom to pursue socially productive activities of one's choosing, the freedom to pursue life projects that one values: these are intrinsic features of complex freedom, which can guarantee a new form of social citizenship and social solidarity (Somers, 2008).

Market Transparency

The final category emerges from the peculiar characteristics of the market system that impede the ability of individuals to comprehend the intricate workings of the market. In the *first* instance, the complexity of the market economy –the decentralized coordination of preferences; the perception that economic outcomes occur as the result of atomized individual decisions and vast impersonal forces of supply and demand (what Polanyi called the "blind action of soulless institutions"); the distance (geographically, cognitively and socially) between production and consumption- makes it harder to recognize the market's core imperatives and to identify the actual interplay of power within market relations. In these circumstances, the true nature of production and exchange can be obscured and commodities, as writers in the Marxist tradition have long argued, become endowed with the power to dictate the conditions of economic and social life, subordinating individuals to things and masking the social and ecological relations that are integral to the operation of these seemingly neutral market processes (Goodman, 2004. When an individual buys a toy manufactured in China, the coerced labor it took to make it remains invisible; when someone shops at an expensive furniture store, the criminal pillage of the land required to make an exquisite mahogany dresser is not immediately apparent; when people leave their offices, they do not give a great deal of thought to the workers (often low paid, immigrant laborers) who clean up after them. This *structural* mystification therefore underpins market dominance in two ways: it makes it harder to directly attribute responsibility for exploitation and inequality to capitalist dynamics; and by transforming social relations between people into social relations between things, it is destructive of human flourishing and social cooperation.

Second, markets over time tend to become naturalized and normalized. As highlighted in our earlier discussion of *market insulation*, institutional practices and social relations that might once have been the site of considerable political and social contestation become normalized as business prerogatives and their founding principles and rationales no longer conceived as controversial forms of domination. As an example, workers do not exercise ownership rights over the products they make and have no automatic right to make decisions about the allocation of investment or the organization of production (the conditions of work, how products are made, what gets made) because of the historical development of property rights and the way in which these rights were or were not inserted into appropriate regulatory institutions (Anderson, 2017). Indeed, one of the hallmarks of a capitalist democracy, argues Joshua Cohen and Joel Rogers, is that the very institution of private property rights removes a range of choices and decisions of collective importance from the realm of public deliberation (Cohen and Rogers, 1983). A corporate decision to shutter a factory (even one that is profitable) and relocate abroad (where profits could be higher) can wreak material and emotional havoc on a local community: those made unemployed will likely suffer from depression and anxiety, struggle to make house payments and provide for basic necessities while the ripple effect on small businesses, house prices and social networks and friendships can be equally devastating. Clearly, if those workers being displaced had the right to intervene into such decision-making, their accounting of the real social and human costs and benefits of the closure would differ markedly from managers deciding on the basis of narrow private interest.

Market economies are opaque in a final important way, in that its victims are often hidden from full view and their injuries discounted by economic, social and political elites. At the heart of Polanyi's impassioned argument about the *hidden injuries* detailed in Chapter 3 is a decommodification critique: an interrogation of what the basis of economic activity should be and whether markets can provide the basic needs and goods that every decent society requires. Contemporary corollaries of these "hidden injuries" are rife in the world of neoliberal globalization. Health researchers have uncovered a direct link in Eastern Europe and the former Soviet Union between mortality rates from tuberculosis and IMF loans, where each one percent increase in credit was associated with a 0.9 percent increase in mortality whereas leaving the IMF lending program lowered mortality rates by 31 percent. The precipitous rise in sexual trafficking, the dark underbelly of the global service economy, has trapped tens of thousands of women worldwide in virtual slave labor. In Mexico, the *maquiladora* (small factory) sector, reeling under the ferocious onslaught of Chinese competition, witnessed a brutal series of unsolved murders of women totaling well into the thousands in the region; a character in Roberto Bolano's magnificent novel, *2666*, which describes the region as "globalization's charnel house", laments that "no one pays attention to these killings but the secret of the world is hidden in them" (Bolano, 2009, 348). In summary, each of these forces of structural and historical amnesia operates as a fierce constraint on the societal ability to contemplate decommodified alternatives. "In this sense, 'capitalist hegemony'", writes J. Gibson Graham, "operates not only as a constituent of, but also a brake upon, the anti-capitalist imagination" (Gibson-Graham, 1996, 90).

A diverse range of counter-hegemonic initiatives, attempting to challenge these forces of structural ignorance and market insulation, has flourished in recent years. What unites all of them is their insistence that production/exchange/consumption should be viewed as a single interdependent circuit; that relations of power, coercion and domination are deeply inscribed within these so-called neutral market processes; and that in making the "invisible hand" visible once more, the social, cultural and environmental character of commodity production and exchange can be fully revealed. Campaigners for alternative food production highlight the terrible conditions under which so much of our food is produced: commercial battery farms, brutal treatment of animals, appalling work conditions, heavy use of poisonous pesticides and growth supplements. Anti-sweatshop organizers and campaigning groups attempt to reveal the true costs of the popular obsession for brand names by tracing the exploitative conditions along the clothing and apparel commodity chain. Transnational links between trade unions, which serve as vital information and solidarity exchanges, are also important forums where the hidden damage of exploitative workplaces, or brutal land enclosures dispossessing thousands of peasants from their indigenous lands, or environmental degradation of waterways and land, can be given a full public airing.

Organs Watch, a human rights group established to monitor the flourishing black market trade in body organs (especially kidneys), has used ethnographic research to expose these worldwide transplantation practices and to document the horrific costs of this grisly harvesting and distribution of body parts. The Covid-19 pandemic offered a salutary lesson in how work is valued/devalued, especially the way in which labor skills, from short order cook to grocery worker to caregiver, were now regarded as "essential" even if salary levels or work conditions in these jobs still left much to be desired. All in all, these initiatives have proven invaluable for inserting into the heart of capitalist processes – consumption choices, conditions of work, nature of production and exchange – a concern for wider social ends beyond profit and self-interest; in their very insistence on uncovering exploitation, inequality, domination inscribed within capitalist processes, they implicitly envisage a future world in which these would no longer hold sway.

These various schemes for increasing market transparency and undermining market hegemony are also limited in several important ways. First, greater knowledge and understanding does not always proceed seamlessly to action or transformative practices.[16] A more profound recognition of the plight of the exploited farmer or worker in the developing world might not be sufficient to entice consumers, buffeted by the gales of a recession, to choose a higher cost ethical option. Indeed, it could be difficult for individuals to comprehend their own culpability in these arrangements – the insight that our consumption *here* is inextricably linked to someone else's misery *there* – unless a more encompassing sense of obligation within a shared imaginary community can be constructed (Goodman, 2004). This empathetic leap is rarely achieved simply on the basis of improved knowledge mediated through the market but rather requires a fundamental ethical and emotional transformation. As the social movement literature has amply demonstrated, individuals often need to undergo a process of "cognitive liberation", itself a product of "moral shocks" that reorient individual identity and behavior in the direction of collective identity and struggle, before such connections between understanding and action are understood and mobilization becomes feasible (Jasper, 1997; McAdam, 1982). But in the individualized, balkanized world of consumer sovereignty, ethical consumption will remain isolated unless individual preferences can be aligned with a collective project and ethos.

The growth of a new politics of consumption, fusing cognitive empowerment, moral fervor and social mobilization alike, attempts to fill this gap by linking consumption directly to issues of social justice and to harness ethical consumption as a vital force of political engagement (Barnett et al., 2011). These non-profit groups and campaigners are attempting to create an institutionally entrenched structural knowledge that both mitigates the harm of the market and maximizes the likelihood of extending the reach of decommodification. Consumer groups and NGOs have called for the ethical content of all products to be incorporated directly onto the information available at the point of purchase in order to pressure global brands to improve their labor and environmental practices. Others have called for a more comprehensive and rigorous certification process that would set universal standards for work conditions, child labor, environmental standards for producers of all commodities. Of course, there is the recurrent dilemma that these information gathering and standard setting activities could well become a new site of corporate profit in their own right, which would likely not challenge the existing framework of private power (Locke et al., 2009).

However, as a design for enhancing social capacities and democratization of information, they acutely postulate the process of social learning as an integral process of decommodification: how knowledge about these various market processes can be aligned with a proper moral stance and then transmitted collectively in a way that underpins the wider decommodification program. As Hilary Wainwright emphasized:

> "this assumes a view of knowledge as a social product, distributed, valued and appropriated in ways that are potentially transformative; and in turn, implies that the possibilities of radical and democratic social change depend to a considerable extent on democratizing and socializing the organization of knowledge."
>
> (Wainwright, 1994, 8)

The Politics of Decommodification

It is worth highlighting that there could be considerable overlap across each of these decommodification categories. Some safeguards against boundary invasions might well be accomplished through the provision of public goods; public goods, like open source software, might also constitute alternative economic circuits; reducing market dependency through a social protective measure such as a basic income could strengthen the efficacy of public goods such as caring activities; ethical consumption represents not only a distinctive social and moral embedding of consumption circuits, it can generate a different sort of knowledge that illuminates the terrain of market hegemony. The wider lesson, as so often appreciated by activists in previous eras, is that progress on specific projects for social justice might well require innovative action across a range of these decommodification processes.

To take a single social problem as an exemplar, one of the pernicious effects of a rapacious consumer society is that it traps individuals in a destructive work-spend cycle: having to work excessive hours in order to buy more things (leaving them less time to enjoy them, to play with their kids, look after their sick parents and relatives), running up unsustainable credit card debt and engaging in a soulless pursuit of happiness through acquisition that is unrealizable. A reversal of this process on behalf of wellbeing and sustainability would implicate multiple decommodification programs: improving access to higher quality public goods (libraries, recreation centers, parks, community festivals); actively promoting alternative circuits such as collaborative consumption predicated on sharing, gifting and mutuality (ride shares, free cycles, community and self-provisioning, barter exchanges); sparking other-regarding activities like volunteering and community service via a reduction in work hours or comprehensive work-sharing; and inserting within all contract negotiations the right to choose work time reductions or leave in lieu of a salary hike (Schor, 2010).

Nevertheless, it could be the consequence of the structure of the previous section, as much as its underlying premise that these categories are usefully conceptualized as component features of a single process, that contributes to the impression that all of these movements and initiatives will necessarily combine in ways that replicate a virtuous circle of decommodification. This familiar pitfall of progressive thinking was deemed the "synergy solution" by Albert Hirschman who warned that the belief that all advances are mutually reinforcing obscured the necessary recognition that some methods of struggling for reform made it more difficult to fight for others (Hirschman, 1991). There is no doubt that some initiatives can be designed to generate spillover effects that aid other decommodification projects but cross cutting trade-offs will persist as well. Local authorities might seek to encourage fair trade in their purchasing strategies because of a desire to promote global justice but this can marginalize the local sourcing of food products and the cause of sustainability. Even if some of these dilemmas might be resolved by the strategic action of decommodification advocates or by the brokering role of the state, others might prove to be more resistant. To be successful, Polanyian reforms will need to impact on the entire capitalist institutional order at multiple political levels (local, national, global) and across multiple social spheres (political economy, nature, social reproduction, democracy) (Fraser, 2015).

What this reveals is the immense political complexity of constructing a compelling case for decommodification. Whereas previous egalitarian projects were explicitly conceived in terms of a single leading agent of change (the worker's movement or the Keynesian welfare state as exemplars), decommodification reform will unquestionably involve a plurality of social agents, including the state, civic associations, non-profit groups and social movements. While certain agents enjoy a comparative advantage to accomplish particular decommodification aims – as an example, states possess the encompassing scope and authority to enact boundary protections and to finance public goods while establishing alternative circuits is more likely to be the province of civil society associations that can marshal the social solidarity and tactical acumen required to achieve such social collaboration- harnessing the virtuous collaboration of multiple social actors will necessitate thorny issues of social coordination (Locke, 2009). While decommodification campaigners might well succeed in establishing durable alliances with other progressive activists (for participatory democracy, anti-austerity, human rights and the like), its primary social base remains the vast populace, cutting across social divisions and communities, that are afflicted by the pervasive forces of commodification and inequality (Evans, 2008).

There is no doubt that a decommodification pathway will necessitate a thorough going democratization of the state and its relationship to civil society (Cohen and Rogers, 1996; Offe 1996; Siriani, 2009; Wright, 2010). It will not be easy for governments, which might have actively colluded in earlier rounds of marketization, to instantaneously acquire the political will and the adaptive capacity to sustain reform. They will need to be willing to disperse political power across civil society and institutionalize regular consultation with the public. They will need to mobilize a wide community of interest in the design of programs and harness local knowledge via participatory and deliberative forums into collective instruments of citizen problem solving. Even as they devolve power, states must at the same time extend and deepen their strategic capacity: to monitor and evaluate new programs; to enforce compliance across dispersed sites and multiple policy domains; to improve and disseminate best practice; and develop innovative approaches to scale up the most successful projects to a wider audience. If, as I argued in Chapter 5, all reform projects within capitalism face the same undermining/destabilizing dilemma, then states must learn to anticipate these tendencies and design institutions and policies that will cushion the impact of these impairments. States therefore need to inculcate a reflexive capability for democratic experimentalism premised on a growing capacity for adaptation, improvisation, and creativity (Unger, 2006; Wright, 2010).

Indeed, because of the inherent tendency for crisis and because cooptation and defection back to the market remains an ever-present threat, decommodification advocates will require much greater attention to questions of institutional design. As Hacker and Pierson have long contended, robust social policies have to create supportive political dynamics if reforms are to be entrenched and expanded over time (Hacker and Pierson, 2010). There are reinforcing institutional features – lock-in effects, positive feedback loops, network effects, easy to understand benefits, and the like – that can enhance government capabilities, actively reshape citizen expectations and motivations, facilitate durable patterns of social cooperation and alliance formation and generate popular support and mobilization across a diverse universe of popular movements. A program that actively encourages the participation of the local populace in the design, construction and maintenance of a new playground will likely build a strong vested interest and constituency for this public good. Networks of cooperation that create resilient non-market circuits, such as the open science movement, create strong incentives and commitments that can entrench initial success and constitute a permanent alternative to the market.

Of course, Cohen and Rogers offer the salutary reminder that "no social design is 'strategy proof'. No matter how carefully designed the scheme of social cooperation, no matter how ingenious its incentives to behavior that produces egalitarian outcomes, individuals motivated only by self-interest will find a way to muck it up" (Cohen and Rogers, 1996, 98). In order to minimize defections from social cooperation and mischief from adversaries, decommodification proponents will need to encourage the development of a diverse culture that nurtures an egalitarian ethos, seeks to integrate these commitments as an integral component of people's daily lives and moral imagination, and conceives of specific initiatives as part of a wider campaign for social justice and emancipation (Fraser, 2014, 2018).[17] When individuals and groups see themselves as engaged not in a separate cause but rather a common struggle, the more likely they are to estimate that their chances of success will be dramatically enhanced. Once people are convinced that they are engaged in a common endeavor, they look for strategies to diffuse best practices and generate positive spillover benefits across various non-market domains; they exchange practical advice about how best to sustain their initiatives against the relentless pressures of the market; they explore ways to build the social and political constituencies that can permanently entrench reform. In other words, they begin to constitute a critical social reservoir for further reform and actively contribute to its everyday governance, which would enable citizens to develop their full capacities for democratic citizenship.

The ideological argument for decommodification will be equally challenging. All transformative projects require a compelling vision that offers an outline of the good society to come and a clear idea of how to get there. It must persuade people with differing conceptions of the good life, different motivations and different ideas of social justice that their projects are feasible and persuade them to bind their "habits of the heart" to this new vision. It is of immense benefit if the objectives they support already have widespread cultural resonance; if the slogans they espouse can be easily recognized, comprehended and expressed in clear terms; and if they can be embraced as a habitual common sense. Perhaps my greatest reservation in terms of constructing a counter-hegemonic ideology is that the term decommodification, even if analytically expansive in the ways previously outlined, is still a rather unwieldy word to capture the collective imagination. The chant of "what do we want-decommodification-when do we want it-now!" does not roll off the tongue so easily and those looking to develop appropriately catchy rhymes would surely be flummoxed! Despite my call for a return to an older progressive tradition, our first task might well be to find a better vocabulary for depicting it.[18]

Lastly, even if we are able to resolve these prodigious political, social, and ideological complexities in a way that entrenches a decommodification logic within market life that is both popular and durable, it is by no means certain that this will necessarily mark the demise of the double movement. These initiatives might very well constitute small, pragmatic steps that can tilt the double movement in an emancipatory and egalitarian direction but, as Polanyi knew full well, pathways to social change are always unpredictable. A scholar with such a keen eye for irony and paradox could not help but appreciate that all projects for social reform remain at the mercy of unintentional consequences and unforeseen contingencies that have the potential to derail even the best designed and most popular reforms. Meaningful social change is bound to require gradual, painstaking determination aligned with an open minded scrutiny of our hard won capacity for democratic experimentation and social learning. As such, this Polanyian inspired vision of decommodification represents what Erik Olin Wright calls a "compass point", a moral principle that orients us in the direction of egalitarian and emancipatory objectives even though it is not possible to decipher the precise contours of this long journey (Wright, 2010). A world beyond the double movement represents a feasible pathway not a dogmatic blueprint, an open ended process with multiple destinations rather than a single end point. We embark on this road not with certainty but rather with a modest faith that a world beyond the double movement lies within our reach, an ambition that Polanyi himself would surely have embraced.

Notes

1 It is worth highlighting at the outset that decommodification programs might also generate inegalitarian effects. Fair trade and micro-credit programs might unintentionally foster insider-outside relations and exclusionary practices; day care cooperatives or hospices managed by non-profit faith based groups could practice discriminatory hiring practices; ethical consumption movements might find participation is sharply circumscribed by the ability to pay. However, I would maintain that these unequal relations are essentially an artefact of other social processes rather than an intrinsic feature of decommodification initiatives themselves. All reform programs are necessarily embedded within a world that is systematically fractured by entrenched social divisions so it is not entirely surprising that these initiatives will be considerably limited by existing inequalities. In other instances, it might be the fundamental nature of the non-market sector being shielded from market imperatives that is antithetical to egalitarian aims or a faulty institutional design. The wider point to emphasize is that decommodification, like commodification itself, is politically and normatively complex even if I hope to demonstrate that on balance its egalitarian and emancipatory benefits are considerable.

2 The way in which Polanyi links complex freedom to a process of emancipation closely parallels the work of other social theorists who similarly conceive of emancipation as the ability to pursue life projects free of unnecessary impediments.

In this vein, Roy Bhashkar emphasizes the "progressive removal of *unwanted* determinants" (Bhashkar, 1998, 6); Nancy Fraser seeks "to remove obstacles that prevent some people from participating fully, on a par with others, in social life" (Fraser, 2011, 199); and Erik Olin Wright highlights the enhancement of "social power", which he envisages as the "capacity of actors to accomplish things in the world" (Wright, 2010, 111). All of these perspectives share a close affinity with the capabilities approach of Amartya Sen and Martha Nussbaum, who argued that freedom was not merely a question of which rights a person enjoyed, but rather the capacity to exercise these rights in everyday life (Sen, 1999; Nussbaum, 2000).

3 Marx's early writings exercised an abiding influence on this discussion as exemplified by the following quote from *The German Ideology*: "Only in community with others has each individual the means of cultivating his gifts in all directions; only in the community, therefore, is personal freedom possible" (Marx, in Tucker, 1974, 126; Dale, 2010).

4 In the years before the writing of his masterpiece, Polanyi entered into a spirited discussion with fellow socialists about how to organize a post-market society, much of which was contained in what is known as the "socialist calculation debate", most famously between Oscar Lange and Ludwig von Mies to which Polanyi was an avid contributor. Gareth Dale has a fascinating summary of these writings and a lucid account of how the themes of many of these papers were incorporated into the main arguments of *The Great Transformation* (Dale, 2010, chapter 1).

5 Past critiques of Esping-Andersen's work often focused obsessively on classificatory minutia, at times more closely resembling arcane Talmudic disputes rather than debates that actually advanced our understanding of the underlying conceptual issues. However, there are notable exceptions to this overall tendency. Graham Room (2000) stressed the link between labor commodification and self-development and argued that decommodification proponents did not sufficiently address how greater autonomy and creativity could be ensured in the sphere of paid work. In an influential critique, Ann Shola Orloff (1993) argued for the positive effects of commodification on women's lives and proposed an alternative category, *defamilialization*, which explored the extent to which women could secure an independent livelihood without recourse to the household. Claus Offe similarly envisioned decommodification in the wider manner proposed in this chapter: "areas of social life that have been decommodified by welfare state interventions can be developed, through political struggle, into relatively autonomous sub-systems of life oriented to the production and distribution of use values" (Offe, 1996, 265).

6 For contrasting definitions, Colin Williams defines the decommodified realm as any form of economic activity that is non-exchanged, non-monetized or without a profit motive (Williams, 2005). Andrew Sayer uses decommodification to refer to what he calls the "recontextualizing moment" of consumption (the move from functional attributes of things [exchange value] to the symbolic aspects of status, identity and personal liberation that people intentionally attach to products [use values]. "The continued success of commodity production therefore", he writes, "depends on successful decommodification by the consumer, usually with a cultural steer by the producer" (Sayer, 2003, 346). J. K. Gibson-Graham includes as part of the non-commodified realm independent commodity production of small businesses as well as for-profit partnerships where the surplus is jointly appropriated and decisions about its distribution are jointly made (Gibson-Graham, 1996).

7 Marion Fourcade has emphasized how the introduction of cash payments in Latin America, South Africa and India has been accompanied by a rapid, widespread financialization and recommodification of public services. "As the government replaces social processes with cash disbursements", she writes, "and physical

services are transformed by the introduction of virtuality, social policy becomes another 'collateral', ripe for extraction by the financial system, either as interest money, or, increasingly, as data" (Fourcade, 2021, 157).

8 Nancy Fraser, to the contrary, argues that Polanyi's model of the double movement conspicuously lacks a moral and emancipatory critique (Fraser, 2013). This holds not just for the important omissions in his analysis (the failure to address anti-colonial struggles, peace movements, and women's emancipation) but because struggles for emancipation, she insists, do not map very well onto the processes of the double movement. For Fraser, an emancipatory perspective must offer a fundamental opposition to oppression and domination; scrutinize all social relations from the standpoint of non-domination; and assess the potential for non-market forms of economic activity. I have tried to highlight some of these same kinds of inconsistencies in Polanyi's approach but, as detailed previously and in this chapter, I believe that there is a strong emancipatory and egalitarian thread in Polanyi's framework that should be more openly acknowledged and appreciated.

9 The discussion in this section draws extensively upon Vail, 2010.

10 Of course, there can be differing degrees of non-rivalness. My consumption of a book from a library might well mean that someone else is unable to read that same book until I am finished with it. Similarly, my enjoyment of the beautiful vistas of a national park wilderness or a beach, not to mention the quality of the good in question, could be severely impaired if too many other people pursue their right at the same time. In those instances, restrictions on usage may be necessary, and these can be accomplished by both bureaucratic procedures (registration requirements, waiting lists, etc.) and monetary fees (user charges to defray expenses of park management), which need not imply commodification in every instance.

11 David Miller (1989) insists that there is still a "first order question" to decide, namely which goods society deems is necessary to make public. Given that certain groups might benefit more from certain public goods than others, public goods are subject to the same kind of social justice considerations as any other forms of social wealth. Indeed in an era of widespread fiscal constraints, the debate about which public goods might be sacrosanct from the inevitable public sector cuts rages on both side of the Atlantic.

12 Political culture plays a significant role in whether public goods develop such a politics of the common good. The example of public pools in the United States is instructive in this regard (Klinenberg, 2018; McGhee, 2020). In the 1920s and 1930s governments built thousands of public pools across the nation, which were viewed quite intentionally as social melting pots, similar to public schools as a way of creating common identity and solidarity. But from the 1950s onwards, once access to these amenities were guaranteed to African Americans as a result of desegregation and political protest, white officials across the American South drained their pools rather than share them with their Black neighbors; or created new private companies to operate the pools on a membership only basis that excluded Blacks. As Heather McGhee notes, once public goods were transformed into a racialized zero sum game – if things were better for Blacks, it could only be at the expense of whites- sustaining them across a range of goods and services (parks, schools, zoos and the like) was crippled (McGhee, 2020).

13 This does not preclude that the enactment of public goods might very well enrich private beneficiaries. This could be the result of intentional action – a means of ensuring legislative passage by arranging side deals with potential adversaries - but, more likely, it is a natural byproduct of creating such goods within a capitalist economy. When a government decides to commit funds for public libraries, public health clinics, or high speed rail, they do so in the full knowledge that it is likely

that the construction of these entities will be undertaken by private firms which will derive substantial profits from their participation. Yet private enrichment should not obscure the wider societal benefits from enacting such goods in the first place nor should it invalidate the underlying belief that providing more public goods would have strong egalitarian effects.

14 During the pandemic, drug companies agreed to forego copyright protection on their vaccines, which would supposedly allow nations to produce, manufacture and distribute the vaccines. But this largesse was largely symbolic. The immense complexities of production mean few nations had the technical or organizational expertise to mass produce vaccines. A far more effective and egalitarian program was the G7 announcement in June 2012 that they would purchase 1 billion doses to distribute to developing nations in need for free.

15 One could reasonably inquire whether this definition strays very far from the familiar argument within economic sociology that emphasizes the "embedding" of markets (see Krippner and Alvarez, 2007). When we argue that a market is embedded (in social, political/institutional, cultural, cognitive forms), it could mean various things: that financial markets are influenced by symbolic relations and by theories of financial markets themselves; that commodity prices are formed not only by market interactions but by branding, status, and taste; that global trade is regulated by a dense web of rules, standards, and political agreements. However, not all instances of embedding directly impact on the functioning of core market imperatives in the manner I am suggesting and more importantly, many forms of embedding are designed to improve the functioning of markets (by improving information flows, reducing price volatility, lowering transaction costs, managing uncertainty) in order to aid efficiency and enhance profitability rather than to promote egalitarian and democratic outcomes as I am arguing a decommodifying effect must accomplish.

16 Peter Jackson makes a similar point: "Yet there is something hollow about the call to 'unveil' the commodity fetish as though the provision of such knowledge would automatically lead to widespread shifts in consumer behavior or to significant changes in working conditions at the point of production. There is little evidence to suggest that commercial culture works in this way" (Jackson, 2002, 6–7).

17 This brief for a wider oppositional culture on behalf of egalitarianism also arises from the prudent recognition that expanding the mobilizational capacity of civil society does not always privilege associations that act as a positive force for egalitarianism rather than particularistic forms of solidarity (a point we emphasized in the discussion of Polanyian countermovements in Chapter 4 and 6).

18 Fred Block throws his support to an even older ideological tradition but one that has a somewhat more attractive resonance – the "moral economy". See Fred Block, "A Moral Economy," *The Nation* (March 20, 2006). See also Andrew Sayer's important work in re-establishing the concept (2000, 2007).

Bibliography

Abercombie, Nicholas et al. (1980) *The Dominant Ideology Thesis*, Allen and Unwin.

Abraham, David (1986) *The Collapse of the Weimar Republic* (Second edition), Holmes and Meier.

Allen, Robert (1994) *Enclosure and the Yeoman*, Clarendon.

Anderson, Elizabeth (1993) *Value in Ethics and Economics.*

Anderson, Elizabeth (2017) *Private Government*, Princeton University Press.

Appelby, Joyce (1978) *Economic Thought and Ideology in Seventeenth-Century England*, Princeton University Press.

Appelby, Joyce (2010) *The Relentless Revolution: a History of Capitalism*, W.W. Norton & Co.

Arrighi, Giovanni (1994) *The Long Twentieth Century*, Verso.

Arrighi, Giovanni and Beverly Silver (2003) "Polanyi's 'Double Movement': the Belle Epoques of British and U.S. Hegemony Compared", *Politics and Society*, 31(2), 325–355.

Atkinson, Anthony (2015) *Inequality: What Can be Done*, Harvard University Press.

Azmanova, Albena (2020) *Capitalism on Edge*, Columbia University Press.

Baker, Dean (2003) *The Artistic Freedom Voucher*, Center for Economic and Policy Research.

Baldwin, Peter (1999) *Contagion and the State in Europe, 1830–1930*, Cambridge University Press.

Bales, Kevin (2000) *Disposable People: New Slavery in the Global Economy*, University of California Press.

Barber, Bernard (1985) "All Economies are 'Embedded': the Career of a Concept and Beyond", *Social Research* 62(2), 387–4113.

Barnett, Clive, Paul Cloke, Nicholas Clarke and Alice Malpass (2011) *Globalizing Responsibility: The Political Rationalities of Ethical Consumption*, Wiley-Blackwell.

Beckert, Jens (2009) "The Great Transformation of Embeddedness: Karl Polanyi and the New Economic Sociology", in Chris Hann and Keith Hart, eds, *Market and Society: The Great Transformation Today*, Cambridge University Press.

Benkler, Yochai (2006) *The Wealth of Networks*, Yale University Press.

Berg, Maxine (1994) *The Age of Manufactures, 1700–1820*, Routledge.

Berman, Marshall (1982) *All That Is Solid Melts Into Air*, Simon & Schuster.

Berman, Sheri (2006) *The Primacy of Politics: Social Democracy and the Making of Europe's Twentieth Century*, Cambridge University Press.

Berman, Sheri (2021) "The causes of populism in the west", *Annual Review of Political Science.*

Birchfield, Vicki (1999) "Contesting the Hegemony of Market Ideology: Gramsci's 'Good Sense' and Polanyi's 'Double Movement'", *Review of International Political Economy*, 6(1).

Blackburn, Robin (2007) "Plans for a Global Pension", *New Left Review*, 47(Sept./Oct.), 71–92.

Blaug, Peter (1963) "The Myth of the Old Poor Law and the Meaning of the New", *Journal of Economic History*, 23, 151–184.

Block, Fred (1990) *Postindustrial Possibilities*, University of California Press.

Block, Fred (2003) "Karl Polanyi and the Writing of *The Great Transformation*", *Theory and Society*, 32, 275–306.

Block, Fred (2006) "A Moral Economy", *The Nation*, March 20, 2006.

Block, Fred (2007) "Understanding the Diverging Trajectories of the United States and Western Europe: a Neo-Polanyian Analysis", *Politics and Society*, vol. 35(1), 3–33.

Block, Fred and Margaret Somers (1984) "Beyond the economistic fallacy: the holistic social science of Karl Polanyi", in Theda Skocpol, *Vision and Method in Historical Sociology*, Cambridge University Press, pp. 47–84.

Block, Fred and Margaret Somers (2003) "In the Shadow of Speenhamland: Social Policy and the Old Poor Law", *Politics and Society* 31(2), 282–323.

Block, Fred and Margaret Somers (2014) *The Power of Market Fundamentalism: Karl Polanyi's Critique*, Harvard University Press.

Blyth, Mark (2002) *Great Transformations: Economic Ideas and Institutional Change in the Twentieth Century*, Cambridge University Press.

Blyth, Mark (2004) "The Great Transformation in Understanding Polanyi: Reply to Hejeebu and McCloskey", *Critical Review*, 16(1), 117–133.

Blyth, Mark (2013) *Austerity: the History of a Dangerous Idea*, Oxford University Press.

Blyth, Mark (2018) "When it is Rational to Learn the Wrong Lessons: Technocratic Authority, Social Learning and Euro Fragility", *Perspectives on Politics*, Vol. 16(1), 110–126.

Bolano, Roberto (2009) *2666*, Picador.

Boltanski, Luc and Laurent Thevenot (2006) *On Justification*, Princeton University Press.

Bond, Patrick (2000) *Elite Transition: From Apartheid to Neo-liberalism in South Africa*, Pluto Press.

Bourdieu, Pierre (1990) *The Logic of Practice*, Stanford University Press.

Bourdieu, Pierre (1998) *Acts of Resistance: Against the Tyranny of the Market*, New Press.

Bowles, Samuel (2011) "Is Liberal Society a Parasite on Tradition", *Philosophy and Public Affairs*, vol. 39(1), 46–81.

Bowman, John (1989) *Capitalist Collective Action*, Cambridge University Press.

Boyer, George (1990) *An Economic History of the English Poor Law*, Cambridge University Press.

Boyle, James (2009) *The Public Domain: Enclosing the Commons of the Mind*, Yale University Press.

Braudel, Ferdinand (1982) *The Wheels of Commerce*, Harper & Row.

Brenner, Robert (1977) "Origins of Capitalist Development: A Critique of Neo-Smithian Marxism", *New Left Review*, 104, 25–93.

Brenner, Robert (1986) "The Social Basis of Economic Development", in Roemer, J, *Analytical Marxism*, Cambridge University Press.
Brenner, Robert (2006) *The Economics of Global Turbulence*, Verso.
Brewer, John (1989) *The Sinews of Power: War, Money and the English State, 1688–1783*, Knopf.
Brie, Michael and Claus Thomasberger (2018) *Karl Polanyi's Vision of a Socialist Transformation*, Black Rose Books.
Briggs, Asa (1968) *Victorian Cities*, Penguin.
Bronner, Stephen Eric (1990) *Socialism Unbound*, Routledge.
Brubaker, Rogers (2017) "Why Populism", *Theory and Society*, 46, 357–385.
Burawoy, Michael (2003) "For a Sociological Marxism: the Complementary Convergence of Antonio Gramsci and Karl Polanyi", *Politics and Society*, 31(2), 193–261.
Burawoy, Michael (2010) "From Polanyi to Pollyanna: the false optimism of Global Labor studies", *Global Labor Journal*, vol. 1(2), 301–313.
Cain, P.J and A.G. Hopkins (2000) *British Imperialism, 1688–2000*, Taylor & Francis.
Calhoun, Craig (1982) *The Question of Class Struggle: Social Foundations of Popular Radicalism in Industrial England*, University of Chicago Press.
Calhoun, Craig (2012) *The Roots of Radicalism*, University of Chicago Press.
Callon, Michel (1998) *The Laws of the Market*, Blackwell.
Case, Ann and Angus Deaton (2020) *Deaths of Despair and the Future of Capitalism*, Princeton University Press.
Cassidy, John (2009) *How Markets Fail*, Farrar, Straus, & Giroux.
Chasin, Alexandra (2000) *Selling Out: the Gay and Lesbian Movement Goes to Market*, Palgrave.
Cohen, G.A. (1978) *Karl Marx's Theory of History: A Defence*, Oxford University Press.
Cohen, G.A. (1986) "The structure of proletarian unfreedom", in John Roemer, ed., *Analytical Marxism*, Cambridge University Press.
Cohen, Joshua and Joel Rogers (1983) *On Democracy*, Penguin.
Collier, David and Ruth Collier (1991) *Shaping the Political Arena: Critical Junctures, the labor Movement and Regime dynamics in Latin America*, Princeton University Press.
Crouch, Colin (2009) *Post-Democracy*, Polity Press.
Crouch, Colin (2009) "Privatised Keynesianism: An Unacknowledged Policy Regime", *The British Journal of Politics and International Relations*, vol. 11, 382–399.
Crouch, Colin (2011) *The Strange Non-Death of Neoliberalism*, Polity.
Dale, Gareth (2008) "Karl Polanyi's *The Great Transformation*: perverse effects, protectionism and *gemeinschaft*", *Economy and Society*, vol. 37(4), 495–524.
Dale, Gareth (2010) *Karl Polanyi: the Limits of the Market*, Polity Press.
Dale, Gareth (2010) "Social Democracy, Embeddedness and Decommodification", *New Political Economy*, 1–24.
Dale, Gareth (2012) "Double Movements and Pendular Forces: Polanyian Perspectives on the Neoliberal Age", *Current Sociology*, vol. 60(1), 3–27.
Dale, Gareth (2016) *Reconstructing Karl Polanyi*, Pluto Press.
Dale, Gareth (2016) *Karl Polanyi: A Life on the Left*, Columbia University Press.
Davis, Mike (2001) *Late Victorian Holocausts*, Verso.
Degrazia, Victoria (1981) *The Culture of Consent: Mass Organization of Leisure in Fascist Italy*, Cambridge University Press.

Deutschmann, Christoph (2019) *Disembedded Markets: Economic Theology and Global Capitalism*, Routledge.

Diani, Mario and Donnatella Dellaporta (2003) *Social Movements: An Introduction*, Wiley,.

Drezner, Daniel (2014) *The System Worked: How the World Stopped Another Great Depression*, Oxford University Press.

Eagleton, Terry (1991) *Ideology*, Verso.

Eichengreen, Barry (1992) *Golden Fetters: The Gold Standard and the Great Depression*, Oxford University Press.

Eichengreen, Barry (1996) *Globalizing Capital: A History of the International Monetary System*, Princeton University Press.

Eichengreen, Barry and Douglas A. Irwin (2010) "The Slide to Protection in the Great Depression: who succumbed and why", *The Journal of Economic History*, vol. 70(4), 871–897.

Eichengreen, Barry (2015) *Hall of Mirrors*, Oxford University Press.

Elson, Diane (2000) "Socializing Markets, Not Market Socialism", in Leo Panitch and Colin Leys, *Socialist Register*, pp. 67–85.

Elster, Jon (1986) *Making Sense of Marx*, Cambridge University Press.

Ensminger, Jean (1992) *Making a Market: the Institutional Transformation of an African Society*, Cambridge University Press.

Espeland, Wendy and Mitchell Stevens (1998) "Commensuration as a Social Process", *Annual Review of Sociology*, vol. 24, 313–343.

Esping-Andersen, Gosta (1990) *The Three Worlds of Welfare Capitalism*, Polity Press.

Esping-Andersen, Gosta (2009) *Incomplete Revolution: Adapting Welfare States to Women's Changing Roles*, Polity Press.

Evans, Peter (2008) "Is an Alternative Globalization Possible", *Politics and Society*, 36 (2), 271–305.

Farrell, Henry (2015) "Piketty in Three Parts", *Crooked Timber*, December 15, 2015.

Ferguson, James (2009) "The Uses of Neoliberalism", *Antipode*, vol. 41(1), 166–184.

Ferguson, Niall (1998) *The World's Banker: the History of the House of Rothschild*, Weidenfeld & Nicholson.

Folbre, Nancy (2001) *The Invisible Heart: Economics and Family Values*, The New Press.

Fourcade, Marion (2021) "Ordinal Citizenship", *British Journal of Sociology*, 72, 154–173.

Fourcade-Gourinchas, Marion and Sarah Babb (2002) "The Rebirth of the Liberal Creed: Paths to Neoliberalism in Four Countries", *American Journal of Sociology*, 108, 533–579.

Fourcade, Marion and Kieran Healy (2007) "Moral Views of Market Society", *Annual Review of Sociology*, vol. 33, 285–311.

Fourcade, Marion and Daniel Kluttz (2020) "A Maussian Bargain: accumulation by gift in the digital economy", *Big Data and Society*, vol. 7(Jan./June), 1–16.

Fraser, Nancy (2013) "A Triple Movement: Parsing the Politics of Crisis after Polanyi", *New Left Review*, 81(May/June), 119–132.

Fraser, Nancy (2014) "Can society be commodities all the way down? Post-Polanyian reflections of capitalist crisis", *Economy and Society*, vol. 43(4), 541–558.

Fraser, Nancy (2014) "Beyond Marx's Hidden Abode: for an Expanded Conception of Capitalism", *New Left Review*, 86(March/April), 55–72.

Fraser, Nancy (2015) "Legitimation Crisis? Or the Political Contradictions of Financialized Capitalism", *Critical Historical Studies*, 2(2), 157–189.
Fraser, Nancy (2016) "Contradictions of Capital and Care", *New Left Review*, 100 (July/August), 99–117.
Fraser, Nancy (2018) "Why Two Karls are Better than One: Integrating Polanyi and Marx in a Critical Theory of the Current Crisis", in Brie and Thomasberger, *Karl Polanyi's Vision of a Socialist Transformation*, pp. 67–76.
Fraser, Nancy (2021) "Climates of Capital", *New Left Review*, 127(Jan./Feb.).
Fridell, Gavin (2007) *Fair Trade Coffee: the Prospects and Pitfalls of Market-Driven Justice*, University of Toronto Press.
Frieden, Jeffrey (1992) *Debt, Development and Democracy*, Princeton University Press.
Funke, Manuel, Moritz Schularick, and Christoph Trebesch (2016) "Going to extremes: Politics after financial crises", *European Economic Review*, vol. 88(C), 227–260.
Gallagher, John and Ronald Robinson (1953), "The Imperialism of Free Trade", *The Economic History Review*, vol. 6(1), 1–15.
Gallarotti, Guilio (1985) *The Anatomy of an International Monetary Regime: the Classical Gold Standard, 1880–1914*, Oxford University Press.
Gemici, Kurtulus (2008) "Karl Polanyi and the Antinomies of Embeddedness", *Socio-Economic Review*, 6(1), 5–33.
Gibson-Graham, J. (1996) *The End of Capitalism (as We Knew It)*, Blackwell.
Gidron, Naomi and Peter Hall (2020) "Populism as a problem of social integration", *Comparative Political Studies*, vol. 53(7), 1027–1054.
Glasman, Maurice (1996) *Unnecessary Suffering: Managing Market Utopia*, Verso.
Gorz, Andre (1967) *Strategy for Labor*, Beacon Press.
Gourevitch, Peter (1978) "The second image reversed: the international sources of domestic politics", *International Organization*, vol. 32(4), 881–912.
Gourevitch, Peter (1984) "Breaking with Orthodoxy: the Politics of Economic Responses to the Depression of the 1930s", *International Organization*, 36(2), 379–415.
Graeber, David (2002) *Toward an Anthropological Theory of Value: the False Coin of Our Own Dreams*, Palgrave.
Gramsci, Antonio (1971[1929–35]) *Selections from the Prison Notebooks*, eds, Quintin Hoare and Geoffrey Nowell Smith, Lawrence and Wishart.
Granovetter, Mark (1985) "Economic Action and Social Structure: the problem of Embeddedness", *American Journal of Sociology*, 91(3), 481–510.
Granovetter, Mark and Richard Swedberg (1992) *The Sociology of Economic Life*, Westview Press.
Gray, Robert (1996) *The Factory Question and Industrial England, 1830–1860*, Cambridge University Press.
Grusky, David, Peter A. Hall and Hazel Rose Markus (2019) "The Rise of Opportunity Markets: How did it happen and what can we do?", *Daedalus*, 148(3), 19–45.
Hacker, Jacob S. (2006) *The Great Risk Shift*, New York: Oxford University Press.
Hacker, Jacob and Paul Pierson (2010) *Winner-Take-All Politics*, Simon & Schuster.
Hacker, Jacob and Paul Pierson (2016) *American Amnesia*, Simon & Schuster.
Hacker, Jacob, Phillip Rehm and Mark Schlesinger (2013) "The Insecure American: Economic Experiences, Financial Worries and Policy Attitudes", *Perspectives on Politics*, vol. 11(1), 23–49.
Hall, Peter A. and David Soskice (2001) *Varieties of Capitalism*, Oxford University Press.

Hall, Peter A. and Michele Lamont (2013) *Social Resiliency in the Neoliberal Age*, Cambridge University Press.
Halperin, Sandra (2004) *War and Social Change in Modern Europe: The Great Transformation Revisited*, Cambridge University Press.
Hann, Chris and Keith Hart (eds.) (2009) *Market and Society: The Great Transformation Today*, Cambridge University Press.
Harvey, David (1999) *The Limits of Capital*, Verso.
Harvey, David (2005) *The New Imperialism*, Oxford University Press.
Harvey, Mark, Sally Randles, and Ronnie Ramlogan, eds (2007) *Karl Polanyi: New Perspectives on the Place of the Economy in Society*, Manchester University Press.
Hechter, Michael (1981) "Karl Polanyi's Social Theory: A Critique", *Politics and Society*, vol. 10(4), 399–429.
Hejeebu, Santhi and Deidre McCloskey (1999) "The Reproving of Karl Polanyi", *Critical Review*, 13(3–4),285–314.
Heilleiner, Eric (1994) *States and the Re-emergence of Global Finance*, Cornell University Press.
Heilleiner, Eric (2019) "The life and times of embedded liberalism: legacies and innovations since Bretton Woods", *Review of International Political Economy*, vol. 26(6), 1112–1135.
Hing, Leanne Son, Anne Wilson, Peter Gourevitch, Jaslyn English and Parco Sin (2019) "Failure to Respond to Rising Income Inequality: Processes that Legitimize Growing Disparities", *Daedalus*, 148(3), 105–135.
Hirschman, Albert O (1982) *Shifting Involvements*, Princeton University Press.
Hirschman, Albert O (1991) *The Rhetoric of Reaction: Perversity, Futility, Jeopardy*, Harvard University Press.
Ho, Karen (2009) *Liquidated: an Ethnography of Wall Street*, Duke University Press.
Hobsbawm, Eric (1994) *The Age of Extremes: the Short Twentieth-Century, 1914–1991*, Vintage.
Hobsbawm, Eric and George Rude (1969) *Captain Swing*, Lawrence and Wishart.
Hobson, John M. (1997) *The Wealth of States: a Comparative Sociology of International Economic and Political Change*, Cambridge University Press.
Hochschild, Arlie (2016) *Strangers in Their Own Land*, The New Press.
Hollingsworth, J. Rogers and Robert Boyer (1997) *Contemporary Capitalism: The Embeddedness of Institutions*, Cambridge University Press.
Hollis, Aidan and Thomas Pogge (2008) *The Health Impact Fund: Making New Medicines Accessible For All*, Incentives for Global Health.
Holmes, Christopher (2012) "Problems and opportunities in Polanyian analysis today", *Economy and Society*, vol. 41(3), 468–484.
Holmes, Christopher (2014) "Whatever it takes: Polanyian perspectives on the Eurozone crisis and the gold standard", *Economy and Society*, vol. 43(4), 582–602.
Hopkin, Jonathan (2020) *Anti-System Politics*, Oxford University Press.
Hudson, Pat (1992) *The Industrial Revolution*, E. Arnold.
Humphries, Jane (1985) "Women's Labour Force Participation and the Transformation to the Male-Breadwinner Family, 1790–1865", *Economic History Review*, 48(1), 89–117.
Ishay, Micheline (1995) *Internationalism and Its Betrayal*, University of Minnesota Press.

Jackson, Peter (2003) "Commercial Cultures: Transcending the Cultural and the Economic", *Progress in Human Geography*, 26, 3–18.

Jaffee, Daniel (2007) *Brewing Justice: Fair Trade Coffee, Sustainability and Survival*, University of California Press.

Jameson, Fredric (1984) "Postmodernism, or the Cultural Logic of Late Capitalism", *New Left Review*, 146(July/August), 53–92.

Jasper, James (1997) *The Art of Moral Protest*, University of Chicago Press.

Joyce, Patrick (1991) *Visions of the People: Industrial England and the Question of Class, 1840–1914*, Cambridge University Press.

Judt, Tony (2010) *Ill Fares the Land*, Penguin Press.

Kalecki, Michal (1943) "Political Aspects of Full Employment", *Political Quarterly*, vol. 14(4), 322–330.

Katznelson, Ira (2003) *Desolation and Enlightenment*, Columbia University Press.

Kaul, Inge, Pedro Conceicao, Katell Le Goulven and Ronald U. Mendoz, eds (2003) *Providing Global Public Goods: Managing Globalization*, Oxford University Press.

Kelty, Christopher (2008) *Two Bits: The Cultural Significance of Free Software*, Duke University Press.

Kindleberger, Charles (1986) *The World in Depression, 1929–39*, University of California Press.

Klein, Ezra (2021) "Ezra Klein Interviews Adam Tooze", *The New York Times*, September 17, 2021.

Klein, Naomi (2001) "A fete for the end of the end of history", *The Nation*, March 19, 2001.

Klein, Naomi (2002) *Fences and Windows: Dispatches from the Frontlines of the Globalization Debate*, Flamingo Books.

Klinenberg, Eric (2018) *Palaces for the People*, Vintage.

Konczal, Mike (2021) *Freedom from the Market*, The New Press.

Krippner, Greta (2001) "The Elusive Market: Embeddedness and the paradigm of Economic Sociology", *Theory and Society*, 30, 775–810.

Krippner, Greta, et al. (2004) "Polanyi Symposium: A Conversation on Embeddedness", *Socio-Economic Review*, 2(1), 109–135.

Krippner, Greta and Anthony Alvarez (2007) "Embeddedness and the Intellectual Projects of Economic Sociology", *Annual Review of Sociology*, 33, 219–240.

Krippner, Greta (2011) *Capitalizing on Crisis: the Political Origins of the Rise of Finance*, Harvard University Press.

Krippner, Greta (2017) "Polanyi for the Age of Trump", *Critical Historical Studies*, Fall, 243–254.

Krippner, Greta (2020) "Disembedded markets and the problem of economism", *Socio-Economic Review*, vol. 18(4), 1199–1212.

Kuttner, Robert (1997) *Everything for Sale: The Virtues and Limits of Markets*, Knopf.

Kuttner, Robert (2018) *Can Democracy Survive Global Capitalism?*, W.W. Norton & Co.

Lacher, Hannes (1999) "The politics of the market: re-reading Karl Polanyi", *Global Society*, 13(3), 313–326.

Lacher, Hannes (1999) "Embedded Liberalism, Disembedded Markets: Reconceptualising the Pax Americana", *New Political Economy*, 4(3), 343–360.

Lacher, Hannes (2006) *Beyond Globalization: Capitalism, Territoriality and the International Relations of Modernity*, Routledge.

Lacher, Hannes (2019) "Karl Polanyi, the 'always-embedded market economy', and the Re-writing of The Great Transformation", *Theory and Society*, 1–37.

Lamont, Michele (2012) "Towards a Comparative Sociology of Valuation and Evaluation", *Annual Review of Sociology*, 38(21), 201–221.

Lamont, Michele and Paul Pierson (2019) "Inequality as a Multidimensional Process", *Daedalus*, 148(3), 73–104.

Lie, John (1991), "Embedding Polanyi's Market Society", *Sociological Perspectives*, 34(2).

Lie, John (1993) "Visualizing the Invisible Hand: the social origins of 'Market Society' in England, 1550–1750", *Politics and Society*, vol. 21(3), 275–305.

Lindblom, Charles (1982) "The Market as Prison", *The Journal of Politics*, vol. 44(2), 324–336.

Lindblom, Charles E. (2001) *The Market System*, Yale University Press.

Locke, Richard, Matthew Amenguel, and Akshay Mangla (2009) "Virtue out of Necessity: Compliance, Commitment and Improvement of Labor Conditions in Global Supply Chains", *Politics and Society*, 37(3), 319–351.

Lonergan, Eric and Mark Blyth (2020) *Angrynomics*, Agenda Publishing.

Luebbert, Gregory (1991) *Liberalism, Fascism or Social Democracy: Social Classes and the Political Origins of Regimes in Interwar Europe*, Oxford University Press.

Lukacs, Gyorgy (1971) *History and Class Consciousness*, The MIT Press.

MacKenzie, Donald (2006) *An Engine, Not a Camera*, Princeton University Press.

MacPherson, C.B. (1962) *The Political Theory of Possessive Individualism*, Oxford University Press.

Mandler, Peter (1987) "The Making of the New Poor Law Revisited", *Past and Present*, 117, 131–157.

Mann, Michael (1986) *The Sources of Social Power*, Cambridge University Press.

Mann, Michael (1993) *The Sources of Social Power: Volume 2: The Rise of Classes and Nation States, 1760–1914*, Cambridge University Press.

Marglin, Stephen (1974) "What do Bosses Do?", *Review of Radical Political Economy*, vol. 6(2), 60–112.

Marglin Stephen and Juliet Schor (1990) *The Golden Age of Capitalism*, Oxford University Press.

Marquand, David (2004) *Decline of the Public*, Polity Press.

Marx, Karl (1973[1867]), *Capital, Volume* 1, E. P. Dutton.

Matthijs, Matthias (2016) "The Euro's Winner-Take-All Political Economy", *Politics and Society*, vol. 44(3), 393–422.

Mayer, Arno (1978) *The Persistence of the Old Regime*, Princeton University Press.

Mazzucato, Mariana (2021) *Mission Economy: A Moonshot Guide to Changing Capitalism*, Allen Lane.

McAdam, Douglas (1982) *Political Process and the Development of Black Insurgency*, University of Chicago Press.

McAdam, Douglas, Sidney Tarrow and Charles Tilly (2001) *Dynamics of Contention*, Cambridge University Press.

McGhee, Heather (2021) *The Sum of Us*, One World.

McNally, David (1993) *Against the Market*, Verso.

McRobbie, Kenneth (2000) "Vision and Expression: Literature and The Great Transformation", in Kari Polanyi-Levitt, ed., *Karl Polanyi in Vienna: the Contemporary Significance of The Great Transformation*, Black Rose Books.

McRobbie, Kenneth and Kari Polanyi-Levitt, eds (2006) *Karl Polanyi in Vienna*, Black Rose Books.

Mendell, Marguerite and Daniel Salee, eds. (1991) *The Legacy of Karl Polanyi*, Macmillan.

Merton, Robert (1987) "Three Fragments from a Sociologist's Notebooks: Establishing the Phenomena, Specified Ignorance and Strategic Research Materials", *Annual Review of Sociology*, vol. 13, 1–29.

Milanovic, Branko (2019) *Capitalism Alone*, Belknap Press.

Miller, David (1989) *Market, State and Community*, Clarendon.

Millett, Kris (2021) "On the meanings and Contemporary Significance of Fascism in the Writings of Karl Polanyi", *Theory and Society*, 50: 463–487.

Mintz, Sidney (1985) *Sweetness and Power: The Place of Sugar in Modern History*, Viking.

Moore, Barrington (1966) *Social Origins of Dictatorship and Democracy*, Beacon Press.

Morgan, Phillip (1995) *Italian Fascism, 1919–45*, Palgrave.

Mudge, Stephanie (2018) *Leftism Re-Invented: Western Parties from Socialism to Neoliberalism*, Harvard University Press.

Muller, Jann-Werner (2016) *What is Populism*, Allen Lane.

Munck, Ronaldo (2002) "Globalization and Democracy: a New 'Great Transformation'", *The Annals of the American Academy of Political and Social Science*, vol. 581 (May), 10–21.

North, Douglass (1977) "Markets and Other Allocation Systems: the Challenge of Karl Polanyi", *Journal of European Economic History*, 6(3), 703–716.

North, Douglass and Barry Weingast (1989) "Constitutions and Commitment: the Evolution of Institutions Governing Public Choice in Seventeenth-Century England", *The Journal of Economic History*, vol. 49(6), 803–832.

Nussbaum, Martha (2000) *Women and Human Development: the Capabilities Approach*, Cambridge University Press.

Nussbaum, Martha (2018) *The Monarchy of Fear*, Oxford University Press.

O'Connor, James (1988) "Capitalism, Nature, Socialism: a theoretical introduction", *Capitalism Nature Socialism*, vol. 1(1), 11–38.

Offe, Claus (1984) *Contradictions of the Welfare State*, The MIT Press.

Offe, Claus (1996) *Modernity and the State*, Polity Press.

Offe, Claus (2015) *Europe Entrapped*, Polity Press.

O'Neill, Martin (2017) "Philosophy and Public Policy After Piketty", *The Journal of Political Philosophy*, vol. 75 (3), 343–375.

Orloff, Anna Shola (1993) "Gender and the Social Rights of Citizenship: The Comparative Analysis of Gender Relations and Welfare States", *American Sociological Review*, 58, 303–328.

O'Rourke, Kevin and Jeffrey Williamson (1999) *Globalization and History*, Cambridge University Press.

Ostrom, Elinor (1990) *Governing the Commons: The Evolution of Institutions for Collective Action*, Cambridge University Press.

O'Toole, Fintan (2019) *Heroic Failure*, Head of Zeus.

Pantich, Leo and Sam Gindin (2010) "Transcending Pessimism: Rekindling Socialist Imagination", *Socialist Register*, 1–29.

Panitch, Leo and Sam Gindin (2012) *The Making of Global Capitalism: The Political Economy of American Empire*, Verso.

Parry, Jonathan P. (1999) "Lords of labour: Working and shirking in Bihar", *Contributions to Indian Sociology*, vol. 33(1–2), 107–140.

Peck, Jamie (2013) "For Polanyian Economic Geographies", *Environment and Planning A: Economy and Space*, vol. 45(7), 1545–1568.

Pierson, Paul (1994) *Dismantling the Welfare State? Reagan, Thatcher and the Politics of Retrenchment*, Cambridge University Press.

Piketty, Thomas (2014) *Capital in the Twenty-First Century*, The Belknap Press.

Piketty, Thomas (2020) *Capital and Ideology*, The Belknap Press.

Polanyi, Karl (1944[1957]) *The Great Transformation*, Beacon Press.

Polanyi, Karl (1947) "Our Obsolete Market Mentality", *Commentary*, 3(2), 109–117.

Polanyi, Karl (1968[1957]) "Aristotle Discovers the Economy", in Karl Polanyi, *Primitive, Archaic, and Modern Economies*, ed. George Dalton, Doubleday Anchor, 78–115.

Polanyi, Karl (1977) *The Livelihood of Man*, ed. Harry Pearson, Academic Press.

Polanyi-Levitt, Kari (2013) *From the Great Transformation to the Great Financialization*, Zed Books.

Pollard, Sidney (1981) *Peaceful Conquest: the Industrialisation of Europe, 1760–1970*, Oxford University Press.

Pomerantz, Kenneth (2000) *The Great Divergence: China, Europe and the Making of the Modern World Economy*, Princeton University Press.

Popkin, Samuel (1979) *The Rational Peasant*, University of California Press.

Przeworski, Adam and Michael Wallerstein (1988) "Structural Dependence of the State on Capital", *American Political Science Review*, 82(1), 11–29.

Randles, Sally (2003) "Issues for a Neo-Polanyian Research Agenda in Economic Sociology", in Harvey et al., *Karl Polanyi: New Perspectives on the Place of Economy in Society*, Manchester University Press.

Raynolds, Laura, Douglas L. Murray and John Wilkinson (2007) *Fair Trade: the Challenges of Transforming Globalization*, Routledge.

Reddy, William (1987) *Money and Liberty in Modern Europe: A Critique of Historical Understanding*, Cambridge University Press.

Reinhart, Carmen and Kenneth Rogoff (2009) "The Aftermath of Financial Crises", NBER Working Paper 14656.

Richards, Thomas (1990) *The Commodity Culture of Victorian England*, Stanford University Press.

Ridgeway, Cecelia (2017) "Why Status Matters for Inequality", *American Sociological Review*, 70, 1–16.

Rodrik, Dani (2011) *The Globalization Paradox: Democracy and the Future of the World Economy*, W.W. Norton & Co.

Rogan, Tim (2017) *The Moral Economists: R.H. Tawney, Karl Polanyi, E.P. Thompson and the Critique of Capitalism*, Princeton University Press.

Room, Graham (2000) "Commodification and Decommodification: A Developmental Critique", *Policy and Politics*, 28(3), 331–351.

Rosenberg, Justin (2001) *The Follies of Globalisation Theory*, Verso.

Ruggie, John (1982) "International Regimes, Transactions and Change: Embedded Liberalism in the Postwar Economic Order", *International Organization*, 36(2), 379–415.

Sabel, Charles and Jonathan Zeitlin (1985) "Historical Alternatives to Mass Production: Politics, Markets and Technology in Nineteenth-Century Industrialization", *Past and Present*, vol. 108(1), 133–176.

Sampson, Robert J., Stephen Raudenbush and Felton Earls (1997) "Neighborhoods and Violent Crime: A Multi-Level Study of Collective Efficacy", *Science*, 277 (August 15, 1997), 918–924.

Sandel, Michael (2012) *What Money Can't Buy: the Moral Limits of Markets*, Allen Lane.

Sandel, Michael (2020) *The Tyranny of Merit*, Allen Lane.

Satz, Debra (2010) *Why Some Things Should Not Be For Sale: the Moral Limits of Markets*, Oxford University Press.

Sayer, Andrew (2011) *Why Things Matter to People: Social Science, Values and Ethical Life*, Cambridge University Press.

Sayer, Andrew (2013) "(De)-Commodification, consumer culture and moral economy", *Environment and Planning D: Society and Space*, 21(3), 341–357.

Scharpf, Fritz (1991) *Crisis and Choice in European Social Democracy*, Cornell University Press.

Schumpeter, Joseph (1950 [1943]), *Capitalism, Socialism and Democracy*, Harper.

Sen, Amartya (1999) *Development as Freedom*, Knopf.

Sennett, Richard (1998) *The Corrosion of Character: The Personal Consequences of Work in the New Capitalism*, W.W. Norton & Co.

Sewell, William (2008) "The Temporalities of Capitalism", *Socio-Economic Review*, 6, 517–537.

Sewell, William (2014) "The Capitalist Epoch", *Social Science History*, 38(1), 1–11.

Sewell, William (2014) "Connecting Capitalism to the French Revolution: the Parisian promenade and the origins of civic equality in 18th century France", *Critical Historical Studies*, 1(1), 5–46.

Sewell, William (2021) *Capitalism and the Emergence of Civic Equality in Eighteenth Century France*, University of Chicago Press.

Shaw-Taylor, Leigh (2001) "Parliamentary Enclosure and the Emergence of an English Agricultural Proletariat", *The Journal of Economic History*, vol. 61(3), 640–662.

Shiva, Vandana (2001) *Protect or Plunder: Understanding Intellectual Property Rights*, Zed Books.

Silver, Beverly (2003) *Forces of Labor: Workers' Movements and Globalization since 1870*, Cambridge University Press.

Sirianni, Carmen (2009) *Investing in Democracy: Engaging Citizens in Collaborative Governance*, Brookings Institution Press.

Slobodian, Quinn (2018) *Globalists: the End of Empire and the Birth of Neoliberalism*, Harvard University Press.

Smelser, Neil (1962) *Theory of Collective Behavior*, Routledge.

Smelser, Neil and Richard Swedberg (1994) *The Handbook of Economic Sociology*, Princeton University Press.

Snell, K.D.M. (1985) *Annals of the Labouring Poor: Social Change and Agrarian England*, Cambridge University Press.

Somers, Margaret (2003) "Citizenship and the Place of the Public Sphere: Law, Community and Political Culture in the Transition to Democracy", *American Sociological Review*, 58, 587–620.

Somers, Margaret (2008) *Genealogies of Citizenship: Markets, Statelessness, and the Right to Have Rights*, Cambridge University Press.

Somers, Margaret (2018) "Utopianism and the Reality of Society: Decoding Polanyi's Socialism, Freedom and the Alchemy of Misrecognition", in Brie and Thomasberger, *Karl Polanyi's Vision of a Socialist Transformation*, 91–109.

Somers, Margaret and Fred Block (2005) “From Poverty to Perversity: Ideas, Markets, and Institutions over 200 Years of Welfare Debate”, *American Sociological Review*, 70(2), 260–287.

Somers, Margaret and Fred Block (2021) “Against Polanyian Orthodoxy: A Reply to Hannes Lacher”, *Theory and Society*, vol. 50(3), 417–441.

Standing, Guy (2011) *The Precariat: the New Dangerous Class*, Bloomsbury Academic.

Stansfield, J.R. (1989) *The Economic Thought of Karl Polanyi*, St Martin’s Press.

Steinberg, Marc W. (1996) “The Labour of the Country is the Wealth of the Country: Class Identity, Consciousness and the Role of Discourse in the Making of the English Working Class”, *International Labor and Working Class History*, no. 49 (Spring), 1–25.

Steinberg, Marc W. (2016) *England’s Great Transformation: Law, Labor and the Industrial Revolution*, University of Chicago Press.

Stephens, John D. (1979) *The Transition from Capitalism to Socialism*, Macmillan.

Stiglitz, Joseph (2013) *The Price of Inequality*, Penguin.

Stinchcombe, Arthur (1968) *Constructing Social Theories*, Harcourt Brace.

Stone, Lawrence (1989) *The First Modern Society*, Cambridge University Press.

Streeck, Wolfgang (1997) “Beneficial Constraints: On the Economic Limits of Rational Voluntarism”, in Hollingsworth and Boyer, *Contemporary Capitalism*.

Streeck, Wolfgang (2008) *Reforming Capitalism: Institutional Change in the German Political Economy*, Oxford University Press.

Streeck, Wolfgang (2011) “The Crises of Democratic Capitalism”, *New Left Review*, 71(Sept./Oct.), 5–29.

Streeck, Wolfgang (2014) *Buying Time: the Delayed Crisis of Democratic Capitalism*, Verso.

Streeck, Wolfgang (2016) *How Will Capitalism End?*, Verso.

Streeck, Wolfgang and Kathleen Thelen, eds (2005) *Beyond Continuity: Institutional Change in Advanced Political Economies*, Oxford University Press.

Stiglitz, Joseph, Amartya Sen and Jean-Paul Fitoussi (2010) *Mismeasuring Our Lives: Why GDP Doesn’t Add Up*, New Press.

Swaan, Abram de (1988) *In Care of the State*, Polity Press.

Swenson, Peter (2002) *Capitalists Against Markets: The Making of Labor Markets and Welfare States in the United States and Sweden*, Oxford University Press.

Tawney, R.H. (1922) *The Agrarian Problem in the Sixteenth Century*, Ballantyne.

Tesler, Michael (2016) *Post Racial or Most Racial? Race and Politics in the Obama Era*, University of Chicago Press.

Tett, Gillian (2009) *Fool’s Gold*, Little Brown.

Therborn, Goran (2013) *The Killing Fields of Inequality*, Polity Press.

Thirsk, Joan (1978) *Economic Policy and Projects: The Development of Consumer Society in Early Modern England*, Oxford University Press.

Thompson, E.P. (1966) *The Making of the English Working Class*, Vintage.

Thompson, E.P. (1993) *Customs in Common*, The New Press.

Tilly, Charles (1978) *From Mobilization to Revolution*, Addison Wesley.

Tilly, Charles (1979) “Proletarianization: Theory and Research”, CRSO Working Paper 202.

Tilly, Charles (1984) *Big Structures, Large Processes, Huge Comparisons*, Russell Sage.

Tilly, Charles (1995) "To Explain Political Processes", *American Journal of Sociology*, 100, 1594–1610.

Tilly, Charles (1995) *Popular Contention in Great Britain*, Harvard University Press.

Tilly, Charles (1997) *Roads from Past to Future*, Rowman & Littlefield.

Tilly, Charles (2007) *Democracy*, Cambridge University Press.

Tilly, Charles (2008) *Explaining Social Processes*, Paradigm Publishers.

Tooze, Adam (2018) *Crashed: How a Decade of Financial Crises Changed the World*, Allen Lane.

Tooze, Adam (2021) *Shutdown: How Covid Shook the World's Economy*, Allen Lane.

Trotsky, Leon (1977[1930]) *The History of the Russian Revolution*, Pluto.

Tucker, Robert (1972) *The Marx-Engels Reader*, W.W. Norton & Co.

Tufekci, Zeynep (2018) "How social media took us from Tahir Square to Donald Trump", *MIT Technology Review*, August 14, 2018.

Unger, Roberto (2006) *What the Left Should Propose*, Verso.

Vail, John, Michael Hill, and Jane Wheeelock (eds) (1999) *Insecure Times: Living With Insecurity in Contemporary Society*, Routledge.

Vail, John (2010) "Decommodification and Egalitarian Political Economy", *Politics and Society*, 38(3), 310–346.

Van Parijs, Phillipe (2006) "Basic Income versus Stakeholder Grants", in Bruce Ackerman, Ann Alstott and Phillipe Van Parijs, *Redesigning Distribution: Basic Income and Stakeholder Grants as Cornerstones of a More Egalitarian Capitalism*, ed. Erik Olin Wright, 199–209.

Wade, Robert (2008) "Financial Regime Change", *New Left Review*, 53(Sept./Oct).

Wainwright, Hilary (1994) *Arguments for a New Left*, Blackwell.

Wallerstein, Immanuel (2002) "New Revolts Against the System", *New Left Review*, 18(Nov./Dec.), 29–38.

Weber, Isabella (2021) *How China Escaped Shock Therapy: the Market Reform Debate*, Routledge.

Webster, Edward, Robert Iambert and Andries Bezuidenhout (2008) *Grounding Globalization: Labour in an Age of Insecurity*, Wiley.

Weiss, L. and Hobson, J. (1995) *States and Economic Development*, Polity.

Williams, Joan C. and Viviana Zelizer (2005) "To Commodify or Not to Commodify: That is *Not* the Question", pp. 362–382, in Martha Ertman and Joan C. Williams, *Rethinking Commodification*, New York University Press.

Wilkinson, Richard and Kate Pickett (2009) *The Spirit Level: Why More Equal Societies Almost Always Do Better*, Allen Lane.

Williams, Colin (2005) *A Commodified World: Mapping the Limits of Capitalism*, Zed Books.

Williams, Raymond (1983) *Keywords* (revised edition), Croom Helm.

Wolf, Martin (2020) "Covid has exposed society's dysfunctions", *Financial Times*, July 14, 2020.

Wood, Ellen Meiksins (1986) *The Retreat from Class*, Verso.

Wood, Ellen Meiksins (1995) *Democracy Against Capitalism*, Cambridge University Press.

Wood, Ellen Meiksins (1999) *The Origins of Capitalism*, Monthly Review Press.

Wood, Ellen Meiksins (2002) *The Origins of Capitalism: a Longer View*, Verso.

Woodruff, David (2016) "*Governing by Panic: the Politics of the Eurozone Crisis*", Vol. 44(1), 81–116.

Wright, Erik Olin (1998) "Introduction", in Sam Bowles and Herbert Gintis, *Recasting Egalitarianism*, pp. xi–xiii, Verso.
Wright, Erik Olin (2010) *Envisioning Real Utopias*, Verso.
Wright, Erik Olin (2019) *How to be an Anti-capitalist in the 21st Century*, Verso.
Wrightson, Keith (2002) *Earthly Necessities*, Penguin.
Yarrow, David (2017) "Progressive response to populism: a Polanyian critique of liberal discourse", *The Political Quarterly*, vol. 88(4), October–December, 570–578.
Young, Michael (1994) "Meritocracy revisited", *Sociology*, 31(6), 87–89.
Young, Michael (2017[1948]) *The Rise of the Meritocracy*, Routledge.
Zelizer, Viviana (1994) *The Social Meaning of Money*, Basic Books.
Zelizer, Viviana (2005) *The Purchase of Intimacy*, Princeton University Press.

Index

For Product Safety Concerns and Information please contact our EU representative GPSR@taylorandfrancis.com Taylor & Francis Verlag GmbH, Kaufingerstraße 24, 80331 München, Germany